Backyards
to
Ballparks

More Personal Baseball Stories
from the Stands and Beyond

5/23/2022

To Francesca,

I hope you enjoy all the stories in this
collection and that you have great baseball
memories of your own. Tell me your story!
See Charles on p. 254

Eric C. Gray

Eric C. Gray

Palmetto Publishing Group
Charleston, SC

Backyards to Ballparks
Copyright © 2022 by Eric C. Gray

All rights reserved.

First Edition

Printed in the United States

Paperback ISBN: 979-8-88590-465-0
eBook ISBN: 979-8-88590-466-7

Back cover photo by Lisa Allen

Here's my unsolicited testimonial for Eric's book - It's well worth your time and a few coins for it. Buy the book! It's full of good stories that will make you smile and maybe love baseball even more. It is a book of stories you don't have to read from start to finish. You can read most of them between innings. Who watches the commercials anyway?

~David Moriah, Contributor, *Sports Collector's Digest*

Eric's books have helped get people together during tough times.

~Mike Pressman, Lifelong Baseball fan Senior Writer, *Sportico*, and BBWAA Member and Hall of Fame Voter

TABLE OF CONTENTS

FOREWORD

I loved Eric Gray's first book, *Bases to Bleachers*, and the hidden little gems colleagues and fans told about covering and enjoying the game of baseball. It gave me a chance to tell one of my own, which is still a constant source of giggles and laughter between Seattle Times sports columnist Larry Stone and myself.

Stoney always greets me with the line: "Who has more authority, Rosey? You or Barry Bloom?"

The giggles always then ensue. Of course, in that instance it was me, Barry M. Bloom.

Stoney was a baseball scribe back then covering the Giants for the San Francisco Examiner, and I was on the Padres beat for the San Diego Tribune. It was spring training at the old metal and brown-painted wooden Scottsdale Stadium where the current modern facility now stands, and the Giants still use as their spring home. Stoney was sitting in a media trailer down the first base line when I sent in the late Padres pitcher Eric Show to get a sandwich.

In the Cliff Notes version of the story – if you know what Cliff Notes are, it really dates you – I ran into Show (pronounced Sh-ow, like ow) in full uniform, his name and No. 30 on the back of his jersey – wandering through the stands as I was heading up to the ramshackle of a press box. When I asked where he was going, he said, "To get a hot dog."

I sent him into the trailer with its abundance of deli meat and packaged breads on a table and then continued my journey. Enter Show followed closely behind by the late Al Rosen, a Hall of Fame infielder and then Giants president. As Stoney would tell it, Rosen started screaming at Show, who had no idea of the assailant's identity.

"Who are you?" Show asked.

"I'm Al Rosen, president of the Giants. Who told you that you could come in here?"

"Barry Bloom," Show said. "And let me ask you this question: Who has more authority, Rosey? You or Barry Bloom?"

I had a long-time relationship with Rosen, so that shut him up. Show left with the sandwich and that's how legends are made.

In this current tome written by Eric Gray, *Backyards to Ballparks*, Chapter 1 involves stories about when baseball fans attended their first baseball games.

Mine was in 1960 with my dad, Len Bloom, at what I call the original, original Yankee Stadium in the Bronx. The edifice that Babe Ruth actually built and where he played when it opened in 1923. It was replaced by a sad facsimile in 1976. And the most recent version that opened in 2009 is across the wide boulevard of 161st Street.

My father was a big ball fan and catcher of some repute, but I'll get to that a little bit later. I was nine. We saw the Yanks of Mantle, Maris, Ford, and Berra play the Cleveland Indians twice that summer. The second time, seated in the buck-fifty reserve seats in the upper deck behind home plate, the original Tito Francona hit a pair of homers into the upper deck in right field. It was a nice story to tell his son, Terry, when he managed the Red Sox decades later.

But that wasn't the most memorable live Major League Baseball experience of my early life. That happened across the Harlem River at the venerable Polo Grounds on June 1, 1962.

The long and the short of it was the Giants and Dodgers left New York after the 1957 season for the west coast, leaving the city without National League baseball. A threat to establish a new Continental Baseball League with New York teams at its hub led to MLB expanding by four teams, and in 1962 the Metropolitans – Mets – were one of them.

For the seasons of 1962 and 1963, the Mets played at the Giants old home across the river from Yankee Stadium as Shea Stadium was being built in Queens, named after the lawyer – Bill Shea – who had spearheaded the nascent and never-to-be CBL. On the above-mentioned date, the Giants of San Francisco returned to play their first game back at the Polo Grounds since their final game in New York on Sept. 29, 1957, a 9-1 loss to the Pirates in front 11,606 tearful and mournful fans.

My father grew up in Harlem a short distance from the Polo Grounds. He was a good stick catcher for nearby George Washington High School in upper Manhattan near Hill Top Park where the Highlanders once played, around the turn of the 19th to 20th centuries, and the Giants had to also utilize when one of the many versions of the Polo Grounds burned down.

As legend would have it, my father told the story of trying out for the Giants during the World War II years at the Polo Grounds and even hitting the ball into the upper deck in left. He said he was assigned to the lower minor leagues, but then was drafted into the army and sent to Europe. And that was all she wrote for his budding professional baseball career. There's no way of confirming or denying this story, so I've always gone with it. And why not? The Giants seem to have a life-long connection to all these stories.

On this Friday night in 1962, my father grabbed me, my eight-year-old red-headed brother, Steve, and a group of his friends from our Riverdale neighborhood in the Bronx and headed by subway to the Polo Grounds to see the Giants of the two Willies – Mays and McCovey. Mays was born as a New York Giant at the Polo Grounds and my Uncle Eddie really adored him. A rejected and neglected Giants fan, he said that night all he wanted to see was three things: Mays make a basket catch, Mays hit a home run and Mays run out from under his cap making a play in center field. That all happened. And McCovey hit two homers.

We sat in the left-field upper deck in fair territory just above the spot where nearly 11 years earlier, on Oct. 3, 1951, Bobby Thomson had hit his walk-off homer to defeat the Brooklyn Dodgers. Of course, there was no such thing as a walk-off homer back then. "The Giants win the pennant, the Giants win the pennant," Giants radio voice Russ Hodges crowed out of the small boxes that were tuned in across the city. I was born 23 days later.

Memories? During the middle of the 1962 game, some fan came up the isle by our seats looking for a friend of his.

"Fagan, Fag-an," he screamed.

In an instant, to much merriment, our entire group started also calling for "Fagan." He never materialized. Or so it seemed. The Giants defeated the Mets that night, 9-6. Billy Pierce earned the win, Roger Craig the loss, Stu Miller the save.

The game drew 43,742, a bigger crowd than any that attended a game at the Polo Grounds during the entire 1957 swan song season. It makes me wonder what might have happened back then if fans had come to the games.

Enjoy the book *Backyards to Ballparks*. Enjoy the stories. I know I do.

~Barry M. Bloom, Senior Writer, Sportico, and BBWAA Member and Hall of Fame Voter

INTRODUCTION

My first book, *Bases to Bleachers* was born of a simple question posed to other fans at a baseball game: "What was your favorite game?" Writing a book about baseball was as little of a thought as a batter has about swinging on a 3-0 count against a pitcher who just walked the bases loaded… although like so many things, that has changed in this home run-happy era. Then I asked the slightly revised question over and over again, with growing confidence, like DiMaggio who knew he would get a hit every game (56 straight), "What was your favorite game, or moment, relating to baseball?" The odds were good I'd get a great, funny, emotional, or bizarre story others would love to read.

Equipped with a ton of great stories not in the first book, and an ongoing collection of email and Facebook messages relaying memories, it was clear to me there would be at least one sequel, maybe more. Think of this book as the second in a series.

How can I say this in a confident and honest, but somewhat humble manner…?

The stories in the first book, and now in this one, are simply wonderful. I don't take credit for them; I owe them all to the contributors, the people who had great memories they were happy to share. I became, I suppose, the Casey Stengel of curation. My dad believed anyone could have won World Series championships managing the '50s through '60s Yankees. I don't think that is quite true, although it was a lot easier to accomplish with that great lineup. Someone had to write the names on the card, know which player to put into the game at the right time. In writing my books, I, too, had great players—in this case stories—to work with; it was just a question of which ones to use in the right chapter and in the right place.

So, there you go, me and Casey, the Ol' Perfessor, with whom I happen to share a birth date. Yes, I am talking about month and day, but he did have a few years on me.

My first impulse in writing this introduction was to repeat a lot of what I wrote in the intro to *Bases to Bleachers* for anyone who did not read that book. Why baseball is important to me, thoughts about the game, why I think it is sometimes undervalued, how the idea for the book came about, and the various steps involved in putting together that first book. My better instinct was that would be a cheap, lazy, thoughtless, effortless, and boring way to begin this book. So, I won't do that. I decided to "Let It Be" (no cite necessary).

For the most part.

What I will talk about, though, are things that evolved from that first project, with a few diversions into the past. In a nutshell, *Bases to Bleachers*, born that afternoon in August of 2011, was a life-changing experience. It began with one simple question to my wife, Lynn, daughter Rachel, and friend Cheryl, followed by hundreds of emails to friends, random meetings on the street, at games, in airports, and enhanced by uncountable numbers of Facebook exchanges. "Day After Day," "Everyday" (Badfinger, Buddy Holly). I ultimately collected 1250+ stories to choose from, only a relatively small portion of which I was able to fit in the first book, though many so clearly deserved a place. It was a soul-crushing dilemma. Feeling guilty, hurting feelings—I mean, man, I experienced a whole record collection of anxiety. The title of a relatively unknown Who album said it best: "It's Hard." Many additional stories followed, after and because of the first book, leaving me again with that gnawing-in-the-gut crisis I ultimately chose to confront, fight through, and hopefully conquer. Which stories? "Here I Go Again," "Déjà vu" (Hollies and CSNY, tied together, of course, by Graham Nash).

The first book set me off on that path of meeting people, getting to know many of them, getting their stories. Was it fun? Mostly. Was it easy? Not always. I proved to myself that I am very good, or at least diligent, at something I am not particularly proud of—being a really good nag.

Was it worth it? I am not aware that I lost any friends because of it, and for absolute certain, I made a slew of new ones. My friendship team roster grew far larger than most teams' injured lists did in the 2020-21 covid-affected seasons. I received amazing stories.

I didn't have to follow up with Jesse; his story came two days after I met him. Ironically, he was an afterthought, what I figured would be a consolation prize, as I really had been focused on a young woman (relax, Lynn was with me) who was wearing a Wrigley Field T-shirt in a NYC coffee shop. It is hard to believe she might have given me a better story than Jesse's. Did I have to—and I will be gentle here—follow up with Dan K? Yes, for years, but man, the wait was worth it. He provided a story of such emotional impact, decades-spanning memories that, like Jesse's, is on perennial rotation on my set list when I do readings. (While never a rock star, I was a college and career-aspiring DJ and always think in terms of music, if you haven't noticed.) Because I asked that question at a Brewers game, Dean and Debbie not only became our good friends, it turns out we are related by marriage—second cousins-in-law three times removed or something like.

Which brings us to the stories that were *not* in the first book, and *not* because they weren't good enough. My first draft was literally more than twice as long as I'd been told it was supposed to be. Yes, I was that college student who was frustrated when there was a maximum length for a college essay. It was an absolutely gut-wrenching, ulcer-inducing—though, honestly, that is more figurative than literal—exercise, trying to figure out which stories I could fit in a book someone would be able to carry, or hold, without the assistance of a Sherpa. But it soon became clear that my publisher wanted to do a second volume, so with this safely tucked away in my mind the way Bob Costas keeps a Mickey Mantle card in his wallet, I knew—especially since Lynn repeatedly hammered me with this point—that I had to save enough great stories to make book two just as good as book one. Some were omitted from book one because the chapters they would be in were DFA'd (Designated for Assignment), for whatever reason, to book two. Some were in chapters I knew would have to be repeated, as I felt they were the core of the book: Family. What Baseball Means to Me.

Meeting the Stars. Did you see and love the film *Ghostbusters*? Great movie, right? How many of you liked the 1989 sequel, *Ghostbusters II*? Anyone? I did not want my own sequel to be a book people regretted reading.

It hadn't been easy for me to omit Scott's tale of meeting the legendary Hank Aaron, but I knew there would be a chapter on Mickey, Willie, and the Greats of the Golden Age of Baseball. I never intended to include a chapter about games watched on television, listened to on the radio. But then my Uncle David told me the story about when he, my dad, and their other brother, Richard, crowded around the radio to listen to the famous 1934 All-Star Game, and I knew that story, with some others, was destined for book two as well. Andy's amazing tale about catching a ball? Book two. My First Game? A chapter astonishingly, and for reasons I still don't understand, not in the first book. I have tried, only to some degree successfully, to resist my urge to feel guilty that they weren't in the first, but I am glad my friends generally understood. I mean, I even left out *my own* greatest memory, going to Mickey Mantle's retirement ceremony.

Of course, I received many new stories as a result of the first volume. After my NPR interview with Robin Young on *Here and Now* (talk about a life-changing experience—thanks Gail!), I got Nancy's story. She didn't remember we had actually met at a Giant's game several years before. Out of the clear blue I received a great email from Charlie, whose daughter had bought him the book. I was supposed to meet Wilmer at a reading in St. Petersburg, Florida, that was cancelled at the last minute because of the pandemic. His story is in here, as well. And Brillo (Gary), I *finally* got yours!

What has happened or changed since the first book came out? The Astros and Red Sox scandals were revealed. Covid-19 scuttled the beginning of the 2020 season and when it returned, well, it was like you'd done a Rip Van Winkle and awoke to find you had a whole new roster of players on your favorite team and very different circumstances inside the ballpark. When play resumed, you simply weren't in the stands unless you were a cardboard cutout. Only players not in the starting lineup and grounds crew could sit there. Everyone was supposed to wear a mask, although that seemed to be enforced about as much as the strike zone. Who knew if, when this book was originally due to be published in 2021, you'd be getting your peanuts and beer at the stadium or still in your den? There were lots of on-field changes as well: designated hitters in each league, and relief pitchers had to throw to at least three batters unless they ended an inning. Doubleheaders—inevitable with game postponements not because of rain-outs but COVID-outs—were seven innings long, like a standard Little League game...which quickly resulted in the MadBum no-hitter controversy. And get this, beginning in the 10th inning, a runner starts the inning on second base. Haha, hilarious. Wait, what? (For you, LA.) True.

What hasn't changed? Pitchers throw, batters swing, runners run, fielders catch and throw. There are still five tools to make a complete player: he must be able to run, throw, field, hit for average, hit with power. The beauty of a 6-4-3 double play, the elation of a stand-up triple. Thankfully, there are still no ties in baseball to end a game. I still plan my trips to D.C. and NYC around when the Giants will be in town, and usually suffer through uncomfortable, hot, muggy, July and August weather. But uncomfortable is what I am used to living in San Francisco, albeit on the freezing side in those same months.

But other, more important things haven't changed, at least as far as the storied collective national experience and history of this game, and the feelings that everyone from elderly people to young children, hipsters and nerds, strait-laced folks and goths, have about our national pastime. Young boys and girls will still be told "Lights out!" and sneak under the covers not a transistor radio but a cell phone, to listen to the end of the game, and read the box scores the next morning not in the newspaper, but on that same phone (thanks, Stavros). Through technology, they won't discuss with their parents and schoolmates the next morning the one play the umpire missed last night, but the scores of plays they'd seen on ESPN, MLB, and internet highlights of *every* game, especially because of the umpteen number of slo-mo and different angled reviews of any play. Older folks will still reminisce about the old-timers and "back in my day," although they will be talking about Mantle and Mays, Koufax and Aaron rather than Ruth and Gehrig, Ty Cobb and Cy Young. The next generation will one day talk about Griffey and Trout and Mariano.

Then once you were finally allowed back inside the park, you know what else hadn't changed? The wide expanse of green grass, the dirt infield interrupted only by white bases and chalk marks down the baselines, the peanuts and crackerjack and hot dogs and beer. Okay, that has kind of changed, beers are $15 now, rather than $1.50. But you get the point.

My love for baseball hasn't changed. It is still (usually) a sunny afternoon or balmy evening at the park—though still not in San Francisco—sitting with your partner or your kids, or your dad or your friends, or with people you don't know but might become friends with. The game recap and box score are still the first things I read in the paper with my morning tea. Admittedly, I am not likely to watch a Dodgers vs Cardinals game—I have my team biases, and there are lots of things to do in life—but I will always watch Giants and Mets games.

I know, I get it, baseball isn't everybody's cup of tea. It is the game that many kids stop playing first because it is "too boring." Many adults don't like the inaction and sometimes low scores. But hello? Forty-five seconds between snaps in football followed by eight seconds of action, and regular 1-0 soccer scores? And people are aggravated by the length of games. The thing is, a lot of people don't—or don't take the time—to *get* it. Baseball is a cerebral game; there is far more going on than appears on the surface. My friend Andy, who is totally disinterested in baseball yet ironically provided me with the story that inspired the first book, came over one day to watch a game. It was terrific for me, as I had the chance to talk for three nonstop hours, explaining all the strategy and nuance. He left with a splitting headache, caused, he said, not by my incessant babbling, but because, "I never realized this game was so complicated."

The most important thing that has not changed, for me, is that baseball continues to be one of the unifying factors for my family. See my story about how Matt Cain's perfect game confirmed that. Lynn and I are still season ticket owners, and our goal, although not a hardcore bucket list item, is to see all the major league parks—six to go. Daughter Rachel is now in her 23rd year working for the Giants, where everyone from the Giants broadcasters to the team president knows her. She comes to the occasional game, and she and her partner, Steve, make a point of merging this with another great love on Star Wars Night at Oracle Park. Our son and daughter-in-law, David and Lisa, living in D.C., also are big Giants fans, and I continue to visit almost every year when the Giants are on the schedule, and we collectively endure mostly losing games. *But,* as I'd hoped for and even conjectured in the first book, they have brought a new generation of baseball and Giants fan, Juliet, onto our team and into our lives. And, David, wasn't that catch we had last summer just great, even with a few misthrows?

As said, *Bases to Bleachers* changed my life, as it did, to some degree, Lynn's. Suddenly I was setting up book tours. Okay, to be honest, that is far too grandiose a term. We planned trips to see family and friends, and figured out places, libraries, living rooms, and bookstores where I could do readings. But what the heck, I can pretend I had my little rock star journey, unlike Mike C. who provided an *epic* story in book one that truly encompasses that sacred Come Together (Beatles) of rock star and baseball. I think Mike still doesn't recognize how great a story that is.

How has this changed Lynn's life? There are obvious tasks for which she was professionally trained and particularly adept at—bookkeeper, accountant, tech support. But she also took on roles with which she had no prior experience—book promotion, producer of online readings, plus design and maintenance of my website, basestobleachers.com, and my FB page, @basestobleachers. And she has been my partner on our travels and in meeting new friends. You know who you are.

This is not a scholarly book, a biography, or a look at a franchise, but it is a ton of fun. For those of you who have read *Bases to Bleachers,* I hope you will find this second volume, *Backyards to Ballparks,* filled with as many funny, emotional, entertaining, and remindful stories as the first. If you haven't read the first book and don't find the need to do so but would like to read all those amazing pearls of wisdom in that book's introduction, contact me at eric.baseballstories@gmail.com and I will email it to you. Or just look at my website, where it's posted.

And please continue to send me your stories.

Or anything about baseball.

Or, you know, just say hi!

A couple of programming notes. There are a handful of people with more than one story in this book, and a few more who have stories in each. There are several stories about both Matt Cain and Willie McCovey; it just worked out that way. My hero, Mickey Mantle, also makes several appearances. Stories were often written at a particular point in time, so in some cases, the ages of the people and circumstances have changed—yes, the Red Sox finally won one, er, I mean four World Series. And while the book skews to my g-g-generation (The Who, again), it was not for lack of trying to get stories from younger fans. But more important, it doesn't matter. It is the stories that count, and they could have been about any player or team.

The horror of COVID-19 is thankfully abating, but none of us will forget so much about that lost year, including the 2020 baseball season. Here is a permanent reminder of how the games were played in that crazy year, written by my good friend, and sung to the tune of "Take Me Out to the Ballgame."

Time to start playing some ball games
But the crowd won't be loud
Vendors, announcers, will not be brought back
No one but players will hear the bats' crack
It's a poor substitute for the real thing
With cardboard fans in the stands
Could be 2, 3, 4 months of this
'Till we snag that foul with our hands.

The collateral damage is daunting
Employees will not be there
Roosting pigeons are feeling abused
Hungry seagulls will be so confused

If the game's going bad on the TV
We can head to the kitchen for snacks
The game then can turn on a dime
All it takes is a couple of jacks

We're finally getting some ballgames
There won't be much of a crowd
No buying our peanuts and Cracker Jack
No one knows when we'll ever get back

Still we root, root, root for the home team
Not being there is a shame
Wonder when we'll get out
To the old ball game

~Steve G., San Francisco, California

BONUS STORIES FROM BASES TO BLEACHERS

*I ended my first book with "Coming Battractions", a couple of stories from chapters specifically held for book two. It seemed only fitting to lead off this book with this chapter, Bonus stories from **Bases To Bleachers**... containing a couple of extra stories from chapters that were in book one. Enjoy!*

Love and Baseball

My husband, Joe, didn't follow sports at all until we met, so his favorite teams are those I follow. I have been an Atlanta Braves fan since I was a kid because that was the team my dad's family followed while living in Panama City, Florida. I ended up in the D.C. area because Dad was stationed at Joint Base Andrews. I stayed in the area because my husband's family is local and most of my family is within a day's a drive, as well. I have lived in Florida, Germany, England, Sacramento, and Plattsburgh, NY. The Braves have remained my team.

Joe decided to propose to me at a ballgame on September 11th, 2005, at RFK stadium. He couldn't do what he'd originally planned—have the event shown on the scoreboard—because the Nationals didn't own the stadium. The only person with us that day was my future mother-in-law—my parents were invited to a wedding and forgot about having tickets to the game. It was a warm day in D.C., and during the seventh inning stretch I mentioned I wanted something to drink. Joe said he would get something, but first put his arm around my shoulder and said, "I want to spend the rest of my life with you, will you marry me?" Completely surprised, I of

1

course said yes and proceeded to text friends and family while he went on his drink run. The day was extra wonderful because the Braves won 9-7 thanks to a game-tying home run by Chipper Jones and a 2-run homer by Andruw Jones.

I called my parents to let them know my happy news, but they first asked about the score. I told them about the game, but as I tried to break the good news about the engagement my phone died, so I had to call back on Joe's phone. I told Dad first. He asked me what I'd said, and I replied, "What do you think I said?" He handed the phone to my mom so I could tell her. She later told me that she'd looked over and Dad had tears in his eyes. I've always been Daddy's little girl.

~Brandy Copsey, Waldorf, Maryland

On July 17, 2010, the summer before I proposed to my now-wife, Lauren, she had bought tickets to a Cardinals game against the Dodgers. I was so excited to go. I always look forward to a great game at Busch Stadium, and with Adam Wainwright starting, it promised to be an extra-special day. This was my first birthday celebrated with Lauren, and in addition to the tickets, she bought me a David Freese jersey to wear to the game. Of course this was awesome, but what let me know she really loved me was that despite being a big Cubs fan, she also got a Cardinals shirt to wear at the game! I knew then and there she was the one for me.

~David Butch, Louisville, Kentucky

The question is, David, has Lauren worn it to a Cardinals vs. Cubs game?

In 1973, working for Department of Housing and Urban Development in Washington D.C., I was given a one-week assignment in Boston to gain regional office experience. I met a pretty girl in the office and invited her to a Red Sox game at Fenway Park, the baseball cathedral of a team rich in baseball history. I felt honored, in a way, to be there in the oldest park in Major League Baseball. I could feel that history, and still do 43 years later. And it didn't hurt to be sitting next to...I'll call her "Marie". I recall sitting there listening to the Boston accent of the stadium announcer say the names of the players coming to bat. Fisk, Yastrzemski, Petrocelli, Aparicio. Some of the names were mouthfuls, representative of so many ethnic groups and cultures.

Marie lived in the Italian section of the city and made it very clear that the neighborhood guys watched out for her whenever she left or came back to her apartment. I don't recall if I had secret plans in mind... Needless to say, when I heard that, I did not even think about going home with her. Which is probably how she wanted it, as I think back on it...

~Marc Ordman, Oceanside, California

I was set up on a blind date with Diana in June of 1984. Within a few dates, I knew she was the one, and we were married in July 1986. When you meet someone and the relationship develops, you begin to see similarities and differences. There were some big differences—an Italian Roman Catholic girl from Brooklyn and a Jewish guy from Long Island—but that ended up not being a big deal, especially as my mother adored Diana and made it clear she wanted her as a daughter-in-law.

As our relationship grew, Diana and I realized there was one major difference on which we would never agree: Diana is a Yankees fan and I bleed blue and orange, a hardcore fanatic Mets fan from their inception in 1962. When we first went out the Mets were on their way back and the Yankees were in the doldrums. I took her to Shea Stadium for opening days in 1995 and 1996, and was too smitten with Keith Hernandez, Daryl Strawberry, and Doc Gooden to worry about this difference. We were at Shea the night Bill Buckner couldn't handle Mookie Wilson's groundball. Diana being Diana, she took it all in stride, and I was glad I'd married someone who liked baseball…even though on many summer evenings she would watch the Yankees game while I watched the Mets. By the time interleague games started, the Mets were down in the dumps, so when the two teams played it was no big deal to her if the Mets took a few. The Yankees were dominant again, and a loss to my Mets was just a bump in the road.

Baseball in New York often has one team up and one down, but 2000 was the year all real New York baseball fans were waiting for—the first Subway Series since 1956 (and that was the Dodgers, not the Mets). I was so psyched I even found a six-pack of Rheingold beer, since some brewery had relaunched that brand. Diana said to me, "We have an interfaith marriage," and I replied, "Yeah, I know," pausing to reflect on our wedding day with its two ceremonies. "No," she said with emphasis, "We have an interfaith marriage." Meaning the Yankees and Mets. I guess that was okay since I knew she adored Tom Seaver, and any NY baseball fan had to love The Mick.

~Mike Roberts, Edison, New Jersey

Let's Beat the Traffic

I grew up in Hawaii watching the Hawaii Islanders of the old Pacific Coast League, going to games with my father at the old Honolulu Stadium. Chuck Tanner managed the Islanders. When I left Hawaii to go to college at Valparaiso University in Indiana, he was selected to manage the Chicago White Sox, the reason I am still a Sox fan. He brought some of the Islanders with him, notably Bill "Iron Glove" Melton. I have something in common with President Obama: we're both Hawaiian-born White Sox fans!

I have worked for the YMCA for 30 years, and as a gift they gave me Diamond Level seats right behind home plate. My wife and I went to an A's vs. Angels night game that eventually went 19 innings, the longest playing time in A's history. We were going to leave in the 8th because the A's were behind, but they rallied and tied the game in the 9th. We decided to stay a few more innings, and eventually it became clear we were not leaving. The Angels scored a run in the 15th, and the A's tied it up. Free food and beer came with the tickets, but darn, they stopped serving in the 7th. Brandon Moss hit a walk-off home run to end the marathon. We got home at 2:30 in the morning.

~Don Lau, Richmond, California

Born and raised in Spokane, WA, my family moved to San Diego when I was 10, only to return to south of downtown Seattle three years later. I had been to a few Padres game, but the game I went to when I was 17 was one of the most memorable...for all the wrong reasons. My dad had taken to me to Safeco, a ballpark I had come to love, a beautiful stadium in a beautiful city. The Mariners hosted the Oakland Athletics that night. It was a very close game through 8½ innings, tied after the top of the 9th. Dad looked at me and said we were leaving, he didn't want to get stuck in traffic at the conclusion of the game. I couldn't believe it. To say I was disappointed is an understatement. We got up and headed for the exit. By the time we were in the car and on the freeway, Dad looked over at me and could tell I wasn't in a very good mood. He turned on the radio to hear the game. It was the bottom of the 10th by this point, and Bucky Jacobson, the hometown hero that season for the Mariners, was up to bat. Not more than two minutes after the radio was turned on, Dave Niehaus' voice erupted on the other end in excitement as Jacobson hit a walk-off home run to win the game. A blank stare settled over my face. Dad looked over at me and turned off the radio. Not another word was spoken on the way home. I still remember that moment like it happened last night. That was 12 years ago. I guess baseball has that effect on me. I have a hard time remembering what I ate for breakfast, but I can recall what happened during an obscure regular season game more than a decade ago. Win or lose, I love the game of baseball.

~Brad Benesch, San Diego, California

Women IN Baseball

In June of 1979 I was a 10-year-old baseball fan, having been entranced by the 1978 Yankees vs. Dodgers World Series. Dodger Blue all the way! On Little League sign-up day, I was a girl with a plan. I naturally got in the baseball line—I wanted to play baseball. But then I noticed the line was all boys. All the girls were in the softball lines. What to do? Should I take the hard path, play the game I wanted to play and be the only girl, or take the easier path and switch to the softball? It was the decision of a lifetime and, alas, I caved and switched lines.

So, I played softball all through Little League, and middle and high school. I loved it, and even made some all-star squads, but it wasn't *baseball*, it was a different game. My heart wanted to play baseball. In 1996 I tried out for a men's baseball league, the only woman to do so. I was placed on the scraped-together "Bad News Bears" team that featured those men not good enough for the regular teams, plus me, the Tatum O'Neal. The Tornadoes were 3-17 that season, and two of those wins were by forfeit. We did win one outright, 3-2, and that crackerjack woman at second base made a mean diving stop and throw to first to save a run and chipped in a single and an RBI! Batting stats for the year: 3-37. Not pretty. I'd struck out in the first game of a doubleheader five times in a row and begged the coach to take me out for the second game. He wouldn't, and I struck out three more times. It was humiliating, but I really didn't care; I was playing baseball. *Baseball!* Ten years later in 2007, in another men's league, I improved to 6-26, catching half the games. I was accepted and treated well. The men respected a woman willing to get behind the dish, and that was the only place I wanted to be.

I ultimately played baseball on three continents. In Australia, I mentored the women of the Canberra Ainslie Bears in the inaugural year of their women's league. These women had never played baseball before. I helped teach them our national game, and we made it to the grand finale. It was the first and only time I ever felt like a hotshot, my proudest baseball moment ever.

I've made hundreds of new friends through the game, including play-ers from the All-American Women's Professional Baseball League through years of attending their reunions. It's been the thrill of a lifetime to get to know these pioneer women who also lived my dream by playing profes-sional baseball in the 1940s and 50s. I give advice at tournaments to young girls who now have that precious chance I didn't take to play baseball while they are kids. It still astounds me and makes my heart glad that I got an-other chance, at age 27, to reinvent myself as a baseball player.

The one thing that never changes—each time that 10-year-old girl, now a woman, steps onto a baseball field, sees that green grass and gorgeous field, grips the ball that completely, perfectly fits into her hand, smells the air, smiles at her teammates, flops in the dirt behind the backstop, and dives for a ball at third base that she (probably) won't come up with, she is transported. She is home. She is playing baseball! *Baseball.* Imagine that! She still pinches herself each and every time. She is playing the greatest game in the world!

~Debbie Pierson, Eugene, Oregon

The most memorable baseball game I have played in was when I was a girl of 15, and the first time I'd made it onto a boy's representative base-ball team for my hometown of Brisbane, Australia. It was July 10, 2016, the grand finale day for the inaugural Timber Jacks Tournament, played just north of Sydney in New South Wales. My team, Brisbane Metro, was playing for first place after what had been a pretty successful tournament. As a player, though, my tournament was not so eventful. The only girl on the team, I wasn't anticipating much playing time, although I was excited to finally be selected for the team I'd been trying to break onto for years. As expected, I played little, not figuring to be called upon from the bench, especially for the championship game. Over six games, I'd only had five at-bats, just one hit, and one put out at second base.

I sat on the bench most of that last game. The score was tied, and I was playing the role of ultimate bat girl and cheer-er...until the top of the 9th inning. To my surprise, the coach decided it would be a great idea to put me in at second base. Internally, I was freaking out, scared and mentally unprepared. To this day, I remember the stress I felt walking onto that field knowing that any error I'd commit could possibly lose the game…and probably some friends on the team. This was the situation I was thrown into:

Tied ball game at 2-2, 1 out, runners at first and second.

The batter was 3-3 that game against our pitching

This was in itself a stressful situation for a 15-year-old in a championship game. As the game played out, the batter hit a line drive above my head, and by some insane means I caught it. My team was just as shocked as I was. Without even thinking I threw the ball to first where the runner had taken off without tagging up since the ball was expected to be out of my reach. I had just rolled a double play to save the game. We scored in the bottom of the 9th to win the championship.

That play instilled confidence in my coaches, teammates, and even myself for years to follow. After that day, I made every boy's representative baseball team I tried out for. That grand finale day also taught me a very important lesson: If you're on the bench, always be prepared for any situation. Now, navigating through the college baseball ranks in the U.S., where I play for West Los Angeles College, I am mentally and physically ready for whatever the game—or life—may throw at me.

~Luisa Gauci, Brisbane, Australia

My daughter, Breanne Olsen, started playing with a bat and a ball at the age of one. By 18 months, she wasn't allowed to play with her plastic bat and ball inside the house because she nearly broke a window. We enrolled her in a local tot program, Lil' Baseball, and she shined. Being the only girl wasn't the only reason she stood out, her skill level ensured that. She hit a coach in the face. He'd underestimated her batting ability and got too close when pitching to her, and she blasted one right at him. He will always remember that.

At four, Breanne began playing T-Ball, after we dealt with administrative obstacles. When we tried to enroll her, our payment was refunded. They told us, "Sign her up for softball." After I put up a fight, making calls to the Little League headquarters in Southern California, she was allowed to play. She excelled and had a fan club. Now in her fourth year, she is still the only girl on the Single A team and has gained the respect of all her teammates. She was voted MVP in two consecutive years.

Breanne trains at a baseball facility, Total Player Center which several major leaguers, including the Giants' Brandon Crawford, attended. She loves going to practice, gaining knowledge, and improving her skills. She was invited to Level 2 testing one March, an assessment usually done for older boys. The coaches and trainers told us that, based on her skills, they thought it would be better for her to advance to the next level. To do so, she had to take verbal and skill tests. She had to learn every routine drill and be able to demonstrate and explain their purposes. Both the hitting instructor and pitching coach tested her, and she passed on her first try. Few kids do. Breanne was the first seven-year-old girl to be invited and to pass the test. We were so ecstatic for her!

Breanne loves to play baseball and dreams of becoming a professional baseball player. We support her in every way we can. Many little sisters on the team look up to her, and she is making a name for herself in our city. She is recognized at the grocery store, theme parks, and other places. So many people support her. She's one tough cookie!

Update: Breanne is now 11 and the only girl to make the Little League Minors All-Star team. She then became the only girl drafted into the Majors, where she pitches, catches, and plays third base. She prefers to catch and has a great throw down to second base. She has hitting, pitching, and catching coaches to help her in all aspects of her development. She also plays on an all-girl baseball team, the East Bay Oaks, through a program called Baseball for All. A slogan has been created for her, "Brea Aggressive," and she is developing a clothing line with that name. She is still recognized around the community. One firefighter said to her in a grocery store, "Oh, you're Brea? You struck out my son." As an afterthought he said to me, "Oh, you must be Brea's mom."

I am. And ever proud.

~Roxanne Mena, Pleasanton, California

My Time on the Field

Who is your favorite baseball No. 28?

My Grandpa Al was the general manager of the Dodgers when I was in high school just north of Angels Stadium in Orange County, CA. It was the middle of the high school baseball season in early April, and also the end of spring training when the Dodgers and Angels play the Freeway Series.

Grandpa asked me if I wanted to take batting practice with the Dodgers and field grounders with the shortstops. I said, "Yes!" After suiting up in a Dodger uniform, I looked at the bulletin board and saw my name in the first batting group. I borrowed a wooden bat and jumped in the cage when it was my turn. I hit pretty well—enough to get compliments from the players.

Then it was time to get out to shortstop to field grounders, but my arm was barking from pitching in a high school game the day before. I told Bill Russell, the Dodgers longtime shortstop, about my arm and he said there's no reason to air it out in fielding practice. On the first grounder, Russell fielded it smoothly and fired a strike to first. Then it was my turn. Joe Amalfitano hit a grounder, I fielded it cleanly, took a shuffle step and lobbed it over to first. Again, Russell fielded one and fired a strike, and I lobbed the next one over again.

That's when Amalfitano started screaming at me to fire the ball across the diamond. Russell piped up about my arm, but he didn't care. He hit me another one and I decided to show him I did have a good arm. I took the shuffle step and fired a bullet to first—and realized it was high, so high the first baseman didn't even jump. He just watched fly over his head. Everyone started screaming, "Heads up!"

The ball kept sailing all the way into the dugout where the Dodgers announcer, Jerry Doggett, was interviewing my favorite No. 28 and the best hitter on the Dodgers—Pedro Guerrero. Neither saw it coming. As Pedro answered a question, the ball nailed him right in the collar bone and down he went.

It was chaos. All the trainers were scrambling to help Pedro. Russell was laughing his ass off and screaming, "He nailed Guerrero! He nailed Guerrero!" I wanted to dig a hole and hide, mortified by what I had done. They rushed Guerrero into the clubhouse to be checked out more closely by the trainers.

I was scheduled to be the bat boy that game, so I sat in the dugout waiting to be kicked out for what I had done. A lot of players were giving me crap, and I knew I deserved it. I just smiled and said it had gotten away from me. Guerrero emerged from the dugout, walked over to me and said, "Did you throw the ball that hit me?" I cringed and nodded. He then showed me his collar bone; there was a clear lace mark on it. He gave me some crap, and all I could do was apologize.

Then he said, "You are lucky you are a Campanis—your grandpa has been very good to me." He told me that when he was a minor leaguer, in the off-season he saw Grandpa walking on the beach in his Dominican hometown. He went over to say hello, and Grandpa asked how he was. Pedro said he was working out but didn't have enough food. He told me Grandpa pulled a few hundred dollars out of his pocket and told him to eat healthy so he could make the big club soon. That meant so much to Pedro, I could tell.

So, instead of kicking my ass, Pedro Guerrero gave me a pass because of my grandpa. He immediately became my favorite No. 28 of all time.

~Jim Campanis, Jr., Phillips Ranch, California, author of *Born into Baseball*, where this story was first published.

MY FIRST GAME

First games are very special memories for most baseball fans. The excitement of getting to the game, the wonder of seeing the unbelievable expanse of grass, the smell of hot dogs, the pregame activity of batting and fielding practice, all of these contribute to the magic of the day. Even if the game turned out to be nothing special, it is still a day to remember. Of course, I can't remember mine…I can barely recall the game I saw last week. I do remember, clear as a bell, the first game I took my kids to in 1992 (that story was in the introduction of my first book). Fortunately, many other folks remember their maiden journeys to the park. To be honest, I have literally no idea how this chapter did not lead off the first book. So, it is leading off the second.

In truth, I am not exactly sure if this is my story or my son's to share. I am the baseball fan in the family; my husband is more of a football fan, although he appreciates the sport. I grew up rooting for the Phillies with my dad…who never stopped complaining about 1964…and I didn't care about the Cardinals until I moved to St. Louis in the '70s. That turned me into a loyal Redbirds fan.

In the summer of 1980 I was pregnant, and as always, it was hot, humid, and not at all pleasant. I already had two children, aged three and five at the time. I wasn't feeling well and took myself to the doctor, who told me rather matter-of-factly that I had actually miscarried. My instructions were to go home, stay inside, and rest. Not wanting to wallow in sadness, I decided that my kids should not be deprived of fun. Instead of following the doctor's orders, I took them to Busch Stadium for a game. The next day I decided to get a second opinion on my medical condition, and lo and behold, I was still pregnant. Now, I am not a doctor, but I choose to believe that it was the Cardinals that sustained the boy we named Ari. His first official game was before he was even born. If *that* doesn't make Ari a lifetime fan, I don't really know what would.

I only wish the doctor who was so cavalier regarding my condition was alive to read this story and to see my 6'5" tall son sporting his Cardinals cap, sitting with his similarly-uniformed sons on his lap.

~Ellen Stein, Modi'in, Israel

I saw my first game on June 10, 1970, when I was seven years old. It was the Pittsburgh Pirates vs. the San Francisco Giants at Candlestick Park in a game featuring five future Hall-of-Famers—Mays, McCovey, Perry, Stargell, and Clemente. A sixth, Juan Marichal, did not pitch that day.

My dad is from Canada and hates cold weather. I am sure he picked this one because it was a day game. Candlestick at night was not a place he would go, but that afternoon the whole family was in tow—Mom, Dad, my older sisters Laurie and Kristy, and me. We started the day in the cheap seats but had moved down behind home plate by the eighth inning when the game was tied 2-2. Laurie asked what happens if the game ends in a tie. Dad explained there would be extra innings because baseball games don't end in ties. This information was received with much consternation, moaning, and groaning from my sisters. They were done and wanted to go home.

I told Dad not to worry. Mays was up first in the bottom of the eighth and he wanted to go home, too. He was sure to hit a home run. Dad started to tell me baseball didn't work that way, that even Willie Mays couldn't hit a home run anytime he wanted. Mid-explanation, there was a mighty *crack* from Willie's bat, and the ball flew over the fence and into the bleachers for a home run. The Giants went on to score a second run in that inning on a homer by Ken Henderson. The final score was 4-2 Giants, and my sisters were spared the agony of extra innings.

I was a fan for life.

About 40 years later, I met Mays and told him the story, that in my first game he hit a homer in the 8ᵗʰ to break a 2-2 tie. "Bob Moose," Willie said. "They said I was no good in 1970." I assured him that in my eyes at the time and now, he was the greatest. I am still amazed he was able to name the pitcher he'd hit that home run off—one of 660 lifetime homers—with so little information. I'm still a Giants fan thanks to Willie.

~Tim Willson, San Francisco, California

My father was an avid Yankees fan, as am I. When I was five, he would take me to baseball practice. I told him that for Father's Day I wanted the whole family to go to a game as a gift for him. To my surprise, that Father's Day Dad organized a bus trip to Yankee Stadium for a game against the Indians. We sat up high behind home plate. Tino Martinez came up to bat and the crown roared, "Tino! Tino!" That day I found my favorite Yankee and all-time player. I've since been to hundreds of games, including game 1 of the 2009 World Series. I've sat as close as seven rows behind home plate. Not one memory comes as close to meaning so much to me as that first game with my dad. He'd turned my dream into a reality.

~Daniel Marino, Phillipsburg, New Jersey

The first baseball game I saw in person was at Connie Mack Stadium, the 1957 season finale. The Phillies hosted the Dodgers, the very last game the Dodgers played representing Brooklyn. What really sticks out to me, something I have often thought about, is what a shame that kids today probably won't ever get the feeling of their first game like many of us did back in those times. There weren't many games on TV back then, and those that were televised were in black and white. I will never forget walking into the ballpark as an eight-year-old together with my father and heading up the tunnel to the seating area. Once through the tunnel it was like magic, with all the colors, the green grass, the uniforms of both teams, and the ballpark itself. It was breathtaking, the first of many great baseball memories. I had a pretty good feeling that I was going to love the game of baseball from that day on. I was right.

To put an even brighter light on this story for me, although I admit I don't really remember, I recently discovered that in addition to this being the last game the Dodgers played representing Brooklyn, Sandy Koufax was the last pitcher to throw for the franchise. He pitched the 8th inning. The Phillies led 2-1 after 8½ innings, so no other Dodger pitcher got into the game. A Koufax appearance for my first game!

~Sam Schiff, Philadelphia, Pennsylvania

One of my fondest memories from growing up is when my dad chose me, yes *me*, a girl, over my two older brothers to go to with him to a Cincinnati Reds baseball game. I was so excited! It was my first ever major league game and Dad had gotten tickets from a friend. It was September 1978, and I was 13. Pete Rose had just ended his 44-game hitting streak the month before, which was devastating to Dad. In my house, he was simply known as "Pete" because we all knew who Dad was referring to. He seemed like just one of the family since he was the topic of many dinner conversations.

I'll never forget loading up the car for the two-hour drive to Cincinnati from Louisville, KY, feeling special as my brothers waved us out of the driveway. The whole way there, Dad talked about the sights and sounds of the ballpark with almost giddiness in his voice. The day was beautiful, cool, and clear. When we arrived, the crowd of fans was unlike any I had ever experienced. I remember Dad leaning over to me for more than half of the game pointing out players, spouting statistics I didn't quite understand. I'll never forget him yelling, "There's Pete! There's Pete!" as Rose headed toward home plate to take his swings. We ate hot dogs and peanuts and smiled and laughed all the way through the seventh inning stretch and the final catch of the last out.

Dad is now 84 years old. That experience is one I will never forget, but it was Dad who made that day at the ballpark truly memorable, and I will forever hold that dear. I still have the ticket stub, along with many others that came after, to remind me how lucky I am to have a dad like mine.

~Sherry Harris, Phoenix, Arizona

In 1985, at the age of 12, having lived in San Francisco for two years after moving to the States from El Salvador, I went to my first base-ball game. I was a motivated student and had won two free tickets from school because of good grades. I took my big brother, Ulysses, to the game. At that time I did not follow baseball and knew basically nothing about it. It was a night game in May or June vs. the Houston Astros. It had been a beautiful day, but Ulysses told me to bring warm clothing. We were sitting in the bleachers. I recall Ulysses buying hot dogs and peanuts and such.

As the game wore on, it got colder and colder, and I was glad I'd brought the warmer clothing. He obviously knew about San Francisco summer nights. At about the 7th inning, Candy Maldonado came up to bat and hit a ball toward the bleachers. Everyone rose to watch the flight of the ball, and when it cleared the fence everyone ran for it, scrambling and screaming. Knowing nothing about baseball, I asked my brother why everyone was screaming. He said, "You cheer when a Giants batter hits a home run." I naturally asked him, "What is a home run?"

I have since become a baseball and Giants fan but will never forget my first experience with the Roger "Hummm Baby" Craig Giants.

~Juan Reyes, Oakland, California

I grew up within walking distance of Ebbets Field. On one corner of my block was a Catholic Church with a large Italian-American congregation, on the other an Orthodox Jewish shul. That was Brooklyn in those days. One summer night in 1956, we went to the Feast which the church sponsored—a street fair with food and games and all the energy of the neighborhood, held in honor of a saint. Suddenly, there was a buzz in the crowd, and there was Gino Cimoli. Gino played outfield for the Brooklyn Dodgers. He was Italian and lived in the neighborhood, as so many players did back then.

I attended my first baseball game, probably in '57, the Dodgers' last year in Brooklyn, against the Cardinals. My dad, brother, and I walked to the stadium from our Crown Heights apartment. We had saved Borden's ice cream wrappers to get in, a promotion in those days, and stopped along the way for ice cream to pick up a couple more wrappers to have enough to gain admittance. I was very young, but I recall Dad pointing out Stan Musial to me as an important player I should keep my eyes on. And I remember seeing Gino Cimoli in the outfield, the guy from the neighborhood whom I'd met at the Feast!

When the Dodgers and Giants became traitors and left New York for the West Coast, Gino was the first batter when the Dodgers played the Giants in San Francisco at Seals stadium. He struck out.

~Ira Leibin, Oakland, California

Right around my seventh birthday, Dad came home with the exciting news that he had five tickets to a Phillies game. It would be the very first game any of us ever attended. There would be enough ducats to allow the whole family to pile into our '64 Ford Falcon and head to good ol' Connie Mack Stadium to watch big leaguers at play—I've never considered baseball to be work.

The Phils were hosting the Atlanta Braves, facing the legendary Tony Cloninger. Tony Cloning…who? Dad, more of a University of Minnesota and Big 10 football fan at heart, but who did enjoy a little baseball, explained, "Tony Cloninger—a pitcher, no less—hit two grand slams in the same game earlier this season!" I knew enough about baseball to be wowed by that feat. Amazingly, 50 years later, he is still the only major league pitcher to do so! Of course, the Braves also had an all-time great in right fielder Henry Aaron. Hammerin' Hank was by that time already my first sports idol, while my older brothers, Dan and Josh, chose Roberto Clemente and Willie Mays, respectively, as theirs. Keep in mind that this trio comprised quite the National League All-Star starting outfield for much of the 1950s and 1960s. I still love, and try to incorporate, the number 44 in day-to-day life in honor of Hank.

It was 1966, and I was just becoming a huge baseball fan. My dad's Minnesota Twins had been in the previous year's World Series, losing a tough seven-game classic to the legendary Sandy Koufax and the Dodgers. This year's Phillies was a decent ballclub, but already 16 years deep into a 30-year stretch without a Series appearance. The 1950 Whiz Kids had charmed the locals until getting outclassed and swept by the Yankees. The 1980 bunch, led by Steve Carlton, Mike Schmidt, and Pete Rose, would finally bring a baseball parade to this uniquely sports-crazed town. Most famously, the '64 Phillies carry the dubious reputation of going from underdog feel-good story to choke artists who blew a 6 ½ game lead with 12 left to play. I was a little too young to witness this, but the embarrassment has been hard-wired eternally into my Philly sports DNA.

The ballpark was located in the rough-and-tumble streets of North Philly; perhaps it was good that this was an afternoon game. Our middle-class suburban New Jersey home was only a half-hour's drive from the ballpark, but we had arrived in a different world. Dad parallel parked the Falcon in front of the row homes surrounding 21st and Lehigh, and I recall being greeted by a youngster not much older than me. "Watch your car for a quarter," he said. I thought that was kind of cool, if a little costly. Dad thought it was a very good investment. The kid did a good job of watching; we arrived back to a car in the same condition as we'd left it.

Now, for the game itself.

We didn't purchase a program. It wasn't until I was preparing this piece that I thought to look up the particulars of that August 7th contest between two non-contenders. Baseballreference.com will tell you my Goldberg family was joined by only 14,577 other fans that day, and that Cloninger pitched a five-hit shutout. Not only that, but this latter-day Babe Ruth also doubled home a run. What of the other big sluggers I was dying to see? The immortal Aaron and the Phils' mercurial Richie (later, Dick) Allen went for a combined 0-8.

What no box score could capture was the impossibly gorgeous expanse of green grass that came to life so beautifully in the North Philly shrine. The late, beloved Hall of Fame player and broadcaster, Richie Ashburn, once said of Connie Mack Stadium, the former Shibe Park, "It looked like a ballpark. It smelled like a ballpark. It had a feeling and a heartbeat, a personality that was all baseball."

I'm not sure my just-turned-seven-year-old self realized just how much personality it had, although I did try to take it all in. I sensed immediately that the ballpark was immense. At that time, it was 447 feet to dead center, and more than 400 feet to both power alleys. While the 3-0 Braves victory featured only one home run, by a fine, pure hitter from the Dominican Republic, Rico Carty, and four doubles, including one by Joe Torre, every crack of the bat was impossibly loud and resonant.

As I look back, I recall the pure joy of screaming, "We want a hit!" with the other fans—and usually not having our request granted—and I remember being intrigued by the name Woody Woodward. The Braves utility man booted two balls at short that day, while his Hall of Fame partner at the hot corner, Eddie Mathews, also kicked one. Cloninger, not content to merely pitch a shutout and stroke an RBI double, also uncorked his 19th and 20th wild pitches of the season on the way to a National League-leading 27. Another wow!

So, what became of some of the main characters of this story?

Our 1964 Ford Falcon ran another four years until we traded it in for a 1970 American Motors Ambassador. Why would I lie about that?!

Hank Aaron? I think you know that the then 34-year-old slugger would still not only make nine more All-Star Game appearances but would best Babe Ruth's iconic 714 homers by another 41. I chose my first sports idol quite well.

Tony Cloninger didn't have the same longevity as No. 44. His last game would be pitched in 1972, just prior to his 32nd birthday. He finished with a respectable 113-97 career record and 4.07 ERA, and no doubt, the immense satisfaction that no other pitcher, maybe even player, will ever break his record of two grand slams in a single game. If anyone does, I'd love to be there to see or write about it.

Connie Mack Stadium would make it through the 1970 season, after which the Phillies moved into one of those horrible, cookie-cutter, all-purpose artificial turf stadiums in South Philly. Yes, most of my ballpark memories came to be realized at The Vet, but what's intended to be progress often comes at the expense of personality. We wouldn't catch too many more games at 21st and Lehigh, but I do remember that my brothers and I earned some free games there via our school, thanks to our excellent report cards. From one of those games, I recall neighborhood buddy Jackie Carpenter flying a paper airplane onto the field and watching Phils' southpaw hurler Grant Jackson stuffing it into his back pants pocket.

The things one remembers! You can't Google every fun fact.

And what of the kid that did such a great job of watching our Falcon? He only had four more seasons to cash in on parking fees but was still able to sock away enough money from those rounds to put himself through college and eventually become a renowned multimillionaire businessman who is also a wonderful philanthropist. How do I know that? Well, I don't, exactly.

The beauty of baseball goes beyond runs, hits, and errors to fathers and mothers, sons and daughters, neighbors and friends. It goes to the very heart of dreams and aspirations.

A seven-year-old boy could scarcely dream up a ballpark so massive and uniquely beautiful, servicing a team that never won much of anything. I'm still thankful that I was there to witness an otherwise meaningless 1966 ballgame with Cloninger, Aaron, Allen, and Johnny Callison. I was there with my brothers, and my parents of blessed memory, indulging an early love affair with a sometimes-silly American pastime.

Ours is a love affair that has never died, despite all the changes the game has embraced and endured.

~Matthew J. Goldberg, Cherry Hill, New Jersey, co-author of *A Snowball's Chance: Philly Fires Back Against the National Media*

When I was nine or 10 years old in the mid-'70s, my dad took me to my first Boston Red Sox game at Fenway Park. I was an avid Little Leaguer, and Dad was an umpire for the older youth (Babe Ruth) league in my hometown of Worcester, MA. I had my glove with me, ready and eager to catch a foul ball. Accompanying us was a guy who worked with Dad, and his daughter who was about 12 and not at all knowledgeable about the game, which I found rather off-putting. We went to the park early and watched batting practice. Because Fenway was rather empty at this early time, we were able to go down to the very edge of the stands next to the dugout. One player broke his bat and a grounds crew member brought it to the dugout. He saw us, came over, reached out over the low wall, and gave the bat…to the girl! I was so upset, I think I cried and was miserable the entire game. I guess the whole episode was an inauspicious start to my dealings with the opposite sex, as well.

~Jeff Turgeon, Northborough, Massachusetts

Years ago, as part of a small group, I took a girlfriend to her first major league game at Shea Stadium. I impressed them all by "buying" *her* Mets an additional out. There was a high foul pop that the opposing team's left fielder and third baseman closed in on. I drew from years of experience, where I'd learned how an individual fan in the stands can affect the outcome of the occasional play. I knew what to yell, and when. The stereotypical thing the average fan yells in such situations is, "I got it!" a simple attempt to confuse the fielders, but one that rarely works. Why? Because "I got it!" is *not* how a pro ballplayer calls a teammate off. Likewise, I did not time my yell at the initial roar from the crowd reacting to the ball in play. I waited a second, knowing that I had a better chance to be heard if I yelled on the offbeat. And what I yelled was one word, "Mine!"

The ball dropped between both fielders, either of whom could have easily caught it, but didn't. Instead, they looked up at the stands and shook their heads, muttering to themselves about how they had been called off by a fan.

As for my girlfriend? We had been dating awhile, she was newly hooked on the Mets, and I can say that at least for a while, I was truly lucky.

~Michael Bouton, Woodside, New York

My love for baseball started as it did with so many other young kids, when their fathers took them to their very first game. We lived in Las Vegas where there was no major or minor league team in the 1960s. We visited Candlestick Park in San Francisco during a summer vacation, and there are a few things I will never forget. It was *cold!* I was four or five at the time, and Dad carried me around the stadium on his shoulders. After the game we stood outside a ballpark gate waiting for players to exit. Cars pulled out from the players' parking lot and fans tried to stop players to get autographs. I liked the excitement. But my dad was a patient man. We stayed for quite some time, and finally a car pulled out. Dad smiled big! A ball player handed me a small round piece of paper in the shape of a baseball, his autograph was plain to read—Willie McCovey.

~Nina Green, Salt Lake City, Utah

My father, Jim Holman, is a *big* baseball fan. Being a good Canadian kid, he loves hockey, but baseball is his passion. In 1990, one week into the season, I called him and asked if he had watched any games yet. His response was, "I haven't really seen many. I think I have caught five games so far." It takes me a whole year to watch that many games. I grew up in the small town of Hanna, Alberta. Dad would take my brother and me to the ballpark to watch our town's teams. When we went to Calgary, we would see the AAA Cannons play. I loved sitting in the stands with Dad, learning about turning double plays, how far the base runner should be leading off, and how you can leave peanut shells all over the place and it was more than okay, it was expected…and fun! It was also Dad's best sport; he was still playing slo-pitch in his mid-60s with much younger guys. He hits fewer homers these days, but still often goes 4-4 to complement a good glove and arm at third base.

In 2014 when Dad turned 65, he still had never been to a regular season major league game. One of my bucket list items was to take him to catch a few. I offered him several options, and he chose a trip to New York and Boston. We took in two Red Sox vs. Yankees games in the new Yankee Stadium, complete with a tour of the ballpark. He loved going behind the scenes and hearing about the players he watched as a kid. The Sox (my team) won the first night; the Yankees (his team) won the second. We were thrilled to see Jeter hit a home run in his final season. The most fun we had was singing "New York, New York" when the Yankees won. We even kicked up our heels like can-can dancers. We laughed along with everyone around us. The next day, we hopped on a train to Boston to see the Sox play Toronto. Rather than a tour of Fenway, I was able to get him onto the field to watch batting practice. He loves the Blue Jays and spent the whole time grinning from ear to ear as he stood five feet from his heroes.

Dad has asked to go on another baseball trip with me to Chicago and St. Louis. I can't wait to share another wonderful experience sipping beers, razzing batters, and making a huge mess eating peanuts.

~Paul Holman, Lindell Beach, British Columbia

I was a 12-year-old Yankees fan in 1963, living in Tucson, Arizona. That summer we went on a vacation to New York to see relatives. At a family get-together in Mount Vernon, things were going quite slowly and I was enduring kisses from old lady relatives, and such. Suddenly my older cousin, Steven, showed up with an extra ticket to the Yankees game that evening. Before I knew it, we were walking into the upper deck behind first at Yankee Stadium. The place was lit up like a fairyland, and I especially remember the emerald, green grass. Mantle hit a homer, we won, and my first big league game was unforgettable. Postscript: I got fed up with Steinbrenner, moved to San Francisco, and became a Giants fan.

~Joe Goldmark, San Francisco, California

Although I've been a lifelong Phillies fan, my first game was actually watching the old Philadelphia A's play. It was on July 11, 1954, their last year before moving to Kansas City, and later, Oakland. I was not quite five, and my dad and Uncle Ben who lived next door were watching me one Sunday afternoon because Mom was very pregnant with my younger sister-to-be. It is more accurate to say they were watching the first game of an A's vs. Red Sox doubleheader, not me. I was just hanging around in the living room trying to keep myself occupied. I remember my uncle saying to Dad, "Why don't we try to catch the second game?" Dad said, "What about Jerry (me)?" Uncle Ben said, "Let's take him."

The next thing I knew, I was sitting in what seemed like an enormous other world, where the grass was so long and wide and flat, and a beautiful shade of bright summer green. I grew up in a row home with 80 houses on the block. I was not used to this wide expanse of perfection.

The following is from a story regarding that doubleheader. I don't remember the game details, but Dad would always tell me that Gus Zernial got injured that day, so I Googled it.

"The A's most embarrassing loss of 1954 was in game one of the Sunday twin-bill, an 18–0 Red Sox rout. Gus Zernial broke his left collarbone after he tripped on a water spigot trying to catch Billy Consolo's double. Some A's fans booed Zernial as he came off the field. The Red Sox then took game two of the July 11 doubleheader by a slightly less embarrassing 11–1 margin."

So, my introduction to sports, Philadelphia-style, was a prophetic one. Results-wise, it did not get much better for a long time and successes were few and far between. But that was not what was important. What resonated with me was that both my dad and uncle, two very serious and hardworking men, were enjoying themselves to an extent I had never seen before. They weren't talking about work, or family health issues, or anything burdensome. They were focused on the game and cheering. I had never known cheering existed! What a concept! The other fans were, too. I was hooked. Forever!

I was fortunate to have had a dad who loved sports, played sports, taught me how to play, and took me to games. This was where it started.

~Jerry Shinfeld, Philadelphia, Pennsylvania

While visiting my 75-year-old dad, Joaquim, in St. Louis, Game 1 of the 2014 National League Championship Series was about to be played in Busch Stadium against San Francisco. As a lifelong Giant's fan, I insisted on taking Dad to the game. Without tickets, we marshaled our way to the sold-out stadium. As I was checking out the sights and sounds, Dad struck up a conversation with someone in the crosswalk. Next thing I knew, he yelled out, "Raymond, this guy here will sell us two tickets at face-value." I bought them on the spot. As we made our way to the seats and started to watch soon-to-be labeled baseball legend Madison Bumgarner take the mound, Dad leaned over and said, "This is my first professional baseball game." *Wow.* How come I didn't know that?! The man I've known my whole life.

That's why I love baseball. It has a way of bringing us back to rediscovery.

~Ray Limon, University Park, Maryland

I had never been to a professional ball game before. I actually hadn't been anywhere before. Other than the traveling carnival and a drive-in movie now and then, I'd had very few exciting childhood experiences. Born and raised in L.A., I had never been to Disneyland, Magic Mountain, or any theme parks. So, hopping in the blue and white mini-station wagon with my older brother Michael on the way to Dodger Stadium was the joy of my life. I was equally excited about the drive as I was about the game. I stuck my head completely out of the car window to let the cool L.A. breeze and smog hit my face. It was quite rare for me to be inside a car, and I savored the ride. My other brother, Ronald, just a little older than me, complained to Michael to make me sit back and relax. It seemed that everything I did was embarrassing to him, but I didn't care. I was enjoying the moment.

Like any kid in the world, I will never forget the experience of my first big league game. I was so excited as we pulled up to the stadium, I couldn't even get my seatbelt off. I remember the joy on Michael's face as the provider of this rare treat. Although he had been to several Dodgers games times by then, he knew it was Ronald's and my first time and was proud to share it with his younger brothers. From the taste of my first foot long Dodger Dog to the smell of the diamond's green grass, and finally seeing my favorite players live and in person, that day will forever be imprinted in my memory.

We were there early enough to see our favorite players in a relaxed mode prior to the game. One of the most famous infields in big league history was there in the flesh—Steve Garvey, Davey Lopes, Bill Russell, and Ron Cey. We stayed the entire nine innings, which I haven't done since. I don't remember if the Dodgers won, but they were playing the Angels. I'm not sure what it actually cost Michael, who was a student at UCLA, but it was a priceless experience for Ronald and me.

These rare but joyful childhood experiences drive me, as a father and now a grandfather, to fill my children's lives with rewarding experiences. I often encourage parents, particularly young fathers, to be cognizant of the fact that emotional experiences form the longest lasting memories. To quote the poet Maya Angelou, "A person may forget what you say or forget what you do, but they will never forget how you made them feel." What emotional memories would a parent prefer their child have of them? I'm not sure if Michael knew it at the time, but this experience was, and still is, one of the brightest moments of my childhood.

~Deon Price Oakland, California, author of *Raised in Hell*, from which this story is excerpted

On August 13, 1957, on a car trip to Massachusetts from Louisiana, my dad, my oldest brother, and I stopped in Philadelphia to go to Connie Mack Stadium to watch the Phillies play the Pittsburgh Pirates. It was my first Major League Baseball game. I will never forget the men bringing paper sacks with bottles inside the ballpark, sneaking contraband alcohol into the game. I was 12 and still remember the outfielders and pitchers in the outfield shagging fly balls and talking amongst themselves. The Pirates won 6-0, Bob Friend defeating Warren Hacker for the win. The highlight for me was Bill Mazeroski hitting a home run that hit the tin roof over us in the left field bleachers. Maz was 2-3 and drove in four of the six Pirates runs. Roberto Clemente was 1-5.

I was reminded of that night three years later, listening on the radio at school, when Mazeroski hit the walk-off home run in the ninth inning of the 1960 World Series to bring the Pirates the title.

~Andrew Godfrey, DeRidder, Louisiana

May 28, 2005 shouldn't have been anything special, just a date on the calendar, but it is special for me. That date has become one of those times that make you achingly wish to have things be as they were in earlier, happier times. That day, my father, my four-year-old son Mitchell, and I experienced that precious piece of Americana, the multi-generational trip to a Major League Baseball game.

Mitchell already had a mitt, and he confidently caught a tennis ball. He often wore a Cincinnati Reds cap, alternating with others we had bought him. Thanks to my wife, as a toddler he had been photographed in that Reds cap along with his mitt and a Louisville Slugger mini-bat in hand. He was familiar with Babe Ruth and a handful of current and past Reds players. A love for the history of the game, as well as appreciation for the best players in the mid-2000s, was being cultivated in the blond towhead, and I adored every second of his indoctrination. The affinity for the game that he displayed at such a young age, combined with his propensity for behaving well in public, bolstered my confidence when planning that special multi-generational outing. On that day, the Reds would finally honor legendary former manager George "Sparky" Anderson, retiring his No. 10 uniform number in a pregame ceremony. I won't recite Hall of Famer Anderson's credentials, or the team and personal accomplishments of the mid-1970s Big Red Machine. He was part of my childhood and the baseball memory trove that my father and I shared.

It was a gorgeous, warm day. We lived just outside of Indianapolis and drove two hours to my parents' house—my Hoosier childhood home—to pick up my dad, who had taken me to Reds games at Riverfront Stadium before the Great American Ballpark. Dad grinned as I strapped Mitchell into the back seat and we headed for the Queen City. Mitchell gazed out the window like a little adult until his eyes got heavy. Asleep by North Vernon, he snoozed until we neared the Ohio state line and the hilly terrain overlooking the Ohio river in the tri-state region of Indiana, Ohio, and northern Kentucky. We parked, and I took Mitchell's hand to make the trek across the highway to the ballpark. The crowd and pregame atmosphere had the youngster on wide-eyed sensory overload. His head swiveled and he stopped a few times to absorb all that he was witnessing. We took our time and allowed Mitchell to take it in.

We made typical ballpark lunch purchases. Mitchell had a hot dog, soft drink, and requisite bag of peanuts in shells to enjoy during the number-retirement ceremony and game. By the time the fanfare and applause for Anderson had concluded, Mitchell had been in his seat high up in the stands for more than 45 minutes. He'd watched the ceremony, asked a few questions, chuckled at scoreboard graphics and sounds, pointed at boats passing by on the river beyond the right-center field seats and munched on peanuts while drinking soda. I asked periodically if he was doing okay, and he always nodded his head affirmatively and continued being a fan. When the seventh inning stretch rolled around, Mitchell hadn't once squirmed in his seat or left it for the six-plus innings of baseball and long pregame festivities. I urged him to make a trip to the restroom with me during the song-filled extended break in the action and he agreed. As we made our way back to our seats, he pulled up short. I looked down to see his little face peer up at me and he asked, "Daddy, can we go home now?"

That young man had been amazingly well behaved and attentive for more than three hours of stadium time plus the long journey. More important, he had shared in a special time with his father and grandfather, the first Major League Baseball game of his life. If he now wanted to be a four-year-old and release himself from exceeding societal expectations, it was fine with me. He had earned it.

We partially scaled the steps to get my father's attention and waved him down to meet us. When I told him Mitchell had asked to leave, Dad shared my beaming pride in the little man who had been so tuned in to baseball and the ballpark experience while still three months shy of his fifth birthday. We began our walk out of the stadium to the garage. Following a postgame meal of chicken fingers and fries on top of all the peanuts he'd consumed during the afternoon, he settled into his seat and snoozed again on the way back home.

Mitchell and I have been to several Reds games as well as minor league and independent league baseball games in the ensuing years. But May 28, 2005, is special for me. It always will be.

-Troy Guthrie, Jonesborough, Tennessee

When I was seven or eight years old, in 1965 or 1966, my neighbor, Archie Rose, invited me and my dad, Don Rascoe, to go with him and his son, Richard, to a San Francisco Giants game, a scheduled double-header against the Braves. Archie, a great guy, *always* had great seats, often right behind home plate. This would be my first major league game at Candlestick Park. *Everything* I did that day was a first—the drive to the ballpark, parking in the lot, the long walk to the ticket booth, the longer walk up the ramps into the stadium. In those days, you could look out past right field through a cyclone fence out to the shipyards. There were no seats out there back then, and the wind really blew through that fence.

While I remember a lot about that day, what is seared permanently into my memory is what I saw when I walked up and through those big double doors leading to our seats. I still clearly remember how bright and vivid the colors were—the orange seats, and the scoreboard lights. But the field is what gave me goose bumps and does so even today. That grass was so green and perfectly manicured, I recall standing at the top of the steps and just gawking. I am a baseball worshiper. At that moment, I knew I had arrived at my church, my place of worship. Candlestick had a lot of drawbacks, but I have always loved that place. That love began the day I first pushed though those big double doors.

Final note: as touching and big an experience as that was for me in my journey as a baseball fan, the game was a *rainout!* I didn't see a single pitch thrown. It didn't matter, though, the damage was done!

~Ric Rascoe, Santa Rosa, California

At 12 years old, along with everything Star Wars-related, there was, of course, baseball with my friends. Random broken windows resulted from batted baseballs, so we began to make balls with newspaper and duct tape, in retrospect a genius move. We couldn't care less if we lost the ball, and there were no more broken windows along with the inevitable grounding and ass-tanning that came with them.

I went to my first major league game on September 26, 1987. My grandfather took me for "Reggie Jackson Day." Reggie was his all-time favorite player. Details have been blurred through time, yet I remember—confirmed by research—being disappointed that Reggie batted only once this day in a pinch-hit role, popping out with runners on second and third in a 3-2 loss to the Chicago White Sox. After the game Reggie was in a bad mood. "I'm not into talking about how wonderful things are for me when we've lost four in a row," he said. "I'm embarrassed. If we had won, it would be different. But right now, my esteem is low. My self-importance is microscopic."

I remember little of that game, but my memory was refreshed by looking back at the box score. I recall my 12-year-old self wondering, "Who in the hell is Walt Weiss?" Just 1988 Rookie of the Year. I don't recall Curt Young pitching seven strong innings, or any feelings or ballpark details, except for the expansiveness of the field, my grandfather chain-smoking Marlboro Reds, and peeing in a trough for the first time. I do remember Reggie's at-bat. This probably destroyed my belief in pre-destiny and prepared me for the heartbreak and disappointment of being an Athletics fan for years to come.

Without my grandfather's fondness for Reggie—his brash attitude and high strikeout rates aside—I would probably never have found my love for baseball and the A's. To me, Reggie was a legend, a mystifying one since he retired just as I was learning to love and appreciate the game. He was a Ruthian figure, honored by someone I loved, which made me open my eyes and try to figure out just what made this guy so special.

When my grandfather died, I sadly watched his children argue and bicker over his possessions. I decided right then that I didn't need an earthly remembrance of this man who was the biggest father-figure in my life. A couple of months later, my grandmother handed me an autographed Reggie Jackson ball. I knew it well; it had the most prominent spot in the case where grandpa kept his baseball memorabilia. It was the gem of the collection. "I saved this for you," she said. "Grandpa would have wanted you to have it."

I love when baseball existentialists come together to sing their anthems of praise about the serene rhythms and mystic qualities of the game. It gives me a warm feeling. As much as I love and adore the game, sometimes I feel as if those are all illusions because of a time and an innocence that I miss and cherish, and that I'll never see again.

~Gary Trujillo, Austin, Texas

My most memorable game was my first Major League Baseball game. I was a freshman at UCLA and getting my first taste of freedom…or as much freedom as my student loans could afford me. Three high school friends and I got nosebleed seats at Dodger Stadium for a whopping $8 a pop. This was also the price of a movie ticket, but the game gave us a sunny sky, the ability to talk to each other, and copious amounts of peanut shells with which we could litter the floor. We were not old enough to buy beers, but for a kid living away from home for the first time, I felt like an adult.

Since then I've been to many games more exciting and with better seats, but the first is still the most memorable.

~Terry Im, Hillsborough, California

In 1955 my family lived in New Brunswick, NJ, where my father, a young army officer, was stationed after four years in Bamberg, West Germany, amidst the rubble and restoration of that country in the wake of WWII. I was introduced to baseball in Germany, watching games played by U.S. servicemen. Then, living in the shadow of New York City, I began to follow Major League Baseball and the local teams—the Yankees, Dodgers, and Giants. I confess that I didn't know the history of those three great franchises, and when forced to choose a team to attach my allegiance to, I picked the Yankees because the Yanks had defeated the Rebs during the Civil War!

My pestering to be taken to a real game paid off when Dad and I set off for Yankee Stadium on September 11, 1955, to see a doubleheader against the Cleveland Indians. The Indians had dethroned the five-consecutive championship Yanks the previous year for the American League pennant and the two teams were now locked in a tight pennant race. Through the magic of the Internet, I rediscovered the data from those games. The crowd was 65,310, the third largest in baseball that year. The other two were also Cleveland games in New York. The teams split the doubleheader, with Tommy Byrne defeating Early Wynn, and then Don Mossi beating Whitey Ford. Mickey Mantle hit a home run.

Dad and I walked across the field after the game—permissible back then—pausing at Monument Park to view the plaques to Yankee greats, then again in center field. For a long time I couldn't figure out how my father had gotten such great seats, right behind the Yanks' dugout, in that sold-out park. He hadn't had tickets when we left for the game. Much later, I learned that the Yanks had a tradition of comping active duty serviceman with the best seats available. My father, not only on active duty, but a WWII vet, got the best seats in the house.

-Nick Sebastian, Emeryville, California

It was April 1958, and the vision will remain with me until the cows come home. Grass so green it shocks the eyeballs almost into being blinded, I remember. It was what I saw as a 10-year-old whippersnapper with his favorite aunt who loved baseball and everything about it—the players, the drinking, the smells, the scorecard. My dad worked a couple of jobs and had little free time, although he dearly wanted to take his two sons on an outing like this. When I got wind that "Aunt Rita" was going to Opening Day, it was all I could talk about. She had two extra tickets and asked Mom to allow me and my older brother, Jack, to skip Catholic school to go with her. WooHoo! We even got permission from the nuns, who seemed to understand the sanctity of the moment. Aunt Rita, I learned later on, wasn't really our aunt; she was one of Dad's old flames before he married Mom. For some reason, Rita kept in contact with Dad after WWII, to Mom's annoyance. Nevertheless, Mom allowed this relationship to continue. It seems odd today, to say the least, but at the time she was our favorite aunt, period.

I did not sleep one wink the night before. We slept in bunk beds, and I continually bounced a ball off Jack's bunk above me. He finally grabbed the ball and said, "Go to sleep, Mickey." Morning couldn't come fast enough. Finally, Aunt Rita came to pick us up in her Pontiac convertible. We had moved to the D.C. suburb of Silver Spring, and it would take about 30 minutes to get to Griffith Stadium, and then park nearby for the cost of $1—an enormous sum of money in those days. With the neighboring Wonder Bread Bakery emanating the most delicious smells, we were already hungry as we went to pick up our tickets at the window. I remember asking, "Can I eat three hot dogs?"

As we entered the stadium, I couldn't begin to imagine the thrill and the blinding green color I was to experience. Jack and I were mesmerized, watching all the funny-looking people doing the same thing as us—going to the ballgame. Some had transistor radios held to their ears, some were well-dressed. We followed Aunt Rita to a long, narrow hallway with a light at the end of the tunnel, and there it was, the most beautiful green lawn I'd ever seen, with players on it throwing and catching. We were so close we could hear them talk. We had box seats by first base! I was so amazed Jack told me to close my mouth or I was going to catch flies. I was carrying my new Rawlings baseball glove, a Coke, and some peanuts. As the players took batting practice, they would make the turn at first, and you could almost touch them as they ran by. Eddie Yost came by— evidently, he'd had a few dates with Aunt Rita.

I will never forget the excitement of that day watching Harmon Killebrew, Roy Sievers, Camilo Pascual, and Jim Lemon, or even Clint Courtney, the veteran catcher they used to call "Scrapiron." He was unbelievably old at the time, I think 32. These were my true heroes of the day. To watch them in person, well, it was much better than Christmas because I only had to share the moment with Jack, and not five other siblings who didn't even begin to understand what a sacred moment this was.

Of course, the Senators didn't do very well, but the experience wasn't about the final score. Aunt Rita showed us how to keep score, which Dad verified when we got home, changing a few symbols to make sure we got it exactly right. What a science. We learned so much more than we could have learned in school that day. It is a day, as I said in the beginning, that I will never ever forget.

~Michael O'Malley, Washington, District of Columbia

TO CATCH A BALL...OR NOT

What baseball fan doesn't want to catch a ball? A home run, a foul ball, a batting practice home run, it doesn't really matter. That is why so many people bring their gloves to baseball games. Maybe when you catch it you will hold it up high, like a conquest, for some camera time. Sometimes you will give it to your girlfriend, or the little kid sitting next to you. Sometimes you may even throw it back on the field in defiance of a home run by a visiting player. But everyone wants to catch a ball once in their lives. I never have, not in all the games I have gone to. Rachel has, and David has twice, all when sitting no more than two seats away from me.

Here are stories of fans when they caught that treasured ball...or didn't.

July 29, 1990, I was at Candlestick Park with my wife, Diane. Our seats were 12 rows up from first base, an area where you had to be ready to catch a foul ball at any time. In the bottom half of the first inning, I noticed a rather large fan carefully picking his way through the maze of legs, feet, beers, and peanut shells to get to his seat while carrying a large beer and a Polish sausage. Just as he was about sit down, I head the crack of a bat and looked up to see a towering foul ball headed his way. With one hand clutching his beer, and the other cradling the polish sausage, you could clearly see the panic and indecision on his face. At the last second, he set his beer cup and Polish on the cement between his feet and reached up to catch the ball, but he was too slow to make the catch. The ball passed between his outstretched hands and, like a guided missile, it scored a direct hit on the sausage, sending up a cloud of meat, mustard, and relish that thoroughly covered the unlucky fan and knocked over his beer. The ball then squirted about five seats to the left where another fan made an easy catch of the mustard-slathered ball. Needless to say, we all felt sorry for the poor fellow as he trudged back up the aisle, covered in the remnants of what should have been a fine ballpark meal. The Giants won that day, shutting out the Reds 4-0. This fan, too, was shut out, from his lunch and a ballpark's greatest souvenir.

~John Akin, Pinetop, Arizona

A few years back when my partner, Bobby, had access to corporate front row seats behind the Giant's dugout at Pac Bell Park, we were watching a very fast-moving game with a lot of pop flies. Suddenly, a ball was hit right at Bobby. He stood up calmly—along with those behind and beside us—and caught it in his bare hands. We were shocked. Beside him was a little girl and her dad, and she looked up at Bobby with envy. He knew what he had to do, and he handed the ball to the father who in turn gave it to her. She held it with both hands before chatting with her dad. A moment later she nudged Bobby, and he looked over at her to find she was holding up a half-empty box of Cracker Jacks. Her father said she wanted to give them to him because he had given her a ball hit by a Giant. She held onto the ball all through the game, clutching it close to her chest. She wasn't going to drop that ball for anything.

~Bob Welch, San Francisco, California

It was the 2008 home opener for the Rangers against the Baltimore Orioles. My son, Adam, and I were sitting in our usual front row bleacher seats in center field. With two out in the top of the 7th, Josh Hamilton made a crash-into-the-wall catch right in front of us to end the inning. He took a few steps away from the wall, locked eyes with Adam, and threw him the ball.

~Richard Guay, Dallas, Texas

I still not only *have* that ball, but I keep it with me wherever I go, either in my car or in my baseball bag. The ball took on extra special meaning for Dad and me—and we have a good collection of autographed balls, including Hall of Famers we personally obtained—when three years later, a fan, Shannon Stone, died falling from the same area we were in while reaching for a ball thrown up to him…by Hamilton.

~Adam Guay, Aubrey, Texas

I went to a game in Seattle in 2001. The Mariners, the team of 116 wins, were hosting the Tigers. Jose Lima was pitching for the Tigers, and Ichiro had two singles in the 1st inning of a seven-run explosion. I caught a home run ball hit by Mariners' first basemen John Olerud, the first and only ball I have caught to this day. But I knew this one girl, Jamie, was trying to get a ball for her dad, Robert, who was in the hospital dying of cancer.

I made my way to the dugout between innings, and the officer stationed there let me speak to Manager Lou Pinella. After explaining the situation, Lou obtained the signatures of every player in the dugout. The officer then escorted me to the bullpen to get the signatures of the pitchers, making it a ball signed by the entire team. I gave it to Jamie. She was so surprised, and it made Robert so happy. He passed away two weeks later.

Jamie and I became best friends and remain so until this day. She keeps the ball displayed in a case.

~Michael Lust, Phoenix, Arizona

At a game in 2003, my constant personal battle between my love for baseball and for ballpark food came to a head. In college, a professor had offered me his Club Level tickets for a beautiful, sun-drenched day game at the yard. They were aisle seats behind home plate, and a buddy and I had just settled in with our beers and nachos when a screamer of a foul ball flew in our direction. In a split second I had to analyze whether to duck and cover while protecting my ice-cold beverage and steaming nachos or attempt to catch the ball. I got caught somewhere in between, kicking my beer over, flipping my nachos off my lap into the aisle and fumbling the ball. I got pelted directly in the chest, but the ball bounced into my buddy's lap and I was left with no food, drink, souvenir, or dignity. While my ego was crushed for failing so amazingly, I could have done without the attendant walking down *not* to check on my health, but to yell at me for spilling nachos and beer all over her aisle.

~Bryan Dow, Burlingame, California

Although I grew up in Los Angeles, we were Yankee fans because my older brother loved Mickey Mantle. So we hated the Dodgers. Through my British dad's influence, we were also track fans, and when the Dodgers came in and ruined the Coliseum for track, we hated them even more. Even so, to games we went. I had gotten into baseball partly by reading my brother's old Dell baseball magazines. I became a Cincy fan because of the Murderer's Row of sluggers.

I think it was 1960 when we saw Cincy vs. L.A. Because of the shape of the Coliseum, there was a very high left field screen which made home runs more difficult, but then it went straight down to normal level, shaped like an L. The drama of this game involved Wally Moon, a Dodgers star. He managed to single, double, and triple in his first three at-bats. In his last, he hit the ball hard, right at the corner of that L. The great Frank Robinson came running from left field, the almost-great Vada Pinson from center. They smashed into each other right at that corner, both temporarily knocked out. Moon ran around the bases—but no one in the stadium knew what had happened. Was it a home run, Moon hitting a home run for the coveted cycle? Was it an inside the parker or over the fence? Or did one of the guys lying out there have the ball? Finally, Frank got up…and showed the ball in his glove. Wally didn't get his circuit…or the cycle.

~Stephen Owen, Augsburg, Germany

I caught my first and only foul ball at a Texas Rangers game at the Ballpark in Arlington in July of 2004 against the Toronto Blue Jays. We were sitting halfway between third base and the left field wall in the field level seats, just under the next level above us. This was important because around the 6th inning there was a rain delay, and the covering allowed us to stay dry and enjoy the best chili dog I've ever had at a ballpark, while many people left the stadium because they were getting wet. The rain delay lasted 45 minutes. Once they resumed play, I trotted down and grabbed a seat two rows behind the Rangers' dugout. I was hoping to get a ball when the inning ended since I was 16 years old and could still easily grab balls tossed by players. After five to 10 minutes, a man and his son came to where I was sitting, the man saying I was in his seats. I promptly apologized and moved over a few seats to give them some room, and he angrily said, "No you can't sit in this entire row! Do you work for Price-Waterhouse Cooper's? No! Get out!"

Flabbergasted, I got up, looked at the man, and moved out of "his row" up to the fourth row, first seat. Two rows behind this very mean man, I was talking to someone behind me about what a jerk he was when Gary Matthews Jr. came up to bat for the Rangers. Knowing he was a lefty, I kept my eye on him as we chatted. He fouled off one of the first pitches to right behind the dugout. As it came off the bat, I knew it was coming in my direction. Time seemed to slow down, and the speeding ball seemed to be in slow motion. As it got closer, coming right toward me, I put my hands up and caught it bare-handed. The ball would have hit me right in the chest had I not caught it. I was surprised, but this was one of the happiest moments in my life. I got a standing ovation from the crowd around me. I stood, held up the ball, and enjoyed my moment. I barely got to savor the look on the man's face who had booted me out of the seat in his row, which ironically resulted in my catching the ball. Looking back on it, as much as I wanted to rub the karma in the man's face, I'm happy I didn't. It would have diminished the elation of my feat. I went back up to sit with my dad and asked him and the nice couple sitting next to us if they had seen the foul ball. I told them that it was very close to me, then pulled the ball out and told them the whole story. To this day, I tell this more than any other baseball story. It is one of my proudest moments.

~Brendan Paskach, Boise, Idaho

At Game 5 of the 2002 World Series, I was sitting in the Club Level and went to the concession area to buy a souvenir for my teenage daughter, Kate. We had to wait for the batter to complete his at-bat before we could return to our seats. I was standing just behind a fan holding a cardboard tray with three or four beers in it. The batter hit a high foul ball toward us and it landed, no lie, right in the beer tray, sending a shower of beer all over the fan. He didn't have any beer left, but he did have a souvenir ball.

~Cindy Gilman Redburn, San Francisco, California

At a Giants game at AT&T Park in 2010, I was with my dad sitting in our regular seats down the first base line. Edgar Renteria, the Giants shortstop, hit a foul ball which was caught by the person right in front of me. While I had previously caught a ball in a different part of the stadium, these seats in prime foul ball territory hadn't produced the same luck for me. Disappointed but undeterred, I watched the right-handed Renteria get back in the box with my glove religiously on my hand. Who would guess that on the very next pitch, he would hit a screaming line drive right at *me*? In a *Sandlot* moment, I reached out my glove among a sea of hands and silently sent the thought, "Please catch it!" Sure enough, I felt contact and squeezed my hand like my life depended on it. The force, and the bodies surrounding me, literally spun me around, and my hat flew off my head. Instinctively, and possibly still in shock from my Gold Glove-caliber defensive catch, I bent down to search for my hat, forgetting to let the crowd at home and in the stadium shower me with applause. Since all the great catches are shown on TV, I naturally assumed mine would be too, with special commentary from Kruk and Kuip.

We went home and watched the game replay. There it was, the foul ball into the stands. But there was no highlight reel-worthy catch. All they showed was a brief moment of my back, head down, looking for my hat, and an attempted high five from my dad sitting next to me. I got no special attention, no respect, and no praise from Kruk and Kuip.

Lesson learned. When you catch a ball, ignore all else and hoist that ball high up in the air. Maybe give a shout, or a fist pump. Oh, and that wouldn't ever happen again in our seats. They are now blocked off by a screen.

~David A. Gray, Washington, District of Columbia

On May 20, 2012, I went with friends to a Dodgers game, who were playing my World Champion St. Louis Cardinals. It was a great, close game, with the Cards leading 5-3 going into the bottom of the 8th. We were sitting in the left field bleachers, I in my red Cardinals cap, somehow not getting beaten up and put in a coma. I am sure my blue Dodgers sweatshirt compensated; that had been my plan. As my friend, José, and I discussed, it was an unlikely night for left field home runs, with right-handed starting pitchers dealing to lefty-heavy lineups.

The Dodgers put two men on, and up to pinch-hit came recently-promoted right-handed rookie, Scott Van Slyke. His father, Andy, was a Gold Glover and All-Star with the Cardinals and Pirates in the '80s. I didn't notice at the time, but the Cards had put in their only left-handed reliever, Mark "Scrabble" Rzepczynski. With the count 3 and 0, the batter would be taking, of course. But then he swung. *Crack!*

It's high. It's deep. It's—oh, shit, it's *right at me*! I kid you not, this was the easiest home run grab in the world. All I had to do was stick my hand out like I was waving goodbye, just reach my right hand up maybe a foot above my head, perhaps two feet. It was a can of corn. Except...maybe not. It wasn't a straight screamer, but still more of a liner than a looper. It took just enough time getting there that in the course of those few seconds I calculated (a) how much it would hurt my bare hand (a lot); b) the likelihood of my bare hand holding contact with a ball hit that hard (not good); and c) how it would look on Sports Center (even worse).

And that, my friends, was when I completely bailed on the play!

If it makes any difference, everyone around me bailed too. People were ducking everywhere. It grazed José's hand—the numbskull had been sitting with a useless glove on his knee the whole game and had set it aside this inning—then hit the concrete and somehow bounced to a guy sitting a few rows back.

That is what makes you live with baseball regret—only made worse by the fact that the fan who caught the ball was pulled out of the stands and offered bribes to give up the ball—young Van Slyke's first major league home run. I not only missed the easy play, but also probably sacrificed free tickets and other goodies—autographed jerseys? Easy access to clubhouse groupies?—all to save my precious hand.

Which will never enter the baseball Hall of Fame.

~David Noller, Los Angeles, California

My son, Tyler, and I attend University of Hawaii baseball games with me standing on a three-step stool with Tyler on my shoulders. People often ask if we would like tickets to go into the stadium to watch the games— that is just how the people of Hawaii are, very generous. We always kindly decline their offers, as watching from the right field foul line just outside the home team's bullpen provides a very good view of the field. This is our place, where we can chase foul balls that leave the stadium. Competition with adults to chase down a ball is tough, especially for a young boy.

One night when Tyler was about 10, on my shoulders as usual, there was a crack of the bat and the ball began heading into foul territory and out of the stadium right toward us. After stepping off the stool and lowering him down so we could chase the ball, others began running to where they felt it would land, as did we. Tyler looked up, saw all the people chasing it, and said, "Dad, I will never get a ball." I replied, "Tyler, we just need to be faster than the others and get to the ball first. Run, run, we still have a chance." As we started to get into stride, the ball smacked into one of the lights on the light pole and deflected straight down to where we were. I said, "Son, stop! Look, the ball is right here." Headed for the parking lot, Tyler caught it on one bounce, raised it above his head, and let out a loud, "Yeah!"

The look on his face was one that will be in my mind for a lifetime. This has given Tyler much hope that he can be just as lucky as other people. He has since grabbed a bunch of foul balls and has them displayed on the sports memorabilia shelves in his room.

~Kerwin Stenstrom, Honolulu, Hawaii

It was March 27, a Wednesday night and the last exhibition game before the season began. Family was visiting us in California from Chicago. Our nephew, Jeff, doesn't care much about sports, but his wife, Karen, is a big Cubs fan. Their son, Sam, age 13, is a *huge* Cubs fan, but his sister, Lucy, age 11, likes baseball even less than her dad. Nevertheless, it seemed like the obvious thing to do to take the whole family to see a stadium other than their Wrigley Field. Lynn and I bought tickets, and off we went.

It was a chilly, weather-threatening evening. Our seats were just a few rows from the field, right near where the visiting A's players were stretching and warming up. Sam was sporting his Little League A's cap and given the circumstances—preseason, chilly night, small crowd, seats close to the field—it didn't seem much of a surprise when he came running up the rows from the rail with a ball. Still thrilling, but I just wasn't surprised.

Lucy turned to me and said, "(Grand)-Uncle Eric, have you ever gotten a ball?" The answer was a simple, "Nope," even though I had been just one seat away three times when my kids, Rachel and David, had scored these prizes. "Never?" Lucy asked, and I repeated my answer. Lucy, sitting in my lap, said, "I want to get a ball for you." I replied that was very sweet, but "That isn't the way it works. Old guys like me are supposed to catch a ball and give them to kids." I added that if she got one, I wanted her to keep it. To which she said, "I don't want it, I want you to have it."

Off she went to the rail, where I watched her constantly for two innings while she waved her hand every time an A's player came by. I looked away for a second, and up the steps she came running, as her brother had done just a little while before, smiling and holding a ball, then handing it over to me. I told her, with all honesty, it was the sweetest thing anyone had ever done for me. I then proceeded to tell the folks around me what had happened, just beaming with pride. At one point Lucy said, "Uncle Eric, are you crying?" I looked at her, not quite knowing if she was seeing something in my eyes, on my face, or if she had somehow managed to figure me out even at her young age, and I replied, "No, Lucy…but I might be."

I told her if she really wanted me to have the ball, I needed her to do one more thing. She did. She signed it. It now has a prominent spot on my living room mantel.

~Eric Gray, San Francisco, California, and Lucy Rhodes, Chicago, Illinois

In the late 1950s, I went to a game at Gilmore Field in Los Angeles to see the Hollywood Stars. I remember seeing slugger Dick "Hands of Stone" Stuart play. He was a tremendous home run hitter, even hitting 66 one minor league season, but on the few occasions I saw him play he mostly struck out. Before I went, my Mom admonished me, "Don't chase any foul balls!" I hadn't planned on doing this, but when the first one came flying up near where I was sitting with my friends, it crossed my mind to go after it. Unfortunately, because of what Mom had said, I hesitated. When I finally reached out to scoop up the ball, someone else beat me to it. To this date, that is the closest I have ever come to getting a foul ball.

~Marc Orozco, Windsor, Colorado

My memorable, if not fond, experience occurred about 20 years ago when I was seven or eight. If it had been a newspaper headline, "Innocence Shattered at Candlestick" would've been appropriate. I was sitting about 25 rows up from first base with my brother and father, glove in hand as usual. Suddenly, there was the crack of the bat and everyone was standing. I couldn't believe my luck as I looked up and saw the ball coming straight down toward me. My area wasn't packed to capacity, but a man occupied the seat directly behind me. He deftly reached forward and caught the ball inches above my glove, then calmly sat down as if nothing had happened.

Having watched countless games in person, on my couch, or from a bar stool, I've always enjoyed observing the behaviors of people when a ball is hit into the stands. Oftentimes, the ball becomes a gift from one fan to another, handed to a nearby child or a girlfriend. Nearly every fan hopes to someday catch a foul, or better yet, home run ball. If my day ever comes, I'll always remember that there are some things more important than a dream deferred.

~Michael S., San Francisco, California

Sometime during the 1990s, I was on a business trip to Houston. The Astros were playing at home, so I went to a night game on a whim. I forget the opposing team, but the Astrodome was memorable—dark, empty, and cavernous. It was really depressing. You could hear the umpires' calls all the way in the upper deck! I was able to get a $300 seat for about $25, the lower box right behind home plate. The place was empty, no one near me except a group of about 10 die-hard fans in their Astros gear. I must have had a Giants cap on because in the early innings I looked up, and there I was on the Jumbotron beyond center field. Okay, I was thrilled, but didn't think much of it until the group in front of me started giving me looks. One guy said, "We have been coming to every lousy game for years and never been on the Jumbotron." It was kind of funny, until a couple innings later when I grabbed a pop-up. I just walked over to an empty row and picked up the ball. Boy, the entire group had daggers in their eyes. "We have been coming to every lousy game for years and never got a foul ball!" It wasn't long before I took my ball and quietly left the 'Dome with my souvenir and my story.

~Bob Johnston, Taylorsville, Utah

In August of 1969 when I was nine years old, my dad caught a foul ball for me in one of the first games he ever took me to. It was at Shea Stadium, Mets vs. Dodgers. The following June, he caught a batting practice foul ball off the bat of Hall of Famer Orlando Cepeda. He tossed it to me, and I said, "Wow, Dad! Another one!" An old man—to a 10-year-old boy he was old—saw this and exclaimed, "Another one? I've been going to baseball games for 50 years and I never got a foul ball!" My dad smiled, maybe a little too smugly, and said, "Well, you've got to go for another 50 years, then."

He put the whammy on me, I'm certain. That was 48 years ago, and I've never gotten another foul ball. But I guess I've still got another two years…

~Paul Rabin, Clifton, New Jersey

On April 11, 2003, in Detroit, as my friend, Jason, posed for a picture, a hard line drive sailed right past his head. I was taking the shot, so I'm not exactly sure how close the ball came to actually killing him, but I do know it was smashed. I also know I was the first one to get to it. My first major league foul ball!

A bunch of junior high girls swarmed me like I was a celebrity. I guess for a moment, to them, I was. But we didn't have long to celebrate my accomplishment. Jason and I had to drive nearly 200 miles to catch the night game in Cleveland. We left the Tiger's game in the 8th and managed to get to our seats in Cleveland before the 2nd inning was over. By "our seats" I mean the ones we snuck into for the game. The ones we'd purchased were nowhere near home plate, but much more affordable.

With Jason catching a foul ball a few days earlier in Milwaukee, and mine hours earlier in Detroit, we now felt we had a legitimate chance every time a foul ball was headed in our direction. Just an inning after we sat down, a ball was popped up behind home and was coming our way! It was hit the exact distance of our seats, but unfortunately about 10-12 feet to our left. The fan there was not able to make the play; it bounced off his hands and headed right toward us. The ball went over the aisle, passed Jason, and I snatched it up!

We were barely over a week into our epic trip, and there I stood with my second foul ball of the day! With some confidence, I believe I can say I'm the only fan ever to catch a major league foul ball in two different stadiums, in two different states, on the same calendar day! Where were my middle school fans now?

As this California boy sat there in his three pairs of pants, two pairs of socks, three shirts, a jacket, ski mask, beanie, and scarf, I realized something. With all my clothing, I had forgotten to take the first ball out of my pocket. So even though I looked ridiculous, I held both balls up for a photo inside Jacobs Field. A guy near me saw me catch the foul ball but was skeptical when I told him I'd also caught one earlier in the day. He later overhead us talking about our plans for the next stadiums on our trip and said, "So, were you serious about getting the ball in Detroit too? I thought you were just joking around."

Yep, I was serious.

That was just the beginning of our five-month journey where I was basically homeless, traveling the country and going to baseball games. Jason and I managed to make it to 17 stadiums in 30 days, and I picked up the other 13 over the next four months. We had some weird weather that year. Despite being spring, the game in Detroit was already our second game cancelled because of snow, Chicago being earlier that week. Thankfully, it had been cancelled, or I wouldn't have the story from the long-distance doubleheader.

My trip was full of adventure, fun, craziness, and all kinds of baseball, but nothing more noteworthy than my foul ball record in the first week.

~Kevin Burrill, Elk Grove, California

Did you catch any others on the journey? That was already two more than I've caught in my life.

51

AN AUTOGRAPH, A PHOTO, A CHAT WITH A STAR

Having idols is part of the American pop-culture landscape. Musicians, actors, and athletes top the hero list. They don't have to be superstars—they can even be relatively unknown—but they mean something important to you for whatever reason. I personally don't care that much. Would I have loved to meet Mickey Mantle? Even more so, John, Paul, George and/or Ringo? Well sure, but I am not certain what I would have said other than, "You were my hero." I once met Claire Hamill, a great British singer/songwriter whose music I played as a college DJ—you may not know her name, but I love her music—and we are still friends 45 years later. A hero doesn't have to be a superstar, they have to be someone who mattered to you for whatever reason. Here are some lucky fans' stories.

My earliest recollection of baseball is attending a game at Connie Mack Stadium with my father in 1966. I recall vividly that it was bat day, a great bonus for a kid. I couldn't have been more than four or five years old, but I remember happily walking under the stadium to our seats with my Tony Taylor baseball bat. Dad and I had tickets along the first base line and were watching the pregame practice. I was looking up at the Ballantine Beer advertisement in center field with the three-ring symbol that I still today make in the condensation from a bottle of beer. All of a sudden, a ball got past the first baseman and rolled right in front of me. My father was obviously distracted as I climbed over the fence to get it and fell onto the field. To my surprise, it was Tony Taylor himself who came to my rescue. He put me back in my seat and even let me keep the ball. Tony remained my baseball idol for the longest time after.

~Peter J. Calvo, Glassboro, New Jersey

My dad was a fanatic Red Sox fan and really loved Ted Williams. He took me to my first baseball game when I was eight and couldn't stop raving about him. I thought this guy couldn't be *that* good a hitter. As fate would have it, Ted hit a home run his second at-bat. The crowd went wild. Dad jumped up and down like a maniac, gave me a big hug, and told me that Ted hit a home run just for me. Thus, Williams became my first sports hero.

I met my hero some years later when I was with Dad's best friend, a friend of Johnny Pesky, at a Boat Show in Boston that Ted Williams appeared at. I was awestruck! He said to me, "Ronnie, find your passion and you'll never work a day in your life. My passion is hitting, so I go to everybody I can—people like Ty Cobb and Rogers Hornsby—and ask them questions about hitting. Always learn from the best, Ronnie. Don't be afraid to ask questions, and when you become a success, pass on everything you know to any young person who sincerely wants to learn. Hey, one last thing, I want to be the best that ever lived! But never forget that Teddy Ballgame told you the greatest baseball player of all-time was, and will always be, Babe Ruth."

I found my passion. It was music, and still is, but I never forgot what my hero said to me. As a young man starting my position as choral director of the new John F. Kennedy High School in Plainview, New York, I sought out the best choral directors on Long Island. They loved my energy, enthusiasm, and passion for choral music and shared their "secrets" with me. They were instrumental in introducing me to other wonderful choir directors who encouraged me to build something great at Kennedy. Not a day goes by that I don't appreciate what my hero did for me. Thank you, Teddy Ballgame.

~Ron Cohen, Swampscott, Massachusetts

I was in that choir. I can still practically sing the Hallelujah Chorus note for note

On September 8, 2005, I was working for Michael Andretti as a nanny for his youngest son, Lucca, who was almost six. Mike, retired from IndyCar racing, was now a team owner, and I traveled with Lucca to races. We usually stayed inside the racetrack in Mike's tour bus, but one time in Chicago we were staying downtown. Lucca and I had been out and about discovering the town, and as we entered the hotel lobby, we noticed it was packed with people. It took about two seconds for me to spot Hank Aaron—I had *no* idea he was so big and tall! I told Lucca who he was, and we went up to the room to get my Atlanta Braves Chop Talk magazine and hurried back to the lobby, hoping we could meet Mr. Aaron and he would sign it. I was already wearing a Braves jersey. We made our way over to him and I introduced myself, telling him I was a huge fan. I was so excited, but I felt he perceived me to be some nutty fan and I didn't get much of a response. I introduced him to Lucca, telling him whose son he was. I told him I was doing my best to make sure Lucca would be a Braves fan and not a Phillies fan even though he lived in Pennsylvania. Hank's face lit up then, and he gladly signed my magazine. That day became the greatest sports memory I have. I didn't have either a camera or a phone with me, so I have no picture of the experience, but it was awesome anyway to meet the *true* home run king.

I've met lots of Braves players, including Dale Murphy and Otis Nixon as well as more current players, so I have lots of autographs. But nothing compares to meeting Hank Aaron.

~Jan Insinga, Fort Mill, South Carolina

Growing up in the Detroit suburbs in the 1960s, it was almost impossible not to have Al Kaline as your hero, or at least your favorite baseball player. But another favorite of most guys was then-Tribe star, Rocky Colavito. When we'd play in the schoolyard, we'd duplicate his bat-behind-the-head stretch, followed by grabbing the crotch and pointing the bat straight at the mound. How great it would have been to get close to those guys! But all we had were baseball cards to hold, putting our heroes seemingly millions of miles away.

Two decades later, I was a sportswriter in a small town 30 miles south of Albuquerque, New Mexico. Bob Feller came to the Duke City to sign autographs before a Class AAA Albuquerque Dukes ballgame, and I set up an interview for the next day. At the appointed time at the hotel, Bob welcomed me up to his room. I sat on his bed, enthralled, as the Van Meter, Iowa, native demonstrated his old double-pump windup. I remember thinking, God, how envious those "Greatest Generation" guys would be of me! Even better, Bob needed a ride to the ballpark, so I gave him a ride in my wife's car, apologizing for him having to ride in a Pinto. He told me not to apologize—he drove a Maverick.

Today, who doesn't have a Feller autograph? Nobody. But who's given the Hall of Famer a ride to the ballpark? Far fewer people, and I'm among them.

~Gary Herron, Albuquerque, New Mexico, author of *Baseball in Albuquerque*

I was eight when I saw the 1963 All-Star game. My dad was a big Indians fan, but most of all, a baseball fan. Mays, Clemente, and Aaron were all in the National League outfield and Dad was going on about the three future Hall of Famers. Mudcat Grant was the only Indian chosen for the game. Being an Indians fan, and Grant being the first Indians player I ever saw live, he was the only one I really cared about in that game. Back then, pitchers warmed up in front of the bleachers. I yelled to him from the front row, and he came over and asked my dad for a pen. He never got in the game, but he signed the ball he warmed up with and handed the pen and ball back to Dad. I still have that ball today, along with the scorecard and press pin from the game.

~Bruce Wood, Cleveland, Ohio

In 1976 when I was 17 years old, I went to Dodger Stadium to see Cincinnati's Big Red Machine play the Dodgers. The Reds had future Hall of Famers Joe Morgan, Johnny Bench, and Tony Perez; Dodgers had Hall of Famer Don Sutton and solid players like Smith, Garvey, Lopes, and Cey. I lived 90 miles away and went early to watch batting practice. Down by the left field foul pole with no one else around, Joe Morgan came up to me and just started talking. I don't remember much of the conversation, but I recall him saying, '"Stay in school, get a degree." I did. I got a BS and an MBA.

It meant a lot to me that a famous athlete took the time to talk to a stranger, and by doing so made an indelible impression. Even though my parents stressed school and I was going that way anyway, Mr. Morgan had an impact on me and made a difference.

~Rodger Long, Huntington Beach, California

As a 10-year-old in the summer of 1971, my daily obsession was the Philadelphia Phillies. The team was not very good, finishing last in the National League East, even behind a Montreal Expos team in only its third year of existence. But on June 23rd, one Philly—my favorite player— almost singlehandedly beat the Cincinnati Reds. I was watching the game on television when Rick Wise no-hit the Big Red Machine at Riverfront

Stadium, winning 4-0, and walking only one batter. In addition, he hit two home runs with three RBI. Pete Rose was the final batter, and I was so concerned he would break up the no-no that I went into another room and prayed. For this 10-year-old, it was to be the Summer of Wise, a bright spot on a bad team. Rick would go 17-14 with a 2.88 ERA and a memorable slew of pitching and hitting exploits, including two home runs—one a grand slam—to beat the Giants, and a 12-inning complete game against the Cubs, retiring 32 batters in a row and singling in the winning run. At just 26 years of age, Wise appeared to be coming into his own...so the Phillies traded him! They got a pretty good pitcher in return, Steve Carlton, but who knew how that would turn out. Besides, Wise was my guy! But that is not what this story is about.

Wise had many other career highlights, prior to and after this season. His first major league victory was on Father's Day, June 21, 1964, in game two of a doubleheader over the Mets at Shea Stadium. Game one had been a perfect game tossed by teammate Jim Bunning. The Phillies next no-hitter was the Wise gem I watched on TV nearly seven years later to the day. In 1973, Reds' manager Sparky Anderson selected him as the starting pitcher in the All-Star game, and Wise was the winning pitcher. Two years after that, pitching for the Red Sox in the World Series, he would be the winning pitcher in Game 6 when Fisk hit a home run off the foul pole in the twelfth. Who doesn't remember that? But again, not what this story is about.

Here is the story. In 1982 I began a career in radio broadcasting, working for WMVB-FM, a station in South Jersey. The station was on the Phillies radio network, and I covered home games at Veterans Stadium. In 1986, the Phillies celebrated Old-timers Day by bringing back their 1976 NL East winning team to take on a team of 1970s NL stars, including, you guessed it, Rick Wise. After all those years, I finally had the pleasure of meeting and interviewing my boyhood hero. During the interview, I started naming all of the above deeds off the top of my head and asking Wise about them. Finally, he smiled and said to me, "How do you remember all these things?" I told him I was 10 when he threw the no-hitter, that he was my first hero in Phillies pinstripes, and I thanked him for the memories. What a great night and a great memory that I will always remember.

~John Spahn, Boyds, Maryland

On September 24, 1972, my family made the three-and-a-half-hour drive from upstate New York to Shea Stadium in Queens, where the Phillies were in town to play my favorite team, the Mets. It was a classic pitching matchup, Steve Carlton vs. Tom Seaver, whom Carlton called his greatest rival. Carlton was having a Cy Young year, and Seaver would win it the next. The matchup lived up to its billing, Seaver out-dueling Carlton 1-0.

I was nine years old, and after the game I waited outside the stadium for player autographs. Carlton came walking over to the team bus. I figured he would be upset over the loss, but still I held out my ball for him to autograph. He literally pushed me aside and walked onto the bus without signing.

Twenty years later I was snowboarding in Durango, Colorado. Waiting in the small airport for my flight home, I saw someone who looked familiar. Sure enough, it was Steve Carlton. We were the only two in the waiting area. I found a pen and asked him if he would sign my ticket envelope. I told him that I grew up a Mets fan but admired the way he pitched. After he signed my envelope, I mentioned that I saw him pitch against Seaver and the Mets. I said, "You lost 1-0 but it was a great game." He forced a smile and began reading his magazine.

~Jeff Schorr, St. Petersburg, Florida
You wisely waited until after he signed the envelope, Jeff.

In 1977, my mom worked for a van conversion company. Marty Pattin, a pitcher for the Royals, did a great Donald Duck impersonation, and wanted a color drawing of Donald Duck in a pitching motion wearing a Royals uniform on his rear tire cover. He provided Mom tickets to a

Royals-Yankees playoff game, but mom wouldn't let me go, concerned that I would not show proper respect to the folks in the Yankee players' section where the seats were. In truth, I was just learning the game, crazy about the Royals players, and might not have been a good sport. She went with her friend and sat next to Darrell Porter's parents. To say I was angry with my mom would be putting it mildly.

The next summer, Mom lost her job during hard economic times. We moved in with friends for a while, but then my sister went to live with my aunt and I lived with my father. He was not a big part of our lives so I didn't know him very well. I liked my younger stepbrother and half-brother, and we spent a lot of time outside in the apartment complex. I missed Mom a lot. My stepmother was not happy I was around, and Dad wasn't loving or caring. It was a miserable summer, although it had one great outcome. Some Royals lived in this complex during the season, and one of them was Marty Pattin. I babysat his sons, Jon and Jeff. Marty was very sweet and kind. Marty became like a dad to me, not so much the way we see dads today, but just listening and being kind, someone I could look up to. His wife was the same way.

In 1979, my best friend, Cheryl, and I went to Picture Day, when fans were allowed on the field before the game to take photos with the players. I was into ceramic painting and had found a statue of a catcher. I painted it in Royals colors and put No. 15 on the back, with the name Porter over the number. Cheryl had a big crush on Darrell Porter so I let her carry it to give to him. As we walked near the dugout, I heard my name called. Jon and Jeff were calling and waving to me. I hugged them and they asked Marty if they could hang out with me. He said yes, so we walked around with the boys, eventually joined by Brian McRae and several other players' kids. Can I say I was in my element? Yes, I was. And we were able to give Porter the statue. But my best memory was being able to see Jon and Jeff one more time.

~Rhonda Berry, Garland, Texas

In March of 2013 at the Dodgers spring training complex at Camelback Ranch, I went to see Sandy Koufax who was working with some of the Dodgers' pitchers. It was a cold day, and I wore the Christmas present I had received, a great Dodgers jacket with their World Championship years on the left sleeve and World Series stadium logos on the right.

When the players go to the clubhouse, they pass through a gauntlet of autograph seekers, everyone shouting out their names. I don't do that or stick merchandise in their faces just for an autograph. I patiently waited for Sandy to get to me. When he approached, I politely asked if he would sign my jacket, on the sleeve with the championship years. I said, "Between '63 and '65," because we all know he starred in both.

He took my sharpie with a big grin and signed a very nice autograph next to '63. I thanked him and since I had a ball in my hand, I asked if he would sign it, as well. He gave me a big smile and said, "Na-na-na-na," while shaking his finger back and forth the way you would tell a kid "No", smiling the whole time. Oh, well. I went home and put the coat away. It will be my daughter's to do with as she wishes.

~Larry Waters, Phoenix, Arizona

When Barry Bonds hit homers number 71 and 72, I found myself sitting two suites away from my hero, Willie McCovey. I told him I try not to bother famous people, but he was my exception. He said, "No problem, Fawd, it happens all the time," in his gentle Alabama drawl. I told him that when I married my beautiful and very funny wife, she asked me if I loved her or Willie McCovey more. So, I lied. He thought that was *very* funny.

We spent some comfortable time in that tight, crazy, painful ballgame evening telling stories and laughing. I was so grateful for the time with my hero. He did not disappoint!

~Ford Goodman, Sonoma, California

As a Giants fan, a picture of me wearing a Dodgers jersey is worth a lot more than 1,000 words.

Red Adams was a longtime Pacific Coast League pitcher, a Los Angeles Dodgers scout, pitching coach, and my friend. He died on January 19, 2017, at the age of 95. Adams was a baseball lifer who spent over 50 years working professionally in the game. His baseball resume very impressive. However, who he was as a man was even more impressive. Without exaggeration, he was one of the best men I have ever met.

Born in Parlier, California, Adams pitched 19 seasons professionally, 1939 to 1942, and '44 to '58. In 16 Pacific Coast League seasons, he compiled a 153-138 record with the Los Angeles Angels, Portland Beavers, San Diego Padres, and Sacramento Solons. His best record, 21-15 in 1945 with the Angels, resulted in a promotion to the Chicago Cubs the following year. He saw only brief big league action, posting an 0-1 record over eight games in relief in 1946. At the time of his passing, he was the oldest living Cub. Other Pacific Coast League career highlights included leading the league with a 2.17 earned run average in 1952 and contributing to three championship teams with the Angels—1944, 1947, and 1956.

Following his playing days, Adams spent 33 years with the Dodgers, 1959-1991, in numerous scouting and coaching roles. This included pitching coach from 1969-1980, overseeing a staff that frequently led the National League in ERA, with the team winning three pennants. He was praised by many Dodgers pitchers for his coaching abilities. In Don

Sutton's Hall of Fame induction speech, he stated, "Red Adams is the standard by which every pitching coach should be measured. No person ever meant more to my career than Red Adams. Without him, I wouldn't be standing in Cooperstown today."

I first met Adams as a young teenager through my great-uncle, Larry Powell. Larry and Red were teammates on the Angels in 1947-'48 and had kept in touch. Since I loved baseball and lived relatively close to Red, Larry suggested I reach out to him. Red was always very accommodating. We spoke on the phone occasionally, regularly traded letters, and he had me over as a guest at his home a few times. Our conversations focused primarily on baseball, but as I got older, they evolved into more important topics like marriage, family, and life. Me being a Giants fan, we often joked with each other about our preferred teams.

For a decade or so, I was focused on my career and family, and we lost regular contact. I spoke with him by phone in mid-2015. That fall his birthday card was returned. I tried calling a few times the following spring and summer, but eventually got a notice that his phone had been disconnected.

His important role in Dodgers history inspired me to attend Vin Scully Weekend in Los Angeles at the end of the 2016 baseball season. For the first time in my life, I wore a Dodgers jersey at the games—Red's 1980 game-used home jersey. It seemed a fitting way to retire the jersey and say goodbye to Red, since I never expected to see him again.

Upon returning home from that nostalgic and emotional trip, I decided to try to track him down, regardless of how unlikely my success would be. I knew his wife had passed away in 2010, so I looked for her obituary online. Luckily, I found it. In the obituary, there was reference to his surviving children. After some online searching, I found a few phone numbers and called them. The next day I got a call back from his oldest daughter, who updated me on his condition and location. He was in an assisted-living and memory-care home in Fresno.

I am very thankful that in the last three months of his life, I had the opportunity to enjoy four visits with him. I thanked him for the positive impact he'd had on my life and introduced him to my wife and kids.

Despite not remembering many details of his baseball career, he was the same man. He hadn't lost his sense of humor or welcoming nature and ability to lift up everyone around him with his encouraging personality. During those visits, we didn't talk much about his experiences as a baseball player or coach. That was no longer important. We spoke about what was important to him at his core as a man.

Since his passing, I established an annual tradition of wearing a Red Adams Dodgers jersey at Dodger Stadium. I call it my annual "It's a Red Adams Jersey, Not a Dodgers Jersey" game.

~Zak Ford, Sacramento, California

It was the summer of 1954 and all the guys were on bikes coming back from McNally Park in Skokie, Illinois. Jay, Terry, Mel, and I had our baseball gloves on the handlebars. A couple of guys had their bats on their shoulders. We played baseball from morning to night, excited about sports in general. It was starting to get dark as we turned down Lawndale Avenue from Main Street, headed toward Lee Street. Suddenly, Jay yelled out, "Look! It's Jimmy Enright, my neighbor." Enright was a big executive with the Chicago Cubs. Driving a big black Cadillac, he recognized Jay and slowed down, and said to us, "Hi boys. I've got something very special for you and I'm sure you'll be surprised." The back window rolled down and there before us sat the two most talked about rookies in baseball—especially in Chicago—young Ernie Banks, shortstop for the Cubs, along with his teammate, Gene Baker. We were floored. Mr. Enright told us to run home and get some baseballs to sign, promising he would wait for five minutes. We were all back in two. Ernie and Gene could not have been nicer. They got out of the car, shook our hands, and autographed our baseballs. We asked for advice on playing, and I remember two things. Ernie told us all to put more snap in our wrists when we batted, saying that was the key for him. Looking at him, he was very thin and wiry but his wrists were incredibly strong, so we understood his point. Gene gave us a fielding tip. "When a ground ball comes at you, immediately put your glove to the ground and let it come up to the ball." He said, "Never let the ball play you, play the ball with your glove to the ground, then lift it up on a bad bounce to make the play." We all put that in our defensive bibles. They shook our hands again, got back into the car and drove off. We sat on the curb talking about how exciting it was to be mingling with the stars of the Chicago Cubs on our own street. It was something we would never forget. I can still see their faces over 60 years ago, just as if it were yesterday.

~Jerry Dulkin, Rolling Meadows, Illinois

I became a fan of class-act Jamie Moyer after the Boston Red Sox traded him to the Seattle Mariners in 1996. The difference between watching a power pitcher blow a 95 mph fastball by a hitter, and Moyer's Bugs Bunny change-up lollygagging to home plate blew my mind! I was hooked!

By 2008, Jamie had been traded to Philadelphia. That year I took a baseball tour which included a stop in the City of Brotherly Love. As our group walked into Citizens Bank Park, I looked out onto the sun-bathed field and saw barricades snaking around the warning track, fans packed along them. It was Photo Day, and Phillies players and coaches were making their way around the stadium. I nearly lost my shoes running down the stairs, I was so excited! I was told Jamie had not yet come out, so I kept watching and waiting. He was one of the last few to come by. I raced onto the field, proudly sporting my Mariners' Moyer jersey, got my camera set up, and hoped someone would take the photo for me. Jamie came toward me, kindly stopped, and I found someone to get that hoped-for picture. The 8x10 photo I printed out when I got home was then proudly displayed on my desk at work.

Three years later, my sister heard that Moyer was coming to our hometown. His son was playing for our semi-pro baseball team, the Bellingham Bells, and Jamie was coming not only to give the players a pep talk, but also to meet with fans. I took time off work, brought my photo, and hoped for a chance to meet him again and ask for his autograph. I got both. He met with 75 of us, reminiscing about his playing career, telling us about the work of The Moyer Foundation, and finally, offering to sign memorabilia. When it was my turn, I handed him the photo. Three years and 3,000 miles had passed between meetings, and here we were, face to face again. It definitely caught him off guard! The keepsake, along with the ticket from the game on Photo Day, are now framed and preserved as very special memories for me.

~Diane Ecker, Bellingham, Washington

Growing up on Long Island, New York, in the 1960s-1970s, I was a huge Yankees fan, somewhat of an anomaly, as most kids on the Island were Mets fans...especially after the 1969 Miracle Mets went from worst to first and defeated the powerhouse Baltimore Orioles in the World Series. The star pitcher of that Amazin' Mets team was, of course, George Thomas "Tom" Seaver who went on to a long Hall of Fame career.

Fast forward to the spring of 1990, and to New York's LaGuardia Airport, where I was a very young and very junior Eastern Air Lines Boeing 727 captain, assigned a West Palm Beach morning flight. Unfortunately, there were a few normal airline issues preparing for departure, so we pushed off the gate around twenty-five minutes behind schedule. I flew the airplane a little faster than planned, and fortuitously got a couple of air traffic control shortcuts. We ended up landing right on schedule.

The plane was a three-pilot aircraft, so after blocking in at the gate I opened the flight deck door to stand and say goodbye and thanks to the customers while the first and second officers completed the parking checklist. As I opened that door, sitting right in front of me in first class aisle seat 1B, was none other than "The Franchise", hero of the 1969 Mets, Tom Seaver. I instantly recognized him, and without thinking, immediately exclaimed, "Tommy Seaver!" He bounded up out of his seat, vigorously shook my hand, and said, "Thank you for busting it. We're here on schedule. Great job." He walked out of the open aircraft door into the West Palm Beach jetway. No bags, no carry-on, just The Franchise heading off to the Mets spring training camp in nearby Port St. Lucie, Florida, for his retirement job as—I think—an instructor and/or announcer.

After the rest of the passengers left the aircraft, I asked the two young flight attendants why they hadn't told me Tom Seaver was aboard our flight. They both responded, "Tom who?" When I told them they had just served a Major League Hall of Famer, star of the 1969 Amazin' Miracle Mets, one of my boyhood heroes, they explained that they weren't even born until 1970! The two attendants working the back of my plane had similar birthdays. To top it off, when I returned to the flight deck and excitedly told my officers that we had just flown Tom Seaver, they too, sadly, had no idea who I was talking about.

I couldn't believe it. I had just flown The Franchise and had no one to share it with. Amazin'.

~Bill Sablesak, Hollywood, Florida

In early 1960, just before leaving for a dentist appointment with my mother, my father flipped a baseball to me and said that Jimmy Piersall would be at J.J. Newberry's—an old retail store—and Mom was taking me there before my appointment. It was a school day, and I was the only boy in the store when Piersall walked in. He was promoting a batting device that he was selling with Willie Mays and Roger Maris. Seeing about a dozen women and me the only boy, he immediately came over, asked my name, and signed the baseball that I still have today. He was unbelievably friendly and gave me batting tips when he found out I played Little League. Years later while announcing White Sox games, he got in hot water for criticizing players' wives. I sent him a letter letting him know I was in his corner, recounting the events of that day when he signed my baseball, "To Ricky, your pal Jimmy Piersall." He thanked me in a return letter and sent two autographed pictures. Some months ago, I saw a picture of him using a walker to get around, and it broke my heart to see him that way. As long as I live, I will never forget how nice he was to me on that day.

~Rick Risley, Zephyrhills, Florida

My first Major League Baseball game was in 1950 at Sportsman's Park between the Cardinals and the Brooklyn Dodgers. I was 13. I had talked my dad into an out-of-Iowa vacation, going to St. Louis since it wasn't too far—or so I said—from my grandfather's farm in Van Wert, Iowa, where we usually spent our vacations.

As many say about their first game, the sights of the green grass and lights shining brightly as we walked up the ramp to our seats were amazing. Little did I then realize that I would be seeing so many future Hall of Famers in action at the same time. Playing that day were Jackie Robinson, Duke Snider, Roy Campanella, Pee Wee Reese, Stan Musial, Enos Slaughter, and Red Schoendienst. I don't remember much about the game other than the Cardinals won 5-3. That, of course, paled in comparison with the experience of seeing all those great players. It was quite a day, one I'll never forget.

A couple of years later on a trip to Milwaukee, we saw the Braves play the Giants, another game featuring several future Hall of Famers, including Aaron, Mathews, and Mays. After the game we were caught in a massive traffic jam outside County Stadium. Cars were not moving. I happened to glance out our car window at the car next to us. I couldn't believe my eyes! Caught in the same traffic was Braves pitcher and future Hall of Famer, Warren Spahn. I grabbed my game scorecard, jumped out of our car, and approached Spahn's. I very politely ask him if he would sign my scorecard, and without hesitating he said, "Sure, kid." I thanked him and returned to our car. I still have that scorecard and treasure it greatly.

~Errol Brown, Mountain Home, Arkansas

In 1964, the Cards played the Yankees in the World Series. But I did not know until recently what a classic that Series was. I was 12 at the time, and hailed from St. Louis where everyone knows baseball, regardless of your age. I lived a half a block from the hotel hosting the Series, where the teams, media, and enthusiasts were all staying. This was my backyard, so we knew every entrance, exit, and service elevator. I can't say the security staff welcomed our familiarity, but for God's sake, the Beatles stayed there, too, and there were many fun conventions.

My sister Markey and I decided to check out the action and get autographs. Just home from school and pressed for time, we wore our school uniforms. We first saw Harry Reasoner—a national news anchor!—and knew his autograph was one we wanted. Before he signed, he checked to see who we had so far, and informed us we had gotten autographs from hotel guests not connected to baseball! As it turned out, Harry had seven children and recognized the Catholic school uniforms we wore, so he adopted us for the day. As only a national news anchor can, he got us a table in the cafe overlooking the lobby. His companion that afternoon, who was just as impressed as we were, was Mel Stottlemyre, a rookie pitcher for the Yankees. Harry ordered sodas for the three of us and a cocktail for himself. Harry and Mel pointed out every one of interest. The autographs in addition to theirs that I got, and still have, included: both Boyers—Ken, Cards, and Clete, Yankees,—Roger Maris, Mickey Mantle, Yogi Berra, Bill Dickey, Whitey Ford, Cal Hubbard, Tony Kubek, Phil Rizzuto, Casey Stengel, and bat boy Tony Florio. I also got one from legendary announcer Jack Buck, who later worked with my brother-in-law. Years later I said hello to him when the Cards played the Giants in the 1987 playoffs and showed him his 1964 autograph. Wanting to see how much his signature had changed, he asked to sign it again, so I have two Jack Bucks!

The next day I returned and hung around the pool where Mantle and Maris were relaxing. I met a group of boys my age who were trying to get their autographs, but M and M wouldn't sign for them because they were being obnoxious. For $5 each, I got the boys' baseballs signed for them. I made $20 that day, but foolishly did not get any signed balls for myself. They would be worth far more than that today.

~Mimi Morgan, San Francisco, California

Growing up in a very small town, McLean, Illinois, population 750 people, we played baseball all the time. A Cardinals fan, my mom and I would listen to the games on the radio whenever we could. One day in 1966, a group of us were playing a pickup game along Hwy 136 which runs parallel to Route 66. It was late February, still quite cold with light snow on the ground. We had been playing for a couple of hours and were picking new teams when we noticed a guy had pulled off the highway and was watching us. When he saw that we had noticed him, he walked over and asked who was winning, a question to which I don't think he got an exact answer. Then he asked us if we knew who he was. When we said no, he asked if we ever listened to the Cincinnati Reds. Of course, now came all the answers, no we were mostly Cardinals fans, with a few Cubs fans. He asked if we knew the player Pete Rose. Of course, we did!

Who didn't know Pete Rose? He told us he was Pete, and that he was traveling to Florida for spring training. He saw us out in the cold playing baseball and had to stop. So, here is Pete Rose talking to a bunch of seven to nine-year-old's about baseball. He gave each of us his '65 Topps baseball card before he left.

It's kind of funny, back then it wasn't as big of a deal as it would become when I got a little older. Now I am 56, and even though I am a devoted Angels fan, with the Cardinals still my National League team, Rose has always been my favorite player.

~Mike Farrar, Norwalk, California

In 1956, I was still in the innocence of my baseball fandom. A year later, the Dodgers left Brooklyn and I became a disillusioned eight-year-old.

One day we received a phone call from my mother's brother, not a usual occurrence. He worked for an airline in some faraway place called Kansas City, and it just so happened that one of his responsibilities was setting up charters for professional sports teams. In fact, he announced, one he'd recently arranged was for the St. Louis Cardinals baseball team, and they would be leaving from New York's Idlewild Airport, now John F. Kennedy, the following day on an early morning flight. If we got there early, we could see the whole team arrive at the terminal!

You mean the *whole* team, I asked? Like Red Schoendienst, Dick Schofield, Bobby Blalock, Bobby Del Greco, and "Stan the Man"? *That* whole team? "Yep," was the reply. When mom hung up there was a silence. But it was the silence of, "We're going to do this!" not, "Well, that's nice."

I don't remember sleeping, but I do recall getting up the next morning way earlier than I normally had to for Mrs. Bennett's second grade class. My father and I ate breakfast and headed for the airport. We knew the terminal well. Sometimes in the summer we'd go to the outdoor observation deck so I could watch the airplanes. We knew exactly where we would stand.

We parked close and went to our station. We were there early; we were ready. Of course, it seemed like a very long wait to a seven-year-old. But finally, a big bus like a Greyhound bus but with other words on the side, pulled up. The door opened, and there was a pause. I said to Dad, "It must be them!"

It *was* them.

But something was wrong, horribly wrong. They were wearing *suits*! Gray suits! Where were their numbers?! I knew them from their batting stances, the positions they played, their baseball cards, not their *faces*! The gray suits made them all look alike as they filed into the terminal in ones and twos. I didn't recognize a single player, not a one. I couldn't ask for the autograph of someone I didn't recognize, what if he was a coach or a trainer? I'd be an idiot.

The team began to bunch up near an agent handing out tickets in the center of the ticketing area. And then I saw a face that no fan could not recognize—it was Stan. As I walked up to him he saw me coming and held out his hands. A quick scrawl, and he was done.

And that was it. I got only one autograph. I got Stan Musial's autograph. And over the years, whenever I looked at it, I couldn't help but think of all the autographs that I didn't get, because the players didn't wear their numbers.

~Allan Kemp, Littleton, Colorado

Growing up several hours outside of Milwaukee, the first baseball team I followed was the Braves. My first game was at County Stadium in May 1961. Now, after seeing maybe a thousand ball games, I still have such a vivid memory of that one, watching Warren Spahn, Hank Aaron, and Eddie Mathews. I went to the game with my cousins, not knowing then or for years after that they were asked to bring me because that was the day of my grandfather's funeral and it was determined that I was too young to attend.

Sometime in the '80s, I went with four friends to an Indians game at the old Municipal Stadium. It was July 5, a doubleheader against the A's, and we had great seats near the A's dugout. Don Baylor was an A's coach. As part of our baseball-fueled conversation, we tried to name all the teams Baylor had played on. Sheldon Green and I recognized one of the security guards, Dick, who also worked at our office building, so we called him over and asked if he could identify Baylor's teams. He thought for a moment, disappeared, and then came back with Baylor. We went over the list with Baylor who, leaning on the rail, would confirm or deny with "Yes," or, "No, you left this one out." He then asked, "Was there a bet on this, by any chance?" Later on, during the game, he popped up and asked, "Did I mention..."

~Tom Sudow, Shaker Heights, Ohio

I was 13 years old in 1962, already a die-hard Yankee fan. Why was a small town Iowa kid a Yankee fan? I was simply mesmerized by the Yankee mystique. I loved Moose Skowron. I read the Des Moines Register every day checking the box score to see how Moose did and who the Bombers had beaten.

Our family had experienced a sad year-and-a-half. My great-uncle Hiney had passed away suddenly at age 60. He was the person who'd fueled the fire of my obsession with sports. I loved him and my great-aunt Ione more than nearly anyone in my life. To make matters worse, Ione had a heart attack, and for the next year I literally lived with her, doing my best to keep her spirits up.

My father, Jim, and Ione planned a surprise for me. Dad called the Minnesota Twins ticket office and bought tickets for the Saturday and Sunday games in June against the Yanks! Ione suggested that she and I, plus two of my friends, would take the train from Greene, Iowa, to Minneapolis. We took a taxi to the Leamington Hotel where we were staying…and more important, where the *Yanks* were staying!

I got the signatures of Hector Lopez and Luis Arroyo while they ate breakfast. I headed outside to stand by the team bus that would take the Yankees to Met Stadium. A large group of kids stood by an open window of the bus, and to my amazement, Mickey was leaning out the window giving autographs. As the kids waited, an adult pushed them out of the way to get to Mantle, who saw what was happening. My respect for No. 7 increased tremendously when, as the man got close, Mickey grabbed his pen and paper, wadded up the paper, broke the pen, and tossed them onto the street. He said, "I will never give an autograph to anyone who pushes kids out of the way." I then waited patiently for his autograph thinking, "Boy, what a great guy he is, I really like him!"

The weekend games were epic. We beat the Twinkies twice, and Moose got a couple of hits. But I was mad that Twin fans booed my team. One disappointment was that one unnamed Yankee star was incessantly booed at each plate appearance and was booed again when he caught a fly ball and ran to the dugout. As he reached the dugout, he raised his right arm and gave the finger to the entire crowd! My 13-year-old mind thought, "That's not the right thing to do. He's a poor sport."

That special weekend experience is something I will never forget. My love for the Yankees and baseball has never stopped, some 53 years later.

~John Allan, Cedar Falls, Iowa

I was in high school in Kenosha, Wisconsin, during the 1982 World Series when my favorite team, the Milwaukee Brewers, was battling the St.

Louis Cardinals. My English teacher knew I loved the Brewers, especially the third baseman. Every day she brought me newspaper clippings about the game and the adorable Paul Molitor. One day her church was having a special function at which Paul was to be the guest of honor. You can imagine how ecstatic I was when she invited me to come along. Not only did he autograph a baseball for me, but he kissed me on my cheek! I thought I would never again wash that cheek. I treasured that baseball and left it in my desk drawer at home when I went off to Washington University in St. Louis—ironic, after the Cards captured that '82 Series over the Brewers. While I was away, my brother, Patrick, borrowed the ball to play with his friend Joel. Not only would that ruin my precious ball, but to make it worse, Joel stole it! It took over 20 years for Patrick to admit that he'd played a role in the disappearance of the autographed Molitor ball. He knew how much it meant to me, and he felt horribly guilty about Joel running off with it. He never spoke to Joel again. Over the years, Patrick is still my favorite (albeit only) brother.

~Sue Huser, Redwood City, California

In 2012, my son, Evan, and I went to a Toronto Blue Jays game. It was Lady Jays Day, and the players' wives were raising money for a food bank. At Gate 6 there was a table holding mystery bags with two young women selling them. We bought one, and the lady who sold it started to chat with Evan. She asked if he would like to meet Brett Cecil, and his eyes lit up. She explained that he would be out momentarily. Evan asked me what he should say. I told him just to say hi. I knew that Brett, too, had been a Little Leaguer. Soon Brett appeared and walked over to the lady we had spoken with, his wife, Jennifer. She pointed in Evan's direction. Evan was by now pretty nervous. Brett walked over, knelt down, and said, "Hi Evan. Thanks for coming today." Evan was thunderstruck. He had told me he wanted to ask if Brett had met any big leaguers when he was a kid but was so nervous that I had to ask for him. Brett said, "Yes, BJ Surhoff and Don Mattingly." Evan opened up a bit, told him he played baseball, too, and asked Brett to sign his cap. Evan then said he wanted to talk more but knew other kids wanted to meet Brett. We'd always taught him to share. Jennifer is popular on Twitter, and months later we tweeted and she remembered the meeting.

Later in 2012, Brett Cecil entered a game against Boston in the 7th inning, allowed two runners, then struck out the side. Catcher JP Arencibia threw the ball into the crowd. A guy caught it and handed it to Evan, who was sitting in the 100s with my brother. He sprinted up the aisle at full speed holding the ball over his head screaming, "Dad! I got Brett's ball!" The crowd of 45,000 was going nuts, but all I heard was my boy.

At Lady Jays Day the next year, in 2013, at Gate 6, Jenn was selling hats. Déjà vu. When I showed her the picture of Evan with the ball, she recognized him immediately. We chatted and passed on our congrats on Brett's outstanding season and hopes he would be picked for the All-Star Game. I doubted a middle reliever would be picked, but Evan replied, "I think he makes it." When we heard the news that Brett, Joey Bats, and EE were selected, Evan looked at me with a big smile and said, "I told you so!"

Jennifer and I kept in touch, and she arranged a quick meeting between my family and Brett before a Dodgers game, giving Evan an opportunity to have Brett sign his ball for him. Brett came out to meet Evan and my daughter, Julia, for five minutes. He is such a classy guy. He signed the ball, listened to Evan's story, signed Julia's baseball card, and my kids played with his son. We took a family picture with him, and I congratulated him on being an All-Star.

Going to our seats, we bumped into Duane Ward. Staring at him starry-eyed, I said, "Evan, meet the greatest closer the Blue Jays ever had." My boy looked at me, a confused look on his face and said, "That's not Tom Henke." Wardo and everyone in the elevator let out a big belly laugh. It was quite a day.

~Mark Vendramini, Toronto, Canada

MAKING OUT THE LINEUP: THE MANAGING EXPERIENCE

Whether in the workplace or on the diamond, we have all had our share of bosses or coaches and can attest they come in a wide variety of styles and attitudes. We remember our best coaches, and our worst, who left impressions to last a lifetime. Ever notice that when a team fires a manager, they tend to go towards someone with a totally different mindset? Let's go to someone more player-friendly, or what's needed now is a disciplinarian. We all have our ideas about what makes a great coach, and how to act as one. In this chapter, we see what motivated these folks to write in the starting lineups.

I spent 15 years coaching Rock Island High School baseball. We had great players, great kids, and because of that, a lot of success. All my teams and boys were special for me, but one holds a particular place in my heart. Our neighboring rivals had a great team that had come close to reaching the Little League World Series. As my group entered their sophomore season, our rivals had just won the summer state title. We knew how good they were, how they were expected to beat up on us. Despite everyone's expectations for the kids two years behind us as being our school's best hope, my assistant coach and I knew our talented group out-worked everyone else. They loved the game and played it the right way. We knew we had a chance and didn't have to wait two years.

That season we did beat our rivals, sweeping them in a doubleheader at their home field to win our conference title! But that is only the start of this tale, and why "special" doesn't do justice to this group. In the spring of 1997, in a story that seems part "Casey at the Bat" and part *The Natural*, this team was immortalized in Illinois baseball lore. We were very good, but from a small river town in western Illinois. In Illinois, many people don't seem to think that baseball is played beyond the Chicago suburbs. Those teams are always underdogs to Chicago-area teams, with the tournament played at the Kane County minor league stadium in their own backyard.

In December 1996, my father passed away. He had been a huge fan of my teams, going to all the games. All the guys knew and loved him. When he was buried, something inspired me to grab some of the dirt from his grave and take it with me in a container. I am still not sure why I did this, but soon it would play a part in Rock Island baseball history.

My squad, now the varsity team, made the state tournament and matched up with a frequent state champ suburbs team, Tinley Park Andrew. I gave our player Bob Van Hoorebeck, to whom I was close, the bag of the special dirt so my dad could be there with them. I watched from behind the dugout—as the sophomore team coach, I did not dress for this game so as not to change the karma. It was a tough battle and we struggled to get anything going. In extra innings, I knew Bobby was due up. As he took some practice swings, I called to him to rub some dirt on his bat. He said, "I put it at home plate." I told him to grab some and rub it on his bat. With one on and one out, he came to the plate and did as I suggested. On a 2-0 count, Bob sent a rocket toward the left field wall. In the newspaper article the next day he said he knew he had hit it well but had lost it in the clouds, so he just ran! Maybe in those clouds there was help from a special angel, or maybe it was just meant to be. Whatever the case, that ball easily cleared the fence and Bob's first ever home run had just won an extra inning state tournament game. That team finished third in the tournament, losing to the eventual champion in the semi-finals. It is still the highest finish by an area team in the Illinois State Tournament.

The next day, the Chicago Tribune ran an article that spoke of the magical dirt and how it had helped Rock Island advance at the state tournament. It sealed the story of a team that two years before had been overlooked, and now held the spot as the best team ever to play from our area.

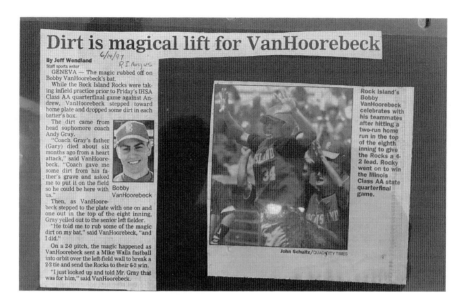

Dirt is magical lift for VanHoorebeck

By Jeff Wendland
Staff sports writer

GENEVA — The magic rubbed off on Bobby VanHoorebeck's bat.

While the Rock Island Rocks were taking infield practice prior to Friday's IHSA Class AA quarterfinal game against Andrew, VanHoorebeck stepped toward home plate and dropped some dirt in each batter's box.

The dirt came from head sophomore coach Andy Gray.

"Coach Gray's father (Gary) died about six months ago from a heart attack," said VanHoorebeck. "Coach gave me some dirt from his father's grave and asked me to put it on the field so he could be here with us."

Then, as VanHoorebeck stepped to the plate with one on and one out in the top of the eight inning, Gray yelled out to the senior left fielder.

"He told me to rub some of the magic dirt on my bat," said VanHoorebeck, "and I did."

On a 2-0 pitch, the magic happened as VanHoorebeck sent a Mike Walla fastball into orbit over the left-field wall to break a 2-2 tie and send the Rocks to their 6-2 win.

"I just looked up and told Mr. Gray that was for him," said VanHoorebeck.

Bobby VanHoorebeck

Rock Island's Bobby VanHoorebeck celebrates with his teammates after hitting a two-run home run in the top of the eighth inning to give the Rocks a 4-2 lead. Rocky went on to win the Illinois Class AA state quarterfinal game.

John Schultz/QUAD CITY TIMES

~Andy Gray, Rock Island, Illinois

The Denver Bears, a Minnesota Twins farm team, was the team I grew up with. It was a perfect fit since my dad, Robert, was from Colorado, and my mom, Diane, was Minnesota-born. I loved going to games at Mile High Stadium with Dad. However, there was a different baseball experience that is more memorable…if maybe a bit uncomfortable. Dad coached a women's softball team in the '70s called The Damn Yankees, named for the musical. Mom and I both played on that team, which was so great. However, as the team became more competitive, Dad actually had to cut Mom. It was unbelievably awkward to live in my house for the next few weeks. Dad felt so guilty, he created a new team called The Yankee Doodles… And so, it went on.

~Sheryl Phipps, Oakland, California

Coaching players across many age groups, 5U (and under) to 18U, I've learned that at each age level, players tend to understand things differently...*very* differently. I had tended to steer clear of the younger players (8U and lower) until I was picked to direct a T-ball league.

For the first time ever, I had no idea what to do when I stepped onto the field. The first day of practice, which I remember quite clearly, was eye-opening for everyone involved, players and coaches. Gathered together in the pre-practice huddle, these kids were looking up at me just waiting for me to say or do something. In turn, I was looking down at them with absolutely no idea where to begin. All I could think was, how do you even coach a kid who has never actually played before? I started with the easy part, running and stretching.

Then came catch. That was a whole other story, and where things really started to get interesting. Here I was, assuming these kids knew what "catch" was. I mean, what five-year-old doesn't know what catch is? I lined them up and spoke on the basics of throwing and catching. After a few minutes, I told them I'd count down from three, and on "Go" they could start playing catch with their partners. In that moment on "Go," I finally realized that none of these kids had any idea of what they were doing. Half of them dropped down and started building dirt castles and a couple others threw their gloves off and started playing tag.

I think we were all a little lost, but I promise you, we all walked away learning something new that day.

~Ryan Rohmiller, St. Louis, Missouri

The all-time baseball memory for me is the moment before the last out of the 2010 World Series. I was the third base coach for the San Francisco Giants. It's hard to describe...it was tough to breathe...but the feeling that there were no teams left to beat was pretty amazing. I have many great moments, with 33 years in and three World Series championships, but, well, that one wins.

~Tim Flannery, San Diego, California

I coached my kids, to varying degrees, in their various sports. I helped coach Rachel's T-ball team and was head coach in her one year of basketball. I co-coached David's first several years of soccer and baseball with his best friend Jeremy's dad, Jeff, stepping aside when it became clear they needed better skill development and, in my case, someone who actually knew what he was doing. I continued as an assistant coach, but everyone knew I was basically the team mom, coordinating logistics, snacks, and tracking substitutions. Still, it kept me on the coaching side of the field, away from screaming parents. It was always, for me, about being with my kids.

When David started Little League, I continued as a coach, although my duties were to "keep book." I clearly recall one at-bat with David at the plate. The pitch came in ankle high and the umpire called, "Strike one!" David gave me a look as if to say, "It was a ball!" and I shot one back saying if the umpiring is calling that, adjust. Pitch two, same spot, same outcome, and then, with little surprise, strike three, and he hit the bench. After the inning, he complained that they were balls. I said, "No, they were strikes. They should have been balls, but you should have figured out after the first pitch that this was this umpire's strike zone. Maybe they were impossible pitches to hit, but if you didn't swing, you sure weren't going to hit them."

I never have considered myself to be particularly wise, but this was a lesson that seemed important to me. In my career, working with Job Corps programs which provided job training to disadvantaged youth, students often complained about their instructors. I listened to their concerns, raised them with management when appropriate, but I always felt that the biggest thing I could teach them was that in their professional lives they would come in contact with all kinds of supervisors, and they would need to adjust to the realities facing them.

They just needed to adjust.

If only David had swung at the third pitch...

~Eric Gray, San Francisco, California

I cherish the relationship I have with my children more than anything in the world. A child of divorce, I didn't have a close relationship with my father, so I promised myself I'd be the most involved, dedicated father ever, and strive for this every day. I knew that common interests would help forge relationships with my kids. Of my many interests, the one I love most, is baseball. It took many years into adulthood to realize this, but once I achieved clarity on that front it's been a sensational love affair.

My grandfather, Willard Raymond Hurst, had a poor, tough life in the hard country of central Texas, forged by work in the cotton fields and fighting in World War II. He was a bad man, simply put, but he realized I was his opportunity to get it right. He did. He loved me and introduced me to baseball, watching games together on television. A Cincinnati Reds fan, his favorite player was Johnny Bench, followed by Mickey Mantle, two Oklahoma boys, close enough to Texas to earn his respect. Our time watching baseball together was special to me; I didn't realize how much so until it hit me like a ton of bricks, 30 years later, when my first son gave me the greatest baseball moment of my life.

When Rhett was born, I hit the ground running sharing my love of baseball with him. His first professional game was at five months old, a night game between Rangers and Astros AA affiliates in Corpus Christi Hooks. It was as difficult as I expected, but I don't regret a second of it, planting a seed being watered by his tears. I vividly recall the day I registered him for youth baseball. I had been a decent catcher (remember, Bench?), a good glove, and average hitter. Rhett, my physical opposite, is short, skinny, and fast, and a contact hitter. He catches, and is a vacuum behind the plate, quick and decisive. In the fall of 2012, he began his first season in kid-pitch baseball. A productive hitter for the Flower Mound Giants in coach-pitch, how would he transition to the wild, inconsistent pitching of nine-year-old peers? He struggled that season.

I enlisted the help of a pro, Angels' draft pick catcher Jonathan Walsh, and Rhett made huge strides. In the 2013 opener, the Giants faced the

Reds, who had beaten us the previous fall. Now an assistant coach, I passed Jonathan's ideas to Rhett's teammates. We felt confident. Rhett led off the game with a walk, disappointed not to get a hit. As he reached first, where I was coaching, I put my hand on his shoulder and told him, "Great job, that's what a leadoff hitter does, he gets on base." As a coach, I was pleased, as it helped the team—he scored. As a father, I was relieved he didn't strike out. The see-saw game dragged on to the 75 minute time limit. With the score 8-8, the bases loaded, and two minutes left on the game clock, Rhett stepped into the batter's box with a chance to drive in the winning run. With a 2-2 count, I could tell he was over-thinking, one of his characteristics, letting the moment overtake him rather than the reverse. Although very much alive in the count, he knew he was beaten. He swung wildly at a slow rainbow a foot outside the strike zone and missed. Still, it was a moral victory to tie the team that had beaten us badly the previous season.

I'm harder on Rhett and expect more from him than from his teammates. I don't expect him to be Mike Trout; I understand his age, capabilities, strengths, and weaknesses. I do expect him to be more mentally prepared because of our discussions about practice and game performance. I'm sure he gets tired of my voice. I emphasize my philosophy of beating your opponent with mental aspects of the game and discipline if your physical tools are inferior. On our drive home, I promised him that the next time he had an opportunity to win a ballgame for us, not only would he *not* be swallowed up by the moment, he would *own* the moment and deliver for his team.

The Giants improved, as did Rhett's batting average. The playoffs were a one-day single-elimination tournament. We drew the 4th seed, avoiding the dreaded Saturday 8:00 a.m. game. We would play at 11:00 a.m. against the Rangers. We'd beaten them during the season, and they had that early game. We won 6-3, sending us into the semi-finals against the Astros at 1:00 p.m. in the brutal late-May North Texas heat. The number 2 seed, the Astros had beaten us 11-5 in the regular season. They were confident and rested after their game hours earlier.

At the 1:02 p.m. first pitch, it was 92 degrees with 90 percent humidity, tough conditions for nine-year-old boys.

The score was 3-3 going into the 6th, an inning rarely reached before the clock runs out. With this being a playoff game, it was unclear how time rules would be applied by the umpires. When the temperature reached 95 degrees, we felt the umpires wanted to get the hell out of there, and we agreed. As we prepared to hit, heading to my spot in the coach's box I glanced at our batting order, and realized Rhett would likely get an at-bat. I walked over to him, put my hand on his shoulder and said, "You're going to win this game for us, Rhett!" and walked away. I didn't look back to see his reaction. Four batters into the inning, he came to bat with game-winning run at third and one out.

I will never forget the next moment. Rhett's ritual was to step into the batter's box, look to the third base coach to get his sign, and then look at me, taking a deep breath to settle his nerves. I know he is often apprehensive, with his desire to please me often mentally taking him out of his game. This time he did something different, and I immediately knew my prediction would come true. He stepped into the box, looked to third for his sign, but instead of that deep breath, he looked at me, winked, and gave me a head nod. There was no doubt in my mind we would go to the championship. He decided that on this day, *he* would be victorious. I had never seen that confident look in his eye before. I was so certain of what was about to happen that as the ball left the pitcher's hand, instead of exhibiting my own nervous rituals, I started a slow walk to our dugout. Almost there, I looked up to see his single to left field drive in the game-winner and propel the Giants into the championship game immediately following. Halfway to first when the winning run crossed home plate, Rhett peeled off and ran to join the jubilation. His teammates tackled him and they rolled around the grass celebrating the walk-off win. In the dugout, I grabbed a Gatorade fruit punch from the cooler and sat down on the bench, more than happy to let the kids have their moment. We coaches had a championship game in 25 minutes to plan for.

The Giants lost that game 11-2 to a great Bulls team, but it didn't matter. Our championship was getting there. That 2nd place trophy is prominently displayed in Rhett's room. He has played on very talented championship teams, but that 9U trophy sits higher than his 12U championship one. I've never asked him, but I think that win means as much to him as it does to me. He knows that of all the baseball I've experienced over my 46 years on earth, that trophy symbolizes the favorite baseball moment of my life. I wish my grandfather had been here to see it.

~Dennis A. Lokey, Flower Mound, Texas

When I was 12 years old, I played in a girl's Little League All-Star Tournament. Our manager was away, so my dad, Kevin, managed the game. We were facing a more talented team, and two of the umpires were friends of my dad, who was also an umpire. We were ahead as I pitched the third inning, and the other team loaded the bases. I struck out the last batter to end the inning and, as is customary, the catcher, Ceanna Johnson, rolled the ball back to the pitcher's mound and my team walked off the field.

The girls on base started sprinting around the bases, all of them scoring before we knew what was going on. Dad asked the umpire, Larry, his friend and mentor, for an explanation. Larry told him that he'd thought the catcher had dropped the ball, so it was still in play as it dribbled out to the mound. Dad looked very upset but really controlled himself. He asked Larry to consult with the other two umpires. Dad saw how this was going to go, as they were walking toward home plate with their heads down. When they were asked if they saw what happened, they both apologetically said, "No, I am sorry."

You could see that Dad was doing his best to keep calm although he was actually furious. All our players were really pissed, saying the umpire cost us the game. At that point, Dad admonished us, saying we needed to keep playing hard, move on, and deal with the situation. Dad said to me, "It was just a mistake. You know he volunteers a lot of hours so you girls can play softball."

Ultimately, we did lose the game, but we had played our best. You always hear about the important lessons we are supposed to learn from competitive sports. We were alternately angry and very sad, but we did learn a valuable lesson about how to behave with pride in the face of a hard situation we couldn't control. We owe that to my dad.

~Emma Macho, Rexburg, Idaho

When I managed 11 to 12-year-old boys in the Little League Majors, I had one player, Mason Weaver, who had not yet fully developed his defensive skills and had few chances to shine in the outfield. In our last game of the season against our rival city team, we had a one run lead toward the end of the game, and Mason was playing left field. Our team and I encouraged him on. With two out in the top of the last inning and runners on second and third, the batter hit a hard sinking line drive to left. I thought there was no way Mason would get to that ball, but he read it perfectly and on a dead sprint made a shoestring catch. Mason sprinted all the way to the dugout, anticipating the congratulations but perhaps not anticipating being carried onto the field by his teammates.

Events like these in the lives of young men and women stick with them for a lifetime. Sports give kids a chance to learn, experience teamwork, and be amazing, even when they don't think they can be.

~Kevin Macho, Stansbury Park, Utah

After coaching in Atlanta's Buckhead Little League system at the T-ball and rookie levels, I was invited to join the major league Athletics as a coach. My stepson, Bill, had played for them as a nine-year-old, and had three years of eligibility left. My son, Toby, could join the team after the tryouts and draft of new players.

At that time, Buckhead Baseball's rules allowed teams to "over-draft", selecting up to three players more than they could keep on the 14-player team. All drafted players could practice with the team for a week or so before coaches made their final roster decisions. Players not kept were assigned to a minor league team. This approach was controversial; some coaches refused to overdraft, thinking about potential damage to a player's self-esteem if he was cut from a roster. The A's manager and I believed we could make the overdraft work. We didn't disclose the order in which we had selected players and told all new players they had been selected for extended tryouts. We were looking for those important intangible attributes like desire, coachability, etc., which are hard to detect during the massive tryouts.

Tryouts were absolute cattle calls. The weather was usually cold, and most kids were somewhat intimidated by having to perform in front of so many coaches. We had developed an elaborate scoring system to rate players' basic skills of hitting, fielding, throwing, running, and speed. We understood that once we drafted a player, he would be part of our team until he was 12. That long-term relationship made the selection process a critical aspect of coaching.

The 1979 Athletics had eight returning players, so we needed to elect six new ones via the draft. We chose eight kids to complement the returnees, over-drafting by two players, and had a couple of weeks to make very difficult roster decisions. We quickly realized that one of the 10-year-olds was not ready to play at the major league level. The last slot was to be a choice between a nine-year-old who obviously would become a very good ballplayer, and George, a huge 12-year-old youngster playing organized baseball for the first time. After considerable agonizing, we sent the younger player to the minors, giving the 12-year-old the opportunity to play in the majors level in his only year of eligibility.

At mid-season, we were questioning our decision; George had not made contact with a pitch during our first ten games—not even a foul ball. When he finally got a hit, however, what a hit it was! His screaming line drive hit the center field fence on the fly. It was one of the hardest hits I saw in my 15 years at Buckhead Baseball. For the rest of the season, George was our leading hitter. As his batting average improved, so did his self-confidence and his posture.

Our new star had joined the team as a big, awkward kid who shuffled rather than walked, seldom made eye contact, and rarely initiated conversations. By season's end, he walked with obvious confidence, laughed freely and often, and talked openly with teammates and coaches. I never saw a more complete transformation in so brief a time period, and I don't think it would have happened without the support he got from everyone on the team. I've coached a lot of players and most improved over the years, but George's development was special. I get a warm feeling inside every time I think of him.

~Wynn Montgomery, Erie, Colorado
Every good coach's dream, Wynn. Glad you had it come true.

Eddie Pellagrini was born in Boston, attended Boston College, and played for the Boston Red Sox in his first two years in the majors, 1946-47. His claim to fame was hitting a grand slam in his first at-bat with the ol' home team. Things looked bright for "Pelli in Boston, except that Johnny Pesky (of Pesky Pole fame) was the starting shortstop. Pelli played for eight years in the majors, a life-time .226 hitter.

Pelli began his coaching career at Boston College in 1958 and retired in 1988. I played for him from 1977-81. He was a game-time coach, leaving preparation of his boys to assistant coaches and captains. Even more so than for his grand slam, Pelli was known as a masterful storyteller, and he was old school all the way. Rain-outs or delays were never an issue with my teammates—we loved sitting around listening to him spin his stories of baseball days of old with players who wore sharp spikes, head-hunting pitchers, and bullshit calls. He had a few favorite sayings, like, "It's all right to carry a piano on your back as long as you don't stop to play it," and "If you're going to throw the ball away, throw it away good," and "That's bullshit." He told every pinch-hitter, "Get up there and hit a home run."

His storytelling went further than the locker room. He was a legend in Winter Haven, Florida, where the Sox trained in the spring and where our team began its seasons far from the snow and cold of New England. Pelli would schedule pool time between the hours of 2:00 to 4:00 p.m. at our hotel and entertain the baseball snowbirds coming for spring training. After pool-time, we would run through our evening scrimmage or practice. Pelli met with us each night after the evening session and prompt-ly announced the venue where he would spend his evening. "Boys, I'm going to be at the Holiday Inn on Rt. 6 tonight. See you in the morning," he would say—code, of course, for, "Whatever you do tonight at the clubs and bars, don't do it at the Holiday Inn on Rt. 6!" There were no curfews or bed-checks, no chance encounters with the coach after hours. Just be on the field at 7:00 a.m.

He was a colorful man of a bygone era. Remembering his love of the game, his old-school ways and love of life always brings a smile to my face and a special warm glow in my chest. It seems as I get older, I think more of the old coach. Must be the way these things work...

~Brian Landry, Haddon Heights, New Jersey

Who would have guessed that on a hot July day in 1986 I would be-come part of sports history? I was assistant coach for the West Waterloo High School girl's fast-pitch softball team, and we were in a double elimi-nation, 16-team, Friday and Saturday tournament in Independence, Iowa. The first day was rained out. With Sunday not a possible make-up day, the tournament was reconfigured to be played all in one day. Our first game was in the morning, and we won an uneventful seven-inning game. We were off until 3:30 that afternoon, with our next opponent the number one rated high school team from Garnavillo, a small school with an incredible season record of 28-2. This was to be the historic game.

Home team Garnavillo took the lead in the 1st, and we tied it up in the 4th. And *that* was the only scoring in the game for 30 innings. That's not a typo. Yes, the game was tied 1-1 after 30 innings. The game, of course, was not without incidents. We thought we scored a run in the 6th, but our run-ner ran over the plate without touching it and was then tagged out. Then mayflies invaded the field. These bugs live 24 hours, hatch near water—in this case the Independence sewer treatment plant—and are attracted to light. There was plenty of light at the stadium to draw them. It looked like a blizzard as the insects just fell from the sky and covered the field, with home plate having to be continually cleared off. After a while, I as the first base coach, started warming up our pitcher between innings, to save our catcher's legs. Women's softball fields are generally 225 feet down the lines, but we were at a men's slow pitch complex, so the line dimensions, 275-300 feet, created a much bigger outfield. It would be logical to think that this would have resulted in more hits and runs, but it's baseball, and you never can make assumptions.

Both starting pitchers, high school juniors, Caryn Heise from W. Waterloo, and Tracy Helle from Garnavillo, completed the game. We had 20 hits, they had 23. Some players came up to the plate 14 times. There were 17 walks and 20 strikeouts. There were a lot of exhausted players, coaches, and umpires.

Of course, you are wondering who won the game. We did, scoring in the top of the 31st inning. But our night wasn't over. With the condensed schedule, as soon as the game ended, and as our exhausted players celebrated, the tournament director let us know we would play again at 9:00 p.m., after playing 31 innings and five-and-a-half hours…in 10 minutes. He virtually stuck a pin in our balloon. We lost, 13-1, the mercy rule mercifully ending this game. But, as the TV ad says, "Wait, there's more!" We then had to play an innings-shortened consolation game for third place, beginning around 10:00. p.m.

Just several weeks before, Caryn had had some severe arm issues, but she finished this day with 44 innings—she pitched one of the three inning game if you are doing the arithmetic—and 250,000 pitches, or so it seemed. The next day she said her legs hurt worse than her arm. All the players were exhausted. Our catcher said she could barely walk. We received lots of press coverage, including USA Today, and relatives of our kids from all over the country saw the stories. It was a long, exhausting day, but an historic one. But boy, I am getting tired just thinking about it.

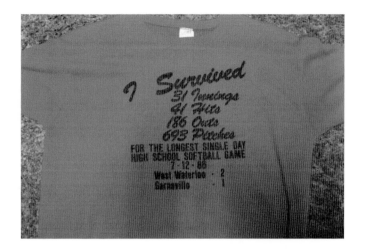

~Errol Brown, Mountain Home, Arkansas

This is a classic Little League story. When my son, Austin, started his Little League adventure at the farm level as a five-year-old, he met Russell. They looked alike, both a little bit big for their age with long, shaggy blond hair. They were both pretty good players and formed a friendship.

91

Every year, kids were re-drafted and became teammates at different times. Austin and Russell had a friendly rivalry when facing each other. At age 10 they became teammates, but it was hard to watch as a parent because Russell was popular and confident, while Austin, who was shy, was teased by Russell. Austin always thought Russell was a neat kid and wanted to be his friend, but Russell turned out to be cruel and did not like Austin, thus starting the rivalry that would last for a couple of years.

As a parent, it's important that your son has a positive experience with sports, so you can imagine my frustration when I saw the things that Russell did to isolate Austin from his teammates. Even during the simple warm-ups before the game, Russell laughed and joked with other teammates while Austin just tried to find someone to play catch with. After watching Austin unable to find anyone to play warm-up catch with, I would be sad before the 10-year-old's game even started.

At 12, in his last Little League season, Austin played Russell's team on the day before Easter Sunday. Russell was pitching and Austin had one of those classic bad days where he struck out all four times at bat. So frustrated, he was swinging and missing at high pitches, not coming close to making contact. In his last at-bat, he struck out on three pitches out of the strike zone, just swinging at anything.

The next day, I grabbed 100 baseballs and said, "Let's go hit and get your confidence back." We tried to drive to the baseball fields located at the end of a park in a canyon, but the whole park was closed for Easter egg hunts and celebrations, and we were unable to drive to the field. So we parked blocks away and carried the equipment on a trail to the baseball diamond. I put the pitching backstop halfway from the pitcher's mound to the plate, and underhanded perfect pitches that Austin could crush. Wanting him to regain his confidence, I didn't throw any hard pitches, just kept everything slow and perfect, right in the middle of the plate.

As luck would have it, the next day we had a game against the same team that had had creamed us two days earlier. It was a close contest. The other coach's son pitched really well, and it looked like we were going to lose again. In the last inning, our first two batters struck out easily and the next drew a walk. Unfortunately, it was then Austin's turn to bat. I was thinking he would surely make the last out. With two outs and a runner on first, the coach called timeout, walked out to the mound to talk to his son, and decided to bring in Russell to pitch to Austin. It was bad enough that Austin would make the last out, but now he had to face his nemesis who had struck him out four times just two days earlier. It was getting dark, the stands were full of yelling parents, and all the other games had ended, so everybody was watching this last at-bat as Russell threw fastballs confidently as he warmed up.

The first pitch was high, and Austin held up his swing. I was proud he didn't chase the same pitch he had two days earlier. The next was high and outside and Austin ripped it for a long foul ball. I remember wishing it could have been fair. The next pitch was high again and Austin hit a high fly into right field that carried and carried over the fence for a walk-off two-run game-winning home run. I couldn't believe it! Everybody went crazy, and Austin was mobbed by his teammates as he reached home plate.

Baseball can be a valuable life lesson. If you have a failure, don't give up, keep trying and keep a positive attitude.

~Jeff

I played baseball in my youth, softball as I aged, then began coaching. I coached my two sons throughout their youth, stopped when they stopped playing, then returned when a friend asked me to help out. My youth coaching experience extends over about 15 years, but my love for the game extends well over 50.

As most coaches know, motivation is a key, if not *the* key factor in bringing out the best in players and teams. I found motivating sayings and actions from major league players and coaches which I utilized regularly, with some success. I then stumbled onto one tactic that proved effective as a rallying point for a number of teams and their players over the years I coached in what is called the Gopher State Baseball League, a league comprised of teams in and around the Twin Cities—Minneapolis and St.

Paul—metro area, that play at a very high level, consistently producing Division 1 college players.

The Gopher State Baseball League traditionally gives baseball caps to the team that wins the seasonal league play. They are quality caps bearing the league logo, but more important, "League Champions" is embroidered prominently on the back. The year I returned to coaching, we were fortunate to have a very good team and we won the league, and thus got the caps. At the first practice the next season, with the next group of young men, prior to distributing the uniforms, I wore my trophy hat. At the team talk to start practice, one player noticed the cool logo and asked if their new uniforms included that hat. Not to let the opportunity pass, I took the cap off, turned it around to reveal the League Champion on the back, and told them, "No, this isn't part of the uniform, this one needs to be earned." Winning a League Champion cap became a core part of the team goals for each subsequent team. Frequently there was talk on the bench and in the field about "earning *the cap*," or "one game closer to *the cap*," or "get a hit or out for *the cap*," that sort of banter. I don't recall the exact number of caps our teams won, but as a motivator, it was many more years than not.

A decade later, I still have a few caps in my wardrobe, though most are faded, sweat-stained, and tattered. I'm thankful to every young man that worked hard and earned a cap for me.

~Robert Kretchmer, St. Paul, Minnesota

BALLS, STRIKES, YER SAFE, YER OUT: THE ART OF UMPIRING

Umpiring is not for me. It seems *like it would be fun, and not that hard except for the close calls. But I remember the one time I was pulled out of the stands to referee my son's basketball game. I have had few situations as stressful as that, and it was only for a small school's seventh grade team. I pretty much forgot I had a whistle in my mouth until five seconds after the call I should have made. They all let me off easy that day, but obviously, umpires take an awful lot of jeering during games. Some of the umpires took stuff…but some gave it right back. Here's to the men and women in blue.*

When my twin sister, Warren, and I started umpiring during the summer of 1981, there was exactly one woman calling balls and strikes in all of professional baseball, so it wasn't as if we had a lot of role models with whom to identify or in whom we could see ourselves reflected. It was our mother, Jaqueline, nicknamed Jack, who suggested that umpiring was something I might enjoy, although at the time I had no idea how she'd arrived at that conclusion, and I certainly had entertained no thought of umpiring on my own. It turned out she'd seen me reading a book, *The Men In Blue: Conversations With Umpires* by Larry Gerlach and traced the image of me reading it back to a song I'd written about an umpire in my earlier incarnation as a musician/composer and former opening act for Bruce Springsteen. In the way only a mother can do, she connected the dots from my song to that book, decided that umpiring was the career for me, showed me the way to the diamond, and pushed me unceremoniously out onto home plate.

Forty years later, I've never looked back.

I started umpiring Little League baseball near where Jack was living in California by sweet-talking my way into the job after she showed me an ad she'd cut out of the local paper. "Indio Needs Umpires!" it proclaimed. After inflating my non-existent credentials rather outrageously to the harried assignor I'd called, who must have hired me out of desperation, I found myself face-to-face with my destiny in the form of a mob of unruly 10-year-old ballplayers and their even more unruly coaches and parents. I'd never been the target of such up-close and personal vitriol in my life, yet there was something mysteriously joyous about being yelled at and told I was terrible. The experience was exhilarating and mystifying, like a puzzle I wanted to piece together, no matter how long it took or how daunting it was to solve. Right away I recognized that to succeed I would need a strong support system, and since few other umpires were clamoring for the chance to work with me back then, at my insistence, the assignor reluctantly agreed to hire my sister as my steady partner.

Warren attended the Harry Wendelstedt Umpire School with me in January of 1982, six months after our first foray onto the diamond, and she continued to call games for a few years until life intervened and umpiring took a back seat to the more conventional goals of earning her nursing degree and raising two sons. Mine is a very different story. Forty years after that first Little League game, I've umpired major league exhibitions in both the United States and Japan, worked the Cape Cod League, assembled a four-woman crew for a major league spring training game, called international tournaments in Taiwan, Hong Kong, and Guam, and seen my picture displayed at the Hall of Fame in Cooperstown as part of the "Diamond Dreams: Women in Baseball" exhibit. I haven't achieved any of that by myself. I've worked hard and made the most of every opportunity that presented itself, of course, but I've also had great partners, assignors who believed in me, and a support system in the persons of my sister and mother that was vital to my desire to keep going when it seemed I would never get anywhere. My natural perseverance and tenacity helped me through some tough times, but if there's one thing I've learned after four decades on the diamond, it's that I'm only as good as my partners. Without the unconditional love of my family to sustain and shield me from the sharp-edged slings and arrows all umpires endure, I wouldn't be telling this story today. If my mother hadn't encouraged me to become an umpire, I may never have started, and if not for my sister, I probably wouldn't have lasted this long.

~Perry Barber, New York, New York

McCormick Field in Asheville, North Carolina, is one of the oldest ballparks in the USA, opened in 1924. No less than Babe Ruth himself called it, "A damn delightful place to play." It's a no-frills, down-to-earth, throwback type of ballpark. The first home run ever hit there was by Ty Cobb during an exhibition game. Professional baseball in Asheville goes back to 1897, when the Asheville Moonshiners first took the field. In 1915 they were dubbed the "Tourists" by local sportswriters, and in 1925 the team officially adopted the Tourists moniker. The scoreboard at the ballpark shows Visitors vs. Tourists. Capacity at McCormick Field is approximately 4000, and a general admission ticket costs $7. I try to make it to a handful of home games every year.

Around 2010, I went to a game with my friend, Ben, a fellow baseball freak. We bought general admission tickets and found seats almost directly behind home plate, maybe a foot or two to the third base side. Only the first 10 or so rows are reserved, so we had prime seats that night for the most egregiously blown call I've ever seen an umpire make. This one was even worse than Jim Joyce's blown call that cost Armando Gallaraga a perfect game, or Dan Denkinger's in Game 6 of the 1985 World Series. Luckily for the umpire, it was a midweek single-A contest in the South Atlantic League, not a major league game on national television.

I don't remember who the Tourists were playing that night, but the visiting team's leadoff batter in the top of the 1st inning hit a long fly ball down the right field line. It sure sounded like a home run, and as I watched the trajectory of the ball, I saw it easily clear the right field wall… at least 10 feet to the right of the foul pole. As Ben and I were sitting behind home plate, pretty much even with the first base line, it couldn't have been more obvious that this ball was *way* foul, but the home plate umpire pointed his right index finger skyward and rotated it in a circle, indicating a home run! Everybody in the crowd was stunned, everyone looking around at everybody else, shaking our heads, and asking with our eyes, "Have you ever seen anything like *that* before?" Nobody had. And to this day, I still haven't.

I don't remember who won the game that night, but for the entire nine innings, *every* time there was a foul ball, even the ones fouled straight back, the crowd would stand up and razz the ump by giving the home run signal.

~Chuck Brodsky, Asheville, North Carolina

My favorite umpiring story has to do with a late friend of mine. It was the best piece of heckling I have ever heard, before or since. I was calling a

16-year-olds Babe Ruth game and I called my friend's son out on a border-line pitch. Angelo hollered out at me "Hey, Lardy! What was your major in college, *Braille?*" I laughed to myself for the next three innings.

~Steve Lardy, Lakeland, Florida

During the Men's Senior Adult Baseball League World Series in Arizona, I was the base umpire for a 35-and-over division game at Goodyear Stadium. At age 65, I was three decades older than several of the players. On a close play at first, I banged the runner out. On his way back to the third base dugout, he turned and yelled loud enough to be heard by everyone, "Thirty years ago, you'd have seen that!" Just as loudly, I replied, "Thirty pounds ago, you'd have beat it out!"

As a home plate umpire for a Little League game, I once called a runner out at the plate on a close play. The player's mother, who had been very vocal all game, chirping on nearly every pitch or call that didn't favor her son's team, yelled from the bleachers behind me, "If you were my husband, I'd ask for a divorce!" I turned around and, with a smile, said, "Lady, if you were my wife, you wouldn't have to ask!"

~Larry Mires, Buckeye, Arizona
Sounds like lines straight out of Winston Churchill's archives!

I was a base umpire in a Putnam County B Little League tournament game between Vaughnsville and Columbus Grove when the Columbus Grove pitcher was hit by a line drive and had to leave the game with quite a welt on his arm. The team had to bring in a new pitcher. This little kid had a glove that was bigger than him. He was so scared I went to the mound to see if he was okay, and he was crying. Columbus Grove was down 4-0 with no outs and runners on first and second. I told the coach to talk with him with no charged visit to the mound. The little boy induced a pop out, then walked a batter to load the bases. He was really scared and shaking. I went to the mound to talk with him, and he told me he wanted to come out of the game. I smiled and said, "You will be fine, and if you get out of this, I'll buy you a pop." I'll be darned, that little guy got a strikeout and a ground out to escape the inning. He got a Pepsi out of that! I told him, "You must have been thirsty," and we both laughed.

In another tournament, I was the home plate umpire. Cloverdale was playing Glandorf, who made five errors in the 1st inning and was down 9-0 before they even batted. Cloverdale took the field and Glandorf's first hitter called time out. I asked him what was wrong, and he said the pitcher had to take the plastic neon bracelet off. A league rule stated that no bracelets or jewelry could be worn. I walked out to the mound and both coaches came out. Explaining the rule, when I got to the mound, I was shocked to see the pitcher was a nine-year-old girl! That must have made her mad. The very first pitch hit the batter in his rear end! I couldn't help but laugh since it didn't hurt anyone. The batter's dad yelled to me that the pitcher did it on purpose. I turned around and told him, "I hope your son doesn't try to date her later in life, because she is going to remember this!" Everyone got a good laugh out of that one!

~Mark Potthoff, Glandorf, Ohio

I was an amateur baseball umpire for 40 years. As an umpire, you have to know every single rule, including those you never see invoked. I think I called everything in the book, including this most unusual one.

I was the base umpire in a two-man crew, perhaps at a high school game. The game was tied in the bottom of the 7th inning of a seven-inning game. The leadoff batter hit a triple, so the visiting team planned to walk the next two batters to set up a force play at the plate. The first intentional walk was completed properly, but I noticed the catcher sliding more and more to the outside when giving the signals. His coach was yelling to him to stay in the box. On the first pitch to the next batter the catcher barely had one foot in the catcher's box when the pitch was delivered. I called time for a quick conference with the plate umpire. He had noticed the same thing. On the next pitch the catcher was totally outside the box when the pitch was delivered. We both called it at the same time. Game over on a walk-off catcher's balk. There was no argument from the coach.

~Dan Lewis, Lakeland, Florida

When I was eight, I had an at-bat that would change baseball for me forever. I was so small I usually walked, since pitchers barely had a strike zone to throw at with me in the box. I walked up to the plate, looked up at the pitcher, and hit the ground screaming. The pitcher had thrown the ball straight at my head, hitting me square in the right eye. My huge coke bottle glasses were hit so hard they ended up stuck in the backstop. I still joke with my coach about it. He says the first thing out of my mouth was, "I never saw it coming!" To this day, I cannot close only my right eye. I continued to play until eighth grade but became that kid who ran from balls hit to him and turned away from the pitch when at bat.

Years later, living in central Florida, I wanted to get back into the game I'd loved so much as a kid, and give back to my community at the same time. I contacted the local Little League as they were looking for umpires. I caught up on the rules and bought the gear I needed so the league wouldn't have to spend money.

My first game involved seven to eight-year-old kids from the same town. The first few innings went smoothly, and then it happened, that darn baseball again! The bases were loaded with no outs. I was behind the catcher when a high fastball came in to the plate. The catcher had done a good job the whole game, so I had no need to worry. I was wrong. He missed the ball and it hit me right in the mask, so hard that I fell on my rear end, my mask twisted half way around my face. I could not see a thing. To make matters worse, I was on top of the ball. The catcher fumbled around, but I could barely see so I called time. The coach at third base ran over and, without asking if I was all right, started screaming because I'd called time. He wanted to send all his baserunners home, which I would not allow in what was supposed to be a friendly game. I told him no runners would advance and that he needed to calm down. That only made matters worse. I wanted to throw him out of the game but didn't want to embarrass him. I told him to go back to third and said I'd fully explain my decision after the game. A few pitches later, the catcher missed another one, the ball just brushing past my leg to the backstop. The catcher got it and covered the plate with the runners only advancing one base. The coach again started screaming, and I wondered, "What now?" He said, "Why didn't you call time on that play?" I gave him a warning, telling him that if he said one more word to or about me the entire game, he could walk to his car and leave. I was surprised he listened. I never spoke to him directly again.

I umpired a few more games during the season. My goal was to do it for the kids, but I think I forgot about the parents. Some parents are ruthless and heckle umpires the entire game. One stood behind the backstop and complained that every call I made was wrong except when his kid threw a strike. I don't think parents realize that I, like most umpires, do this out of the goodness of my heart so their kids can play and hopefully have a better childhood baseball experience than I did.

~Jared Famularo, Anchorage, Alaska

Almost 30 years ago, as a 13 to 14-year-olds umpire in Roscoe, IL, I had to toss the coach of a team of 8 to 10-year-old boys five times over two seasons for swearing and such. He yelled and cursed over balls and strikes and any close call that didn't go his way. The next year I had a game against his team early in the season; I figured he'd last two or three innings, tops. The dugout was quiet the entire game, with not a single complaint. After the game he apologized for his past behavior. He'd started umpiring and it had completely changed his behavior!

Around the same time, I had to toss a coach in the bottom of the first inning for swearing. His players' parents went full-tilt nuts, threatening to beat me up and even kill me after the game. I was the base umpire, and toward the end of the game, I just started laughing at those people. Surprisingly, that kind of quieted them down. My partner lived about a mile from the field and normally walked home after the games. My dad made him ride home with us.

~Derick Rose, Machesney Park, Illinois

I was an umpire for the local Little League. One game, a dad kept yelling at me, apparently because of my strike zone. Since they were young kids, I wanted a wide zone so they would swing. I tossed my counter to him and said, "You do it," and went to sit in the crowd. I got a standing ovation. The dad just sat back down quietly, and I resumed my duties. I know how to hush obnoxious parents—"YOU get behind the plate, big boy."

Was I right? Probably not. The boys liked it, and so did I. I called many base stealers out. They knew they had to run if I was calling it. One kid did a Pete Rose head first slide. I loved it.

~Craig Sparks, Spindale, North Carolina

Several years ago, I was umpiring a very low-level recreational slo-pitch game in Winnipeg. The game was tied 23-23 and the home team had a runner on first with two outs. The next batter hit a ball to right center, and I was watching outfield play when a runner in a white track suit flashed by me, scoring the apparent winning run. I started scratching my head and realized the runner from first was now standing on third, and the batter was on second. Huh? I called time. Amidst all the celebrating, I tracked down White Track Suit and asked from what base he had come. He spoke very little English and his translator explained that he was the third base coach who got excited, stepped on third, and ran home for what he thought was the winning run. I called him *out* for making a travesty of the game. The next batter popped up. It was too dark to continue, so the game mercifully ended as a tie.

~Will Joseph

I have umpired baseball in Canada since I was 11 years old. It seems like Canada has always been ahead of the curve regarding women in baseball (that's right, baseball, not softball), whether playing or umpiring, but we still have a way to go. I've taken part in several groundbreaking games. The Skydome in Toronto was the site of the first women's World Series of Baseball in 2001. Four countries were represented—Canada, USA, Japan, and Australia. In the gold medal game between the US and Japan, all four umpires were Canadian women. What I remember most vividly is how the umpires perfectly executed a seldom-noticed rotation, in which umpires rotate counterclockwise if they have to cover a base being approached by a runner because another of the crew had to leave their position. Our supervisor looked at us and told us, "Well done."

One of the biggest crowds I ever umpired in front of was many thousands of people in Telus Stadium at the women's 2004 World Cup in Edmonton, Canada. It was another groundbreaking game, not just for me but for women players from all over the world competing for an international championship. Before a big game and big crowd, I always look around the field at the crowd, take it all in, and just be present in the moment. The gold medal game once again saw Japan play the USA. I was the home plate umpire. With the US holding a 2-0 lead, a Japanese runner was thrown out at home on a very close play, in a close and intense game. At the time, USA was the perennial power house, winning the World Series and the first Women's World Cup gold medal. Japan has since replaced the US as the most dominating women's national baseball team. The Japanese team most recently had Kitta Megumi take over the managerial helm. In 2016, she led her team to a gold medal, keeping the World Championship streak alive for Japan.

In 2018, the men's Intercountry Baseball League celebrated its 100th anniversary. In 2016, I'd been part of the first all-female crew in the league's history. While partially a statement to help break down gender barriers, all crew members were well deserving of the assignment as we had all umpired in the league for years, just never together in the same game. The players and fans knew and felt the game was different, but after the first ½ inning it was business as usual. A number of players in this league represented various countries in the World Baseball Classic or have played professionally.

In 2016, I was the umpire director at the Women's World Cup in Korea, the first time a woman held this position at a WBSC International Tournament. I also was the umpire director of the World University Games in Taiwan, a men's tournament and another milestone. In the spring of 2020, I was selected by Major League Baseball to umpire at the World Baseball Classic Qualifier in Arizona, the first women to do so. I felt it was the culmination of my years of hard work and training, and beyond any dream I could ever have imagined.

Women involved with baseball in any capacity, whether players, trainers, coaches, or umpires, know that the likelihood of ever having any kind of career with the sport, even getting college scholarships, is small, but thankfully, this is beginning to change. With increasing recognition of women and their talents in baseball, opportunities are becoming more available. There is a realization that women belong in baseball and have contributions to make, given the opportunity. Too many girls and women have been told they can't play baseball. "You'll get hurt, it's not for girls." I was also told that as a child…and ignored it. My story is baseball. I tell the girls and women I meet through baseball, "Your story is whatever you want it to be." For me, my journey in baseball has been one of my greatest accomplishments, doing something I wanted to do, something I love.

Reflecting back on my younger self who was told, "Baseball isn't for you," I think about all the experiences I would have missed, the boundaries I would not have broken, the memories I would not have made. I share some of these accomplishments to encourage everyone to Follow Your Dream.

~Lisa Turbitt, Burlington, Ontario, Canada

I live in South Korea and have been an umpire for many leagues and tournaments. In 2018, I was asked to go to Japan to umpire the Youth Asian Pacific World Series in Japan. The teams were from countries including Korea, Vietnam, Japan, China, and the Philippines, with umpires from Japan, Korea, and China. Games were played at professional Japan league spring training fields. It was a wonderful tournament with a lot of exciting games, right down to the final out of the championship game between Japan and Korea. I was the third base umpire in that game.

I had one close, controversial call. With runners on first and second, the Korean second base runner, with a good lead, took off as the pitcher threw to the plate. The catcher threw down to third as the runner slid into the base, the third baseman's glove between him and the bag. As the fielder stood to show the ball, his glove came off his hand with the ball still in it. I called the runner safe. Out came the Japanese coach, arguing that the runner was out, successfully tagged. I listened to him and explained that the fielder lost possession and control of the ball. Call stands.

He was not happy. Didn't matter. Japan won the game anyway, 7-6.

~John Behrend, Daegu, Korea

I was lucky enough to umpire 3,392 regular season and 59 World Series Major League Baseball games. Imagine being able to go to work every day and not think of it as work. My office was the ballpark, I guess 30 of them, almost all current parks except a few built since 2002, and some no longer with us.

I was there the day Bucky F#*&ing Dent hit his famous home run, and the games when Ripken tied and broke Gehrig's consecutive game record. I umpired—or would have—the Giants vs. A's World Series earthquake game. I gave then-principle owner of the Rangers, George Bush, the lineup cards of the Rangers first win at Arlington Stadium.

On the last game of the '84 season, Don Mattingly and Dave Winfield were battling it out for the batting championship. In that situation, you especially don't want to be anything but correct. Miscalling even a single pitch—ball or strike—could set up a different pitching situation, a different pitch to be thrown, a better or worse chance of the batter getting a base hit or being struck out on a called third strike that *better* be correct. You want to be a part of it, you are a part of it, but you don't want to be *the show*. Winfield went 1-4; Mattingly went 4-5 to win the title. Each one later sought me out and complimented me on a "spot-on job" behind the plate. It felt good to be appreciated and to know my hard work was noticed.

My most difficult game behind the plate was a hot Sunday in Chicago, the White Sox against the Angels. The Angels' Nolan Ryan was firing at 98-101 MPH and Sox knuckleballer Wilbur Wood was tossing 65-70 MPH. How can you reasonably be expected to fully adjust? Hitters have a hard time adjusting to a pitcher's varying speeds pitch by pitch, and so do umpires, all game long. I was never so happy to see two starting pitchers leave the game!

I was the first and only Jewish umpire hired by the American League. Now, all umpires are hired by the Commissioner's office. One day I was calling balls and strikes at the SkyDome in a game between the Brewers and the Blue Jays, on the day of the eve of Rosh Hashanah, the Jewish New Year. Jesse Levis was catching for the Brewers, and Shawn Green was batting for Toronto. All of a sudden, I realized there was something quite rare—three Jewish guys at home plate. I called time out, and as I bent down to clean off the plate, I looked at them and said in Hebrew, "Good Yontiv," Happy New Year. They looked at me, both realizing at the same time the uniqueness of the moment, then smiled at me and each other and wished each other the same. That night may be the only time in baseball history that unique moment ever occurred.

I was the first umpire to wear glasses on a permanent basis. I'd tried contacts and they didn't agree with me. I knew I'd catch hell from fans—you know, a "blind as a bat" sort of thing—but I also knew I would eject players if they got on me. It would be all over ESPN. The Angels' manager, Marcel Lacheman was standing near the third base line and got up, pointed at the glasses, and waved in a disparaging way. He was gone. A few weeks later in Baltimore, in a game against the Yankees, I was working second base. A heavy mist in the air was fogging up my glasses, so I took them off. Yankee 2B Chuck Knoblauch asked for time and I acknowledged it. Chuck came over and said, "Al, would you please put your glasses back on?"

Most of all, I loved the fans. I think of myself as gregarious, and when stationed at first or third base, before the game and between innings I would walk to the stands and inevitably draw a large crowd of 10-12 year-old fans. With a ball in my hand, I'd ask if they liked baseball, then said, "Let's have a contest. I'm thinking of a number between 15 and 30." I'd start with the youngest kid, or the shortest, and look up facing the sky, displaying my uniform No. 24, which I wore in honor of the Yankee player I grew up idolizing, Al Downing, who grew up in Trenton, as did I. Even with that hint, often no one guessed correctly, so I would just hand the ball to one of them. The excitement in their eyes was priceless. Many will remember that moment for a lifetime, and maybe at that moment we made a baseball fan. That still makes me smile. These were times I treasured in my years as an umpire.

~Al Clark, Williamsburg, Virginia, author of *Called Out But Safe*

USHERS AND VENDORS AND BAT BOYS…OH MY

Working at the ballpark is, for so many people, a great way to connect with your team, your favorite players, other fans, and the sport you love. Lynn and I thought about ushering as retirement jobs—I mean, you get paid to watch games for free! Well, at least if you are in a seating section and not dealing with rowdy, drunken people. Granted, for some people it is simply a job, but for others it is thrilling, and maybe even leads to being in a World Series parade as it did for Rachel. Some of these folks have wonderful memories to share about jobs of different types at ballparks—on the fields, in the stands, and behind the scenes.

It seems most sports teams have a signature moment, one that defines the most exciting event in their history. For the Seattle Mariners that moment is known as "The Double." SBNation called it one of the most "important games in baseball history." Of the 57,000 raucous fans, press, and Seattle police who were there on that fateful day, along with just one other person, I had the best view in the entire stadium!

The Mariners were rarely competitive and hadn't had a winning season for their first 18 years in Seattle. During that time, the team played in The Kingdome, labeled by some, "The Tomb." Designed as a multipurpose stadium, it lacked sunlight, acoustics, and warmth. It had hosted Billy Graham, The Rolling Stones, the Seattle Seahawks, Monster Jam, an AA National Convention, and the Mariners.

For many years, I had a casual parttime job at the Dome, much of that time as an usher supervisor. This involved working with 20-25 ushers, the maintenance crew, first aid, and the Seattle Police Department. My primary responsibility was the first-level seating area from home plate to left-center field. These seats, considered some of the best in the Dome, were a favorite of many season ticket holders. I had a well-paying office job during the day which was challenging and gave me an opportunity to make a difference, but it didn't offer the excitement I craved. The Dome did. It wasn't the money that appealed to me but the sheer energy of being involved with so many people in a wide variety of circumstances. It was adrenaline and maybe a little testosterone thrown in. I really enjoyed the work, and it showed.

The Mariners had never played in the postseason and were 13 games back by the beginning of August 1995. Thanks to the pitching of soon-to-be Cy Young Award winner Randy Johnson, the outfield play of Ken "The Kid" Griffey, and Edgar Martinez, along with the late-season collapse of the California Angels, the Mariners found themselves in the postseason for the very first time. To make it even more exciting, they were playing the much-vaunted and equally-hated New York Yankees. The M's lost the first two games of the series and were one away from elimination. Although the crowd was electric on that October 8, there was an undertone of dread, a feeling of "Here we go again." But through the efforts of Johnson, Martinez, Griffey, and a team whose motto was "Refuse To Lose", the Mariners won games three and four. It all came down to the last game...win or go home. Game five did not start out well for the Mariners. They recovered but found themselves down by one run in the bottom of the 11th (Music from the 1950s TV show *Dragnet* might be appropriate here). It was the kind of contest that made you love baseball, a game of finesse and fierce competition. The Mariners manager was Lou Piniella, a crusty old-line manager who had been around the block and won National League Manager of the Year in both 1995 and 2001. The team had two future Hall of Fame players—Griffey, who has been called the best player of the century, and Martinez, the namesake for the Best Designated Hitter in Baseball award. Both were at the top of their game and they brought the team along with them.

An important part of a supervisor's role is crowd control, and one of the biggest concerns is "losing the field." This happens when jubilant—or otherwise—fans take the field. Several days earlier we had been stormed and were determined it would not happen again. To guard against this, ushers were stationed at the bottom of each row and paired with SPD officers. We had this covered! As an extra measure, for the last several innings of the game a Seattle policeman and I actually sat on the roof of the third base dugout, ready for action. I remember us looking at each other smiling and nodding. We had an unbelievable view and we knew it!

Trailing by a run in the bottom of the 11th, Joey Cora came to the plate. In his previous at-bat in the 9th, he'd bunted and reached first on a hotly contested call, the Yankees alleging he had run outside the baseline. The umpire felt otherwise. The leadoff batter in the 11th, he took the first pitch for a called strike, then again bunted and reached first. Next up, Griffey also took a called strike. Then, in the words of the Mariner's announcer, he belted a hard liner just past second base, allowing Cora to advance to third. With runners at the corners, the best hitter of the era, Martinez, came to bat. He also took one called strike, and then it happened, a hard-hit ball to the left field fence. Cora scored and Griffey rounded third, heading for home. Along with 57,000 fans, the policeman and I were standing, cheering, willing The Kid to score. The throw from deep left-center to home was a good one, but Griffey was better. He slid under the tag and was safe. The M's had won a most improbable victory, and this spectacle had unfolded literally at my feet. The sellout crowd went crazy. The officer and I high-fived, and I seem to recall a hug. The future of the Mariners in Seattle was assured.

After being part of such an amazing spectacle, one may be at a loss for words, standing in stunned silence. Not this time! The stadium's noise level, fueled by adrenaline, emotion, and joy, was deafening. It was the best of what sports can be, coming together and celebrating. I don't think there were any strangers in the crowd that day. People were hugging, applauding, crying, laughing, and hoping always to remember the magic they had just experienced. It came to be known as "The Double."

The Mariners went on to play Cleveland and didn't make it to the World Series, but the legacy of that evening was far more important than any Series game. Because of the success of that season, the goodwill toward the team, and some aggressive marketing, a new baseball stadium was built.

I may never have another experience like The Double, but that's okay. It makes the memory sweeter, and who knows...leaves room for another great moment!

~Bill Cecil, Seattle, Washington

Jeff Kent just rode in my elevator. It's happened before, and usually I just smile. But today was destined to be different...

Jeff was going up to the fourth floor, and there were people stopping on every floor on the way up. One of them apologized to everyone, and I seized the opportunity to say, "No problem! It gives me more time in the elevator with my favorite baseball player of all time, Jeff Kent!" (No need to mention Matt Cain or the complexities of my ranking system at that particular moment, I felt.) "Oh, thank you," said the man with the only mustache I've ever liked. "I'm not even kidding," I insisted...okay, I gushed, as I had decided to just let myself go full-on fangirl. "I still wear No. 21. Well, I don't actually play anything, but it's in my email address!" I wouldn't have blamed him for not wanting to respond, but he kindly asked, "Are you stuck in here all day?" I had already embarrassed myself, so I just went with it. "Yes, but it's totally worth it!" He smiled, said, "Good to meet you," and shook my hand. This, quite literally, is what I had hoped for in applying for this job in the first place. Life goal achieved!

So what do I do now? I don't need this job anymore... Ha ha ha.

~Rachel Gray, San Francisco, California

Yes, you do, Rachel. You have lots more interesting people to meet.

In 1953, I was in my living room with my dad when I heard that the Orioles would be playing Major League Baseball in Baltimore beginning in 1954. I turned to him and said, "I want to be a bat boy." In December of 1957, I wrote a letter to the Orioles telling them of this desire. Three days later, I got a reply saying there was an opening for the 1958 season, and to come to the stadium the morning of the first exhibition game against the Reds. As bad fortune would have it, I feared that dream was shattered by a rainstorm that day. Then, as good fortune would also have it, I was told to come two weeks later when the Orioles played the Yankees. I went after school, and at the age of 14, I was given the job. I worked there until 1960, progressing from clubhouse guy who did the laundry and cleaned shoes to ball boy, and then to bat boy.

In a 1959 game against the Yankees, the Orioles' third base coach told me—the bat boy!—that he couldn't see the signs the Yankee catcher, Johnny Blanchard, was putting down. He asked, "Can you see the signs?" I indicated I could, and then began to relay them to him. The Yankees' legendary manager, Casey Stengel, figured out what was happening and went out to complain to the umpire. I, the bat boy, was ejected from the game. Later on, I was in the clubhouse cleaning up the uniforms and sunflower seeds, and Stengel came in, found me, and said, "I am sorry, I had to do that." Then he reached into his pocket and gave me an autographed baseball! A great reward for what might be one of the strangest ejections in baseball history.

Through the years, I got to know so many great ballplayers. I count as friends, to this day, such terrific players and men as Brooks Robinson, Milt Pappas, Rick Dempsey, and Frank Robinson. All of this because as a 14-year-old I wrote a letter asking to be a bat boy.

~Warren Sollod, Baltimore, Maryland

From 1996 to 2002, I had the incredible opportunity to live a childhood fantasy as the statistician in the Mets broadcast booth at my beloved Shea Stadium. Over time, Shea was ill-maintained and became rundown and dingy. Nevertheless, for Mets fans like me, whose childhood included viewing a handful of games with my dad in the field level seats during the glorious 1986 season, it was *our dump*. If someone had told my nine-year-old self in 1986 that just 10 years later I'd be working alongside Tom Seaver, Gary Thorne, and the rest of the Mets broadcast team, I'd have thought the messenger was crazy and would not have believed that was ever going to become my reality.

During those years, I spent time in the Mets clubhouse, in the dugout, and on the field during batting practice. I also had the chance to work some away games inside venerable Fenway Park, old Yankee Stadium, and even classily classic Dodger Stadium. I watched my favorite 1986 Met and later Mets announcer, Keith Hernandez, pluck a cherry off his sundae and flick it into the stands at Coors Field, then laugh like a deviant schoolboy. I even got to enjoy a few innings hanging out with one of my favorite actors, Gary Sinise, visiting the booth to plug his latest flick.

Of all the memories and experiences, the time Vin Scully popped into the booth to share reminiscences with Mets' broadcasting original Ralph Kiner is among my most cherished. I remember it like it was yesterday—pregame, a pink-grey dusk, the crowd filing in leisurely, the requisite stadium smells and sounds, along with my view from the booth of the giant scoreboard, the famous Apple, and the automobile chop shops off in the distance beyond the stadium.

And then, That Voice descended into the booth. "How ya doin' Ralph!" Or was it "Ralphie?" I didn't look over because I already was transfixed by the sound of That Voice, that glorious mixture of jazz with poetry, now not more than three feet from me. I was not alone in my reaction. Glancing over in awe, I realized the Mets play-by-play announcer, Howie Rose, was sitting quietly, having stopped his pregame prep to listen as Vin and Ralph regaled each other and those around them. As Ralph chomped on one of his patented cigars, the two shared stories of vintage baseball, long ago cocktail parties, old flames from the 1950s and 1960s, and even the train rides teams used to take on road trips. Howie was by then a broadcaster of great renown in his own right, yet for those moments he was just like me, doing his best to hear every word, savoring the experience while trying to not be too obvious about it. They must have gone on for 10 or 15 minutes, but at the time it felt like 10 or 15 seconds, over as quickly as it began. But, boy, did that brief moment in time ever sear itself into my memory.

Kiner was indelibly a Mets institution, but to me, Scully was more than an announcer, he was a national institution. Coincidentally, I later learned that Ralph had introduced Vin at his Hall of Fame induction in 1982. Both were a slice of Americana. Vin has retired and Ralph passed away, and both voices are missed, as are my days in the booth at that dump of a stadium, our *dump*, good old Shea.

~JD Friedman, Haledon, New Jersey

While attending college, a friend who owned a hospitality staffing company asked if I could work an upcoming baseball playoff game as security staff. I jumped at the opportunity to see a baseball game free and up close! It was 1986 and the Houston Astros were playing the New York Mets in Game Six at the Astrodome. I was assigned to stand guard by the Mets' bullpen near the bleachers.

In Texas, beer is a beverage consumed like water, so by the 16th inning after almost five hours of playing time, my job ended up dodging beer cups and funny insults from the fans, though always done in an innocent, good ole boy way. By then I had resigned myself to ducking and letting the fans have their say, as long as it was done in a safe way. The Mets won, I had a few laughs, and everyone went on their very merry way.

~Michael Schneider, Oahu, Hawaii

Baseball fans remember that epic series and game. It was Lynn's birthday. As a Mets fan, I was listening to the game at work. At some point I decided I had to go home and watch the end, which could have come at any time. I arrived home in time to see a thrilling 16th inning and had a double reason to celebrate that evening.

I work in guest services at Coors Field. One Sunday afternoon, a dad walked through the door to my section with his son in tow. The boy was about four, and wore a fedora-type hat, golf shirt with matching shorts, flip-flops, and had one hand in his pocket. I said, "How are you today, little man?" He didn't say a word but stuck his right hand—not the one in his pocket—straight out in front of himself and gave me a thumbs-up, all the while looking straight ahead. What a scream!

In this capacity, I've had a chance to see some great and historic games. In August of 2016, the Miami Marlins were in town with Ichiro Suzuki in pursuit of his 3000th career major league hit and only one away. He didn't play Friday or Saturday, and though it was disappointing not to see him play, I figured he was being held out to accomplish this feat in front of his hometown fans. However, on Sunday he was in the lineup. His first at-bat produced nothing more than a strikeout. It was so strange because before every pitch it became extremely quiet in the park, and this continued through his at-bat. I think there was a 2-2 count when he pulled the pitch down the right field line for a triple. For a man his age, 42, he was extremely fast. He was very gracious to the crowd, tipping his hat and bowing for what seemed to be a five minute standing ovation. Not many major league ballplayers belong to that club.

~Dave Bowman, Denver, Colorado

My mom, Buol Dougherty, was one of two females who started the Senior Involvement Ball Dude and Dudette program at Candlestick Park in the 1990s. When the Giants moved to AT&T Park in 2000, I joined the program along with other family members.

Mom had two extremely special memories while she was an active Ball Dudette.

The first memory involved Barry Bonds. Everyone knows there has been a lot of controversy around Barry, but Mom never wavered in her love and loyalty for him, for this reason: During a game in 2005, Mom, who was 73 and had numerous heart-related illnesses and cancer, slowly got off of her stool to try and run down a foul ball that rolled all the way to the left field fence. As she slowly jogged to get the ball, Barry ran to retrieve it and slowly rolled it back to her. She went back to her stool to get ready for the next hitter. When the inning ended, Barry ran over to Mom and whispered in her ear, "Don't worry, I'll get 'em for ya!" Mom melted, as this bigger-than-life superstar showed a very endearing and compassionate side to her. She was on cloud nine. And he kept his promise. Every game thereafter, Mom could always depend on Barry to get the hard-hit foul balls headed in her direction.

The second memory was when they retired her and some Ball Dudes with a home plate ceremony at AT&T with Kruk and Kuip (Mike Krukow and Duane Kuiper) announcing. She was ready to retire because it had become clear that the on-field job of shagging foul balls was becoming much too dangerous for someone with limited mobility and reflexes. But that was her day to shine, and one I will never forget.

Mom passed away in April 2016, from a very short battle with lung cancer. I was her youngest child of nine, and she was my best friend. She was a devoted Bay Area sports fan, especially the Giants. She is so very missed. Each game I work, I see her silhouette on the stool across the field.

~Buol Dougherty, as told by her daughter, Laura Elliott, San Francisco, California

117

Following in Mom's footsteps, I have been a Giants Ball Dudette for 21 years. I worked one game in each of the 2010, 2012, and 2014 World Series. I was asked to be in the championship parade in 2014, an amazing experience. I've met many of the players, and they are all so respectful of me and what I do. However, years ago I had a bad experience with a Giants first baseman, name withheld. I didn't move my stool fast enough as he went for a foul ball. He couldn't make the play, and as he walked back to the field he kicked my stool into the infield. Everyone started booing him. The announcers couldn't believe it. He complained to the umpire, and I received a warning to move my stool while the ball is possibly in play. I later found out that I actually saved the game. The opposing team had the winning run on third who would have scored easily had that foul ball been caught. I was praised later for causing him to drop it. Right outcome, wrong reason!

~Laura Elliott, Danville, California

During the 1969 Mets World Championship year, I was still in high school and worked at Shea Stadium as a parking lot employee for the New York City Parks Department. I was able to see more than 45 games for free. My clearest and greatest memory is of the fifth and clinching game of the World Series. I skipped school that day, went to the stadium early and dressed in my uniform even though I was not working, and got into the game. I stood for the entire game and ran on to the field with the masses of humanity after the game ended. I grabbed a clump of grass and brought it home. No other season could ever be as magical.

~David Kahn, San Jose, California

As a young boy I began following the Pittsburgh Pirates when Ralph Kiner was a rookie. To me, and most Pirate fans, he was the heart and soul of the team. My dad took me to many games at Forbes Field, where Kiner would usually reward us with a home run, maybe more than one. When he was traded to the Cubs in 1953, it was a dark day for me and the rest of the city of Pittsburgh.

In 2001 I was still living in Pittsburgh, a retiree lucky enough to have secured a position with my hometown Pirates in the guest relations department. Baseball had gone on hiatus for several days following the terrible attack on our country on 9/11. The first team the Pirates played after that was the New York Mets. The Pirates were now playing at PNC Park, a very impressive new baseball stadium on the banks of Allegheny River. On the afternoon of the first game, I found myself walking down the tunnel under the park near the visitors' clubhouse. Approaching me were three well-dressed men. As they neared, I noted that one of the men looked somehow familiar…and it finally dawned on me that this man was none other than my boyhood hero, Ralph Kiner. I was so surprised that the only thing I had the presence of mind to do was nod to him as he passed—and he nodded back! To this day, I regret not extending my hand to thank him for all the thrills he had given me as a young baseball fan some fifty years earlier.

-John Stoyle, Pittsburgh, Pennsylvania

I was a vendor for the Minnesota Twins for 10 years, five at Metropolitan Stadium and five at the Metrodome. One day before game time in August 1981, I found out Kent Hrbek had been called up. While I was hanging out with some of my vendor friends—all of us high school kids—we found ourselves in the company of Kent's high school friends, just talking about "stuff." Kent came over and we continued to chat. You know that some of these guys get called up in their early twenties, but when you come face-to-face with it, it just seemed so odd that they were all just a few years older than me.

I joined the Navy, and in 1994 while on shore duty, I had the chance to do some vending for the Norfolk Tides in Virginia. The Tides were then a AAA farm team of the Mets, and this was their third year in Harbor Park. I recall one game very clearly. I was selling the usual stuff—popcorn, peanuts, cracker jack—and in the front row sitting across the aisle from each other were two celebrities. On one side was Pernell "Sweet Pea" Whitaker, professional boxer and native of Norfolk. Across the aisle, was rock star Bruce Hornsby. These guys were talking up a storm. I didn't speak much with Whitaker, just sold him some popcorn. But as I sold popcorn to Bruce, I turned into a complete fanboy, and even started singing his song, "The Valley Road," from his second album. Well, this either impressed him or made him smile because he gave me two passes for his show the next night at the Boat House, a concert venue that shared a parking lot with the baseball stadium.

The next night, there I was in the front row screaming out for him to do my favorite song of his, "Across the River," from his third album with The Range, *A Night on the Town*. Well, the next thing he did was play that tune and dedicate it "To my vendor friend." That was a whole lot better than if I'd sold him an entire game's worth of snacks!

~Lance Smith, East Greenbush, New York

I am not sure, Lance, that I would have sung to him as you did, but I sure loved his albums with The Range.

I am approaching my 80th birthday and cannot remember when I was *not* a huge baseball fan—more precisely, a huge Red Sox fan. As kids, my friends and I often went to day games at Fenway Park. For fifty cents, we would sit in the left field stands just above Ted Williams. In June 1957, a friend asked if I might be interested in working in the visitors' clubhouse at Fenway. Are you kidding me? What 16-year-old Red Sox fan wouldn't jump at that opportunity? But there was one huge problem. I was a junior in high school, and the end of the school year was still three weeks away. As the job had to be filled ASAP, I approached a school administrator the next day and told him of my opportunity. My grades were pretty good at the time, and I guess the administrator was also a huge Sox fan because he actually granted me permission to be released from school three weeks early with that year's graduating senior class.

I went to work at the park, but my tenure lasted all of one series, the Red Sox vs. the Cleveland Indians. My first game was a night game. We were required to be there at two o'clock in the afternoon and weren't allowed to leave until all the players had showered and left. Back then, beer was allowed in the clubhouse *after* the games, and many players would have a couple before showering. It was somewhere around 2:00 a.m. before we were able to leave. The pay was $3.50 per game! By 2:00 a.m. the public transportation system had shut down for the night, and my dad had to drive from our home several miles away to pick me up. I left after that series, not even returning to collect my pay. I think Dad may have been the happiest guy in the city of Boston when I made that decision.

Just three days, but oh, what a three days they were for a 16-year-old baseball nut. Among many others, I met Rocky Colavito, Bob Lemon, Vic Wertz, Mike Garcia, and a coach named "Red" Kress, who was tossed out of one of those games by the umpires. I believe it was the first, and perhaps only, time that had happened to him. I met coach Eddie Stanky, and manager Kirby Farrell. I also met Roger Maris. Most fans now don't realize that Roger came up with the Indians. While people know the Yankees got him in a trade with Kansas City, his Indian days are a mystery to most.

My first day on the job, not quite knowing what I should be doing, I was sitting on an equipment trunk accomplishing absolutely nothing when two guys came by and looked at me sitting there idly. "Get your ass off the trunk and get over there and do something!" snarled one of them. "Yes sir! Yes sir!" I answered as I jumped to my feet. This was followed by a chorus of laughter. The two guys? Colavito and Maris! Welcome to the big leagues! Another day, loading bats onto the bat rack, I thought it would be a whole lot easier rather than taking bats out of the bag one at a time, to empty the bag onto the dugout floor and proceed from there. I did. Just then an Indian rookie, I can't for the life of me remember his name, entered the dugout from the clubhouse, stepped on the bats, and fell on his ass. I thought Stanky was going to kill me! At the end of my stint, Kress gave me a baseball, I guess as a tip. In the hands of a 16-year-old kid, it meant more than a million dollars might have.

Many years later I met one-time Red Sox announcer, Ken Coleman, who, before his days as the Sox announcer, had worked in the broadcast booth with the Indians. We started talking, and when I mentioned I'd worked in the visitors' clubhouse at Fenway Park when Farrell was manager, he said something like, "Charlie, you had to have worked there if you remember Kirby Farrell!" This was music to my ears, for my time at Fenway was so brief that even many of my friends doubted my claim.

Here we are more than sixty years later, and the memories still burn brightly.

~Charlie McGonagle, A Proud Charlestown, Massachusetts, "Townie"
Did you return to classes, Charlie, after that one series…?

In the Maier household, a source of good-natured (I think!) groaning occurs every time my experience as a Cleveland Indians ball boy comes up. In spite of my family's weariness in hearing about it, my days as a ball boy remain a key element of my youth. The following account represents my recollection of the experience.

During my early teen years, I was keenly aware of the contest the *Cleveland Plain Dealer* held every spring to select the Indians' batboy and ball boys. Up to 10,000 kids aged 14 to 17 entered the contest, consisting of a 100-word essay entitled "Why I Want to be the Batboy for the Cleveland Indians." The first prize was a $1000 cash award, a lot of money in those days. I didn't enter until 1962 as a senior at Mayfield High School, searching for ways to pay for college. An after-school job put some money in the bank, but even with a scholarship offer from Ohio State University, I needed more cash to cover expenses. I'd recently purchased a typewriter, a now extinct manual Optima with a very distinct pica font. I sensed a well-typed and nicely laid-out essay would be noticed. I spent one gray, damp weekend writing and rewriting my opus. More than a half century later, I don't remember the details of the essay, but it was about the art and science of baseball—I was to enter OSU's College of Arts and Sciences so the term was on my mind. I enumerated three or four reasons why I should be selected, mentioning my lifelong passion for baseball and the Indians, and how the $1000 would greatly help in defraying college expenses. I sent my essay and didn't think much more about it until I was notified by telegram—in those days, telegrams indicated a sense of urgency—that I was a finalist. I was amazed! My parents and brother were out, but I called everybody I could, so by the next day word got around my school. A few weeks later, the administration got into the act by giving me a special award during Honors Day.

One of twenty finalists, I arrived at the offices of now-departed Municipal Stadium wearing my $45 suit, skinny fake-silk necktie, and my father's overcoat. A bumpy 45 minute bus ride and 15 minute hike had left me nauseous and sweaty. The other finalists, from all over northeast Ohio, looked as dopey and nervous as I did. One by one we were called into the team vice-president's office for a personal interview. The office dazzled me with baseball memorabilia and the largest desk I had ever seen, reminding me of an aircraft carrier. On the wall was a chart with the name of every player in the Indians system, major league and minor league, by position. Several men conducted the interview, including the team VP and Chuck Heaton, a noted sports writer for the *Plain Dealer*. The interviewers were polite and respectful, which I hadn't expected. They were concerned my being at games might interfere with my summer job as a playground supervisor for the City of Mayfield Heights. I assured them repeatedly this was a greater priority.

The interviews ended and seven kids were sent packing. Of the remaining group, one would be the prestigious batboy and the other twelve, ball boys. After what seemed an eternity, the winners were announced. While I didn't win the top batboy job, I was selected as a ball boy, still a great honor. Each ball boy would be given a season pass for two and work 13 games. One of the other guys and I picked the final games of the season, concluding that if the team made it to the World Series, we'd have first crack at home games.

In mid-August I started my stint, a night game. I arrived in late afternoon to prepare and receive an orientation. Greeted by an attendant, I was taken to the primitive locker room reserved for rookies, minor leaguers called up in September, and bat and ball boys. It seemed like a great physical and mental distance to the main clubhouse. I was given a pair of cleats a size too large, and a white flannel uniform with blue pinstripes and blue and red lettering. The uniform, not exactly form-fitting, billowed in the wind. The attendant, trying to make me feel confident, said I looked better than some of the players. In reality, it didn't matter how I looked. As far as I was concerned, I was in the major leagues!

Making my way through passageways, equipment rooms, and offices, I entered the inner sanctum of the players, the clubhouse. The heroes of my youth were standing around in their underwear, many smoking cigarettes. They were regular-looking guys, some chunky or thin, some tall or short. What I couldn't see was their obvious desire to play baseball, their knowledge of the game, and their talent. I was introduced to Ted Skebe, second-year batboy, who would show me the ropes. My first official act was to help carry what seemed like hundreds of bats from the clubhouse to the dugout. I was a designated schlepper! I then stopped to view the field from the vantage of the dugout. The infield was graded to perfection, every blade of pampered grass cut to a uniform length. Unlike all the fields I ever played on, there were no weeds, lumps of clay, or stones. The vast field was engulfed by the massive structure of the 76,000 seat stadium itself. The late afternoon sunlight left dramatic shadows on the field, the late summer wind warming and cooling me at the same time. Enjoying my good fortune, I felt something wet and slimy hit and roll down the back of my arm. Ever so slowly, I looked down to see a glob of tobacco juice on my arm. I turned around and was greeted by center fielder Ty Cline with tobacco juice dribbling down his chin. "Welcome to the team, kid!" he said as he shook my hand. I was initiated!

That night I began my career as right field ball boy. My job was to catch foul balls and not interfere with the game. I managed to catch all of the balls hit my way. After the game, Ted and I lugged the bats back to the clubhouse. When I was done with my various chores, I changed into my street clothes and left the stadium, about the same time the players were leaving. I was swarmed by younger kids asking for my autograph. Happy to oblige, I signed my name on scorecards, balls, and scraps of paper. Most kids didn't bother to see whose autograph they had just obtained, but those who looked asked who I was. When I announced I was a ball boy, they were disappointed. So, I began signing the names of players. Every night I took on a new identity. I sure hope none of those fake autographs survived. I suppose I should check e-bay or go to a memorabilia show to make sure...

As I learned my duties off the field—laborer—and on the field—defensive star—I got to know some of the players and their routines. I was struck by the constant use of tobacco by the players, surprised to see star athletes such as Jim Perry smoke cigarettes, but less surprised to see others chewing and spitting tobacco juice. Many had mastered the art of spitting, and I spent a lot of time dodging those globs. One day, I took a chaw of tobacco to see what the attraction was. I never tried it again.

As a fan, I enjoyed the great Cleveland-New York rivalry. Although I never liked the Yankees, I respected them. When in town, they generated an excitement no other team could match. My favorite game that summer was on September 12. During batting practice, I hung around the batting cage to watch the Yankees up close, finding myself in the company of Bobby Richardson, Tony Kubek, Roger Maris, and Mickey Mantle. I don't remember any conversation, but I was awestruck to be in their midst. After batting practice, Indians' pitcher Pedro Ramos gave me a ball and sent me to the Yankee clubhouse to get it autographed for him. The first person I saw was Yogi Berra, sitting on a stool eating a bologna sandwich. Friendly and cordial, he greeted me with a "Hiya, kid!" I made my way through the clubhouse and got autographs for Pedro, later realizing I should have brought another for myself. I did, however, get one significant Yankee autograph for myself, from none other than the great Mantle. During the game, while stationed at my berth in foul territory adjacent to right field, Mickey hit a home run. The ball landed behind the outfield fence and was picked up by an usher who threw it to me for ultimate delivery to Mantle. With missed connections in this plan, I put the ball in my pocket. Several years later, Mickey was in Cleveland for an event. I stood in line with other collectors and he autographed the ball for me.

Before a game with the Senators, I was sitting in the dugout next to Bob Dolgan, the *Plain Dealer* baseball beat writer that summer. That morning, the newspaper had published his piece somewhat critical of John Romano, the team's catcher, accompanied by a cartoon showing Romano in a dog house. During pregame practice, Jim Piersall, the Senators' volatile center fielder, a former Indian and a personal friend of Romano, ran over to let Dolgan know what he thought of the article, and swore at him for at least five minutes without taking a breath. I'd never heard such swearing before or since. Dolgan just sat there without saying a word. This scene repeated several times, Dolgan continuing to sit impassively. Years later, Dolgan wrote about the incident and I called to remind him that I'd witnessed the whole episode. He said his editor, Gordon Cobbledick, had expected the article and cartoon would anger Piersall and told him to avoid getting into an argument. Romano had seemed unhappy that day, but he'd had a good, supportive friend in Piersall.

Getting to know the players and their quirks was one of my favorite pastimes. Some specific memories were:

Third baseman Bubba Phillips did a variety of tricks with a bat to entertain anyone around.

Max Alvis was a real gentleman and actually called me "sir" when he arrived from the minors. Maybe he thought I was a player, or maybe he was naturally polite. Years later, at an old-timers event, we met again. I told him the story. He had a good laugh and gave me an autograph addressed to his "teammate."

Budding star Sam MacDowell, "Sudden Sam," was far from polite. In his second year with the team, he showed great promise, but I could see he behaved erratically, probably hurting his career. He later acknowledged being an alcoholic. Today he works with ballplayers with similar problems.

My two favorite players were second baseman Jerry Kindall, and Doc Edwards, the backup catcher. Both went out of their way to make me feel a part of the team. Pitching coach Mel Harder, a great pitcher for the Indians decades before, was very pleasant to me, as was radio announcer Jimmy Dudley, a dapper dresser who truly enjoyed his special status with the team.

Most players and coaches were not interested in showing me the secrets of Major League Baseball. I observed talent and hard work, and myriad personalities and quirks. Manager Mel McGaha was quiet and business-like; I had no idea whether he was respected by the players. His only year as Cleveland's manager was 1962.

In addition to the signed Mickey Mantle ball, a family treasure, I have a ball the Indians signed for me. The only other souvenir I still have is a cracked bat used by Indians first baseman Gene Green. I wore my team-issued white and blue sweatshirt until it was nothing more than a rag. I gave my cap and stockings to my cousin Dave, a great baseball fan.

I took pride in cleanly fielding foul balls, learning to field bouncers, smashes, and dribblers, and how to play the carom off the wall. I became perhaps a bit too confident in my foul ball tracking abilities, and as a result had my worst moment. While the Indians were in the field, a batter hit a hard bouncer my way, whistling toward me via a carom off the wall. It was a play I was getting used to. I got a late start, so the ball skipped over my glove and bounded into right field, about three feet in front of the right fielder, Willy Kirkland. Willy didn't move. I had to run onto the field to get the ball. That embarrassing moment was in front of thousands of people.

I had to leave for OSU before the season ended, so I missed a few games, as did my friend Ted. On our last night, Dick Donovan, the team's premier pitcher that year, wanted to give Ted a tip. I was impressed with both the offer and Ted, who probably could've used the money but refused to take it. I said good-bye to Ted, some attendants, and players. My brief, but memorable stint in the major leagues had come to an end. It sure was fun! As the pros would say, I had a cup of coffee in the bigs.

~Howard Maier, Cleveland, Ohio

I have worked at Detroit Tigers' Comerica Park as part of the event staff for eight years, and a tour guide for six. I love being a part of the Tigers family. My favorite fans to interact with are the kids. I love how inquisitive they are and how cool they find everything to be. I have the most fun with them at the statues on the outfield concourse. I love asking them if they can find hidden objects in the statues and quizzing them on different things pertaining to the statue or the person they are depicting. I almost always get at least one, "Are they dead?" question…sometimes the same kid asking at each statue. Their favorite part of the tour is always twirling in the chairs in the visitors' clubhouse. Another popular thing people want to know is how many hot dogs we sell every year (answer: 426,000 in 2017).

One of my fellow tour guides and event staff member, Bill "Foul Ball Billy" Fundaro, spent 52 years as a member of the Tigers family. I loved doing tours with Bill because he always had stories to tell. We'd be waiting for a tour group to show up and he would just talk and talk, telling the most interesting stories. Bill loved to talk to anyone who wanted to listen. When Bill had his 50th anniversary working with the club, the Tigers honored him on the field by letting him throw out the first pitch and presenting him with a plaque and a jersey. After that, fans sometimes came up to me, asking if I knew where Bill was working because they wanted to meet him. He was always happy to talk to fans, so I obliged. One time a friend came to a game and asked me to introduce him to Bill. I did and left them to talk. I walked by about 20 minutes later and they were still chatting. That's just how Bill was, and he loved it. Bill passed away this past year, and he will be missed dearly by his entire Tigers family.

~Barbara Gusway, Canton, Michigan

I am glad I had the opportunity to meet and have a beer with Bill.

THE BATS AND BALLS AND GLOVES THAT BIND: FAMILY AND BASEBALL

This is a core chapter for this book, the previous, and the next. I am not sure my love for this game could ever have been nurtured so thoroughly and satisfyingly if Lynn, Rachel, and David weren't in the on-deck circle. Lynn insisted we jump into the season-ticket partnership offered us. At 14, Rachel began working for the Giants. I coached David from T-Ball through high school baseball, although to a greatly diminishing extent, and he was a bat boy for my softball team. Baseball, to me, is the sport that brings together not just my family, but millions of families all over the world. Moms and dads, brothers and sisters, daughters and sons, husbands and wives, grandparents, all family relationships are covered in this chapter. I wish my mom and dad had lived to see the first book.

In 2007, my much better-looking better half, Valerie, and I were in Chicago while I attended a conference. With a free afternoon available, we decided to do what any sports fans would do, and headed to the ballgame at Wrigley Field. We sat in the right field bleachers—a classic spot if you know Wrigley and its fans. Both our fathers had passed away within the previous 2 ½ years, and both had been avid players and fans throughout their lives. My dad had a tryout with the St. Louis Cardinals. Val's dad, born in Italy but raised in Canada, was enlisted in the army and, while serving overseas, was recruited to play for Canada at the Baseball World

Championships. They finished in second place, and we have the silver medal from that tournament.

We talked about how much they would have loved being at Wrigley, enjoying the history of the park, and the game in general. With our beers in hand, we toasted our dads, "To the ol' boys." At that moment, we decided we should tour all the ballparks in memory of our fathers. We've now completed 20 of the 30 ballparks. We will complete the last 10 ballparks over the next few years, with always the toast, "To the ol' boys."

~Brian Jeffs, Barrie, Ontario

In 2008, my husband, Colin, and I took a tour of six Major League Baseball stadiums in six days with Big League Tours. Something touched us personally at five of the stops. In Philadelphia, everyone was so friendly and suggested we try a Philly cheesesteak sandwich. When we returned to our seats in the 6th inning, the Kiss Cam was on, and to our great surprise, it focused on us for our brief moment of fame as we shared a kiss. In Boston, we sat for a while in the fabled Green Monster section.

The first stop of the trip had been in Baltimore, with our seats 10 rows up from home plate. We simultaneously said, "Wow!" At the time, my son Jesse was expecting his first child, and not disclosing what name he and his wife had selected. As an excited grandma-to-be, I kept throwing out names. Being at Camden Yards that night, I had to suggest the namesake. Several months later, my grandson Camden was born.

We live in Washington State and are Mariners fans, so it was exciting to see the Mariners ace, Felix Hernandez, pitch *and* hit a home run at Yankee Stadium. It was exciting for Colin to attend a game from the team of his youth in their final season in the famed park. It was monumental for him to grab some infield dirt, sit in the dugout, and touch the Babe Ruth monument. However, I could not bring myself to suggest that Jesse name his son Thurman, as Colin requested.

~Kathy Howell, Concrete, Washington
For non-baseball fans, that is Thurman as in Yankee legend Thurman Munson

I was always very close with my grandpa, Ray Boone. He was a huge influence on me, with respect to life and baseball, starting in my very early years when my dad, Bob, was off at Stanford, in the army, and playing in the minor leagues. Grandpa and I were great buddies, but he was very old school, especially about baseball. He was insistent that the players of his generation—Feller, Mantle, and Ted Williams—were simply the best, no debate necessary. When you added in my dad's opinion that the players of his generation, like his battery mate Steve Carlton, were better, well, it was fun for me and my brother, Aaron, to listen to these stories and debates over and over. Later on we would chime in with our opinions about the players of our generation. For me, it was as clear as could be that Barry Bonds was the greatest, most feared hitter of our time and perhaps any other.

Grandpa would come to spring training with me, and I'd get an adjoining room for him and grandma. He came to the ballpark every day and would spend the time talking with reporters and scouts who loved being with him. One day on the way to the park in 2004, he gave me a bag filled with all kinds of baseball memorabilia—things like Babe Ruth and Ty Cobb autographed balls. I asked him why he was giving this to me, and he said something like, "You never know how long you will be around."

Mid-season, I got a phone call that Grandpa had been rushed to the hospital. We had a day game, after which I flew out to San Diego to be with him. He couldn't talk, but he could write on a chalk board. He complained about routine stuff, like the hospital food. He told me that new Padres pitcher, Jake Peavy, was solid. "Bret," he wrote, "this kid has a chance to be a really good pitcher." I agreed. Then Grandpa, he of the firm belief that Williams was the greatest hitter to walk the earth, wrote on that chalk board, "Barry Bonds is a better hitter than Ted Williams." I started to cry. That was a clue to me that my grandpa would be passing soon, and so he did, two days later.

Can you really compare players of different eras? Do we have to? That was not a question to ask Grandpa. You couldn't tell him that as the years went by, players got bigger, stronger, and—there's that word again—better. He defended his generation. But that concession in his final days, along with the foreshadowing earlier in spring training, were telling moments that he knew he wouldn't be around much longer.

~Bret Boone, author of *Home Game: Big-League Stories from My Life in Baseball's First Family. Bret is a member of one of the very few three-generation baseball families. Grandpa Ray was a third baseman, and Bret's dad, Bob, was a catcher. Aaron and Bret were infielders. All had long, distinguished careers, each having been an All Star.*

My memory is a common one, a father and son at a game. My father grew up in Minneapolis and watched the minor league Minneapolis Millers play in old Nicolette Park. Tall for his age, his height sometimes made him stand out in a crowd. At one game, there was a commotion in the crowd, and a policeman came over and smacked Dad hard on the head with a billy club even though he wasn't sure who was involved in the ruckus. Dad always claimed it was the row below his group, but the damage was done. This was in the 1920s, and the last game he attended for many years. I came along decades later and quickly became a huge baseball fan. I pestered him to take me to a game, but there was always an excuse for not going. I repeatedly heard the story of the billy club, clearly a bad memory. I went to a few games with my brother and many with friends, but I still hadn't gone to one with Dad, Then one day in April of 1963, he said, "Come on, we're going to the game today." It was Opening Day and we ended up sitting 20 rows away from President Kennedy at D.C. Stadium. I remember the dignitaries, the packed stadium, the green grass, and nothing at all about the game. My dad's smile at us enjoying a game together stands out brightest of all.

We went on to go to several games together, including picture days where you could take photos of the players and talk to them. Dad took pictures, even winning a prize for one. Clearly, the billy club memory had mellowed, though it never fully went away. Fast forward to the 1990s, and

Dad had since passed away. I had been collecting and dealing in Senators memorabilia for several years, especially active in the pursuit of Senators photos. During one buying experience, I purchased a large group of pictures taken by team photographer Don Wingfield. In the group were photos from picture days. In one of them, there I was—what a surprise! Continuing to search the pictures, I was literally knocked over with shock, for there was my dad taking a picture, looking straight into Wingfield's lens. Today, it remains one of my favorite photos, a permanent link between my dad, me, and the game I love.

~Alan Feinberg, Lake Worth, Florida

I clearly remember the first baseball game I attended with my father. It was Dodgers vs. Cubs at Wrigley Field in Chicago on May 31, 1958. The Cubs jumped out in front early 1-0, and I was thrilled. My father cautioned me not to get too excited, the Cubs had a tradition of throwing away leads. Watching the action was not the only thing to do at a game. Periodically, my father went for a walk and returned with hot dogs, popcorn, peanuts, and ice cream. I did not go hungry! In the end, the Cubs lost 9-4. Disappointed, we left the stadium and walked to the train to return home.

What did it all mean? This was a chance to bond with my father and an opportunity for him to convey his love for the Cubs to me. Up until then, he had waited his entire life for the Cubs to win the World Series. I did the waiting for both of us for another 58 years.

~Mark Levin, Skokie, Illinois

My most memorable game was between the White Sox and Cubs on June 9, 2001. Tickets to the game with my dad, Mark, were a middle school graduation present. My grandfather was a Cubs fan and Dad grew up one, as well. I was the black sheep of the family and became a White

Sox fan when I started to follow baseball. Interleague play gave us an opportunity to see our favorite teams play each other.

Throughout the week leading up to the game, I kept trash-talking about how the Sox would destroy the Cubs. Dad just ignored me, most likely hoping that the result of the game would put me in my place. The game was at U.S. Cellular Field, then known as Comiskey Park. As the teams took the field, the atmosphere was similar to that of a college football rivalry game. They were neck and neck throughout the game until the Cubs broke through and won 4-3 in 10 innings.

Despite the outcome, I enjoyed being there with my dad as we cheered on our favorite teams. Like my grandfather did for him, Dad enjoyed buying lots of food and souvenirs. I learned that we don't have to root for the same team to share the same passion for the game. While my trash talking didn't work for me that day in 2001, I thought I got the last laugh since I only had to wait 18 years to see my favorite team win the World Series in 2005. Then 2016 happened, and the rest is history.

~Steven Levin, Skokie, Illinois

Vin Scully's familiar golden voice saying, "It's time for Dodger Baseball!" always kicked off evenings or lazy weekend afternoons. His routine made me feel at home and, in essence, that I belonged. I recall stories my father told me about the games that he went to as a child and getting autographs from his favorite players—Dodger greats like Koufax, Podres, Drysdale, and Wills. Also born with Blue Blood, I became fond of the team and developed my own loyalty, admiring players like Guerrero, Fernando, Sax, Gibson, Hershiser, and still my favorite Dodger to this day, Mike Piazza. I often went to Chavez Ravine to watch them play. My earliest memory of a Dodger game is when I was two or three years old. I can still see my mother holding me in her arms as she sang, "Take me out to the ballgame." To this day, I make it a point to be in my seat for the 7th inning stretch and think of those times with Mom. I have carried on this tradition, singing it to my daughters, Isabella and Natalia, when we go to games. My loyalty is so strong because of what the team meant to my father and whole family. The Dodgers always brought us together.

During my young adult years, things became strained between my father and me. I was growing up and trying to become independent, and he was doing what good fathers do, trying to guide and direct me. I saw my parents during family gatherings but became involved in exploring and experiencing things outside my city. During these times I often felt distant from them. When I visited, I would find my father listening to the game on radio or watching on television, and during these encounters things between us seemed more stable. When games weren't on to save me, I would break the tension by simply saying, "What about the Dodgers?" Conversation would break out and for a while things would seem normal. My mother, always the glue in my family, worked to bring us all together by purchasing tickets to a game we could fit into our busy schedules. Parents, children, and siblings all came together and were a family again. Dodgers magic has always allowed us to heal and bond. I consider the team a true family member.

This magic extended outside of my immediate family, facilitating a relationship with my paternal grandfather whom I referred to endearingly as "Empa." I often visited him after work, finding him in front of the TV with the game on. We'd sit together discussing a strategy the Dodgers needed to implement to win the game, or talk about players, current or past. Even during the off-season, I would see him and spark a conversation by saying, "Y los Dodgers, Empa?" As the years passed, Empa suffered from degenerative heart disease and his accessibility decreased. He could no longer go to games with us, but he still followed his team. Conversations still magically flourished each time we were together. As his condition deteriorated, afternoon visits to his house were replaced by visits to the hospital. Though his spirits were sometimes down, given his diagnosis, his loyalty never wavered. We talked Dodgers even in his final days. My tradition was to buy him a customized Dodger hat every year for his birthday so we could celebrate not only his day but our bond with each other and the Dodgers. It was also a way of getting back at my uncles, guests at these events, too, as they were fans of the rival San Diego Padres. After his passing, I was given the last hat I had given him for his final birthday. I will cherish it always.

I will always be True Blue, and the Dodgers will always be a part of my family, dear to my heart. Although it is just a game, the team and the memories it has brought to my family are magical and have in their own way been a part of the bond that has always brought us together. It took 32 years for me to see the Dodgers recapture the World Series title, but it was another magical moment when we came together to celebrate the championship. I looked to the sky and said, "Empa, What about those Dodgers!?"
~Adan C. Gomez, Riverside, California

During the 1996 World Series, I was asked by my good friend, Gordo, if on the spur of the moment I would fly with him to Atlanta for games 3-5. Gordo, a successful businessman with great connections, would have tickets to sit in a box with Henry Aaron. This promised to be an opportunity of a lifetime. I told him yes, and that if there was any possibility of an extra ticket—but don't push it—I would love to bring my Yankees fanatic daughter, Laura, with me, even though it meant taking her out of school. As the time drew closer, Gordo found he would not be available, but he told me although the Hank Aaron experience was out, he'd arrange to leave two tickets for me.

Laura had done seemingly six days of homework in advance in case this possibility turned into an adventure. We were ready to go. On October 24, we drove to Philadelphia since you could not get a flight from New York and flew to Atlanta. On a train to Fulton County Stadium, a woman, upon seeing we wore Yankees clothing, said in a Southern accent, "Well, y'all may have won the last two, but we have Smoltzie pitching tonight, so we're going to win this one." My reply was, "Gee, I wish you had told me that before I got on the airplane."

It was a mound duel of epic proportions. Andy Pettitte and Smoltzie were equally brilliant. Smoltz himself would later describe it as the greatest game he ever pitched. The Yankees led 1-0, having scored an unearned run. Chipper Jones doubled to lead off the 9th. The stadium was rocking. If you think the Braves fans' tomahawk chop is overwhelming on television, you have no idea how deafening and echoing it is when experiencing it in person amidst thousands of fans under such tense circumstances. At one point Laura turned to me and said, "Dad, I can't take this, it's making me too nervous." I could only reply, "Neither can I."

With two outs and Jones at third, Luis Polonia came in to pinch-hit against Yankee reliever John Wetteland. Right fielder Paul O'Neill was shifted a few steps deeper by first base coach Jose Cardenal into a no-doubles defense. The Braves had the winning run on first after Joe Torre elected to walk Ryan Klesko. Polonia hit a shot to right-center field. When it was hit, we knew the game was to be decided on whether O'Neill could make the play. He did, thanks to being in the no-double defense, with Laura and I sitting close to the action.

There were relatively few Yankees fans at the game. The YES network, the Yankees local television station, always had a postgame show in front of the Yankee dugout after every postseason game that season. We headed there and coalesced with other Yankees fans, finding ourselves doing a mock of the chop, chanting, "One more ga-ame, one more ga-ame."

There were many great moments regarding this scene. The Yanks went on to their first World Series title in 18 years, beginning another great run for the team. I think strategic errors were made by Braves manager Bobby Cox. This was the last game at Fulton County, and in addition to being the winning manager in the last game played there, Torre had hit the first ever home run there as a Brave. But for me, the most important thing, by far, was to be able to share this amazing experience with my daughter. We were two fanatic Yankees fans surviving and thriving in the land of the tomahawk chop.

-Richie Greenberg, Monroe, New Jersey

Near the end of the 2019 season, Eric and I were in our usual place in Sec 104, Row 8. With us were our neighbor Frank and friend Sid. Eric and I enjoy sharing our love of the game with friends. A big part of the enjoyment is having conversations with the folks around us and making new friends and acquaintances, which seems to happen at every game we attend. We have been part of a season ticket group since the Giant's new stadium opened in 2000, sharing four seats for 81 home games with a varying number of partners. At the beginning, our kids, Rachel and David, generally accompanied us, although Rachel, in high school, was already working for the Giants in guest services. So, whether with our kids, friends of ours, or friends of our kids, we always could find folks to fill the four seats with us for our share of the games.

Now with the kids grown, David having moved to Washington, D.C., in 2010 and Rachel working most games, it has been our practice to invite friends to join us, and our habit is to have them sit between us, so conversations are easier. And so it was at this particular game. With four seats on the aisle, Eric was on the inside, next to him was Sid, then me, and Frank on the aisle. At some point during the game, David texted Eric, asking if it was a good time to talk. Eric texted back that we were at the ballgame. David asked, uncharacteristically, who we were with. After Eric texted him back with the answer, David replied, "Okay, we can talk tomorrow." Eric, being a bit of a worrier, asked if something was wrong. David replied cryptically, "It depends." Not being able to let *that* go, Eric replied, "Worry, worry, I'm a little worried." David responded, "Oh, you are so needy!"

Moments later, my phone rang with a FaceTime call from David's wife, Lisa. These occasional FaceTime sessions come from Lisa's iPhone, David being unwaveringly attached to the Android platform.

With the game on the field in front of us, I answered the call, and saw David sitting rather stone-faced on my screen. He slowly raised a tablet from his lap, and on the screen I read the words in large letters "Hi future grandparents." An involuntary exclamation "Wow!" escaped my lips as Sid, sitting to my right, looked at the screen with me. As I sat there with a big grin on my face, Sid had the presence of mind to suggest to Eric, sitting to his right, that they exchange seats.

That is the story of how we found out that we were going to be grand-parents, fittingly for us while at a ballgame! That is, Sid and I found out that Eric and I were going to be grandparents… As soon as Eric was in on the call, we shared our excitement with David and Lisa, and Sid and Frank and most of the baseball fans sitting around us within earshot. We kept the call brief, as the sounds of the game made it hard to carry on conversation. But I do recall we got a number of "Congrats!" from the folks in the rows above and below us.

~Lynn Rhodes, San Francisco, California

My father became an avid fan of the St. Louis Cardinals, initially be-cause he liked the uniforms. By 1969 when the Expos began to play in Montreal where we grew up, there was no turning back. Dad was not go-ing to switch allegiances. Like a good dad, he attempted to indoctrinate us, ensuring his kids had Cardinal hats, jackets, and T-shirts. Although St. Louis is over a thousand miles from Montreal, he could pick up the distant signal of Jack Buck and Mike Shannon doing the Cardinals play-by-play on KMOX. It worked on me. I listened to games on my clock radio at night, and my room's walls were papered with Sporting News covers featuring Cardinals players. We went to many Expos games, but Cardinals' visits to Montreal were always special. Once, Lou Brock paraded me through the dugout on his shoulders.

In the 1970s, Montreal was safe enough—or my parents were foolish enough—to let me travel an hour by bus and subway to hang out at the visiting team's hotel before games. I'd approach the players and ask if they'd give their complimentary tickets to my friends and me. It often worked with the rookies. We'd get into the stands early to collect balls hit during batting practice. If a player broke a bat, we'd beg for it. By the time I was 13, my glove featured the autographs of many Cardinal players. I'd also get autographs from players of other teams, but never on my mitt. I suppose I was a groupie but didn't know it then. Based on my role model, that type of devotion was normal.

After I left Montreal over 30 years ago, Dad and I remained close, although our interests diverged. Like many fathers and sons we'd argue, and I was too impatient with him. My interests evolved and I didn't care as much about baseball. When he'd visit, I'd struggle to find activities we could both enjoy, but baseball has always been there for us. Going to at least one game per year together became a family tradition that now involves my brother and his kids.

In 1994, my brother and I were both living in Chicago and we arranged to take Dad to Busch Stadium so that he could finally see the Cardinals at home. Flights and hotels were booked, tickets purchased, and even dinner reservations were made. It was going to be perfect. A week before the game, the players went on strike and we never made it to St. Louis. I worried that we might never see the Cardinals at home together. Years passed, and we attended games in Chicago (Cubs and Sox), San Francisco, Oakland, and Cleveland. MLB on cable TV enabled Dad to see almost any game he wanted.

In 2009, my brother and I arranged another try for St. Louis. The weekend started perfectly at Mike Shannon's steakhouse. Tony LaRussa, the then-Cardinals manager, was even seated at a nearby table. Years later now, I can't recall who the Cardinals played that weekend, who pitched, or who won. All I remember is looking over at my father's face during one of the games and seeing his huge grin. It was the greatest baseball game I ever attended.

~Rodney Altman, San Francisco, California

I have been lucky to be at a number of memorable Yankees games. I was at the American League Championship Series game when Chris Chambliss hit the legendary home run that brought the Yankees back to the World Series. I went to many Old Timers' games with my dad and brother Ron and watched Dad's face as he got as emotional seeing Joe DiMaggio announced as I did watching Mickey Mantle's name called. That made me realize that our parents were once kids, too, and they also had their idols. I was at Mantle's retirement day, sitting in the upper deck, cheering and crying for what seemed like hours.

My best baseball memories involve my dad. He was born to a father who was a Brooklyn Dodgers fan, as were most of Dad's friends. I can only speculate that it was Dad's one teenage act of rebellion when he declared himself a Yankees fan. His kids were also raised to be Yankees fans.

I was my parents' firstborn. Dad did not care that I was a girl, he just wanted to teach his kid how to catch, throw, and hit a baseball. *That* was what mattered to him. He wanted to play ball with his kid, regardless of the gender. I grew to love playing baseball, was quite good at it, and was pretty mad I wasn't allowed to play Little League. I threw right-handed but batted from the left side. Dad got angry when my 7th grade gym teacher tried to make me bat right-handed. He always told me I can do anything I want. My bond with him was strong, in no small part because of baseball. When Dad passed away, I began my eulogy by saying Dad was a feminist…even though he did not know it at the time. Maybe I didn't then, either, but I sure do now.

~Rieva Lesonsky, Los Angeles, California

My cousin, Marty "Taco" Perez, an infielder with the Atlanta Braves, was traded to the Giants with Darrell Evans in 1976. My father Alfred, brother Eddie, our friend Jim Stolz, and I went to a Giants game soon after the trade. The Giants were losing, and we decided to leave early. In the parking lot, listening to the game on our radio, we heard that Marty, who had already struck out three times that day, was coming up to hit with the bases loaded. We rushed back to the stadium in time to see Marty hit a bases-clearing double. The Giants lost the game, but it was a great moment and memory.

~Henry Hernandez, Santa Rosa, California

He didn't start out a baseball guy. Nope, not my dad. He had been a busy vaudeville comedian, performing with the Three Crazy Sailors throughout the country from the late 1920s through the 1930s. He loved music—even Lawrence Welk—and Radio City Music Hall. Dad got my sister, Devy, and me into the Peanut Gallery on the Howdy Doody TV show, and he enjoyed the Shore Dinner on Friday nights at his beloved, star-packed Friars Club. He took us to see boxing matches, where we were awestruck at the Ali vs. Frazier Fight of the Century at Madison Square Garden, and we watched Gorilla Monsoon and BoBo Brazil wrestle for the hearts of America. Of course we vacationed at the Concord Hotel in the Borscht Belt—that's where my mom, Margie, and my dad first met—and even when I was barely six we never missed the nightly 10:00 p.m. shows in the Imperial Room with thousands of other guests, being regaled by the likes of Barbra Streisand, Tom Jones, Buddy Hackett, Shirley Bassey, and young Gregory Hines. Solly, as his friends fondly called Dad, loved to entertain and be entertained. He had an indefatigable zest for life and for his family. But when I was little, not for baseball.

My neighbor, Charles, had parents who were wildly enthusiastic about introducing their only child to Little League. Mr. and Mrs. Breel volunteered to coach a proud team of mostly eight-year-olds. I was just seven, but they insisted I join the team. We posed for a black-and- white team photo, arms crossed and chests puffed. However, I felt pretty unprepared, not quite ready for prime time. I recall that during the long 1959 season, I got on base only once—thank God, I was hit by a pitch. It felt really good running to first.

By the time I turned nine we had moved to Plainview—Old Bethpage— and I played in Little League that summer. Mom took me to practices and games. I learned to hit the ball reliably and for a good average. I played catcher, pitcher, first, and sometimes second base, though being catcher seemed to keep me busiest. And, boy, did a cold bottle of Coca-Cola taste good after a dusty, sultry summer's afternoon! My participation faded after I was eleven because I really got into playing bass guitar and singing in rock bands, including The In-Sex. I still can't believe our parents let us use that name! It was prominently on display on Charlie Seiler's bass drum and on our business cards!

Never having thought about attending a big league game before, my very first was in 1961 when my friend Mitchell Allen's dad took us to see the Yankees. His dad had black hair combed straight back with Vitalis, olive skin, one glass eye that gazed to his right, and a stubby, thick cigar sticking out one side of his mouth at all times, lit or not. He usually had the crustiest grin around that stogie. I really liked him, and his wry jokes made us laugh. That first experience at a Yankees game was just as riveting for me as Billy Crystal's recounting of his first stadium visit.

I gushed to my dad about this wonderful professional sport, baseball, and Dad being Dad, we started going to games, mostly watching the— our—Yankees play. We saw about twenty games a year for several seasons, most Sunday or twilight doubleheaders at old Yankee Stadium. When I was just 10 or 11, Dad began to let me take a walk by myself between games—yeah, it was a different era. I tried not to waste that wonderful, grown-up me-time. Sometimes I'd navigate to the mezzanine level, right down to the press box to see Mel Allen or Red Barber or Jerry Coleman. My favorite thing was to go to the field level to see the Yankees' starting pitcher for game 2 warm up with a journeyman catcher crouched just in front of the right side of the screen behind home plate. I'd encamp myself just behind that screen to see Whitey Ford, Jim Bouton, or some other Yankee ace warm up. One Sunday, with eyes pressed up against the screen, I watched young Yankee sinker-baller Mel Stottlemyre hurling pitches. Standing about as close as a home plate umpire, I remember his ball whizzing in, often looking like it fell off a cliff the last few feet it traveled. He had an outstanding sinker. I tried to imagine myself proudly up at the plate batting against Mel…I guess I would have had to get hit by a pitch again to reach first with Mel on the mound.

At 16, I tried out for the junior varsity team at Plainview Kennedy High, the school my best friend, Eric Gray, and I attended. Working out with the junior varsity and varsity squads in the chill of late March, I couldn't hit stuff like curveballs and sinkers. I'd bail out on curves that would end up clipping the plate. Kids hadn't been throwing such pitches when I'd last played organized ball at 11. Too many years had passed since I had played Little League. I do remember connecting with one fastball that I sent deep to right-center, well beyond the reach of a racing center fielder. Even so, Coach Monahan, a teacher I knew and really respected, broke the news gently to me that I hadn't made the team.

Ballplayers from high school to big leaguers showed me the talent and perseverance it takes to succeed at baseball, and Mom and Dad always showed me what it took to succeed as parents...and have an amazing amount of fun along the way. I must have done something right. My daughters, Margie and Sara Remi, often say, "Dad, let's go catch our Yankees."

~Gary Fields, Raleigh, North Carolina

A few years ago, my brothers and I sat in the emergency room with our dad, Paul Holmes, after he had taken a fall and hit his head. He was a bit disoriented, but while awaiting results of many tests, we asked if he wanted to turn on the TV. He said, " Hell yeah, it's Opening Day for the Nats!" Meaning the Washington Nationals.

We tuned in, and it was only the 2nd inning, so we spent the afternoon watching the game and cheering on the team as doctors and nurses came and went. Dad told us one of his fondest memories—which we had heard many times before—about how every once in a while in the spring, our grandfather, Pop Pop, would say to Dad in the morning, "No school today, son, our Senators need us to help beat the bad guys." Meaning the other team, of course. Off they would go to old Griffith Stadium to see players like Heinie Manush and Joe Cronin. He often spoke about Walter "Big Train" Johnson, but I think by the time Dad was going in the 1930s, Johnson was the Senators' manager. Dad told us about his experiences, the crowd stomping the wooden bleachers, eating peanuts, and drinking root beer—just guessing Pop Pop was drinking real beer. Dad was the envy of his older sisters as he returned home with a sunburn and a story. It was always a great time at the stadium, and they went to many games every summer until Dad went off to the Navy.

There is, of course, no more Griffith Stadium, no more Washington Senators, and now no more Dad. He fell into a coma that night and drifted off a few days later. We are glad to know baseball made him happy all his life, and hope he enjoyed us cheerleading with him through the decades. We always picture him smiling in the bleachers with his dad, Pop Pop.

~Nancy Holmes, Rehoboth, Delaware

My fondest memory is of my father and me at a game. A rabid Yankees fan when we lived in NY, he was just as rabid a fan for the Angels after we moved to California. For many years, Dad would bet me that the Angels would end up in first place, a $20 bet each year. I don't think he really ever thought it through. In essence, he gave me the entire league against the Angels. Year after year he paid me $20 as the season ended. When the Angels finally came in first, I gave Dad a choice: $20 or a day at the stadium for a playoff game. I don't remember who won, the score, or how the Angels ultimately fared, I just remember the smile on his face walking into the stadium and having a great day at the ballpark with my father.

~Ira Lowenthal, Petaluma, California

When I was eight, my Nana and Papa often took me to Dodgers games. I knew nothing about baseball, but I enjoyed being able to go with my grandparents. My interest began to grow, but even now I wonder if it was actually the Dodgers peanuts that I liked most. In 1995, at age 15, I turned on the Yankees vs. Braves World Series. Nineteen-year-old Andruw Jones came to the plate and hit a home run on the first pitch, the youngest player ever to do so in World Series history. That hooked me, and I began my obsession with baseball. At 18, I went to my first game alone at Dodger Stadium, rooting not for the Dodgers but for the Braves, booed by those around me. I lost my voice that night. I loved being able to be me! I yelled so much I never wanted the game to end. I knew one day I would have a son and hope he would play baseball.

At 25, my little future major leaguer was born. Despite my efforts as Nathan grew older, all the bats, balls, and gloves I bought for him, and games on TV, he was just not interested in baseball. But in October 2013, as I watched the Dodgers play the Cardinals in the playoffs, Nathan came into the living room and sat watching with me. Within 15 minutes, my dream came true. My seven-year-old began his love for baseball, screaming for the Cardinals. He played the next year, and other parents were amazed at how much he'd learned after only following the sport for five months. On March 19, 2014, Nathan played his very first game. In his first at-bat, the first pitch was a hit I will never forget—a grand slam! It was the proudest moment any baseball mom could hope for. I'd never screamed and yelled as loud as I did that day and have not stopped since. Cheering for him and his team is my happy place. I give Nathan the same speech before every game. "Okay, son, go out there have a good time and win. But win or lose, I am proud of you and I love you, so go get 'em Beast Mode, son." I give him a kiss and walk away to stand behind the dugout and cheer. A lot, and loud. Baseball is my life but being a baseball mom is a dream come true.

~Brianne Aubert, Apple Valley, California

My grandpa, William Benzion, grew up and raised his family in Brooklyn. In 1971, he coached a baseball team made up of 13-year-olds who went 67-3. They went on to the New York City Championship Tournament played at McCoombs Dam Park, across from the old Yankee Stadium. When they won, Grandpa received a championship jacket. He eventually became a huge Mets fan, and in his later years I'd visit him in South Florida after my grandma passed away, and we'd watch Mets games together. At that time they were not very good, but he would still watch just about every game.

When Grandpa passed away in 2007, I received two items—the championship jacket, and his Mets hat. The last time I saw him, he was in his chair watching a Mets game and wearing that hat. I was always a casual baseball fan, but since then I have taken it on as a responsibility to be a *big* Mets fan to carry on his legacy and fandom. I watch most Mets games during the year, and now that I live in Atlanta, I go to as many as I can. Living in Nebraska last year, I paid $253 and traveled 3.5 hours to Kansas City for Game 1 of the World Series against the Royals. Although it was a 14 inning game and I didn't get back to my apartment until after 4:30 a.m. and had to go to work the next morning, it was so worth it, because I knew Grandpa would be proud.

~Kyle Benzion, Orlando, Florida

My son, Tommy, does not resemble me. He has his mom's reddish hair and flashing amber eyes, a handsome face from Greek antiquity, a witty and fun-loving personality...and he is incredibly obstinate. I was nothing like that when I was 10 years old. We have already battled over video games, music, housework, and homework. When he latches onto something, he demands all things from me. He loved his first glove and ball, and given his temperament, it meant playing catch at all times possible. It made no difference to him if Dad had work or other adult interests. The backyard beckoned. If Tommy were to be summed up in one word, it would be "irrepressible." The image of father and son tossing a ball should be idyllic.

What better opportunity to teach coordination, enjoy the outdoors, and impart wisdom? But the ball flew far -and wide, the backyard unable to contain Tommy, so we took to the street with a new set of demands. Home plate had to be where the cars sped around the corner. Tommy dictated grounder, pop fly, or the always unpredictable throw home. Overthrows meant failed races to the storm drain. Neighbors looked nervous. Windows looked threatened.

It was all fun, but a lot of work. To be honest, Little League was a relief. Younger dads lined up to manage and coach, but I helped from the sidelines through T-Ball and Rookie League. Tommy always made contact at the plate but seemed to hit every ball weakly to third base which, at that age, meant a successful trip to first base. He ran like the wind—quite a contrast to his slow-footed father as a kid. First base always seemed like a mile away in my memory.

Around that time, I was trying to buy a house and needed a home inspection, which involved my agent, the sellers and their agent, and in-spectors. Everything was scheduled, but as the day arrived, I realized it conflicted with Tommy's first time pitching. After extended discussions, my agent reluctantly concluded, "I guess you need to be there."

Tommy took the mound with authority, something I'd never done as a kid. He was grim and determined, while I would have looked unsure and deferential. I sat on those god-awful aluminum bleachers watching him through the chain link fence as the first batter stepped in. At that point I noticed what I had not noticed before: Tommy bent in a sideways motion to begin a stretch delivery, not a wind-up. It looked familiar. The arm that reached backward looked uncommonly long and tapered to a wrist that was narrow compared to a relatively large hand. This, too, was familiar. In fact, the entire profile that followed him rocking back, shifting his weight forward, and fluidly whipping the ball forward looked so familiar because it was my own profile, just the way my body had looked when I was a kid throwing a pitch off the mound. I was sure of it, despite differences in the angle—he throws more of a ¾, while I was pure overhand—and the fol-low through—Tommy stops short to maintain balance to field, whereas I finished off further off the rubber with a more extended motion.

That was my boy, after all! My view was partially obscured, but the ball seemed to arrive belt high right on the outside corner. Unfortunately my reverie ended and quickly turned to indignation when the ump called it a ball.

~Tony Bentivegna, Novato, California

In 2007 when I was 16, several weeks before Father's Day, I was at a standstill about what gift to buy for my dad. My mom stepped in after hearing on the radio how the Cleveland Indians were selling vouchers allowing fathers and sons to have a catch in the outfield at Jacobs Field after the Father's Day game. Perfect. I made a mad dash to the nearest team shop, then waited anxiously for June 17 to arrive. The Indians faced the Atlanta Braves that June afternoon, Dad joining my brother and me for a game in another promising season we all assumed would end in disappointment…and it did. But on this day, Fausto Carmona threw a gem, the great Chipper Jones played, and the Tribe came away as 5-2 winners. But it was the catch after that mattered the most.

With the Steve Avery signature glove I'd received through my dad's hard work years earlier, it would be the first catch for Dad and me in years. My below-average baseball skills had kept me from the field following Pony League, and with that went the backyard catches. But tossing the ball felt just like old times, although I had way more accuracy at 16 than 10. Good thing, since the padded wall at Jacobs Field was a lot farther away than the backyard fence ever was. The special-edition ball we each received has been proudly displayed among my top baseball possessions—the only Little League game ball I ever earned, and the Bob Feller autographed ball I received when I was young—and while it is packed away now after a move, the ball and that day will always have a special place with me.

~Andrew Harner, Sandusky, Ohio

Watching WPIX broadcast Yankees games was a huge thing with me and my dad. He was a Yankees fan from way back, and I became one, too. I learned to keep score that way, and Dad told me stories of Yankee greats. Some dads and sons can talk about anything, but with us it was different. We could talk history and baseball, tell jokes all day long, but when it came to adult stuff or father-son lessons, it always ended up in arguments. Yankees baseball was something we could enjoy together. Even after I moved out, I would stop over, sit on the couch with Dad, and watch a game. He worked in the steel mills, and I was that kid sitting on the steps waiting with my glove for Dad to come home to play catch. There weren't many kids my age in the neighborhood, and I was the only child of older parents. We played catch until the street lights came on. We laughed about things Phil Rizzuto said during the broadcasts, stories about golf or some lady making him food. Once he told Bill White he got lost on the way to the press box. White's reaction was, "Hey Phil, how long you been coming here?" Dad told me how Phil played the game. I found Phil's address in a book of ballplayers and sent him a letter describing how much fun we had listening to him. A few weeks letter I got a letter from him, from Florida, thanking me for the kind words. It included two autographed photos, still on the wall in my man cave. One read, "To John, Holy Cow! Phil Rizzuto," and the second said, "To John's Dad, Holy Cow! Phil Rizzuto."

July 2010 was a tough month. We lost my father-in-law, a religious Yankees fan who wouldn't even answer the phone when the Yankees were on TV. He grew up during the Great Depression on a farm in Franklinville, New York, did tours in the Korean War, and brought up a family of five kids. A man of few words, he told stories only when they involved baseball, often telling about the time he was late for work because he was listening to Don Larsen's perfect game in the World Series. He was hard of hearing because of the war and working in machine shops, so I was the perfect guy for him because I was loud and could talk baseball. We got him a Yankee bobblehead, and he loved it so much he gave us his credit card to get as many as we could of his favorite Yankee players, past and present. He built shelves to display these treasures, arranging them in a diamond. After he died I got the bobbleheads, as no one else wanted them. I brought one of them—Rizzuto of course—to my dad, who had been diagnosed with cancer earlier that year. I put it next to his chair to keep him company as he watched the games on TV. He liked it, so there it sat.

Attending my father-in-law's funeral had been a draining day. My wife, kids, and I had a goodbye dinner with Dad. After dinner, Dad walked over to me and collapsed in my arms. As a critical care nurse, I knew this wasn't good. I revived him, called 911, and we went to the hospital. He came around and seemed to be doing a bit better, but never made it out of the ER. He wanted me to pull him up on the stretcher. There, with my arms around him, he breathed his last.

I write this sitting downstairs with my collections of many things—crap my wife calls it. The first and best are the pictures of Phil and that bobblehead.

-John Aiken, Bel Air, Maryland

My son, Bob, and I have had a baseball bond his whole life, beginning with him playing Cal Ripken Little League while I helped coach. Over the years it became our thing. We followed the Red Sox and went to an occasional game at Fenway. As he approached his 16th birthday, Bob told me he wanted to see a game at Wrigley Field. I had recently been through a divorce, and this seemed like a great way to stay connected. After that it became our tradition.

Our first trip was to Detroit to see family and a Tigers game. We invited my Uncle Carl to join us. He was about 75 years old and hadn't been to Tiger Stadium in 20 or 30 years. This was the year before the Tigers started winning again, so seats were plentiful. I was used to Fenway, always sold out, always expensive. I'd planned to pay for Carl's ticket, but he had already pulled his out his wallet to buy them all. We walked up to the ticket window and I asked for the three best available. The woman behind the counter had three right behind home plate, 5th row, and said they cost $60 each. I could actually hear my uncle's wallet slam shut! He couldn't believe the high cost of the ticket, while I was thinking what a great deal that was! For $75 in Fenway, you're hardly even in the stadium, much less right behind home plate—those would be about $450 each. I tease Carl about that to this day. He, of course, bought lunch for us all. The most memorable thing about the game was that Curtis Granderson hit his first big league homer.

Bob is now 30, and we only have seven more parks to go to see them all. We intentionally do NOT follow the Sox so that we can cheer for the home team. We saw Mariano Rivera's last save in Dodger stadium. We've caught foul balls, rather, Bob has—he has better hands than me. We've eaten nachos out of souvenir batting helmets and have seen lots of other sights in our continuing trip across America. Baseball has been the glue that has helped strengthen a bond that can easily fray as kids get older. Bob now has his own place and his own life, but he looks forward to our trip each summer as much as I do.

~Bob Rea, Hollis, New Hampshire

My dad, Louis Tarde, was a professional ballplayer. He spent the 1934 spring training with the Brooklyn Dodgers, but Casey Stengel ended his career before the season started. Stengel, a losing manager with the Dodgers a decade before his Hall of Fame success with the Yankees, was watching Dad execute throws around the infield with the precision of a quality first sacker but not the velocity of a 1986 Keith Hernandez. Casey waddled over and asked Dad, "What's wrong with your arm, son?" That was pretty much the end of Dad's big league hopes. But to say he didn't have a successful baseball career would be wrong. He played semi-pro throughout the East Coast, starring on his New Utrecht Brooklyn team and at New York University. A sturdy left-handed hitter who threw left as well, he was the leader of three generations of ballplayers who all hit from the left side because the man known as Poppy set the standard.

When I asked why left-handed, he'd smile, and with that confident swagger which took my entire boyhood to learn, he'd hold me by the shoulder and say, "A lefty can make it faster to first base, it's as simple as that." He tried to prove it by listing left-handed hitters who ended up in the Hall of Fame—Cobb, Carew, Ruth, Gehrig, Berra, Ted and Billy Williams, Yastrzemski, McCovey, Musial, Gwynn, Foxx, and Bonds. A litany of greats.

When I pointed out there was an equal number of right-handed Hall of Famers, as well as switch hitters like Mantle, Murray, and Chipper Jones, Poppy would wave his hand away and repeat his mantra, "You save a few steps, you dummy. Don't you see that?" And then he'd probably walk away.

When he was through counseling me, he'd point out that a left-handed hitter had a distinct advantage over his right-handed competition and urged me to become the best I could at the art of batting. I fulfilled his wish, becoming the star center fielder of my high school team. I introduced the batting glove long before it became ubiquitous.

My son, Scott, followed me from the left side, and was an amateur standout. He walked away from the game as a youth to pursue a health industry career, a pioneer in the Alzheimer's world, and likely will be the most remembered Tarde. Or perhaps it will be my grandson, Dalton, who broke the lefty string of three generations to swing the stick from the right side. He was a reliable player, but baseball wasn't for him. He might be the next Bill Gates or Mark Zuckerberg. Maybe Dalton's son or my daughter's family will produce the next Tarde ballplayer.

It all seemed implausible when that boat landed in Brooklyn and Louis stepped off on his journey to make a life in America rather than be spat upon in his native Russia.

~Steve Tarde, San Diego, California

In 1999, my brother, Douglas, and I took our dad, Kenneth, to a Father's Day game at Tiger Stadium. To make it a multi-generation event, we also brought our kids—my son Nickolas, who was almost two, and Douglas' daughters, Abigail and Emily. What made that day special was that Dad, on his first replaced knee, had the opportunity to run the bases after the game with three of his grandchildren in the last year of Tiger Stadium. Dad got a bit sentimental, recalling trips with cousins and friends to Michigan and Trumbull, the old home of the Tigers, and some of the ballplayers he remembered seeing play, like Al Kaline, Norm Cash, Don Mossi, and Frank Lary. The day was a sentimental one for all of us.

~Kevin De Ceuninck, Macomb, Michigan

My baseball story starts when I was seven and spans five generations. My grandfather, Raymond, was born in 1905 and lived his whole life in San Francisco. I was very close to him and I believe the key to our relationship was our shared love of baseball. The team he rooted for was, of course, the Giants. His knowledge of the game came from playing while he was growing up and becoming an outstanding pitcher. Legend has it he struck out 20 batters in one game. He played with Dolph Camilli, a former major leaguer, in a league in Golden Gate Park around 1920. The team was named the Ad Club. I still have his glove, which my grandmother gave me. He used to play catch with my brother, Scott, and me in front of his house on the sidewalk, and to this day I have the ball we used. He took us to weekday afternoon Giants games during the summer when Scott and I stayed with my grandparents for weeks at a time.

My dad, also named Raymond, was a big fan and a high school pitcher, too. He was supportive of me wanting to play, managing my teams for several years. I recall one game when Dad got into a heated argument with the other team's manager, a yeller with a difficult personality. I don't recall the details, but it seemed like the game was postponed for a long time. I do remember how Dad reacted afterward. I could tell he was embarrassed and regretful of the incident. I overheard him talking with Mom about it, and what he did next made a lasting impression on me. He decided to talk with the other manager and apologize for how he'd acted. Although Dad helped me learn how to play baseball at a young age, he taught me bigger life lessons through his actions.

Born in San Francisco, I grew up in San Leandro and became an A's fan when they moved to Oakland in 1968. I took every opportunity to watch them on TV and listen to games on the radio. Mom wasn't into sports, but she realized when Scott and I were young not to fight it, and she learned to like the game. My parents took us to many games every year. The early 1970s were an especially exciting time with the A's winning five consecutive division titles and three World Championships. We could only miss school on rare occasions, but one of those times was during the 1973 American League Championship Series when the A's hosted the Orioles. Mom took us to Game 3, but it was rained out and rescheduled for the next day, so we ended up missing two days of school! Besides that break, the most memorable part was an 11-inning game that featured one of my heroes, Campy Campaneris, hitting a walk-off home run. I'll never forget the excitement of the crowd and how special it was that my parents allowed us to experience it all.

I played baseball through high school, taking a break when I went to college then began a career and started a family. In my mid-30s, I discovered an adult baseball organization, the Men's Senior Baseball League. Being able to enjoy the game again in an organized league was incredible. But it wasn't just being able to play again, the friendships made along the way have been wonderful. One player in particular for me was Tony Jackson. We'd been teammates for several years when one day, talking about where we'd played when we were 15, we discovered that not only did we play in the same Babe Ruth league, but on the same team! I later looked at the baseball I'd hit for a home run, and sure enough, all of my teammates had signed it, including Tony!

The Men's Senior Baseball League has also provided me with an opportunity to be teammates in the Father-Son Division with my son, Bryce, who also played through high school. I'm amazed that he can play occasional tournaments so well with limited in-between practice. Several of our teams included college level players, but our manager had Bryce bat third because of his hitting ability. I will take some credit for his hitting since I started pitching to him when he was three. We lost so many balls over the fence that I always proudly said, "We need to buy stock in the Wiffle Ball company." As my folks did for me, I've always enjoyed taking Bryce to A's games. After one Friday night game against the Mariners, walking past the area where the players exit the stadium, a taxi pulled past the crowd to pick up a player, the great Ken Griffey, Jr. As he opened the taxi door he looked over at the crowd. It would have been easy for him just to get in the cab and leave, but he shut the door and walked over to sign autographs. Though he didn't stay long enough for Bryce to get a baseball signed, it was so impressive that he took the time to sign for the fans.

I've been lucky to have such great family and friends who know how much I love the game of baseball. For my 50th birthday, my kids had a fancy cake made for me that was decorated with the Oakland A's insignia and colors. My surprise gift from everyone left me speechless. It was a trip to the Oakland A's Fantasy Camp in Arizona, a once in a lifetime event… that I have now repeated seven times. Meeting many great A's from the past, including Rickey Henderson and Campy, was the greatest gift I could have received. What made the Fantasy Camp experience even better was that Bryce attended the last three with me.

One of my grandsons, Cale, who's now five, shows a passion for the game like his grandpa. At one spring training game, even at the age of three he wanted to be on the field playing on the team. Recently I was playing baseball with him, and while pitching, he hit me with a pitch. I acted like I was hurt, and his quick response was, "Stop crying like a baby, Grandpa!" He didn't want anything to take time away from his playing time! I hope I can continue to instill in him the love of the game, as my grandfather did for me.

~Bruce Fraser, Lafayette, California

I SAW IT ON TV, I HEARD IT ON THE RADIO

The original idea for this book was that it would only contain stories from folks about seeing a game in person. Anyone can write about watching TV and seeing Joe Carter's World Series home run, Seaver's 19-strikeout pitching masterpiece, or Jackie Robinson's World Series steal of home. But, as with so many facets of this book, that concept has changed. This is due, in part, to the way the stories were written, and in part because of that recurring theme—the personal connections. At first it was not possible to include these stories, but it soon became not possible to exclude them. Shout-out to John Fogerty on the chapter title

I did not understand the importance of the following event when it occurred, although I distinctly remember it. Many decades later, I still remember it clearly, but have a much better understanding of its significance.

I was seven years old in 1934 when the second major league All-Star Game was played at the Polo Fields. We couldn't afford going to games, but I sat crowded around a radio with my dad, my brothers George and Richard, and probably a few other relatives, listening intently. Richard was a Yankees fan and George probably was as well, although he wound up becoming a Red Sox fan after meeting their owner, Tom Yawkey. I just knew that I could not follow my older brothers, I had to be contrary, so the New York Giants, along with the Detroit Tigers and Hank Greenberg, became my team.

On that day, July 10, 1934, I was listening as Giants hurler and future Hall of Famer, Carl Hubbell, stood on the mound representing the

National League, ready to face a fearsome fivesome of American League sluggers. To open the game, he allowed singles to Charlie Gehringer and Heinie Manush, and then, as befitting an All-Star Game lineup, he faced the epitome of Murderer's Row. Babe Ruth, Lou Gehrig, and Jimmie Foxx went down in succession, all victims of strikeouts. We could hear through the tinny radio the electricity in the stadium.; Because the game was in New York, there were certainly as many American League and Yankees fans as there were National League and Giants fans, but it seemed to me that every successive strikeout unleashed an even greater roar. Hubbell began the next inning by striking out Al Simmons and Joe Cronin. I felt that my joy, compared to the agony of my brothers, matched the sounds coming through the radio…although, of course, not with the same volume.

In the 2015 All-Star Game, Mets pitcher Jacob deGrom struck out the side on 10 pitches in his one All-Star Game debut inning. That was very impressive. But it brought me back to the amazing day 81 years ago when I sat wide-eyed and open-mouthed, listening to that second All-Star Game. Again, I was not thinking about its meaning at the time, I just enjoyed the action. I sure understand now what it meant to strike out five consecutive future Hall of Famers!

~David Gray, Marlboro, New Jersey

Six or seven years ago, my dad had already passed away, and I was talking to my Uncle David about the book I was writing, **Bases to Bleachers**. *I had never thought of David as a baseball fan, and I don't think he was. But he told me this story and I knew it had found a home. I am sorry that none of these brothers lived long enough to see their story in print. This story is dedicated to the cousins, Kevin, Elizabeth, Mark, Alison, Donna, Steven, and Fredric.*

Our family loves baseball and we follow the San Francisco Giants. But during the postseason, we are happy to watch any teams. My son and his family are Civil War reenactors, and I join them several times a year, putting on a costume and working in the commissary tent to fix and serve food for others in camp. A while back, our last reenactment of the year was over the weekend of October 19 in Fresno, California, and of course we were all in period costumes and sleeping in tents with no electricity. By 10:00 p.m. on Saturday night, "Taps" had been played and the camp was quiet. My son got out his iPhone, found the Yankees vs. Astros game live broadcast, and we sat quietly outside with the volume turned down low as the bottom of the 9th inning started. The Yankees had just tied the game 4-4, so we weren't sure how long we would need to sit at our rickety wooden table if it went into extra innings. The Astros got a base runner, and Jose Altuve came up to bat. As soon as his walk-off homer cleared the field, we suddenly heard yelling from all around us—all the Civil War soldiers were yelling, "Yeah! Altuve! All right!" We were not, apparently, the only ones sneaking a peek with our 21st century technology! These same reenactors also play period-correct baseball at several of the sites during the year, which is so entertaining to watch because the rules are *very* different. It's really fun to see all the guys in uniform as they play just like folks did back in the 1860s.

~Nancy Haskett, Fresno, California

Nancy contacted me after hearing my NPR interview and sent me this story. She had not remembered, until I mentioned it, that we had met before. She once sat behind me at a Giants game!

As a 5th grade student in Brooklyn, I was already a big baseball fan. My dad, and especially my older brother, made sure my loyalties were with the National League. I had no choice but to be a Mets fan, even though they were terrible for the first four years I followed them. For a youngster, I knew a fair bit about baseball. Dad took us to quite a few games every year, mostly losses back then. But my brother and I religiously played the Negamco baseball game, similar to the popular Strat-o-Matic, and I memorized the starting lineups of the 16 teams then in existence. I also had an extensive baseball card collection and had gotten to know even more players that way. Suddenly the players in games had faces.

You can imagine my excitement when, in 1969, the Mets were no longer losers. There would be no long losing streaks with Tom Seaver and Jerry Koosman, and the steady hand of manager Gil Hodges to guide the team. Predictably, we were wowed when they beat the Aaron-led Braves, and incredulous when they took a 3-1 lead over the Orioles in the World Series. My family was moving to a larger apartment the next week so my parents were more concerned about the move than the doings in Flushing, but I knew they had an eye on the Series. They were baseball fans who had lived within walking distance to Ebbets Field.

October 16 was a school day, and back then the World Series had all day games. A long-forgotten classmate brought a radio to class, and our usually strict teacher, Mr. MacFadden, turned a deaf ear. I wondered whether he, too, was a Mets fan. Games were played at a quicker pace then, so as 3:00 p.m. approached, the game was nearing its conclusion. We pleaded with him to let us out a little early, not knowing, perhaps not caring, that he could get into trouble for doing that. Miraculously, he granted our wishes and dismissed us at 2:55. I didn't wait for my friends, flying out as fast as my 10-year-old legs would run, praying that green lights were with me. God must have been on my side that day, as I didn't hit a single red. I arrived home at 3:05 p.m. during a commercial break between the bottom of the 8th and the top of the 9th, and Mom had the game on. With a two-run lead for the Mets, I wondered whether Koosman would come out for the 9th or if Gil would go the bullpen. Sure enough, No. 36 came out, and I held my breath, so zoned in on every pitch that I didn't even realize Mom was in the room. With two outs, the Orioles had the tying run on, and Davey Johnson was up. Koosman threw, and Johnson swung, making good contact. I thought the ball was going to be trouble. The camera shifted to Met Cleon Jones, who casually camped under the ball, caught it, and bent down to one knee. It was as if Cleon was thanking the baseball gods for that moment. Pandemonium erupted, without the security games have today. It was amazing none of the players got hurt. I jumped up and screamed, "Ma, they did it, they did it!" All Mom could say was, "Wow!" followed quickly by, "Be careful of the boxes!" Hebrew School started at 3:30 p.m., but Mom let me go at 4:00. She was not the only mother to do so. The teachers understood and greeted us with wide smiles. I felt like shouting to them, "There is a God!" But I didn't want to risk getting in trouble on what was probably the happiest day of my life to date. A Mets championship, early dismissal from school, and late to Hebrew School. What a great day!

~Paul Berger, Forest Hills, New York

That 1962 World Series 7th game on TV and radio, a couple of perspectives:

My dad was a big baseball fan and he took me to Seals games in the days before the Giants came to San Francisco. Several nights a week we would go to Douglass Park after he got home from work to practice my hitting and fielding, both of us dreaming I would one day be a major leaguer. When the Giants arrived in San Francisco, Dad took me to Candlestick several times a year. At age 10 when I was away at summer camp near Yosemite, Dad sent me a letter talking about an amazing new player he had just seen at a Giants vs. Phillies game. Willie McCovey had come up from the minors and went 4-4 against Robin Roberts in his first game. I couldn't wait to get home, go to a Giants game, and see the new Irishman hit. I'd grown up in Saint Phillips parish which was 50 percent Irish and 50 percent Italian. Upon my return from camp, Dad took me to a game, and I was surprised to discover this Irishman was Black. Dad explained that after the Civil War, many freed Blacks in the South took their former owners' names.

I still recall sitting in James Lick Junior High listening to the radio tuned in to Game 7 of the 1962 World Series that featured the Giants battling their former cross-town rivals, the Yankees. In the 9th inning, McCovey hit a tremendous line drive to Bobby Richardson for the final out and a Yankees victory. Dad, who was at the game, said if the ball had sailed a foot higher it would have been a sure home run, it was hit so hard. I was devastated by that World Series loss. That memory, along with the Kennedy assassinations in 1963 and 1968, sticks with me to this day.

~Lawrence Jacobsen, Mill Valley, California

I skipped a college class to try to get into Game 7 of the 1962 World Series. Unsuccessful, I listened to it on radio because I couldn't even get into a bar to watch. I was too young. Like it was yesterday, I distinctly remember how it ended! Bottom of the 9th, Yankees up 1-0, two outs, Matty Alou on third for the Giants, Willie Mays on second, and McCovey hits a scorching drive up the middle of the diamond...which was snared by Bobby Richardson! How could I possibly forget?

-Jack Best, Reno, Nevada

The Cardinals had last won the World Series in 1982. While technically they'd won one in my lifetime, I had been 18 months old and don't remember it, so it doesn't count. I felt I was missing something I needed but didn't know if I would ever see it. A 24-year Cardinals drought wasn't ending anytime soon, especially after the 105-win 2004 season concluding with a Red Sox Series sweep. And on and on.

In 2006 I was living in D.C., two blocks from my brother Shim and his family. The Cardinals had just won an epic National League Championship Series against the Mets, in one of the best Game 7s I had ever seen. They proceeded to pick apart a Tigers team that had a week's rest before the Series—which turned out to be a little too much time off. The Cardinals led the Series 3-1, and naturally Game 5 was on a Friday night. For observant Jews, Friday night is the beginning of the Sabbath when no electronics may be turned on or off, and the appropriate thing to do is to ignore whatever amazing event may be going on in the sporting world. My father is a huge sports fan, but a Rabbi first, and he wouldn't have approved us even recording the game. But Shim and I were adults, and this was the potential clinching game of the first St. Louis Cardinals World Series victory in 26 years.

By the way, I found out later that my father, who was in a hotel that Sabbath during a part-time Rabbi gig out of town, had gone to the lobby to get a towel and saw a large, noisy crowd around a TV in the bar. He went to see what was happening and watched the last inning. He put it in his Dresha (the Hebrew word for sermon).

Shim ate a quick Sabbath dinner and then came over with his wife, three-year-old, and newborn in a stroller to watch the game. Everyone was decked out in our finest Cardinals gear for the occasion. We all huddled in my room. I had left my TV on the night before so we could watch the game. I can't say there was a sense of nervousness. Even if they lost that game they still would have a 3-2 Series lead. But we wanted to win the World Series in St. Louis, so as the game wore on there was a growing sense of excitement.

Shim and I were not close growing up. We had nothing in common and, separated by four years, we had never really done anything in life at the same time. With utterly different personalities, I never expected us to be close in adulthood. For many reasons, the opposite became true, for which I am grateful. But the tenuous thread between those two periods in our lives was the Cardinals. That, we always did together. The reality is, it was pure coincidence that we got to be together for this magical night, but I prefer to think the universe and the baseball gods had planned it that way. The game ended with an Adam Wainwright fastball, followed by pandemonium on the field and in my room. Out of nowhere—we were all sitting on my bed, mind you—I saw a blurry bottle of champagne in my brother's hands as he vigorously shook it. The smell of champagne stayed in my room for weeks. The stain on my Albert Pujols jersey is still there. And the perfect memories will always be, too.

~Ari Stein, Walnut Creek, California

As a teenager, I worked an after-school job at Long Island Leather and Tweed, a factory that made coats from an assortment of materials. I worked standing at a table, marking pieces of fake fur with a yellow crayon. My tablemates spoke only Spanish and weren't able to communicate more than just encouraging me to "Mark the pattern" as the hours dragged on and on. Most afternoons, the only sound heard was the whir of sewing machines and the *thunk* of the button maker. However, on October 16, 1969, the day the Baltimore Orioles and the New York Mets faced each other in the final game of the World Series, the roar of the crowd, the nasal voice of the commentator, and the crackling of 100 transistor radios added a soundtrack all their own. When the Mets won, the Cinderella team that the newly arrived immigrants so whole-heartedly supported, machines stopped, both Spanish and English cheers filled the crowded room, and fake fur flew like confetti!

~Adele Weiss, Washington, District of Columbia

It was Saturday night, October 25, 1986, and at long last something just about as big as possible was about to happen on the New England sports scene. It was, of course, Game 6 of the World Series between the Red Sox and the Mets. It was tied after nine innings. In the top of the 10th the Red Sox scored two runs and were about to finally break through after three-quarters of a century of waiting. I'd been watching the last few innings on TV upstairs in our bedroom, with my wife, Niki, unsuccessfully trying to sleep through the excitement.

In the last half of the 10th, I began to think that I should wake up the kids and get them in front of the TV so they could witness history in the making. Niki did not like that idea, but I managed to convince her to let me wake the oldest. I went downstairs to his bedroom, rousted Chris from a sound sleep, and plopped him on our bedroom floor in front of the TV. By this time, the Mets had begun to piece together a small rally of their own, but with two outs I wasn't worried. "Chris, the Red Sox are about to win the World Series! You'll be able to tell your grandchildren that you watched them clinch it."

With one run in, Bob Stanley threw a wild pitch, and the tying run scored. I started thinking, damn, this is going to take longer than I thought. Chris, more asleep than awake, wouldn't get back to bed right away, and Niki wasn't happy about it. Then a slow grounder hit to the right side along the first base line... Yeah, I don't need to fill in the names or outcome, every baseball fan knows them.

I'm thinking, maybe there is a curse, after all.

~John Cook, Somersworth, New Hampshire

The Giants played the Indians in the 1954 World Series. I didn't attend the games, but I watched them all on TV. The highlight of the Giants sweep, of course, was Willie Mays' amazing catch of Vic Wertz's line drive. It was stunning to watch, miraculous. But I also recall Dusty Rhodes, Giants left fielder and pinch-hitter, hitting two home runs and being largely responsible for the Giants offense during the sweep. One hit stands out in my mind. Knowing the threat that Dusty was, Cleveland tried to intentionally walk him. One pitch came very close to the plate, and Rhodes swung and connected, knocking in some runs. Swinging on an intentional walk was unheard of—and no longer possible—but to this day, every time I see an intentional walk, my heart races, remembering the alertness of Dusty Rhodes.

~Philip Sterdt, Sarasota, Florida

My bar mitzvah was on Oct 10, 1964. The ceremony was in the morning and the reception followed at the Allison House in Manhasset, New York. We had a radio on at all times because it was the day of a World Series game, Yankees vs. St. Louis. My favorite player was Mickey Mantle. That day, he hit a home run in the bottom of the 9th off Barney Schultz and the Yankees won 2-1. His bar mitzvah gift to me!

The next day we got up early and headed to Yankee Stadium. We waited in line for $3 bleachers seats over the 457' sign in left-center field. The Yankees lost 4-3 as the Cardinals third baseman, Ken Boyer, brother of Yankee third baseman Clete, hit a grand slam off Al Downing. I don't remember much about my Bar Mitzvah, but I do remember the baseball of that weekend. We all have our priorities.

~Mike Pressman, Madison, Wisconsin

On October 13, 1960, I was 10 years old, growing up in a little Pennsylvania farm town on Lake Erie. Baseball had always seemed like a slow, boring game to me. The local high school had football, basketball, and track teams, but not baseball. However, my dad had grown up in Pittsburgh with his beloved Pirates, the perennial losers who'd last won a World Series in 1925. On this beautiful October day, my family was making its annual fall trip across the state to visit family in the Philadelphia area, and miraculously, the Pirates were playing the New York Yankees in Game 7 of the World Series. No one had expected the Pirates to win the pennant, and certainly no one thought the Series would go seven games. But here were Skinner, Groat, Mazeroski, and Burgess playing Mantle, Maris, Berra, and Kubek.

As we drove across the state on the Pennsylvania Turnpike, we listened to the game on the radio. I'd never seen Dad this excited! The game was back and forth, with the Pirates scoring first and leading 4-0 by the end of the 2nd inning. But then the Yankees went ahead 5-4 in the 6th. The problem was that every time we went through a tunnel on the turnpike, the radio would cut out. We'd exit and the score had changed! At the end of the 8th as we came out of the next-to-the-last tunnel, it was 9-7 Pirates. And then in the top of the 9th just as we entered the final tunnel, the Yankees scored two runs to tie the game. We emerged as Pirate Bill Mazeroski was coming to the plate.

The rest is history. Maz's walk-off home run to deep left field is one of the most famous in all of baseball. The lowly Pittsburgh Pirates had defeated the mighty Yankees! It was the only time I ever saw tears in my father's eyes. And I fell in love with the game of baseball. Over 50 years later, that love affair continues, but never has a game been sweeter than that one in 1960.

~Lee Bowers, Villanova, Pennsylvania
I still recall where I was when I heard that home run on the radio. I was devastated.

Most people fall in love with teams when they win. Mine lost. That is how I came to know and love the Mets, as World Series losers in 1973. It was an early and valuable lesson that being a Mets fan meant coping with disappointment. In the early and mid-70s, the Mets were the best baseball team in New York, but as the decade wore on and the Yankees reigned supreme, I stayed loyal to the orange and blue. There was something about the upstart Mets that captured my heart.

I credit my grandfather with turning me onto baseball. He grew up a New York Giants fan, but when they left for San Francisco and the Mets played their first couple of seasons at the Polo Grounds, it was natural for him to start following them. Not knowing I would one day make San Francisco my home and become a Giants fan, my best baseball memories stem from my life as an East Coaster and the hot, sticky, evenings at Shea with my dad and grandfather. However, the one that will forever be embossed in my memory took place on 34th and 1st in Manhattan.

I seemed to have great luck during college vacations. Most people went to Mexico or Florida, but I went to doctors, as this was often when my respiratory system came under attack. During the fall midterm break of 1986 I came down with bronchitis, and when everyone else was heading back to school, I remained in New York City. It was here, in bed, that I watched the Mets vs. Red Sox World Series.

The Mets were heavy favorites, but I was not convinced. I'd learned my lesson. Besides, they were a bunch of knuckleheads and troublemakers, not the good guys from the Seaver days. They'd trashed a plane on the way back from beating the Astros in the National League Championship Series, and their antics were well known to all who lived in New York at that time.

Though not a sports fan in the least, my mom caught some of the Series when she checked in to see how I was feeling. She didn't pay that much attention at first, but with each game I could see her interest pique more. By game six she was sitting on the floor next to my bed watching, just in time for...*Buckner*! That should say it all, right? For those of you who don't know what that means, here is how the play-by-play went down in apartment 4C.

Game 6 was a must-win for the Mets. The Red Sox were one out away from capturing their first title since 1918. It was the bottom of the 10th and the Mets were down 3-2. Gary Carter, the goodie-two-shoes catcher, singled. He might not have been as much fun as the rest of the team, but he often came through at the plate. At this point the Mets motto, "You Gotta Believe," ran through my head. Kevin Mitchell pinch-hit for Rick Aguilera and singled. I could see Mom was getting nervous. I think nearly everyone in New York City was on the edge of their seats, but my mom, *my mom*, was worrying about a *baseball* game? This was an historic event.

It was Ray Knight's turn to be a hero. *Boom!* He hit a single, scoring Carter and sending Mitchell to third. Just one more run to tie the game. Sox manager John McNamara changed pitchers. putting in his closer, Bob Stanley. On a wild pitch, Mitchell scored from third tying the game, and Knight went to second. By now the additional adrenaline was definitely helping me breathe better. On a 2-2 count, Mookie Wilson hit what looked like a routine ground ball to first. Easy catch as it may have looked to anyone watching on TV, the ball rolled through first baseman Bill Buckner's legs into the outfield. Knight scored from second, and the Mets won the game, tying the Series at three all. Both of us screamed and we called my grandfather, who I think, above all, was shocked to hear his daughter, who'd never given a fig about baseball, so excited.

The final game was almost as thrilling. There were a few times when I really thought we were going to blow it. Yet we didn't, and my grandfather, mother, and I were as happy as we were the night before. In the end the "bad guys" won, but they were *our* bad guys.

I don't think my mother has watched a single baseball game since 1986, but during that week in late October, she was a Mets fan. And in spite of starting the Series feeling like hell, I felt much better in every respect by the time it ended.

~Pamela Busch, San Francisco, California

Your wearing of a Mets shirt in the gym was how we met. That was a tough series for me, as a fan of both teams. I remember watching the end of that game, the Buckner play, drinking a margarita with Lynn at Carlos Greenbergs after seeing the movie Peggy Sue Got Married. I didn't quite know whether to be happy or sad!

My dad, "Granddaddy Howard," grew up listening to baseball games with his father, "Granddaddy Lang," who recorded scores and memorable plays in daily diaries he kept from 1929 all the way until 1965. I, in turn, frequently listened to games with my dad. I have some slight memories of the St. Louis Browns, but most are of the Cardinals, including Red Schoendienst and, of course, Stan Musial. The most bizarre incident involved the Browns, a game I listened to with Grandpa Lang. Browns owner, Bill Veeck, a zany showman, did all sorts of things to attract attention to the club. Maybe the zaniest occurred on August 19, 1951, when he instructed the manager to send in Eddie Gaedel to pinch-hit. Gaedel was an entertainer who stood 3'7" tall. Back in those days, it was socially acceptable to call him a midget, but he had dwarfism. He wore number 1/8. It was hard to pitch to his strike zone, and Gaedel was instructed not to swing the bat. He walked on four pitches and was taken out for a pinch-runner. It was a legitimate move; Veeck had Gaedel sign a contract and he was put on the roster, but no one had paid attention. Of course, this became very controversial, the league voided the contract and accused Veeck of making a mockery of the game. Gaedel finished his baseball "career" with an on-based percentage of 1.000!

~Khaki Westerfield, Columbia, Missouri

As I look back upon my life, there are a few people I could listen to for several hours—my Pastor, Walter Cronkite, Paul Harvey, and Tigers announcer Ernie Harwell. Of those four, Ernie most evoked the emotions and memories I will forever cherish. Ron LeFlore swiping bases, Tram and Sweet Lou turning two, Morris pitching another gem, and Big Cecil smashing another long-gone home run—those are only a few of the many pictures embedded in my mind from the countless days and nights listening to Ernie's play-by-play on the radio. Throughout my youth and well into my adult life, nobody helped shape me into the devoted Detroit Tigers fan I am today like Ernie Harwell. When Mom thought I was in my bedroom doing homework or sleeping, I was secretly listening to Ernie on my transistor radio. I remember the sudden fear I often felt waking up in the morning, realizing that Ernie's familiar voice, once again, had gently put me to sleep and the radio was still on.

The 1984 Tigers represent my favorite sport memory. Roaring off to a 35-5 start, my beloved Tigers ran away with the pennant, eventually winning the World Series in five games over the Padres. I never complained if the Tigers were not on TV because I knew I could catch the game on WJR AM 760 with Ernie. Although I admit I always watched all of the postseason on TV, I also rushed to turn on the radio after the games to catch the recap and to share in the sincere enthusiasm and pure enjoyment with the biggest Tigers fan I knew.

I never met Ernie, but I felt I knew him personally. He was there for pick-up games, summer cookouts, trips to the beach, and family vacations. He was, and always will be, part of my family. If there is baseball in heaven, without a doubt Ernie will be doing the broadcasting. I know I speak for many fans who all feel the same across our great state. Ernie was truly a Michigan icon.

The impeccable character Ernie always demonstrated, even when the Tigers were struggling to win games, is what I admired most. In a world where people too often turn their backs on each other because of mistakes and unfulfilled personal expectations, Ernie remained faithful. Whether or not the Tigers are fighting to win the pennant or clawing out from the cellar, I will follow Ernie's example and cheer, "Go Tigers!"

~David Ritter, Flint, Michigan

I am from Pittsburgh, but living in Tempe, Arizona, from 2007 to 2014 I became a Diamondbacks fan in addition to my lifelong love of the Pirates. The player in my favorite moment, Tony Womack, played for both teams during his career. I wasn't there in person at what I call the Father's Day redemption game, I watched it on television. But it is as clear to me as if I were there.

Womack was with the D'backs in their 2001 championship season. His father had been his coach, mentor, number one fan, and inspiration. When his father passed away early in the season, Tony was devastated and had a long slump. He was an established major leaguer player, but there was talk about sending him down to the minors. That Father's Day, you couldn't have written the script for what happened. Tony came up with the bases loaded and, lo and behold, he hit a grand slam! He cried as he rounded the bases, touched the plate, and saluted his dad in heaven. It was very emotional to watch on TV. Even now as I think about it, tears come to my eyes.

Womack went on to get the series-winning walk-off hit in the division Series and would greatly contribute to the D'Backs World Series victory against the Yankees, always sharing those heroic moments with a salute to his dad.

~Bill Gorback, Thousand Oaks, California

The sound of baseball on the radio has been my mantra since 1959. As a youngster, I listened to Yankee games called by Mel Allen, Red Barber, and Phil Rizzuto on transistor radios. Late at night in my Brooklyn apartment, I would tune in, but also occasionally got Red Sox and Phillies games accompanied by a great deal of static. When necessary, I would attach a long wire to the antenna of my portable radio for better reception. I did anything to follow the game. To this day, I listen to games on the radio with great pleasure. With current technology, thankfully I am never out of range and static is a thing of the past.

In 2007, as a season ticket holder—section 140/Bleachers—I was able to get tickets to see the All-Star Game at AT&T park. In the 5th inning of a low-scoring game, I went to the bathroom while the America League was batting. I was alone in the bathroom when I heard a thunderous cheer from the crowd. The radio announced that Ichiro Suzuki had hit the first inside-the-park home run in All-Star Game history. As I mentioned, from one coast to the other, baseball on the radio is my mantra.

~Josh Koral, San Francisco, California

I am a Yankees fan from New York. I remember a postgame interview that famed broadcaster Mel Allen conducted with Casey Stengel and Yogi Berra. Mel asked a pretty straightforward question and pointed the mic at Casey for a response. Casey said a few sentences in Stengelese and Mel looked a little uncertain about how to respond. All of a sudden Yogi started talking, although what he said didn't register with Mel...or the viewers. Casey picked up right where Yogi left off and went into another Stengelese rant. When Casey finished, Mel had a big smile on his face, winked at the home audience and pointed the mic at Yogi. It was clear that Stengel and Berra fully understood each other, even if no one else did. Stengel used to refer to Yogi as his "on-field manager." This went on for a few more minutes before Mel went to a White Owl commercial.

~Rich Lang, San Francisco, California

1996 was a year of firsts for me and my relationship with Cardinals baseball. Growing up in St. Louis, dedication to Cardinal Nation is beyond

G-d and country! I am not sure at what point it becomes that strongly ingrained in most people, but I was 11. The Cardinals were under new ownership after the Busch family sold the team, and new management was led by Tony La Russa.

That year for the first time, I went to a Cardinals home opener, escorted by my two big brothers, Shim and Ari. It was great, just the three of us. No parents, no father begging us to leave from the 3rd inning on, saying, "They are just going to lose." Well, what do you expect from a Phillies fan? My brothers and I had a great time even though the Cardinals lost in 10 innings and we froze throughout the game on that cold March night. We went to many games that season, when kids could afford going without parents and bleacher seats were all of $5. The Cardinals made it to the playoffs that year, the first time in my life I was old enough to remember. It was so exciting! Finally, after hearing about the generations of great Cardinal teams making playoff runs, I was going to experience it for myself. Little did I know how much I was going to experience.

Somehow, Ari managed to get tickets to Game 1 of the Division Series against the Padres. I was ecstatic to leave school early, but primarily to go to a Cardinals playoff game. I will never forget the excitement of Gary Gaetti's three run home run in the first inning, and the ball landing in the bleachers just a few rows in front us. Ari still has the poorly pixilated picture with insanely blurry images of us in the background, hanging on the wall in his childhood bedroom. The Cardinals went on to win 3-1.

With serious Cardinals fever, we knew we had to find a way to get to another game. Soon after, radio station KMOX had a contest to give away playoff tickets, and we started frantically calling. This occurred while our family was hosting a party for friends whose son had just had his ritual circumcision. Hungry for another playoff game experience, Ari and I had the radio on, waiting for a chance to win those tickets. The radio hosts announced a contest, and Ari urged me to call. So, I did. We went to a back room in the house and called until we got through. The hosts were discussing the recent incident of Roberto Alomar spitting in the face of an umpire who had allegedly uttered a racial slur during an argument.

I *finally* got through and was speaking to the hosts. It was clear to them that I was a kid and they asked me how I felt about the spitting incident. Obviously, it was sad, but as a kid, baseball is about the game, who cared about anything else? I somehow managed to express my disappointment in these people I admired, in the best way an 11-year-old could express those thoughts. They told me they wanted to give me something for calling. At that point, I was getting really excited, thinking *this is it!* Playoff tickets! But it wasn't, it was even better! They had a baseball signed by Ozzie Smith from the All-Star Game that year, his last as a player. For sharing my opinion they were sending me the baseball. Before they could finish asking me to hold the line, Ari came running in, jumping up and down, screaming like a madman.

We did not get to another playoff game, and the Cardinals lost the Series in heartbreaking fashion after leading 3-1 games. Now when I see that Ozzie Smith ball on my mantel, I forever think of 1996, the year that, with the help of my brothers, I became a full-fledged member of Cardinal Nation.

~David Z. Stein, Modiin, Israel

On August 7, 2007, I was driving home from work by myself, along the Embarcadero in San Francisco, without a ticket to the Giants game. It was clear that Barry Bonds was going to soon break Hank Aaron's home run record. I was listening to the game on the radio, and Barry was on deck. Finally, he came up to bat. I actually turned the radio volume completely down and sat in the traffic outside the ballpark with the car windows rolled down. Even from there, I could feel the tension from the park. Then all of the sudden the crowd went wild! Barry hit #756! To feel the energy in air was purely amazing!

~Darcy Peterson, Burlingame, California

As an 11-year-old Mets fan, I didn't merely root for my team, I passionately willed them to win. The 1969 Mets championship had predated my interest in baseball and was therefore only a dry historical fact to me. But in 1973 when the Mets reached the World Series, I was verklempt with anticipation.

Attending the Series against the A's was out of the question, but I could enjoy the most important event in the history of my world on TV, right? Not exactly. You see, we only had one TV set, which was shared among my parents, my two sisters, and me. Despite the life-or-death-level importance of the Series to me, I was strictly allotted only my 1/5 share of TV time. To make matters worse, that time did not necessarily coincide with game times.

While the family was happily engrossed in irrelevant shows such as *Kojak or The Partridge Family*, I was relegated to the exotic and unfamiliar realm of radio. When Shea Stadium suddenly thundered its approval over some on-field heroics, I pined for the visual. But despite my frustration, I came to enjoy radio. I'd lie on our forest-like shag carpet and get lost in the call of the game and constant background noise of the crowd. Could it be that my beloved but otherwise mediocre team—including my favorites Rusty Staub, Felix Milan, and, yes, Willie Mays, - would actually become World Champs?

Tragically, no. And for the next 13 years I suffered through comically sub-mediocre years. In 1982, for instance, clean-up hitter Dave Kingman struck out 156 times and batted .204. Being a Mets fan was a dark and lonely sojourn, but at least I got to watch the games on TV after we came to own a second, third, and then a fourth set, until all rooms and persons in the house had their own. Even our cats watched TV.

Finally, in 1986, with a little Divine intervention, my Mets were World Champions again. And I watched every pitch on our then-huge 35-inch Emerson. My sacred mission as a fan at last consummated, I promptly retired from fandom. To this date, I have not watched another inning of baseball.

Coda: My retirement seems to have been prescient, as I have been informed that the Mets have not won another World Series these past 35 years.

~Mark Gray, New York, New York

My love affair with the Boston Red Sox began in the summer of 1959 when I found a baseball card on the sidewalk out in front of our house. The first name on the card was the same as mine—Ted. That was as far as my first-grade education could take me. I took the card inside and showed my dad. It turned out to be a Ted Williams card. Dad proceeded to tell me about the Splendid Splinter, The Kid, Teddy Ballgame, and that he played for the Boston Red Sox. I was hooked. If Boston had the greatest hitter in the game and he had the same name as me, I'd root for them. I've been a Red Sox fan ever since...perhaps the only one in northeast Indiana. It's been quite a journey, filled with ups, downs, and even a little magic.

I soon learned that being a Red Sox fan was a bit embarrassing. My friends rooted for the White Sox, Tigers, or Yankees, all teams that offered something to cheer about. But year after year, the Sox were mired deep in the second division of the American League. Over the years, there were glimpses of hope. I watched all the important games on television, starting with the 1967 Impossible Dream season with Bob Gibson defeating Jim Lonborg, pitching on two days' rest in the deciding World Series game. I was proud, but I wanted more. I watched the 1975 Series, with Carlton Fisk's 12th inning home run off the left field pole in Game 6 pushing the Big Red Machine to the limit. But again the Sox couldn't finish it. I hungered for more, for their first Series Championship since 1918. The Bucky Dent home run in 1978—do we even need to bring up (again) the devastating 1986 loss to the Mets? Aaron Boone's walk-off home run ended the next threat in 2003. I still wanted more.

The 2004 season brought an American League Championship Series rematch with the Yankees, who won the first three games and led 4-3 going into the bottom of the 9th at Fenway in Game 4. The great Mariano

Rivera was on the mound for the save and the trip to the World Series. Would we lose to the Yankees yet again? Desperate, I mindlessly got out of my chair, went to the basement, and picked up my Red Sox batting helmet. It wasn't an official helmet, just a cheap plastic copy I'd won many years earlier tossing baseballs in an arcade. Little did I know there was powerful magic in that helmet. I went back upstairs and moved my chair to within two feet of the television screen. I put the helmet on and started rubbing it. Round and round the top of it I went. Round and round, never stopping, never lifting my hand. Lo and behold, Rivera blew the save as the Red Sox came back to tie the game. Round and round I rubbed that helmet nonstop until David Ortiz hit a walk-off game-winning home run in the 12th.

My attitude changed. I was now filled with confidence, imagining countless reasons why the Red Sox were destined to win this Series, using their new secret weapon, an old plastic batting helmet. In Game 5, from the first pitch to the last, I sat two feet from the television screen, rubbing the top of my helmet. My wife walked in the room and looked at me incredulously, not knowing whether to be disgusted by such nonsense or disappointed by the fact that I was certain it was making a difference. She knew nothing of the spells, charms, and superstitions that appealed to the gods of baseball and determined a game's fate. In the bottom of the 14th, Big Papi came through again with a walk-off RBI single. I continued my ritual in Game 6, round and round, never stopping. Curt Schilling, his right ankle stitched together and his sock soaked with blood, pitched the Red Sox to victory in a game plagued by controversial calls and marred by unruly fan behavior at Yankee Stadium. I rubbed my helmet again throughout Game 7 as the Red Sox completed their four-game winning streak to become the only team in baseball to ever come back from three games down to win a best-of-seven Series.

Boston then swept the St. Louis Cardinals 4-0 in the World Series to win their first championship in 86 years and break the "Curse of the Bambino". I rubbed my helmet from first pitch to last, every game. As Game 4 came to a close, I didn't scream or yell or jump up and down excitedly. I just quietly sat in my chair, serene, contented, and relieved. They had finally done it.

Since 2004, the Red Sox have gone on to win the World Series three more times. The Ted Williams baseball card was lost when my mom threw out my baseball card collection after I left home for college. A few years ago, I was able to replace it with an identical card found on eBay. As for the helmet, its magic now gone and its life's work complete, it rests comfortably on a shelf in the garage, patiently awaiting its call from Cooperstown.

~Ted Sadler, Fort Wayne, Indiana

Baseball players are known for their superstitions. So, too, are the fans, including Lynn who subtly tugs on her Giants earrings when they bat, right side for righty batters, left side for lefties.

BUNTS

As in the first book, this is the first of five consecutive chapters with titles depicting levels of base hits. The original notion of the first book was a compilation of short anecdotes. But stories came in with varying lengths, and it became clear that there was no correlation between length and impact. An adage in baseball is that it is important to get on base, regardless of how. These are short—but they got on base.

Around 1990, I was playing in the Men's Senior Baseball League. I batted against Bob Owchinko, a left-hander who'd pitched for 10 years in the major leagues. He threw me two Linda Ronstadt fastballs (Blew by You) and then a curve. Line drive single to center. So, my lifetime batting average against Owchinko is 1.000. Pete Rose's lifetime batting average against Owchinko is .095. Look it up. Does this mean I am a better hitter than Pete Rose? Really not for me to say. But the numbers do tell a story…

~Doug Tobler, Phoenix, Arizona

As Cincinnati Reds closer Aroldis Chapman enters the ballpark in the 9th inning, the audio-visual folks turn the volume way up and play Led Zeppelin's "Kashmir," a pounding, energetic song. The crowd leaps to their feet, yelling and grabbing cell phones, jumping up and down, waving arms. The energy causes the entire Great American Ball Park to levitate at least three feet off the ground…like the Pentagon did during the anti-Vietnam demonstrations. It happens every single time this fire-breathing dragon enters the game. And I was there when Chapman threw his 106 MPH flamethrower; I'm pretty sure the park rose another hundred feet. It was absolutely thrilling.

~Sally Harrison-Pepper, Ft. Meyers, Florida

This is how you write a compelling story about a single pitch.

On June 4, 1968, Don Drysdale beat the Pirates 5-0, allowing three hits and striking out eight. The victory was Big D's sixth straight shutout, giving him 54 consecutive scoreless innings, both new major league records. His scoreless streak reached 58⅔ innings on June 8.

It was tough for Dodgers fans when he retired just over a year later on August 11, 1969. I was at Dodger Stadium when his retirement was announced. The crowd became absolutely silent for about 10 seconds, then erupted in a two-minute standing ovation for Big D. It was one of the most memorable major league game moments of my life.

As a side note, on the night of that same June 1968, day, Robert Kennedy was assassinated. When Drysdale died suddenly, among his personal effects was a cassette tape of Senator Kennedy's speech that night, which opened with, "I'd like to express my high regard for Don Drysdale, who pitched his sixth straight shutout tonight..." Apparently, Drysdale was so moved by that, and what happened moments later, that he kept the cassette tape with him everywhere he went. I can only imagine that once in a while he would listen to it, reflecting on how fragile life is.

~Rick Lenaburg, Phoenix, Arizona

It was September 3, 1972, toward the end of the baseball season. The Chicago Cubs were having their typical bad season. At the time, our family had two season tickets to games at Wrigley Field. My son Harry, age 13, pleaded with everyone in our family to go to the game with him. Being the softy that I am, I finally agreed. The Cubs were playing the San Diego Padres.

Milt Pappas was pitching for the Cubs. He'd retired 26 batters and was one strike away from a perfect game. With a 2-2 count, umpire Bruce Froemming called the next two pitches balls, even though one definitely was and should have been called a strike. Pappas lost the perfect game but was credited with a no-hitter. Froemming never acknowledged he had blown the call. That was the last no-hitter pitched at Wrigley Field for over 40 years.

~Judy Rhodes, Chicago, Illinois

I grew up in Tucson, Arizona, and baseball has always been a passion for me. From playing Saturday morning sandlot ball—like the movie—with friends, our balls covered with electrical tape and broken bats fixed with nails, to watching the game of the week on a black and white television, announced by Pee Wee Reese and Dizzy Dean, I simply loved baseball.

With no nearby teams in my younger days, I chose to follow the Mets, later liking the new Diamondbacks, as well. In 2001, I was lucky to get to attend my first and, so far, only World Series game, the D'backs vs. the Yankees. Being there with my wife and sitting in great seats high over home plate was a fantastic experience. Arizona won the game, but with this being soon after 9/11, my greatest memory is of hearing Ray Charles sing the National Anthem. That was simply an amazing, inspiring experience.

~Gilbert Rico, Tucson, Arizona

I met Mickey Mantle in 1976, and I have a picture of me hanging with him. He also autographed a ball for me, which I kept in a little glass box. When I was out on tour doing my music, my two girls needed a baseball to practice with. Guess which ball they used? Now when you look at the ball, all you see is Mixxxxxxxxxxxx.

~Mike Murphy, Sun Valley, Idaho

It was in 1970 in Bloomington, Minnesota, during my very first T-ball game at the tender age of six, that I reached the apex of my baseball career. I was playing shortstop. The ball was hit and somehow landed in my glove. Wow, first out. The base runner coming from second ran into me. Two outs! I heard my coach screaming for me to throw the ball to first for a reason unclear to me, but I did as I was told, causing the clueless runner at first—who of us *wasn't* clueless at that point?—who had simply taken off, to be thrown out, making out number three. Incredible! A semi-unassisted triple play!

~Dan Schleter, Davenport, Iowa

I was in the eighth grade, and my friends and I could hardly wait for Game 7, the final game of the 1960 World Series between the New York Yankees and the Pittsburgh Pirates. I decided to take my small transistor radio to school. With the game in the 9th inning, I sat in Mr. Baldwin's social science course. There was an ominous sign above his clock that said, "Time passes, will you?" I put my head down, somehow listening to the game without getting noticed. When Bill Mazeroski hit his momentous home run to beat the Yankees in the bottom of the 9th, I heard a big, "Hurrah!" from Mr. Baldwin's class as well as from many other rooms in the school. I knew then I was not the only one listening to this unforgettable baseball game.

~Jonathan Lampman, Concord California

Old-Timers Days

As a young boy in 1957, I attended Old Timer's Day at Yankee Stadium. I watched in awe as Mel Allen announced Ty Cobb, Tris Speaker, Smokey Joe Wood, Rogers Hornsby, and Bill Terry. The last to be announced was Joe DiMaggio. The widows of Babe Ruth and Lou Gehrig were there as well. The Yankees were playing the Red Sox that day, so the 1946 Sox were there, along with Dom DiMaggio and Bobby Doerr. Jim Bagby had been one of the pitchers who'd ended Joe D's 56 game hitting streak. On this day, he pitched to Joe and walked him. The day was a great experience.
~Warren Woerner, Bellevue, Nebraska

Some 55 years have passed since I attended the 1961 Old Timer's Day game at Yankee Stadium, and my memory is a little hazy. It was retired Yankees vs. retired Dodgers, and as a former Brooklyn Dodgers fan waiting in limbo until the Mets arrived in 1962, I felt like an enemy in the ballpark. Seeing Joe DiMaggio for the first time was awesome and seeing visitors like Jackie Robinson and Pee Wee Reese for the last time was fantastic. The greatest crowd reception was for Mrs. Babe Ruth, and Lou Gehrig's wife got a great reception, as well. Afterward, the Yankees played the Orioles, but I have no idea who won that game.
~Stu Sachs, The Villages, Florida

The game indelibly etched in my memory is the 1978 Old Timer's Day at Yankee Stadium. On the way there, my dad and I were discussing Billy Martin, who had just been fired/resigned/whatever you want to call it. I thought he would make an appearance, but Dad said, "No way, he was just fired." Phil Rizzuto and Yogi were introduced, and later Ford, Maris, Mantle, and DiMaggio—who always insisted on being introduced last. Eleanor Gehrig was announced, as well. But in the middle of all this, legendary stadium announcer Bob Sheppard called out that Billy would be returning to manage in 1980, "Hopefully for years to come." The crowd went crazy, and I told my incredulous father, "I told you he'd be here!" I remember nothing about the game other than that the Yankees played the

Twins. By 1980, of course, Billy had already returned and been fired a second time.

~Greg Chernack, Chevy Chase, Maryland

I grew up an Astros fan watching baseball in the Astrodome. In 1986 while I was in high school, I went to many games with my friends. In late September, the Astros magic number was One, and Mike Scott was on the hill for a Thursday afternoon game against the Giants. At lunch, my friends and I decided to skip the rest of the school day and go to the game. We were richly rewarded, as the Astros clinched the division on the strength of a Mike Scott no-hitter! It was an incredible experience, seeing both a clinching win and a no-hitter at one time.

I don't exactly remember how I explained my attendance at the game to my parents.

~Chris Buchko, Chicago, Illinois

I grew up in a small town, and my dad's filling station was a meeting place. One day in the early 1970s, one of my buddies came by, and I asked him if he wanted to go to the ballgame on Saturday to see Gaylord Perry, one of the top hurlers of the time, pitch for the Indians against the Twins. He declined and, disappointed, I didn't go. However, I later had satisfying Perry experiences.

In 1977, on my annual visit to my cousin in Boston, we went to a few Red Sox games, sitting behind right field. The beauty of Fenway is that fans are close to the players even sitting in the outfield seats. I was in awe. The Sox were playing the Rangers in a twin bill. Perry pitched for the Rangers in the first game, going five innings. Unfortunately, after a rain delay he didn't return. In 1978 when my wife, Sandy, and I married, I planned our honeymoon to Southern California knowing the Padres would be in town. My aunt lived in Lakeside, California, and on a Friday night in San Diego, Sandy, my aunt, and I attended a Padres game against the Astros. J. R. Richard was the starting pitcher for Houston and struck out 12. Mickey Lolich pitched in relief for San Diego. But the biggest highlight of the game? It was Gaylord Perry Night! The Padres had acquired him in the off-season and this was his night. I got to see Perry again. Yeah, baby, Gaylord and me. And I did not see a spitball.

~John Lindberg, Grantsburg, Wisconsin

When I was six years old, my very wealthy buddy and his family, who had access to a club suite at Shea Stadium, took me and some friends to a Mets game. For some reason, John Franco was with us in the box for a few innings. I recall being in absolute awe when he walked in and sat with us. He was a real, live baseball player with an aura around him! I think we were all nervous to speak to him, but he was very friendly and funny. I vividly remember him telling us how hitters were trained to foul off pitches up to the suites where we sat. Of course we all bought it, six-year-olds that we were.

~Avi Rodin, London, England

On July 22, 2009, I was at Dodger Stadium for Manny Ramirez Bobblehead Day, part of a loud, sold-out crowd. Manny was not in the starting lineup, I think due to a hand injury, but in the 6th inning he came in to pinch-hit with the bases loaded. On the first pitch, he launched a grand slam. Not only was this a huge home run, he hit it into "Mannywood" – a specially designated section down the left field line. The crowd was delirious, bobbleheads shaking everywhere, people high-fiving, my buddy and I exclaiming, "I can't believe it, I can't believe it!" This blast became the difference in a 6-2 Dodgers victory.

This is just one example of how wondrous baseball can be. Here was a player with many faults, all well documented, producing a moment in time that we all laughed about and enjoyed to the fullest. This was prime Manny being Manny.

~Paul Giboney, Los Angeles, California

Growing up in Raleigh, North Carolina, the closest Major League Baseball team was the Baltimore Orioles, and few people followed the sport closely. However, my dad, Donald, loved baseball and played throughout college on the North Carolina State team. He had a great sense of humor but was pretty quiet. My mother, Laurie, on the other hand, was very out-going and would talk to anyone anywhere. So, it didn't surprise Dad when, picking up Mom at the airport upon her return from New York City to see her cousin sometime in the mid-1970s, she arrived at the car and told Dad she had met a nice man at baggage claim, struck up a conversation, and of-fered him a ride to his hotel. Dad hopped out to help put all the suitcases in the trunk, the gentleman climbed in the back of the VW Beetle, and Mom got in the front seat. Before they drove away, Dad looked in the rearview mirror and introduced himself as Don Stewart. "The guy" reached over the seat to shake hands and said, "Hi, I'm Mickey Mantle," to which Dad simply replied, "I knew you looked familiar!" They drove him to his hotel and invited him to come over that evening for a drink. They never heard from him, but they had that fond memory, nevertheless.

~Blount Stewart, Washington, District of Columbia

SINGLES

Liners to left, bloops to right, grounders up the middle. All are base hits, solid singles, as are these stories.

I got a call from a good friend saying he had two tickets to Game 5 of the 2010 World Series. At that point, my childhood and lifelong team, the San Francisco Giants, were leading three games to one, and they were trying to close it out in Texas. My buddy asked if I wanted to join him for the game at no charge. My dilemma was that I was on a nationwide tour with my band, Rebelution, but here was the chance to see my beloved Giants finally win a World Series! I played a show on Halloween night in Norfolk, Virginia, then headed straight to the airport and flew to Dallas. When we landed, I went directly to the stadium and watched the Giants, behind a masterful performance by Tim Lincecum, win the championship. We partied for a few hours, and then I went to the airport and flew back to resume the tour in New Haven, Connecticut. Greatest tour disruption of all time!

~Eric Rachmany, Santa Barbara, California

I have known Eric since he and Rachel went to kindergarten together. He is the guitarist, singer, and songwriter for the great California reggae band, Rebelution, a terrific young man and performer. Check out his music!

I grew up in western Minnesota in the 1970s, listening to the Twins on WCCO radio and amassing a large baseball card collection. The Twins weren't very good in those days, but we had heroes like Killebrew and Oliva, Carew and Blyleven, Jerry Koosman and Bombo Rivera. The Twins were rarely on TV, so my images of the players were based on my cards or fleeting glimpses on This Week in Baseball. On a Cub Scout trip in 1976, I saw a Twins game against the Yankees. Our seats were in the "Knothole Gang" section—code for the worst seats in the outfield, 500 feet from home plate—at old Met Stadium. But it was great. We spent the afternoon watching Oscar Gamble and his hair patrol the outfield. Gamble had the best hair and the best cards in the mid-'70s. My buddies and I felt it was an honor and privilege to heckle and cheer Gamble all game long.

Since then, I saw Cal Ripken approach and pass Lou Gehrig's Iron Man streak, and Eddie Murray hit the top of the Humphrey Dome in an All-Star Game home run derby. I attended the first home game of the Washington Nationals. All were fantastic memories, but none beat seeing Oscar Gamble's hair at a real, live game!

~Ross Peterson, Ellicott City, Maryland

On September 25, 2013, I attended the game at which Todd Helton took the field at Coors Field for the last time. Everything about that game was amazing. It was Todd Helton Bobblehead Night. The team presented him with a horse as a retirement gift. His daughter, Tierney, threw the pre-game first pitch to him, and then his daughters literally stole first base—much to his surprise—between innings. Of course, he delivered a heartfelt salute to the fans. It was such a joy to watch him play for one team his whole career while giving everything he had to us fans. On a night that was about appreciating him for all he brought to Denver, to see him turn around and thank Denver was remarkable. And, although the Rockies did not win the game, Helton did hit a farewell home run in his first at-bat.

~Stephanie Olesen, Littleton, Colorado

I lived exactly one mile from Ebbets Field from 1952 until the Dodgers left Brooklyn, but for some reason, in 1950 when I was 10, I'd become a

Giants, not a Dodgers fan. Still, I saw many games at Ebbets Field because I could walk to the ballpark and get into the bleachers for 60 cents, or the grandstand for $1.25. Elsie Milk Products sometimes ran promotions that could get you in even more cheaply. On Saturday May 12, 1956, after my Kiwanis League baseball game at the Parade Grounds, I decided to go see my Giants play the Dodgers. Carl Erskine pitched a no-hitter, and Jackie Robinson made a great play at third base to save it. Even though my Giants were on the losing end, I was thrilled. It was rare and lucky to be at such an iconic game.

I walked home all excited, anxious to tell my family about the great game. As I began my story, my 10-year-old sister, Sheila, piped in with, "I was at the game, too!" Her friend's dad had taken Sheila and her friend. I asked how she liked the game, since she knew nothing about baseball and had little interest in it. Sheila was very blasé when she told us everyone was excited because, "One team got no something." She wasn't sure exactly what that something was.

Naturally, I was apoplexed. My little sister, who didn't care for baseball, went to one ball game her entire life (to that point) and it was a no-hitter. I am still apoplexed 65 years later.

Footnote: I went to nine games at the Polo Grounds in 1957 on seven different days, two of them doubleheaders, including the last game the Giants played there. They lost every game.

~Bob Jacobs, Renton Washington, author of *Stuck in the Dark*

The first major league game I remember attending was on July 18, 1970, at Memorial Stadium in Baltimore. My aunt's family lived there, and almost every summer we visited them. I am sure I'd gone to games before this one but can't recall them. This was a typical Baltimore summer day, sunny, hot, and humid. I remember looking at the field and thinking, "That is the greenest grass I have ever seen!" The colors of the field, the players' uniforms, and the people in the stands were so vivid. My dad bought me an Orioles batting helmet, and even though you could have probably fried an egg on it, there was no way I was going to take it off!

My beloved Orioles were in first place, with future Hall of Famers Brooks and Frank Robinson, and others who went on to achieve lesser fame. The powerful lineup included names such as Boog Powell, Davey Johnson, Paul Blair, and Mark Belanger. My favorite player was pitcher Jim Palmer, but on this day, Dave McNally took the mound against Jim Perry of the division-leading Minnesota Twins.

The memory of the game that most sticks out in my mind involved not my O's, but Harmon Killebrew and Tony Oliva of the Twins. I remember Oliva hitting a line drive home run to center and wondering to myself how anyone could hit a baseball that far with so little effort. He was so graceful and seemed to float around the bases, as well as playing smoothly in right field. Killebrew was another story. I had never seen someone with forearms that looked so much like Popeye the Sailor's, a short, compact man, powerfully put together. His line drive home run to left off of McNally, his 475th career homer, essentially won the game for the Twins.

At the time I didn't realize that I had witnessed a semi-milestone for a future Hall of Famer. Looking back, I'm grateful that I witnessed this bit of baseball history for Killer, who went on to hit over 500 career homers.

~Dennis Vaught, Abingdon, Virginia

When I met Eric Gray, I told him about meeting Rafael Palmeiro and what a great experience that was. That would have been a nice story to tell, but I started thinking about another experience I had that was totally different than joy. It was April 2, 1996, Opening Day for the Cincinnati Reds at Riverfront Stadium against the Montréal Expos. During the 1st inning, I watched John McSherry, crew chief and home plate umpire, die of a massive heart attack. He was taken to a nearby hospital but passed away within an hour. It was a day I will never forget. He was a great man and he died doing what he loved, umpiring the great game of baseball. I know this isn't a happy story. I could have written about Rafael, but I suspect there are many such joyful stories. This one is more poignant and unique, and reflective of life and, sadly, death.

~Jayne Ledbetter, Camden, Ohio

San Francisco is a great baseball town, home to many well-known baseball personalities over the years. One of those hometown boys was my second cousin, Francis Joseph "Lefty" O'Doul. Cousin Frank played in the majors and both played and managed in the Pacific Coast League before the Dodgers and Giants came west. His major league career was good but not great. He helped bring professional baseball to Japan. He was better known in San Francisco as a native son and man about town.

In 1958, Lefty opened Lefty O'Doul's Restaurant and Cocktail Lounge on Geary Street. Over the years, I had the occasional opportunity to visit Frank. The place became famous, *the* place to go for baseball fans from all over the world. In 1998, Jim Bovis, Lefty's longtime friend, was able to purchase the restaurant and keep the historic watering hole afloat. If not for Jim, and later his son, Nick, Lefty's would not have continued. I became good friends with Jim and Nick.

I retired in 2007 and vowed to attend as many Giants games as possible. My granddaughter, Caitlin, once pointed to Oracle Park and said, "That's where Papa goes to church on Sundays." Needless to say, O'Doul's became the place for me to be before and after ballgames. This was great. I could meet, talk ball, and visit with folks from everywhere. It was wonderful to meet Japanese baseball fans who remembered Frank as the Father of Baseball in Japan. Tourists from Europe and Down Under would ask, "How long is a game?" I felt lucky to be able to talk with the media, ballplayers staying at the nearby St. Francis Hotel, and even umpires. I came to think it was my place to act as a PR guy for Lefty's.

You never know who might drop in for a meal or a beer. One day while I was sitting at the bar sipping a cold one, an older gentleman came in and asked if the bar stool on my left, with legs made of baseball bats, was empty. My response was, "Join me!" Soon the conversation turned to baseball. I said I had played as a kid, and he said that he had "played a little ball, too." I instantly knew who he was. "Sh#t!" I said, "you're in the Hall of Fame!" He was none other than the great Bob Feller. You never know who you might meet at Lefty O'Doul's!

I paid for his drink.

~Tom O'Doul, Rohnert Park, California

During the 1986 World Series when my beloved Red Sox were playing the Mets, I was a working singer and guitarist. Unfortunately, I had a gig in a local Boston restaurant the night of one of the games. I wanted so badly to stay at home and watch the game, but the rent was due and I couldn't afford to cancel. As fate would have it, the gig started right at game time. Just before showtime I quietly set up my PA gear and tuned up. The restaurant was full of noisy, happy customers, all waiting to watch the game, so no one noticed me and my pre-gig routine. The ten TVs around the room were all tuned to the World Series. Right at game and gig time I stepped up to the microphone and did a quick, "Testing, one two three." The entire restaurant went suddenly deathly quiet. A hundred faces turned and stared at me as if I were some alien monster who had come from outer space to interrupt their game. I had never seen such hatred in my life! The club manager saw what was happening and came rushing up to the stage. He knew that if I started to play, the crowd would kill me. He told me that he'd still pay me but that it would be in my best interest to pack up and go home. To this day, I credit that man with saving my life. The irony here is that if I had been in that crowd, I would have wanted to kill the singer myself. Hey! It's the World Series! Go Red Sox! Get off the stage!!! Boooooo!!!

~Curt Bessette, Lyman, Maine

My love for baseball goes a long way back. Although my mom grew up in Chicago with a father who was an avid Cubs fan, she somehow became loyal to the White Sox. My father was not into sports, so Mom had to share her love of the game with me and my younger sister, Kelly. We'd get so excited every year when Opening Day came around because Mom took us out of school to attend the home opener. Baseball started to mean more to me than just a day off school, but Kelly was not as focused on the game as I was. Mom wanted baseball to be a fun experience, so she made a game out of it, asking us to guess what each batter would do when they came up to bat. I remember one game when the Sox faced the Royals. Despite my mom's urging for me to be a Sox fan, when a Royals player came up I boldly said, "He is going to hit a home run." The batter soon had two strikes on him, yet I was sure he would do what I'd predicted. Lo and behold, he cracked one out of the park! Being a little kid, I instantly thought he'd hit that home run for me. From then on, I was no longer a Sox fan, but turned my loyalty to the Royals and Mr. George Brett!

Later, I took my love for baseball all the way to becoming the first girl player ever to play in our town's Little League. I wasn't good, and the boys made fun of me, but I stuck it out and managed to get one hit in my baseball career.

Since the early 70s I have been all about baseball, George Brett and the Royals.

~Carrie Walz, Mokena, Illinois

What a great day this'll be! Dad's taking me to Yankee Stadium! The Old Man and I walk over to the IRT and get on the Jerome Ave. train up to 161st Street. He plans to drop six bits each for bleacher seats to see the Yankees beat—sorry, play the Orioles. I'm seven or eight years old.

Walking near the outfield entrance, a voice came at me from a big black car. "Hey buddy, come over here." My old man ignored it and we kept walking. "Sir, you with the little boy, could we speak to you?" That approach sounded better. Dad turned us toward the voice, extending his hand toward me with fingers slightly spread and said, "Wait here." Then he went to talk to the men in the car. "You takin' the kid to the game?"

"Yeah, why?"

"Here's a couple of tickets."

"How much?"

"Free, here, take 'em, we can't use 'em today."

"Hey, thanks a lot!"

Dad turned back to me and said, "If these are legit, we're in for a treat." They were, and we were. They were for the lower deck, where I'd never sat before, the seats owned by the Perry Pink Company. Second row. That's right, one seat in front of us, and then the field! We sat behind third base next to the Baltimore dugout, with a clear view into the Yanks' dugout. I saw a lot of third baseman Clete Boyer. I was so floored and enthralled that I didn't care that the Yankees ended up losing.

Many details have been lost over time, but not the excitement of being so close. Hoyt Wilhelm pitched for the O's, with his knuckleball and his oversized catcher's mitt. Ryne Duren with his thick sunglasses relieved for the Yankees. He threw one pitch up onto the screen.

At the end, we joined the rest of the lower deck in going out onto the field, today a long lost tradition. I recall walking out to the outfield on the way to the train and wandering among the monuments in deep left-center field, right on the field of play. What a great day that was!

~Michael Bobrik, Berryville, Virginia

I was visiting Washington State in 1987 and met up with my friend, Ross, to watch the Bellingham Mariners, a Seattle farm team, hoping to see 17-year-old Ken Griffey, Jr. play. Alas, he was injured. We also missed him the following year when he was in the California League due to injury. However, I had one other chance to go see him in Bellingham, and I did.

I knew he was unlikely to hit a homer that night because there was a 40-knot gale blowing in from the northwest, in from right field, pushing the ball farther fair, but also back. If someone were to hit one out to right, it had to be a low, screaming line drive. Griffey was 17 years old, 6'2" and 165 lbs. Or so they claimed. Maybe in wet clothing…he looked so thin! With his incredibly graceful speed in the outfield, some thought he was lazy because he didn't look like he was running hard…although he always seemed to get to every ball. I think it was his third at-bat on that chilly night. A small crowd of a few hundred at the beginning of the game had dwindled down to 80 or 90. Griffey Jr. showed off his gorgeous stroke, and the ball soared high to right field, never bending its peak as it cleared the fence by a good 40 feet and coming down at least another 75 feet away. That hit is locked in my memory bank forever.

I told my best friend from law school, Steve, that Griffey would be the Mariner's starting center fielder by 1989. Steve said he wouldn't be because they were bringing him along slowly. My response was, "That *is* slowly." Although he had a number of injuries along the way, I was right.

~Mel Emerich, Santa Cruz, California

Around 2002—sometime in those fabled Moneyball years—while driving past the Oakland Coliseum on a Saturday afternoon, I spied a sign promoting that night's game and promising $2 tickets with a fireworks show. With two passionate little baseball fans at home—Danny, ten, and Ben, eight—I knew a great opportunity when I saw one. I called my friend, Mary—a St. Louis native and Cardinals fan, but by then an Oakland resident and adoptive A's fan—and invited her to join us with her son, Nathan, who was nine.

The downside to the $2 tickets was that they were way up on Mt. Davis, the seating area former Oakland Raiders owner Al Davis built for overflow seating at Raiders games. The A's rarely drew enough fans to use Mt. Davis, nicknamed for its nosebleed-inducing altitude above sea level, but tonight, the fans streamed up for cheap family fun.

The game had plenty of action to keep the boys interested between hot dogs and the usual fratricidal conflicts. In the bottom of the 8th, the A's were trailing but threatening with the bases loaded. I wish I could tell you that it was Miguel Tejada who stepped to the plate, or Eric Chavez, or Scott Hatteberg, but I honestly can't remember who it was. I just recall the batter in green and gold promptly swatting a grand slam, much to the delight of our little fans. The next hitter, whose name also escapes me, put icing on the cake by going back-to-back with another home run. A shutout 9th followed, and the A's won the game.

We now revealed to the boys that there would be a fireworks show. They were wide-eyed as the ushers allowed us onto the field. We lay down on our backs on the grass and watched the show, Mary and I both feeling about nine years old, as well. As we exited the stadium, an usher bid us good night. I replied, "I think I got my two bucks' worth." Indeed, I had.

~Brian Brosnahan, San Francisco, California

Growing up, I attended Braves games with my family from 1966 to 1971 at Atlanta Fulton County Stadium. My most memorable experience, sadly, is a negative one, although it should not have been. In '67 we went to a Bat Day promotion. I was a huge baseball nut, excited about the day, while my sisters just enjoyed the atmosphere and watching the good-looking players. We all received bats on the way in, probably Little

League-sized, before they stopped giving those away for safety purposes. My youngest sister got a Henry Aaron bat and my other sister got Joe Torre. I had hoped for one of those, or perhaps Rico Carty or Felipe Alou. Instead, I got the un-famous Clete Boyer, who was in his first year with the Braves replacing the great Eddie Matthews. He had a decent enough season, with 26 HR and 96 RBI, but at the time, early in the season, I was not happy with getting the bat of a "lesser" player. I tried to trade the bat with both of my sisters to no avail, and I recall sulking for most of the game. And yes, I am still bitter! Of course, my sisters disposed of those bats at one time or another in the ensuing years, but I still have my Clete Boyer bat in our garage. I use it as a sightline when parking our car.

~Clint Bastin, Bothell, Washington

Before you get rid of that disappointing bat, let me know. Clete was one of my favorite Yankees growing up!

On September 20, 2006, at Fenway Park, David "Big Papi" Ortiz, a Black man, hit two home runs and broke the Red Sox record of 50 home runs in a single season set by Jimmy Foxx in 1938. I have a complicated relationship with the Sox. They were the last team to integrate, and the owner, Tom Yawkey, was a well-known and notorious racist. I grew up loving the game, though, and when the Sox finally integrated in 1961, signing Pumpsie Green, I finally gave them my allegiance.

On that warm September night, my great friend, Rick Swig, the most passionate and intelligent baseball fan alive, was in town. Rick is a San Francisco Giants fan. When I lived there, he took me to many games. When Rick and baseball got together, something otherworldly happened. True to form, he brought his magic with him that night in 2006. He arranged an evening that is every fan's dream. We walked on the field while the team practiced, he spoke with manager Terry Francona, and we laughed when I got tears in my eyes looking at the 2004 World Series trophy. We sat in a private box. When Big Papi hit his first home run my jaw dropped.

I looked over at Rick, who was wearing a serene smile as if he'd known all along this would be an historic night.

As for me, I'm just human. I stood next to my dear friend, watched a Black Red Sox player break a home run record during a home game at Fenway, and thought smugly of Tom Yawkey spinning in his grave.

~Beverly Mire, Cambridge, Massachusetts

I have been one of the guys in the kayaks in McCovey Cove at the Giants' ballpark since 2007, for 30 to 40 games a year, waiting to retrieve balls hit into the bay. Catching these balls is, like a foul ball inside the park, a competitive sport. Positioning yourself where you think batters may hit balls, listening to the radio to hear if a ball is likely to be a splash home run or a foul hit into the cove, being rammed by other kayakers trying to get to balls before you do, broken ribs, competing with drunk girls jumping into the bay to snag a ball, all of this makes it a nightly challenge. There is an adrenalin rush when you hear the announcers call a possible splash hit, and a sense of vertigo watching the white ball descend from a blue or sometimes foggy grey sky. The ball goes where it goes, and all hell breaks loose with people paddling and swimming toward it. One simple rule in ball retrieval from the Bay: There are no rules.

I have caught foul balls, batting practice balls, and home runs, but one thing that really stands out is the friendships I have made. There is a friendly, competitive camaraderie with the other guys who hang out there, but there are also…seagulls. I know this may sound crazy, but each season there are a few birds who just…know me. They know my yellow kayak, and as soon as I row under the Lefty O'Doul Bridge into the cove, they land on my boat. I feed them wheat bread and recognize their colors and beaks. Even if there are a hundred kayakers on any one day, the same few seagulls will stay with me all season. They are teenagers, and by the next season they have grown up and left, or don't remember me. But there will always be a new group of gulls each spring as the baseball season starts.

~Greg Keeny, Montara, California

I joined a coed softball team after much insisting from my co-worker, Eric Gray. I played various positions, but primarily catcher, a position at which I was not very good. Coach Eric told me not to worry; if I preferred, the pitcher would cover home plate on close plays. We made the playoffs that year, a big deal. Amazingly, we got to the championship round, and our opponents were a bunch of young people out for blood. A young man blasted the ball to the outfield, and after some Three Stooges-like throws by our team, headed for home. Our pitcher, Rich, ran to the plate waiting for the play. The runner slid into the plate, colliding with me and taking me over his shoulder, my mask flying off. I hit the ground. Hard. And I was done playing baseball. I was in my forties, give me a break. Needless to say, we lost that game and the division title.

~Lise Bolden, Atlanta, Georgia

In 2011, the Phillies were on the way to their fifth straight National League East pennant with a 102-win season. With the hitting core of Rollins, Utley, Pence, and Howard, and a rotation including Hamels, Lee, Oswalt, and Halladay, they were a powerhouse team that captured the heart of the city. One Friday afternoon I was hanging out playing video games with a friend, and on my way home I got a text, but I couldn't tell who it was from. The texter said he had free seats behind the Phillies' dugout and a parking pass. If I wanted to go, I should meet him at a specific bar. My interest in baseball had waned over the years, but this sounded like a good deal for my first game of the year.

I arrived at the bar to find the texter was my college friend, Bryan Van Lenten, with whom I had lost touch. He told me he'd been given tickets but couldn't find a girl to go with him, so, "You're it." We got pretty bombed drinking scotch, too drunk to drive, so we took the subway. The train was packed with people pumped for the game and also a nearby concert. It was a perfect summer Friday night. When we arrived, we gave away our parking pass, figuring we would give in return for what we were getting. We got to our seats in the 2nd inning, and they were as I'd been told, right behind the dugout. We were disappointed that with the team I described above, we were seeing Vance Worley pitch...but again, the tickets had been free. The man who'd given Brian the tickets was there with his girlfriend. At one point he mentioned he had been to hundreds of games but had never caught a ball.

During the game we chatted with Howard and Utley. As Raul Ibanez came running toward the dugout, I stood up, beer in my left hand, outstretched right hand, and he tossed a ball...which fell right into my hand. Remembering the earlier conversation, I offered our host the ball, but he told me to give it to the kids in front of him. I gave it to one, and his father asked if I wanted anything for it. I said no and told him to read to his son that summer. Worley threw a no-hitter for seven innings or so, and the game was decided in the bottom of the 9th on a walk-off hit by Ben Francisco. The stadium's Liberty Bell lit up, moving back and forth, fireworks went off, and 45,000-plus fans went crazy.

On the subway back to Brian's place, a nice older woman who'd been to the game sat next to me. She asked if I wanted her Phillies' hat, and I politely declined. She asked the same question about a T-shirt, and I gave the same reply. She then asked me if I wanted her gift bag which contained a towel of the four pitching aces, a T-shirt, hat, and pin. She pointed to a man across the aisle and said he was the mayor of Clearwater, the Florida town where the Phillies have spring training. The Phillies had paid for their trip. She then pointed to a beautiful young woman and said she was her daughter. "Do you like her?" she asked me. "That's her fiancé, and I don't like him." I supposed it would be a little too much, and a *lot* old world, to have her give me her daughter as well as all the goodies in the bag.

It was a great night, one filled with giving and receiving, all things that just happened. There just seemed to be so much karma going around. It was the night I re-fell in love with baseball and the Phillies.

~Shivam Patel, Bensalem, Pennsylvania

DOUBLES

Twin-killing, double play, however you call it, here are pairs of stories that are back-to-back two-base hits.

Kids and baseball

When the Giants relocated to San Francisco in 1958, baseball cards became my passion. Hearing Russ Hodges and Lon Simmons announce the games on the radio turned strange faces on cards into people I felt like I knew—Cepeda, Davenport, Stu Miller. I now had a purpose for my card purchases: to collect the Giants. Of course, the most valued was Willie Mays. Summer was nearly over before I finally saw one…in the hands of my best friend, Jimmy Andrews. "I got it," Jimmy whispered one morning as we chose up sides for a game of Wiffle Ball. I looked at him, he nodded, and I knew exactly what he meant. I couldn't wait for the game to end so I could talk Jimmy into letting me see it, touch it, and maybe even swap for it. It was beautiful. Mays' smiling face on the Topps card looking up out of a bright blue background, his hat tilted back in that familiar way of his— and Russ Hodges would describe how it would fly off as Willie rounded first base, his eyes sparkling with pride. The same pride each of us young kids imagined we would feel if we could just play ball like Willie.

"What do you want for it?" I asked Jimmy. Swapping was a familiar ritual for us. "I ain't swapping Willie," he said, taking the usual position of the holder of a prized card, making me want it so badly I'd give up something more valuable. "I'll give you Mantle—the most valued card in the '50s—straight up." Jimmy had once offered *all* his Giants cards for Mickey alone. Now I offered Mickey for one, Willie—one hero for another. Jimmy wasn't biting, though, and he never did, instead taunting me with, "Ha ha, I got Willie and you don't!"

I had nothing of comparable value until the summer of 1960, when my father took me to one of the first games at the Giants' new stadium, Candlestick Park. It's a long story. Let's just say it was a typically windy Candlestick afternoon. Dad bought me a Giants' cap. Our seats were high up above first base, I vividly remember the stadium itself, the players in bright uniforms, the sound of ball meeting bat, the smell of hot dogs, and the roar of the crowd so large and noisy, filled with characters you wouldn't find in my little neighborhood. And more Black people than I'd ever seen, sipping from thermoses, waving pennants, arguing about the game, and shouting at the players like they knew them personally.

One woman I will never forget sat a couple rows in front of us, a Giants hat pinned to her massive head of hair and a pennant in her hand. She was wide, nearly taking up two narrow seats, and loud. When she yelled, people turned their heads twenty rows below us to see who had such a powerful voice. "Hit dat ball, Willie!" she cried out when Mays came up to the plate. Her voice, her dialect, her enthusiasm, and the familiar way she addressed the famous Mays constituted my introduction to what we now call African-American, but back then Black, culture. She was the largest, the loudest, and the darkest-skinned human being I'd ever seen. And how she loved her Willie Mays! "Hit dat thang, Willie!" I remember nothing about the game or Mays' performance, but I still hear her voice ringing out every time he came to the plate. I learned that day what the source of the word "fan" sounded like, and what it meant for San Franciscans to finally have a major league team of their own.

The next time I saw Jimmy, I had something he didn't—the memory of a game. He somehow sensed I was no longer interested in dealing for his Mays card. Something had changed. "Where'd you get that?" he asked when he noticed my new Giants cap.

"I seen Willie Mays."

"Really? You were there? Candlestick?"

"Yup."

"What was it like?"

I told him, about the stadium and uniforms, the hot dog and peanut vendors, the National Anthem and the seventh inning stretch, the wind and the cold, and even the final score—but I didn't utter a word about the Black woman who shouted at Willie Mays to "Hit dat ball." Not a word about her. She was my secret, my memory, better than any old baseball card.

~Bob Mayberry, Oceanside, California

I grew up in a small Midwestern town outside of Chicago during what many fans consider the golden age of baseball, listening to games on a transistor radio the size of an iPhone. That radio bought me a box seat to the games of my heroes. It was the time of Mantle and Maris. For a 10-year-old, summers seemed forever, but especially in 1961 when Mantle and Maris took aim at the legendary Babe Ruth's home run record. My friend, Billy, and I spent afternoons discussing who would break the record first, and then play Wiffle Ball for hours in my back yard. I would be Mantle because I could switch hit, and Billy would be Maris. The neighbor's bushes were the boundary marking a home run. The rules were simple—if it wasn't a home run, it was an out. Day after day, in rain or shine, we played out our personal duel. It was almost anti-climactic when Maris hit that 61st home run to beat both Ruth and Mantle. Billy had reached the mark a week before Maris. Paying rapt attention to the games as deep-voiced announcers painted visual descriptions of each hit or out with their vivid language, it was the beginning of a love affair with baseball that has lasted a lifetime.

~Doug Baltz, San Diego, California

The Wait is Over for Mom

In 1945, I went to my first Cubs game with my cousins who were a couple of years older than me. We sat in what is now the green section of the bleachers. This was the last year for decades that the Cubs would make it to the World Series. I don't know why my cousins weren't going, but I wasn't going to miss the Sunday World Series game. My mother would not let me set out for Wrigley as early as I wanted to—the night before—to get in line early. So I was on the Irving Park streetcar at 7:00 a.m. on Sunday morning with $3 in my pocket. This was the World Series, and bleacher seats were $1.20.

I was 10 years old. In those days, nobody thought anything of kids that age, even younger, riding public transportation alone. I got in line, and not being very big, I have no idea how many people cut in front of me. Before I got to the head of the line, the bleacher seats were sold out. There was standing room only for $3.60. I did not have that much with me, so I went back to the streetcar and went home.

I trudged up to our second floor apartment. When my mom saw how dejected I was at not getting into the game, she tried to make me feel better. She said, "Don't worry, you'll go next time." Little did she know it would be 71 years until I'd get the chance again, and that the tickets would be much more expensive. Of course, I had to go, to make an honest woman of my mother.

Mom passed away in August of 2003 at the age of 98, the year of Bartman, when the Cubs were five outs away from going to the Series. Before *that play*, I was thinking she was looking down and bringing the Cubs home that year. It was not meant to be, but like so many others who finally saw that elusive championship thirteen years later, and for countless others who did not live long enough to see the day, I cherished that day in 2016 when they finally won it all. I was there to see it, Mom's promise fulfilled at last.

~Allen Sered, Chicago, Illinois

Baseball has been treasured in my life. My dad often got complimentary tickets from work and took me to Red Sox games. I loved going to the games with my dad. We took the Boston and Maine train from Lowell to old North Station. Once in 1954 when I was 12, I got to go on the field and meet Ted Williams, Jimmy Piersall, Jackie Jensen, Sammy White, Billy Goodman, and a young Harry Agannis. Williams was gruff but shook my hand and mumbled hello. Jensen was a good guy, with red hair like mine, who didn't say much. We loved the antics of Piersall. Fans would yell out that he was crazy—no, not politically correct even back then.

I later moved to California and variously became A's and Giants fans, but never at the expense of my beloved Red Sox. My mom said she could die at 95 when the Sox finally won the World Series. She did.

~Donna MacLean, Sequim, Washington

Reliving the Dream

In January 2016, I went to San Francisco Giants Fantasy Camp at Scottsdale Stadium in Phoenix after not playing hardball since 1972. I trained for six weeks and went 6-8 in the tournament with three runs batted in. My favorite moment was hitting a stand-up double in the semi-finals. The Arizona weather was gorgeous, and it was great to meet and make friends with other Giants fans from around the country. Nine women were in camp, and they could all really play.

Our coaches were all former Giants players. I was on a team coached by Jeffrey "Hack-Man" Leonard and pitcher Scott Garrelts. Hack-man had not lost his intensity and will to win and was a very helpful batting coach. I pitched for the first time ever and had one good outing and two bad ones. I spent about a half hour talking with Mike McCormick, who pitched for the Giants at the Polo Grounds, Seals Stadium, and Candlestick. Mike, a Cy Young winner in the '60s, showed me his left arm, crooked from years of pitching. Vida Blue pitched batting practice to me one day. That was a thrill. I got great batting tips daily from Joel Youngblood, who started his sessions at 7:00 a.m. sharp. It was wonderful, after all these years, to swing a wood bat and connect with a baseball. What a sound!

~Jon Leonoudakis, Los Angeles, California

In March 1987, my in-laws gave me a trip to Randy Hundley's Cubs Fantasy Camp. His was the first of its kind, arising from two principle ingredients—the baffling loyalty of Cubs fans, and the genuine bond among his one-time teammates. The fact that these former players truly enjoyed reuniting in Phoenix each spring made the experience special for the "civilians" who participated. The 40-50 of us attendees were split into four teams, each managed by two ex-players from among Kenny Holtzman, Glenn Beckert, Gene Oliver, Jim Hickman, Fergie Jenkins, Ron Santo, Billy Williams, and Larry Bittner. Each morning, we'd meet in the locker room at the Cubs spring training facility and hear about whatever the players had in mind—rules of the locker room, that day's upcoming drills, how to treat the prior days' injuries, what to order for lunch, and especially our questions and their reminiscences of their experiences in baseball.

Holtzman recalled his rookie spring training, facing the Dodgers and pitching against Sandy Koufax. When Koufax got to the plate, he took two fastballs for strikes. The retelling was unclear whether his catcher pranked the rookie pitcher, or Holtzman himself decided to throw an 0-2 curveball. Either way, Koufax swung awkwardly, struck out to end the inning, then stood at the plate, his gaze following Holtzman all the way to the dugout. Shortly thereafter, Holtzman was in the batter's box facing Koufax who, by Holtzman's own report, threw three of the sharpest curveballs he'd ever seen, in the most rapid succession possible, each for a called strike. Koufax hadn't once looked for the catcher's sign or checked the defense. Through the entire at-bat, on-deck circle to dugout, Koufax never ceased staring at Holtzman.

~David Rosenbaum, Pleasant Hill, California

The 14th Inning Stretch

Everyone knows there is a seventh inning stretch at every ball game, but what many people *don't* realize is that if the game goes another seven, there is also a 14th inning stretch. The Chicago Cubs have a tradition, since Harry Caray passed away in 1998, of having a guest singer lead the crowd in the singing of "Take Me Out to the Ballgame" in the middle of the 7th. On August 1, 2003, former Cub Bill Madlock did the honors. After he sang he spent a half-inning in the television booth, and then went on his way. As luck would have it, the score was tied after 9, and the game went into extra innings. Arizona scored two in the top of the 11th, but the Cubs answered with two of their own. After 13 innings, the score was still tied. Apparently, someone in the Cubs' organization somehow discovered that Ernie Banks was in the neighborhood, so the team rushed him to the ballpark to lead the crowd in song for the 14th inning stretch. Ernie stuck his head out of the window, waved to the crowd, and said, "It's a beautiful day for baseball, so *Let's sing two!*" It must've brought the Cubs luck, because Sosa, Alou, and Ramirez all singled in the bottom of the inning to win the game 4-3.

~Bart Wilhelm, Traverse City, Michigan

It was a chilly evening for the inaugural home opener at Coors Field on April 26, 1995. Fans had to wait for this late start to the season due to the players' strike the previous year and the belated spring training it spawned. I attended this Rockies vs. Mets game with my good friend, Joe Lewis, as part of a capacity crowd for this historic occasion. The game was a seesaw affair, with plenty of offense—a harbinger of things to come at Coors Field during the pre-humidor era. By the bottom of the 9th, the score was tied 7-7, and it stayed that way until the 13th, when each team scored a run. The Mets went ahead in the top of the 14th, 9-8. In the middle of the inning, I turned to Joe and said, "Looks like we're stretching again." Sure enough, all the fans were on their feet for the second seventh inning stretch of the game, once again singing "Take Me Out to the Ballgame," and loudly cheering the home team to come back against the visitors. When Dante Bichette stepped up to the plate in the bottom of the 14th with two on and one out, he hammered a Mike Remlinger pitch into the right field stands for a three-run homer, sending the delirious Coors Field fans home, cold but happy.

~Sam DeSiato, Denver, Colorado

To be an extra

The year after the San Francisco Giants won their first World Series, I received an email about a contest to appear in a Giants commercial for the 2011 season. I had to describe why I was the Giants' biggest fan. I wrote that, even though I was originally from Rochester, Minnesota, Barry Bonds has always been my favorite player and I love the Giants. I explained that when I moved to California after high school, I was overwhelmed with excitement and joy being at my favorite team's home, AT&T Park. I submitted my essay and waited a few weeks for a response. Finally, an email arrived stating that I'd been chosen. I jumped up and down, freaking out at work, when I received the message. I obsessed about what to wear and what time to arrive. It was my first commercial, and I was nervous.

The next morning, I went to AT&T for the casting call and stood in line with about 500 other people. It was great talking to everyone about how the Giants had just won their first Series, and about all the players we had met. It was fun networking. I got to the gate, super nervous, not knowing what to expect. I had to sign a waiver and get my picture taken with a call number. At that point everyone went straight to the top of the bleachers, where the first video was shot. The director told everyone where to sit and what to say. People held pompoms, signs, and flyers. After the first shoot, some were told they weren't needed anymore, but I remained, and the second shoot was staged near the Giants' dugout. Buster Posey came on the field and everyone chanted, *"Buster Posey."* The third and last shoot was with Pablo Sandoval. I sat behind home plate, cheering for him. It was an exciting and awesome experience to cheer on my Giants!

~Ashley Garcia, Antioch, California

Baseball has always been a game of relationships for me, a game that has value primarily in the company I'm keeping. Growing up in Capitola, south of San Francisco, baseball was a family event. My mother, born in Edmonton and raised in Seattle, was a Yankees fan, a data geek before anybody talked sabermetrics. My brothers were fervent Giants fans. In the late fifties, we would drive to Candlestick Park for games, my brothers rooting for the Giants, and my mother and me usually rooting for the other team while she taught me the ins and outs of the game. In college, in the late sixties, baseball at Candlestick revolved around the man I loved along with his assorted, always astonishing, family members who were simultaneously abject fans and sophisticated critics. They sometimes seemed more concerned about beer than bats. I remember one "new Giants" and "old Cubs" game. Did Joe Pepitone really change wigs between innings?

I later returned to the Bay Area from Oregon, woefully under-committed to baseball, to work for a friend. Armando was somehow both an A's and Giants' fan with a wardrobe array to make each team proud. I loved being with him as Barry Bonds roused the crowds and learned to love the story of the A's. My interest in baseball diminished when he moved away.

When I received an email inviting me to be an extra in Moneyball, I didn't revel in the thought of sitting in the stadium with no game, but I thought Armando might, providing us more extraordinary moments of shared reverence. I contacted him and when, with great joy, he said yes, I signed us up. The instructions came, all was well, and then, days before the shoot, he had to cancel.

Should I go anyway? Why go? Why not? What the hell, I went, and in the throes of the Moneyball movie-making crowds, I regained my love of baseball. The 300 of us extras walked time and again across the bridge from the BART station, stood in long lines, sat where they told us, ate what they told us, drank what they gave us, held signs, yelled crazy stuff, all while real and pretend players mixed it up on the field. People all around me knew every game of that year's 20-game winning streak. We were in the audience for the 20th game, and when we got to be part of the Hatteberg home run, the crowd really did go wild.

Energy waxed and waned during the night. Movie-making can be a tedious process. Staff worked hard to generate crowd electricity. Jonah Hill came out to hurl hilarious insults. Real and fake old school food guys took care of us constantly—maybe to get on screen? Once begging us to get more excited when they needed a little more, they brought out Maddox Jolie-Pitt to have a conversation at home plate. I thought, "Well, that's a cheap trick," but it worked! There was just the right buzz in the crowd and then when they needed the really big roars, they brought out Brad Pitt. But it wasn't Pitt who gave me back baseball, it was the guys sitting around me, thrilled to be a part of the retelling, reciting the tales and the numbers of the A's, yesterday and today, who reeled me back in. And I will always be grateful to them. Baseball is still a game of relationships for me.

~Diane Walton, San Francisco, California

You Never Know Who You'll Meet

While visiting Cleveland for my work promoting college access for underserved youth, I was in line with my friend, Nick, to buy tickets for an Indians game at Progressive Field. The guy in front of us offered us two bleacher seats, and we jumped at the opportunity. In these seats, I was listening to legendary Indians drummer John Adams. We spoke with the father and son in front of us. After learning I was from Honolulu and had a young daughter, Jennifer, he gave me a red Cleveland shirt for her. Nick, a Cleveland native, noticed that then-General Manager Mark Shapiro had passed us and was sitting just a couple of rows back. I went back and introduced myself, again saying I was visiting from Honolulu. A really nice guy, he smiled and thanked me. The whole day was such a warm, wonderful experience. You never know who you will run into at a ball game!

~Carl Ackerman, Honolulu, Hawaii, author of *A Success Story in Public Education*

I was a Little Leaguer in Fresno from 1958 to 1960. My dad was a railroad engineer and we loved the San Francisco Giants. Fresno had the Little Giants. I will always remember my mom keeping score in her book as we listened to the big Giants play in San Francisco.

We also saw a few games in person each year. Dad was a railroad guy, so we'd ride the train to Oakland then take a bus to the City and Seals Stadium where the Giants played before they moved to Candlestick. One summer day we got to the stadium early, and it was all locked up. As we walked around looking at the posters near the ticket booth, a man came up to us and asked if we would like to go into the park. We said, "Sure, we'd love to!" and he replied, "Follow me." We walked over to the huge iron gate, and he pulled out a big key ring and proceeded to unlock the gate. We had no idea who this guy was, but as a kid it was *so cool that he let us in. We followed him and he opened a door with his name on it. He was none other than Horace Stoneham, owner of the San Francisco Giants! While we were there, he picked up his phone and said, "Have the two Willies sign a ball and bring it to me in my office." My parents got a signed ball by Willie Mays and Willie Kirkland!*

~Greg Grant, Fresno, California

A First Aid Visit

In September 2004, we got tickets for a Friday night Giants vs. Padres game, hoping it would be the one when Barry Bonds would hit his 700th home run. As it turned out, it was! We had terrific seats about twenty rows behind home plate. The Giants scored early to take a 3-0 lead, but Bonds failed to homer in the first inning. My wife, Priscilla, had a terrible headache, so she asked an usher where she could get some aspirin. The usher gave her some, and also suggested she go to the first aid station. After the first Bonds at-bat she left, and I reminded her to be sure to return by the time he got up again. The 2nd inning came and went, with Priscilla nowhere to be seen. Bonds got up in the 3rd, hit number 700, and all hell broke loose. Fireworks exploded and streamers came raining down around home plate. Some fans sitting near me asked me where my wife was, and I said I honestly didn't know. About half an inning later, Priscilla came back and told me she had to trek way out beyond left field to get to the first aid station. She had just gotten aspirin from the nurse when Bonds hit the home run. She and the nurse watched it on the television set in the first aid room. We had gotten get terrific seats to see this milestone home run, and my wife wound up watching it on television in left field! She made me swear that I would never tell anyone that she didn't actually see the home run in person...

~Howard Spinner, San Ramon, California

When I asked my younger daughter, Becky—who's now 30—what she wanted to do for her fifth birthday party, she said she wanted to go to a Giants game. I was thrilled to make that happen. Off went the family, including her older sister, Kelli—now 34—and my wife, Debi, to Candlestick Park. The game highlight was Robbie Thompson hitting two home runs and the Giants winning 3-2. That was very exciting, but during the game Kelli, then nine, decided to stick a sunflower seed up her nose. Every time she took a breath it went farther up. Debi took her to the medical tent, and the doctor told Kelli to blow out through her nose. Several adults were in the tent for various ailments, and they all started telling and demonstrating for her how to get this sunflower seed out. Debi said it was hilarious to watch all these people blowing out through their noses to help young Becky.

~Ernie Perez, Clovis, California

3,000

On July 15, 2005, my wife, Patty, and I were present to see Raphael Palmiro get his 3,000[th] hit when Palmeiro's Orioles visited Safeco Field to play the Mariners. He became only the fifth player in major league history to reach 3000 hits and 500 home runs for his career. Aside from the magnitude of this milestone event, I vividly recall the Seattle crowd's overwhelmingly positive response to a visiting player reaching this accomplishment. The Orioles beat up the Mariner's pretty good that night, but the crowd still gave Palmeiro a standing ovation.

~Fred Keene, Lynwood, Washington

Forty years ago this evening, I purchased a standing-room-only ticket at Fenway Park to witness Carl Yastrzemski's 3000th major league hit against the Sox's longtime rivals, the New York Yankees. Three remarkable events occurred in that game. First, while the Yankees' great pitcher, Jim "Catfish" Hunter, had not yet announced his retirement, the Fenway fans that evening, who, as John Sterling once said, have always "gotten it," gave him a standing ovation when he was removed from the game in the fourth inning. Hunter, who officially retired that November, later said that the unexpected gesture was one of his very favorite baseball moments.

Second, in the top of the 8th inning, Bucky Dent, yes, *that* Bucky Dent, fouled off a ball, which skied toward the seats in the grandstand section behind the Sox dugout. "Oh, my God!" I exclaimed, "it's coming right toward me!" I caught it with a one-handed grab, received tumultuous applause from the crowd and a thumbs-up from then-Red Sox TV analyst, Hawk Harrelson, who said on Channel 38, according to my friends, "That kid looks like he's a player!" On the next pitch, Dent grounded out.

A minute later, Yaz came up first in the bottom of the inning, for the fifth time, still needing a hit. On the first pitch, he singled to right, just out of the reach of Yankee second baseman Willie Randolph for his 3000th hit! As players on both teams circled him, I held the ball I had just caught tightly in my left hand. In the end, if Bucky Dent, *Bucky F. Dent!* hadn't fouled off that ball, the ball now in my possession would have been sent to Cooperstown.

I told Bucky the story twenty-four years later when we were filmed together for HBO's "The Curse of the Bambino." He laughed and said, "If I had fouled off that other ball at Fenway in the 1978 Playoff Game, I wouldn't be here with you being interviewed for a documentary on the Cursed' Red Sox!"

Yup.

~Shaun Kelly, Eastham, Massachusetts

Youthful Exploits

As with many others, my baseball activities began in early childhood, playing Little League ball in St. Petersburg in the early 1950s. I progressed to Boys League, designed for those who exceeded the Little League age limit of 12. After that, I pursued high school ball, where my skills were determined to be lacking, and I was cut as a sophomore trying to make the Northeast High School baseball team.

In the fall of 1960, I entered then-Florida Presbyterian College as a Founding Freshman. The total school enrollment was about 150 as we started college at the temporary campus by Bayboro Harbor where the St. Petersburg campus of the University of South Florida is currently located. That first year, intercollegiate sports were initiated with a basketball team that practiced on outdoor courts next to the runway of Albert Whitted Airport. But during my junior year, 1962-1963, with a student population approaching 400, it was determined we needed a baseball team. With my recollection that I had been unjustly cut in high school and figuring my skills had probably not deteriorated *tha*t much over the five years I had not held a baseball or swung a bat, I dug out the same glove and pair of cleats that I had put in the closet before and began my brief collegiate athletics career.

The team was hastily put together and a schedule with junior college teams was generated. Unfortunately, all early records have apparently been lost, but my recollection is that our first game was an away game against Daytona Beach Junior College. Several things about that game stick out in my memory, accurate or not. First, we lost 27-0. Second, I was the starting first baseman in that game. Third, one of my best friends on the team got beaned. To this day, he has ringing in his ears. Unfortunately, helmets were not part of the game at that time.

We completed our brief first season with a record of, I believe, O-7. I'm pretty sure we didn't win a single game. Almost half the season's games were played on a Saturday, and due to one Friday rainout, we once played a *tripleheader*. My one (un)forgettable moment was when I was at bat in what was probably the closest we ever came to winning a game. With the bases loaded, I was the feared batter, and our opponents called for a relief pitcher. I consulted with Billy Wireman, our coach who became the second president of the college, and he gave me good words of encouragement. I still recall the drama of the moment as I worked the count to 3-2. On the next and final pitch of the inning, I still hear the umpire saying to me, "Nothing wrong with that one, son," as he rang me up. On a personal note, I finished the season 0-fer however many times I got to bat, thus ending my brief collegiate baseball career.

~Wilmer LaBrant, St. Petersburg, Florida

Baseball dominated much of my childhood. I was a Yankees fan through and through. I loved to play baseball, but also considered myself a student of the sport. I understood strategy, the responsibilities of each player in every potential situation, and the many nuances of the game. I'd also acquired a detailed knowledge of baseball rules and protocol. I had my share of achievements on the field, but one of my most memorable moments came not with bat or glove, but from my knowledge of the game.

My youth baseball team made it to the first round of the playoffs, due mostly to our dominant pitching. Our ace was on the mound, and as always, I was playing first base. A pitcher's duel from the onset, we squeezed out runs with small-ball tactics and aggressive base running. A home game, we took the field in the top of the 9th leading 2-0, hoping to end it without incident.

Our pitcher's once-untouchable fastball was losing steam, but even at 90%, he was our best chance to close the game. It was a rocky inning. Two were retired but our opponents had managed to load the bases thanks to two hits and an umpire's questionable call. The much-fantasized two-out-bases-loaded-in-the-9th-inning scenario was about to play out. With high hopes and the game on the line, our ace delivered one of his patented fastballs to the next batter. Our hearts sank when he launched a tremendous shot beyond the reach of our center fielder. With no fence, the ball was free to roll until it lost its momentum. Our opponent's bench went wild, filling the air with frenzied yelps as their runners circled the bases.

A first baseman's responsibility dictated that I turn my head to watch the runner round the corner in the highly unlikely event that he'd miss the bag. In my baseball career, I could not recall a single instance when this had happened, yet I checked every time. But this time was different. Clearly, in his excitement the runner cut the corner early and missed the bag entirely as he made his turn and picked up steam on his way to second. My heart raced. After witnessing the misstep, I darted my glance to the field umpire for official corroboration. My observation meant nothing without the umpire as a witness. When I looked over, I saw the umpire's eyes transfixed on the base. He'd seen! He made it his job to confirm the touching of the bag, and I was certain, *certain*, that he'd seen what I had.

My emotions and adrenalin took over as I accosted the umpire and wailed, *"He missed the bag!"* No reaction. Instead of calling him out as expected, he walked away from me, offering not even the slightest acknowledgment. Incredulous, I continued with my tirade. "He missed the bag! I saw that you saw him miss the bag!" The silent treatment continued. I thought, "Why on earth doesn't he call him out?" The visiting team continued their hooting as each runner crossed the plate, completing the grand slam and a tremendous come-from-behind victory. Overcome with rage and injustice, I continued to scream bloody murder...until it finally occurred to me that was not how it's done. Of course! My screaming and flailing would never get the runner called out. The umpire was aware of the misstep, but powerless to help me. He couldn't call the runner out because the runner was not out! Missing a base does not constitute an out; something else needed to be done. The umpire knew this but could not tell me. He had no choice but to ignore my pleas and watch the rest of the play transpire. In a flash, my baseball-rule knowledge kicked in, and I changed my tactic immediately. I knew exactly what to do, having watched countless hours of baseball on television.

The ball was retrieved and tossed back to the pitcher who prepared to face the next batter. Resuming my frenzy, I screamed, "Don't pitch that ball!" My teammates were utterly confused, unaware of the drama about to unfold. Seeing my wide-eyed mania, our pitcher thought I must be onto something, and actually followed my next instructions. As I directed, he went into his stretch, stepped off the rubber, turned to first base, and threw the ball to me. My foot was on the bag, as I reached out my glove. As soon as I squeezed it tightly around the ball, I turned to look at the umpire, who was watching the events closely. He broke his silence with an enthusiastic, *"Ouuttt!"* accompanied by a hearty fist throw for emphasis. The runner was forced out at first since he'd never touched the base. And because that was the third out of the inning, none of the runs from the play had counted.

The celebration on the visitor's bench abruptly ceased, and they looked on in disbelief. "How could he be out?" they cried. My team was just as baffled. Silence and confusion permeated throughout. In that moment, only two people on the entire field understood what had happened—me and the field umpire.

I jumped up and down with my arms flapping and broke the silence, screaming at my teammates like a lunatic, "He missed the bag! He's out!" I wouldn't stop howling that phrase until I saw realization sink in on their faces. Slowly, the significance of the moment became plain to our opponents, as well. In an instant, a spectacular victory had been snatched from their clutches, replaced by an unfathomable defeat. My teammates rushed the pitcher's mound to begin our celebration. We congregated into an impromptu scrum, rejoicing like death-row prisoners with a last-minute reprieve. The several dozen home team spectators showed their delight by joining in with wild cheering.. The instant reversal of emotions on both teams was an extraordinary sight to behold. What would have been recorded as a game-winning grand-slam was ultimately nothing more than a routine 8-6-1-3 put-out. A likely-insurmountable deficit and defeat facing a tough pitcher had turned into a celebration.

I helped secure a victory that day, not by a hit or a catch, but because of passionate study of the game. Let's call it a walk-off technicality. Did I feel bad that I took away a moment of glory from the batter? Sure—but remember, it was a questionable call that had loaded the bases in the first place, and emotions were high on both sides. We did not win the championship, but we experienced an exhilarating win that day.

~Robert Mandelberg, Howell, New Jersey

TRIPLES

In my 40-plus-year softball career, I hit exactly one triple. I immediately ruined it by being greedy and trying to stretch it into the only home run I would ever hit. That marvelous tale is documented in the first book. Triples are, to me, such exciting plays because there needs to be an almost-perfect storm of placement, caroms, and speed. These triads of stories are all related in various ways, stand-up triples.

A Famous Call or Point

I sold programs at Wrigley Field in the 1930s. By the 2nd or 3rd inning, sales came to an end, and I often stayed to watch the rest of the game. Babe Ruth had two famous home run calls, and I was at one of them. It came in the 5th inning of Game 3 of the 1932 World Series. I watched Babe point to center field before he hit this famous home run. It seemed to me that he was calling his shot, indicating exactly where it would land. There was much controversy over whether Ruth was pointing to center or the Cubs dugout, as the Cubs players were riding him mercilessly. Did he call his shot out to center? Or was he pointing to the dugout, indicating he had one more strike to go? Was he annoyed with the Cubs, or just playing with them? There are various opinions and accounts. Newsreels of the event are not conclusive. Even Babe, himself, changed his story over time. Many sportswriters at the time felt Babe was pointing at the dugout, but the more celebrated version, and the one I, and most of the other fans, believed was that Babe was predicting the home run. It really doesn't matter either way. It was a famous and controversial home run, and I was there to see it.

~Harry Bernstein, as told to his son, Jerry, Chicago, Illinois

221

Jerry is my wife's nephew's wife's father, making him, I don't know, let's call it my cousin-in-law twice removed. Harry had told this story, perhaps several times, to Jerry. Because I have to toss in a Beatles reference somewhere, it is like Lucy in the Sky with Diamonds, where only John Lennon would know if it was about LSD or his son Julian's drawing of his friend. The uncertainty about this only serves to increase interest. But like the song, this home run is a classic.

Last Saturday, the morning of my 49th birthday, I woke up a little later than usual. The first thing that came to mind was that I would be turning 50 in a year. My next thought, as always, was of my three kids, P.J., Anna, and Alex. I lay in bed, and as each kid got up from their own bed, I could hear them come down the hallway. Anna and Alex came first. They jumped on the bed, greeted me with hugs and kisses, then were soon off to watch cartoons. P.J. stumbled into the bedroom a little later and plopped down on top of me. I flashed back to when he was a little kid and would put his ear to my chest and listen to my heart. We talked about his game coming up that morning, and what his team needed to do win. He then asked what I wanted for my birthday. I thought about it for a bit, then told P.J. the only thing I wanted was a home run—a Babe Ruthian order. He looked at me and said, "You got it."

We got up, had breakfast with the family, and headed to the baseball field.

It was the 3rd inning of the game, and the second time through the lineup. I was watching out in left field with other dads from both teams. P.J. had a 1-2 count. The pitcher went fastball, low and outside, P.J.'s favorite. The next instant, we heard the crack of the bat and saw the ball flying toward the right-center field wall, clearing it easily. As P.J. rounded second base, he yelled out, "Happy Birthday Dad, that was for you!" Wow! Best present I ever received. Now, if I were in position to catch the ball…

-John Moutzouridis, San Jose, California

My friend, Gary Tinneny, and I were groundskeepers at Veteran's Stadium in Philadelphia. I often stayed at his house after the game.

Gary's mom, Helen, lived across the street and we'd stop by her place before we went to work. Another frequent guest at Helen's house was Dick Allen, who knew her and would drop by on his way to the park. Helen always made meatloaf sandwiches for him. A very outgoing and outspoken person, on June 25, 1976, Helen finally said to him, "You know, Dick, I've been giving you meatloaf sandwiches for a few weeks now. Do you think you could hit a home run for me tonight?" Dick's reply was, "Okay, Mrs. T, let me see what I can do. I will try my hardest." In the 4th inning, Allen hit a solo home run against John Curtis. But he wasn't through. In the 8th, he hit a three-run blast off of Bill Greif, ensuring a win for pitcher Larry Christenson.

This story later surfaced in a newspaper column by Stan Hochman, but Dick never said a word to the media and wouldn't let us tell them, either. It was his little secret. When he hit the first one, after touching home, he looked back toward the Plexiglas window behind home plate and winked at Gary and me. After the second, he looked back and shrugged his shoulders as if to say, "Oh, well, she got a bonus home run." I know it bothered him how he was treated by the press. He often remarked how the media always reported when he was late, but not when he showed up at the park to take extra hitting practice or to help other players, especially Mike Schmidt. He didn't want the attention. That's the way Dick Allen was.

~Helen Tinneny and Mark Carfagno, Philadelphia, Pennsylvania

Check out Chuck Brodsky's song "Letters in the Dirt," the live version. It tells the whole story.

Memories of Dad

My earliest baseball memory is my dad taking me to see the Reds at Crosley Field. They used to sell the popcorn in a cardboard cup that, once the popcorn was eaten, could be folded into a megaphone. I remember cheering on the Reds, but I didn't know the players well since I was only three or four. The only one I remember was Pete Rose. Before the game, he brought out a box of signed baseballs and threw each of them into the stands. I wasn't lucky enough to get one, but even to this day I thought it was a wonderful idea. I don't remember anything about the game, but do recall leaving with Dad, holding his hand as tight as I could and being surrounded by a sea of legs.

~Steve Douglas, Louisville, Kentucky

I saw my first ball game when I was eight. Originally from Alabama, I was a Braves fan since they were the closest team. Of course, the all-time home run king, Henry Aaron, was the other reason. In the late '60s and early '70s, we lived in College Station, Texas, where Dad was doing research to earn his PhD at Texas A&M. We saw the Braves play the Astros in the Eighth Wonder of the World, the Astrodome. I was pulling for Aaron and the Braves while my dad, brother, and neighbor rooted for the hometown Astros. The Braves had been losing for the whole game until Mike Lum came to the plate and hit a three-run homer to put the Braves up 5-3, and they held the lead. It was sweet to be the youngest *and* the winner on our drive home!

I'll always remember how Dad took one step for every three of mine on the way to the game...

~Jonathan Green, Cullman, Alabama

I remember when my dad took the whole family to watch a Dodgers game in 1989. We sat so high up that I remember holding his hand really tight because I was afraid. It was the best game ever. Later that season, I watched my last game with Dad when we saw our Dodgers win the World. Series. My dad died a year later. Memories of my father, that is what the Dodgers and baseball mean to me.

~Michael Zambrano, Highland, California

A Brush with Future Greatness

I had been out of baseball for two years and just gotten back into the game. The summer league team I played for was the Columbus All-Stars, and Tim Hudson was our starting center fielder. He was 5'7" and 119 lbs, but he was fast, could hit, and had a cannon for an arm. One game, I'd hit a double and was on second when Tim came up. The pitcher was cursing at him, calling him overrated. Tim just smiled and got into the box. He fouled off about four pitches. With each one, the pitcher said, "I got you now, bleep." I was on the bag, and the second baseman, now-Colonel Herman Johnson, stood right next to me. I asked him why the pitcher was acting like that. He just shook his head. By now, Tim had fouled off six or seven pitches, and his smile had gone away. Tim hit the next inside fastball so hard no one moved, we just watched it go over the left field wall, some trees, a mom and pop store, a small parking lot, and hit the tin roof on a beauty shop. I'm not sure if it was 500 feet, but it was close. it was the longest-hit ball I've ever seen.

~Bob Johnson, Atlanta, Georgia

We were playing the Green Team, a very fine club. I was 10, and their pitcher that day was 12, a head taller than me, and a legend in the league. He had, after all, made the Little League Majors when he was 8, and hit 19 home runs in 19 games. I, maybe 4'6", and 60 pounds soaking wet, came to the plate knowing, of course, I could not hit him. I was scared to death. I could hear my dad yell, "Don't strike out with the bat on your shoulders!" and there weren't even any strikes yet. Until the first pitch, that is, which sounded like a strike—I'm pretty sure my eyes were closed. The second pitch came in, and I had decided to swing regardless of where it was. I likely started when the ball was still in the hand of the pitcher and I swung as hard as I could. I nicked the ball and it rolled over to the first base dugout. I was so proud that I'd made contact and, until I caught a perfect game thirty years later in a very serious hardball league, this was my most memorable athletic achievement—a pitiful little slow-rolling 45-foot foul ball off a young Mike Schmidt.

I came to know Mike reasonably well in high school and played one game with him three years later. He caught that game, but he was known mostly as a hitter. I can say that I saw him in the one and only game he played in the league. He hit home runs from both sides of the plate and bounced a double over the left field fence. To say at that age he was better than his entire age group is a large understatement. We loved to watch him play. He was special. But playing against him was not nearly as much fun as watching him play other teams.

~Abe Schear, Atlanta, Georgia

I was 13, in my first year on the 90-foot diamond after being on the team that won the Oakland-Fruitvale American Little League championship the year before. I was trying out for one of the better teams in the 13-15 age league. Normally an infielder, in this practice game I was in right field. I was one of those kids who read everything I could about playing the game, so I'd learned how to position myself for hitters. As it turned out, Michael "Tack" Wilson, who would go on to room with Kirby Puckett in the minors during their pro careers, was in center.

A 15-year-old Dave Stewart started the inning and immediately found himself with the bases loaded and a left-handed hitter up. So, as I had read, I positioned myself over toward the right field line, three steps back. I looked toward Wilson and he was moving me over one step toward him and one step in. On the very next pitch, the batter hit a typical screaming, twisting line drive that began slicing away from me. I ran two steps toward the line and back, the drive hit the top of my glove and rolled forever as the hitter rounded the bases with a grand slam off *my* glove.

The inning finally ended, and as I trotted toward the dugout I saw Stewart, a man in a boy's body at 15, waiting outside the dugout, arms folded, giving me a look I would later recognize as the famous Dave Stewart Death Stare. I avoided his stare and told our coach I was in position but that Tack had moved me. Coach said he'd seen that, but it did not keep Stewart from delivering what had to be one of his earliest ever death stares!"

~Victor J. Gonzales III, Oakland, California

Matt Cain Perfecto

In 53 years, I've attended 50 or so major league games, not a huge number. But as luck would have it, there I sat with my 10-year-old son, Lou, in ATT Park on June 13, 2012, as Matt Cain threw his perfect game against the Astros. With emotions totally handed over to the swell of anticipation, I remember not only being consumed by the rarity of Cain's accomplishment, but also the thought of joining a select group of lucky fans.

But this story is not over.

Just 15 months later, Lou and I sat in the very same seats, engrossed in the same consuming electricity of Yusmeiro Petit's run at perfection. While his was stopped short at 8⅔ innings, the emotional charge this time was perhaps even greater than the Cain experience because I couldn't get over what rare air I was about to attain, a second perfect game. I remember thinking I was about to join the tiniest group of fortunates. Vin Scully, Phil Rizzuto, and me. But then Eric Chavez stepped into the box, and I had to be satisfied with slightly thicker air.

~Peter Martineau, Hillsborough, California

In what was one of the luckiest moments in my life, I was able to attend Matt Cain's perfect game in 2012. More important, I went with my then-four-year-old son, Jack. There was a day game the following day and I had expected to get tickets for that game, but a work matter derailed that plan. Still wanting to go, my wife and I contemplated whether Jack could make it through a night game. Ultimately, we decided what the hey, let's try it.

I figured I would hang in there with him for the first four or five innings, make it over to the Coke bottle slide, and be outta there by the 7th. Instead, as the game went on, and as Jack kept asking to go to the slide, I kept explaining that something very special was happening and that we should stay in our seats—probably the best seats, by the way, I'd ever had in the stadium at 10 rows back of the first base bag.

In the 8th, Jack asked one last time to go to the slide. I bent over and explained that what was happening almost never happens—that it was history. He seemed to understand. By this time, everyone was standing, so I held him up for the rest of the game. He cheered as loudly as anyone with the last out. We still talk about this game all the time. It is something we will share forever.

~Richard McPalmer-, Novato, California

It seemed like baseball fate when I moved to San Francisco. I grew up in Richmond, Virginia, home of the Richmond Braves, Atlanta's farm team. The Braves at one point changed to the interesting, somewhat inexplicable name of the Flying Squirrels. When I moved to the Bay Area, imagine my surprise to find my boyhood team had become an affiliate of the Giants. That cemented my Giants fandom.

I can't claim I knew much about baseball at the time. One night, my buddies and I decided to go to a Wednesday game against the Astros. Our seats were down the third base line with a direct view to first base. We were having a good time, and around the 5th inning I decided to look at the scoreboard. It was interesting, so I said, "Wow, look at all the zeros for the Astros." My friends quickly told me to shut up. I did not understand. The people sitting on either side of us, and Jon Miller and Dave Fleming on my little radio, were all going on about the game. I didn't understand the concept of a "perfect game," and I certainly didn't know the unwritten rule of not talking about it!

In the 7th inning, Jose Altuve blasted a hit to left field that Gregor Blanco ran a million miles to track down on a body-parallel-to-the-ground catch. It was otherworldly. At that point, *it was on* in the stands. No one sat, everyone was cheering. Giants field reporter Amy G. came by with her camera crew, taking a shot of the crowd gone wild, and I was in it. I bought the DVD that shows me at the game. With two outs in the 9th, the 27th batter hit a ball that took a weird hop, forcing third baseman Joaqin Arias to stumble back and unleash a throw that, because of our sight line, we could actually see curve as it struggled to get to first.

We watched it fall into Brandon Belt's glove for the final out. The crowd erupted.

I was part of history, and I finally learned the meaning of a Perfect Game.

~Marcus Alphin, Sonoma, California

Youthful Naïvete

During the first year of new Tigers Stadium, I took my nephew to a game. He was seven, and interested in collecting autographs, although he clearly wasn't able to discern who to ask. He leaned over the left field rail at the field level as the grounds crew manicured the field and, one by one, three of them came over and signed his program. During the game, a hot dog vendor wandered too close and gave him an autograph. Later on, needing to use the rest room, he got the Chinese bathroom attendant to give his John Hancock in Chinese characters.

~Eric Schmidt, Bernardsville, New Jersey

I took my oldest son, Myles, to his first ball game at the old 'Stick, along with my wife, Mary. Myles had just turned four and was *very* excited to be going to a Giants game with his dad. It was a classic cold, windy, and foggy Croix De Candlestick night—a button given to fans who braved the elements and remained for extra-inning night games. We typically wore our ski gear, hats, and gloves on such nights. Mary had me try to smuggle in a six-pack, figuring that with a child, no one would suspect. Busted! Mary went into the outraged mom role. "I can't believe you would do that in front of a child. At least let me bring it back to the car." She then easily strolled in through another gate.

The stadium was empty as usual, less than 3,000 in attendance. Close by us were three UC Berkeley male students who appeared to have spent the better part of the day "getting ready" for the game. Obviously fortified by consumption of intoxicants, they stripped off their shirts revealing painted torsos, and proceeded with a form of ancient tribal dancing and chanting. Myles thought that was way cool, and proceeded to strip his shirt off, joining the young men in their pagan rituals. I tried my best to be a good father and get his clothes back on for fear of him catching pneumonia, but to no avail. He was having a great time, and I resigned myself, figuring as long as he was having fun in the present, I shouldn't worry about the consequences.

As game time approached and the players started to take the field, Myles suddenly became morose, slumping down into the seat he was standing on, arms folded in a manner that suggested anger, and was silent. Not understanding what had happened, I struggled to get him to tell me what was wrong. Finally, he looked at me with disdain, and proclaimed, "Daddy, you lied to me!"

"But no, I didn't lie, what do you mean?"

"You said we were going to see Giants!"

Myles, a friend asked me to share this story for a book. Sorry, but you know I will spend the rest of my life as a complete embarrassment to you!

~David Murphy, San Francisco, California

My first baseball game, years ago, was in Arizona to watch the Diamondbacks. I still remember the sights and sounds, looking at how the grass was so green and how everything looked so perfect. Everyone was having a great time. Looking down at the players, it was amazing how everything they did looked totally effortless.

My good friend's father grew up in New York, a Yankees fan. As a young kid he'd gone to a game, and in those days, when the game ended you could go onto the field. He and his dad were out in center field looking at the monuments for Babe Ruth and Lou Gehrig. The little boy thought they were actually buried there. His dad explained what the monuments were for, but the boy didn't believe him for the longest time.

~Jessie Swanson, Phoenix, Arizona

A Near Miss

I have had plenty of magical baseball moments with my beloved Mets. In 1969, my freshman year at Washington University in St. Louis, I watched 19 Mets go down as Cardinals pitcher Steve Carlton set the strike-out record with 19 Ks (strikeouts) strikeouts. But the Mets still found a way to win 4-3 as Ron Swoboda clouted in a pair of two-run homers and made a great run-saving catch. In 1986, in Game 6 of the World Series, everyone praying for a miracle, it happened in what seemed like slow motion, as Mookie Wilson's ground ball went through Buckner's legs.

But one other memory that really stands out was more on the bizarre side. I was on the field in St. Louis during the Mets' batting practice, thanks to my friend who was the college sports radio director. I was trans-fixed by watching my Mets close-up when Tommy Agee ripped a line drive that I didn't see. It was hurtling straight for my head when star pitcher Jerry Koosman yelled, "Duck!" I did, and it thankfully whizzed by an inch or two above my head. As much as I loved the Mets, I don't think I'd have wanted to have been killed by one. I'll forever be indebted to Koos for get-ting me to duck before it was too late.

~Dan Storper, New Orleans, Louisiana

My brother played in a Babe Ruth League, and sometimes I'd tag along. One time I was sitting on a tree stump a few feet to the right of the first base foul line. My brother's coach was a very big man and really nice guy. He walked over and said, "How about letting a tired old man sit down there?" I said, "Sure," and got up so he could sit. The very next pitch sent a line drive straight to his forehead. I will never forget the sound of that ball hitting his head, knocking him off the stump. He was okay afterward, but later he told me he was very glad he had been there instead of me. I was about 10 years old. Probably would have killed me.

~Gary Donahue

My father, George Nethercutt, was an All-American catcher at the University of North Carolina at Chapel Hill in the late 1930s, graduating Phi Beta Kappa. Drafted by the Boston Red Sox after graduation, he played minor league ball in the Midwest, primarily Ohio. Although he fairly quickly decided that pro baseball wasn't for him, his time in the minors was successful, and his batting average led the league. A local newspaper reported at one point that "Catcher Nethercutt is currently batting a strong .440, but this is to be expected, given his lofty 1940 signing bonus of $2,500!"

Equipment wasn't nearly as protective then, especially the catcher's mitt. During his playing career, Dad broke every finger on both hands, some multiple times. The treatment was adhesive tape and a sponge, then put your glove back on and get right back to catching. My father never lost his love of baseball, catching on company-sponsored teams in our hometown for years while I was growing up. He taught me to catch and throw at a very early age. Interestingly, our daughter—his granddaughter—has seemed to acquire the Nethercutt baseball genes. She played softball from the age of eight, going on to captain her high school team in her senior year. Like grandfather, like granddaughter.

Dad never lost his baseball prowess. At a Braves game back in the 1970s, he and my mother were sitting with my husband, John, and me in the third base section about 20 rows up. A Braves batter hit a screaming foul ball straight back into the stands and, without flinching or even moving very much, Daddy caught the ball bare-handed. Once a catcher, always a catcher!

~Helen Parker, Atlanta, Georgia

Where is the Car?

My first big league baseball game was in the summer of 1957. My husband was in the Army Reserves, spending two weeks of training at Fort Leonard Wood, Missouri. I took our two sons, ages four-and-a-half and one-and-a-half, to visit him on the weekend, deciding to spend it in St. Louis. Our adventure began with the long ride to St. Louis early Saturday morning. We had never been to a big league game, so we decided to go that afternoon. I can't honestly remember who played that day, but the regulars included Stan Musial, Ken Boyer, and Wally Moon. Who pitched? Very possibly Larry Jackson, Vinegar Bend Mizell, or Lindy McDaniel.

We managed to get tickets after standing in line with an excited four-and-a-half-year-old helping his mom with the diaper bag and doing very well. The younger one...well, we should have left him home. Needless to say, the storm was about to begin. His crying finally got to me and I decided to take him to the car. I had not paid close attention to where we had entered, and there was a sea of cars in the lot. I walked and walked, passing by a row of houses several times. An elderly man and woman sitting on their porch had no doubt seen me, my crying baby, and the diaper bag pass by all these times. He asked if he could help me, and when I said I couldn't find my car, he said, "I'll go get my machine (his car) and drive you around." We got into his car and he drove around until I finally found mine. I thank God he sent an angel that day. I know you shouldn't get into cars with strangers, but in the desperation of the moment it seemed okay. I'll never forget my first big league ball game in the old Busch Stadium.

~Olena Blackwell, Altamont, Kansas

During my high school years in the late '70s, my cousin Greg and I attended several Kansas City Royals games at Kaufman Stadium. We had a great time watching George Brett and all the Royals. But as much fun as the games were, we always seemed to run into problems after the games. One time, we'd forgotten where Greg's car was parked. Two kids, arriving early to watch pregame activities, hadn't thought about the number of cars that would be in the parking lot afterward. It took hours, but we finally found it when the lot was completely empty. After another game, we were supposed to drive to my parents' house in Topeka. Kansas City always seemed to have road construction and detours, and somehow we missed a detour sign and became completely lost. Driving around, lost for hours in a rough part of the city, we didn't want to stop and ask for directions. We were scared our family would never see us again. We finally were forced to stop and ask for help. For years, Greg and I relived those experiences, always joking about how fortunate we were to make it back safely each time. We couldn't tell our family, though, because we knew they would never let us go again!

~Kelly McGillis, Kansas City, Missouri

I grew up in the New York Metropolitan area, a wonderful environment in which to follow professional sports. I watched Mets baseball on WOR Channel 9, and the Yankees on WPIX 11.

A local dairy company's promotion allowed you to trade in 10 coupons from the sides of milk cartons for tickets to the Mets or Yankees, in the nosebleed section. My grandfather dutifully saved coupons for us, which enabled my dad, my brother Shelly, and me to go see (mostly) the Mets. At one game, our beloved Mets were playing the Giants, with Mays, McCovey, and Marichal. It was of course, a sellout. I don't remember who won, but we had a great time.

As we exited, neither Dad, Shelly, nor I had any clue where we'd parked. The parking lots at Shea surrounded the stadium, all full to the brim. When they finally cleared out, Dad sent Shelly one way and me the other to circle Shea to find our car. I still recall how happy and relieved we were when we saw Dad's midnight blue 1965 Chevy Impala sitting all by itself halfway around the other side of the stadium.

~Rob Hershman, Rome, New York

Gifts for the Fans

At age five in 1989, our daughter, Shelley, always seemed less interested in the games she attended than coloring, or the food we bought. One day, as I wrote the starting lineups in my scorebook, Shelley said, to my great surprise, "Robbie Thompson is batting second. Doesn't he usually hit fifth?"

In 1994, we went to Fan Appreciation Day. We arrived early for autographs, and Shelley grabbed a few Giants magazines on the way in since they were free that day. Prizes were being awarded, and when they started announcing the prizes, we heard, "Open your magazine to page 49, and if Kurt Manwaring signed your Pennzoil ad, you have won a case!" Shelley started flipping through the magazines and said, "Manwaring must have made a mistake! He signed the Alaska Airlines ad on a different page, not the Pennzoil one." I screamed out in joy. We'd won a trip to Mexico!

~Steve Itelson, San Francisco, California

To celebrate my sister Lydia's 10th birthday, the family headed to the ballpark on a rainy spring evening to watch our minor league baseball team, the Reno Chukars. Upon entry at that game, everyone received one raffle ticket and was entered into a drawing. At the end of the game the winner was called, and it was our father! The rain was really coming down, but he raced down to home plate to claim his prize, a brand new mountain bike. Dad was prompted to do a victory lap, riding his new bike around the bases in the rain. The local news station filmed the entire thing, and that night Mom taped the broadcast, which we still have on VHS. The mountain bike has never been used; it's stored in the garage collecting dust. Twice, the tires have gone flat, and even though Dad has never ridden it, he is very protective of his lucky mountain bike and refuses to let any of us take it for a spin.

~McKenna and Lydia Peri, Reno, Nevada

I talked with these two nice young women throughout the game. McKenna told me they loved Angel Pagan, the Giants center fielder, and I told them my daughter thinks he is gorgeous.

But the story continues. This is a post-game message from McKenna:

I want to share our exciting experience after that game. Your daughter will be so jealous! We stopped at the Dugout Store near where the Giants players park. We sometimes stick around to see them drive off. Lydia got a good photo of Posey getting into a car. But the best part was that Pagan came out and got into the passenger seat of an SUV. Fortunately, the windows were not tinted and as the car drove by, he waved at us. I snapped a photo of him smiling our way! Made my day!

~McKenna

I love the history of baseball and was lucky enough to work for Hall of Fame pitcher Bob Feller at his museum in Van Meter, Iowa. Occasionally I got a chance to talk with Bob when he'd pass by or come in and sign autographs. We shared the name Andrew—Bob's middle name—and he always remembered that and talked with me, always super cool. Working there, I had the chance to meet several former baseball players, my favorites being Mark Grace, Bret Saberhagen, Jim Palmer, Andre Dawson, and Billy Williams.

For the last 10 years, I've had season tickets to the Triple-A Iowa Cubs, the top farm club for the Chicago Cubs. Because I attended all 72 home games and every special event, I was chosen as the winner of the 2013 Iowa Cubs Fan of the Year. One of the greatest events I attended was a game between the Cuban national team and Collegiate Team USA. Carlos Rondon started for Team USA, and future World Series star Kyle Schwarber also played. I had my photo taken with Iowa Cubs owner Michael Gardner, who'd created the show Meet the Press, and Sam Bernabe, who won Minor League Executive of the Year. I received free parking for the season, $200 in concessions, and $100 to the team gift store.

~Andrew Pfaltzgraf, Ankeny, Iowa

Rooting for the Visitors

My father was old school. He was never overtly affectionate, nor did he outwardly show emotion to me. I realize that this describes many fathers and their relationships with their sons of my era. We never doubted our love for each other, but there was a polite, emotional distance that we had to traverse, especially during my teens and early adulthood. The exception to this, the common ground that often brought us together, was our mutual love of baseball. It was "safe territory" for us to freely communicate with each other, and we found ourselves relying on this zone of commonality more and more as the years went by.

On a few occasions, we made the trip to Atlanta from our home in Montgomery, Alabama to catch a Braves game. The Braves of the 60's and 70's was an organization that required great patience and long historical perspective. Biff Pocoroba, Rowland Office and Darrel Chaney were the Braves of the era. They were not pretty years, but we loved them anyway, following them regularly, knowing that better days were ahead (they were, though Dad didn't get to stick around to see them).

In the summer of 1978, we were just like every other baseball fan in the U.S.: transfixed by Pete Rose's consecutive games hitting streak. As the consecutive games climbed, so did our fascination and hope that he would break Joe DiMaggio's record. We decided to see the streak continue in person by purchasing tickets to see the Braves play the Reds on August 1st. With great seats behind home plate, we watched Pete go down four times, thinking, "this can't be happening." We realized that he had one more shot at it, as he was due to bat third in the 9th inning against Gene Garber. I won't go into the pitch selection and all that…that's been written about many times. I will share that this plate appearance was "Casey at the Bat" writ large. Everyone in Fulton County Stadium, Braves fans all, was in unison pulling for Pete to get the hit to keep the string going. Of course, he didn't, ending the streak at 44 games. The lasting image I'll take to the grave is Pete walking back to the dugout while Garber did a little "happy dance" on the mound. I've always wished Garber, too had just quietly headed back to the dugout.

The three-hour drive home was subdued. We came to see the streak continue, and left disappointed, like virtually everyone in the crowd that night. But that game provides me to this day a lasting memory of a special evening with my dad, who died nine years later, that time can never take away.

~Dr. Bob Hinds, Lakeland, Florida

I grew up near Boston but was, remarkably, a Yankees fan. My dad was, too, but he had season tickets to Fenway, and we went to many Yankees vs. Red Sox games. None was more remarkable than the game played on September 2, 2001, which saw Mike "Moose" Mussina vs. David Cone in his last full season in the majors, and his only one with the Sox.

Dad had given me his tickets, and I invited along my good friend, Elgin. The game was a pitcher's duel. Around the 5th inning, Elgin subtly pointed out something that I had not been paying attention to. Moose was throwing a perfect game. As this realization started hitting people, the stadium seemed to get progressively quieter, even silent at times. It was a weird feeling, fans knowing they could be witnessing history. Heading into the 9th, the score was 0-0. The Yankees scored in the top of the inning when Enrique Wilson knocked in Clay Bellinger, running for Tino Martinez who had reached on an error. Those two involved in the scoring were not exactly two names for the ages.

With two outs in the 9th, Carl Everett came in to pinch-hit for the Sox. Everett was not a fan favorite, to say the least, for many reasons. His attitude followed him from team to team. He also didn't believe in evolution, and fans continually made dinosaur jokes about him. This at-bat, Everett hit a bloop into left field to break up the perfect game. The fans went crazy booing him. This was the first time in two dozen games against the Yankees that I ever saw Sox fans boo one of their own, screaming at him for breaking up this run at history. It's hard to know whether the fans would have reacted that way had it been another player, virtually *any* other player, who'd gotten that hit. It was very cool to come so close to seeing a perfect game but experiencing Sox fans boo their own player for breaking up a Yankees perfect game was the icing on that particular cake.

~Mark Vieira, Los Angeles, California

I was 13 years old when I finally scrounged enough money together to be able to pay for my first Father's Day gift for my dad. It was 1964, and Shea Stadium was the brand new home of the Mets. I'd become a Mets fan mostly because all my friends were Yankees fans. Reserved seats at Shea were $2.50 each and the subway fare was $0.15. I bought the tickets a couple of weeks in advance at the Mets ticket office at Grand Central Station. When Father's Day rolled around, Dad and I got on the first of three subway trains to get to Shea for a scheduled doubleheader with Philadelphia.

We arrived in time for batting practice. Jim Bunning was scheduled to pitch for the Phillies. I don't remember who started for the Mets, I just wanted them to win, maybe hit a few home runs. The Mets were woeful in those days, so it was no surprise when the Phillies got off to a quick lead. By the middle of the game, not one Mets batter had reached base. As the Phillies' lead increased, the prospect of the Mets winning became less and less likely. It became apparent that Bunning was pitching a perfect game—no walks, no errors, nada, nothing, diddly squat! The bottom of the 9th rolled around, and he was three outs away. At 13, I had been to my share of baseball games, so I found it very strange that a close to sell-out crowd was rooting *against* the Mets and *for* Philadelphia. Dad and I were guilty of this betrayal, as well. Johnny Stevenson, the Mets catcher, made the last out. Jim Bunning had pitched a perfect game for the first Father's Day gift that I'd ever bought for my dad. And yes, the Mets lost game two, too!

~Ron Baum, Marin County, California

Bridging the International Divide

On August 2, 2002, the company I worked for sponsored an outing for employees at Cincinnati's Great American Ball Park, for the Reds vs. the Dodgers. Among the group who bussed to the park were some employees of company contractors from India. There were soccer and cricket fans among them, but baseball was not a sport with which they were very familiar. I was friends with some of them, and happy to answer their questions throughout the game. They really enjoyed it.

It was a great game for a first in-person baseball experience. Our Reds were down 4-0 in the bottom of the 9th, and the Dodgers had brought in their closer, Eric Gagne. He didn't have it that day, quickly giving up two runs before hitting Adam Dunn with the ball, getting ejected, and charging the umpire. I don't recall what my colleagues said about that incident, but when Ken Griffey Jr. came in as a pinch-hitter and potential game-tying run for the Reds, I explained how he was one of the superstars of the game, now playing in front of his hometown fans. They sensed the excitement, but Griffey made an out. The Reds tied it up anyway, but extra innings were not going to be witnessed by us, since the buses had to return by a certain time.

We listened to the rest of the game on the radio during the hour ride home, and my friends from India were shouting as loudly as anyone when Griffey Jr. won the game with a two-run homer in the bottom of the 13th. Some new baseball fans were made that day, and I like to think I was part of that.

~Scott Beckerman, Dayton, Ohio

My wife, Jane, and I rank between a five and a six on the baseball fan scale. We like to watch games on television and try to attend a number of games each season, especially if our favorite team, the Texas Rangers, is having a better than average year. In the summer of 1993, the Rangers were having a good season, attendance was up, and one of my all-time favorite pitchers, Nolan Ryan, would be pitching against the Chicago White Sox. We loaded up and headed to the ballpark.

We found our seats, and right in front of us was a young couple in their mid-to-late twenties from Australia. As we began to chat before the game, they told us about where they had been and what they had seen. They were having an adventure, making friends and memories on their travels. Their mates back in Australia had told them they needed go to a baseball game while in the U.S., and this was the night.

After several innings of strikeouts, walks, popups, and grounders to second base, the score was 0-0. The young man turned to his girlfriend, and in the typical Australian accent said, "This is bloody boring." He could not understand why Americans were so excited about baseball. His next step was to buy a couple more beers from a nearby vendor making the rounds.

Rangers' pitcher Nolan Ryan, a 46-year-old future Hall of Fame right-hander, was having a so-so game for the first few innings. The Sox batting coach was having his hitters crowd home plate to protect the outside corner. Getting frustrated, Ryan started throwing inside, moving the batters back to increase the strike zone. Robin Ventura, an up-and-coming twenty-six-year-old left-handed batter, came up to the plate. As coached, Ventura hugged the plate, and Ryan threw a high fastball on the inside. Ventura jumped back. To show that he was not going to be intimated, Ventura then set up even closer to the plate and, you guessed it, Ryan threw another inside fastball. With the combination of Ventura's location and the speed of the fastball, Ryan hit Ventura in the arm, and the umpire sent Ventura to first base. After two or three steps toward first, Ventura decided to make his infamous charge to the mound. Ryan squared up, and when Ventura reached the pitcher's mound, Ryan grabbed him around the neck with his left arm and proceeded to beat the crap out of Ventura with his right. Both benches emptied, and mayhem ensued. The rest of the story is baseball history.

At that exact moment, the Aussie exclaimed, "This is bloody fantastic, it's starting to make me homesick!" He then said he now understood why Americans loved baseball. To this day, I am fairly certain this extremely excited young Australian believed that having a brawl during a baseball game was a very common experience. I did not want to spoil his baseball adventure.

~Allen Fouty, Dallas, Texas

Years ago, I was a doctoral graduate student at the University of Wisconsin, Madison. A friend of mine taught a special, concentrated English language class during the summer for incoming graduate students from non-English speaking countries. A part of the course was American culture as it related to language. Knowing my interest in sports, my friend asked me to present two lectures for them. One on sports idioms and how their meanings are part of the American-English language inside and outside of sports, and the second on the rules of baseball. Attending a local baseball game would be the final exam for this course segment. At the game, I was to be the instructor, narrator, and leader on when and how to cheer.

My friend got free tickets to the then-Madison Muskies, a Class A team. For two summers in the early 1980s, I held court in the classroom and at the diamond. Most of my students had no clue about baseball at any level, though some from Asian countries knew a bit. For class I used soccer, a sport with which the majority were familiar, as a starting point to describe offense and defense, but then highlighted that in baseball the defense has the ball. Each team has opportunities to play offense and defense. I brought up the purpose of the game: to score more points—called runs—than the opponent. I touched on details such as defense (=fielding), offense (=hitting), positions, batting order, roles of the pitcher and catcher, outs, substitutions, and umpires. I discussed idioms such as doing something well was like "hitting a home run," not accomplishing something is "striking out," and being wrong is "off base." By the way, it's easy to forget how many details there are to the game of baseball. More about that next.

What I remember most are the experiences I had with my class at the final exam each year. I can't recall the games' outcomes, but what happened during each game is etched in my memory. We'd sit in the stands at

Warner Park, and I'd sit in the middle, the students surrounding me. As a game proceeded, the narration, explanations, and questions and answers flew. The progression of the first game went smoothly and had a slow, natural rhythm allowing a lot of discussion and time for more Q & A. We had a grand time and great laughs. The final exam in year two was the complete opposite. I was tuckered out after the first three innings, which included a dropped third strike, an infield fly rule, catcher's interference, three pitching changes, a double play, a run down, and a missed bag during baserunning. Details were flying. Later innings were thankfully calmer with a more relaxed rhythm. However, I needed refreshments, which my students were kind enough to treat me to. As with the first game, we had a great time, which was what mattered most.

Fast forward many years, and I'm now a university professor. A new graduate student arrived from Egypt, and I took him to his first ice hockey game. There I am, describing ice hockey to a new student from the Egyptian desert. Again, thank goodness for soccer. I must be a good teacher; the student became a hockey fan.

~Paul Ranelli, Duluth, Minnesota

HOME RUNS

Calling a story a "home run" is loaded with the inference that it is among the best of the best. Even on the first time around the bases, that was true only to some extent, although no good parent will ever single (so to speak) out a favorite. Others in this book deserve a spot in this lineup, but also fit well in other chapters. But these stories all hit it out of the park.

I just wanted to have a catch. After reading *The History of Baseball in 10 Pitches*, with ball in hand, I, a former college pitcher, just wanted to try out some of the grips, the slider, the curve, even though I hadn't thrown a ball in decades. I needed someone who could catch a hard one, or one in the dirt. I didn't know anyone who could do that.

So, like a mother looking out for her kid, my wife, Alice, a baseball fan in her own right, posted on the neighborhood app Nextdoor, asking for someone who might want to have that catch. The responses started flowing in. A woman called for her son, followed by a couple of guys, all enthusiastic. Another wrote, "What a wonderful way to bring people together and start 2021 with a positive note. This makes me smile."

Alice, in a follow-up post wanting to ensure that this show would go on, suggested a time and place. We showed up early, not really sure if anyone else would. Comments aren't commitments, especially when they are online. I brought some baseballs and an old catcher's mitt which I had repaired that morning. And then people started to arrive. Three students from the North Dallas High School team came with a staff member. A 26-year-old guy, a 73-year-old man from Queens, NY, and several others in between. There was even a spectator in the bunch, as well as a reporter from the local ABC affiliate.

Hellos were said, lines formed, and balls started being thrown and caught, back and forth, like kids at a Little League practice. But something more started to happen, beyond the catches and misses. People started talking to each other, about life, their own lives. Connections were made, perhaps friendships, time will tell. My new friend, Rich, when asked why he came, simply said, "Fountain of Youth. The opportunity to do something I never expected to do again in my life."

This first session ended. Some of us were exhausted, with tired arms and wobbly legs, having not thrown a ball in decades. But I think it is fair to say that most of us were energized. It remains to be seen if these wannabe stars and old diamond warriors will continue to meet. But important things had happened. People had gotten another shot at past glories. They'd had a chance to do something nice to usher in a year with a little more hope than the one just left behind. I plan to do what I can to get some positive attention for the respectful, wonderful kids from that local high school who sometimes get blamed for minor incidents in the community.

Alice, look what you've done!

~Frank Miller, Dallas, Texas

I now live in Germany because I am an opera singer. I sang for a long time in the United States, but there is more work over here. Back in 1985, though, I was hired by the Glimmerglass Opera in Cooperstown, New York. When I arrived, I discovered that singers from the opera were routinely used to sing the National Anthem at the Baseball Hall of Fame. When I was rehired in 1986, I asked to sing at the Hall of Fame Induction Ceremony.

The ceremony takes place outside, but the players wait inside before going out onto the stage. It was pretty amazing to be among all those stars. After a short wait, names were called to line up and take their places. "Ted Williams, Robin Roberts, Stephen Owen." I heard some banter from the line, including Williams saying, "From '48 on, I hit off the slider." I was sitting near the back with my pitch pipe in my jacket pocket, ready to sing a cappella. When it was time for me to sing—ironically, I had never sung the National Anthem anywhere before, and my debut would be on ESPN!—I got my pitch (as it were) and walked up to the front. I thought, "All these guys have heard this song thousands of times. They must be totally bored." And I sang.

The only non-old timer inducted that year was Willie McCovey. As I walked back to my place, I passed him in the front row. He "stretched" out, shook my hand, and said, "That was great!" My hand felt like a little pebble in his. When I got back to my seat, umpire Jocko Conlon said, "Amazing. Not one muscle moved." A man in front of me turned and said, "That was wonderful." Ernie Banks introduced himself to me, (I told him I had been present for his 400th home run.) After the ceremony, Warren Spahn grabbed my hand and said, "Great job." Williams added, "Yeah, great, really great." I ran into Ernie Banks again in the bathroom. He asked where I'd studied, and said singing was his hobby. Then manager Bill Rigney came in and said, "That was fantastic. You should sing at the World Series." Banks started singing, "I could have *dahnced* all night!" and wanted a singing lesson.

Jane Fonda and my hero, Tom Hayden, were in the audience. I would have liked to meet them, but I had to find friends and drive back to New York City. All in all, an amazing, unforgettable experience, singing with the stars.

~Stephen Owen, Augsburg, Germany

Growing up a huge baseball fan in Idaho, it took advance planning to see my favorite major leaguers in person. When I found out the 2001 Midsummer Classic was coming to Seattle, the closest major league city, I decided there was no way I wasn't going. This was before the secondary ticket market took off, so my best and only option was to somehow obtain All-Star Game tickets through Ticketmaster.

On the day tickets went on sale, I stayed home from school and logged onto my slow, dial-up internet, listening for the familiar modem beeps. Once online, I opened as many browsers as I could. I wanted three tickets so I could go with my parents, Jim and Joy. Over and over again I hit the refresh button only to see the "No Tickets Available" message repeatedly. Finally, a miracle struck, and two tickets appeared. I jumped on it.

But now I was torn. I had two tickets in hand and had to decide which parent would accompany me to the game. In my infinite adolescent wisdom, I decided the most fair and impartial way to decide was to administer an exam. For the next few days, I laboriously assembled a baseball test, doing my best to provide an unbiased mix of questions spanning all playing eras. Fortunately, my parents were both good sports and willingly took my "Baseball SAT." In the end, Mom had the edge, and wound up as my All-Star chaperone. It was a very memorable game, with eight of my Mariners voted to the squad and Cal Ripken Jr. winning the All-Star MVP in his final playing year. Sadly, Dad had to watch on TV from the confines of our Seattle hotel room. But don't worry, I've made it up to him in adulthood, taking multiple baseball road trips with just him. And he didn't even have to take another exam!

~Emily Hawks, Seattle, W, via Eagle, ID

I wonder how I would do on your Baseball SAT, Emily. Do you still have the exam?

Throughout the summer of 1985, I played for our local Babe Ruth All-Star team. Against all odds, our team from a very small community beat two of the largest district teams in Vermont to win the Vermont State Championship. Our run would eventually end at the regionals in East Lyme, Connecticut. We didn't fare well, but anyone who has been able to represent their home state in any sport knows it is an honor just to be there and have that experience. Part of our post-tournament reward was a trip to Fenway Park, a New England tradition. Another tradition was receiving our state championship trophy pregame on the field, presented by none other than Red Sox pitcher Bruce Hurst. I was a Sox fan, but at that point, I wasn't the type who watched a lot of games on TV. However, I understood enough to know that being on the field at Fenway was a big honor. Knowing this, my little 13-year-old brain wanted to have something to capture and remember the moment, since the likelihood of my being back on that field in the future was slim to none.

I had a sandwich baggie in my back pocket, remnants of the lunch I'd brought with me. During the ceremony, I bent down and scooped up some dirt and chalk from the first base line. I don't remember much about the game; I just knew this bag of dirt and chalk symbolized a moment I would be able to reflect on for the rest of my life. When I got home, I put the bag on the headboard shelf of my bed where it would sit for years to come. I never moved it and, to be honest, as the years passed I kind of forgot about it. One day, though, when I was a senior in high school, I realized that my bag of dirt was no longer on my headboard. My mom, bless her heart, cleaned my room from time to time, so I asked her if she had seen it. She immediately started to cry. She, too, had forgotten its importance and thrown it out while cleaning. I felt as bad for Mom as I did for my lost keepsake.

Over 20 years later, on Saturday May 8, 2010, I finally made it to my first Red Sox vs. Yankees game. Fun fact, my current license plate is BOSvNYY. I'd received tickets from my very good friend, Bill Hedberg, for amazing seats—Field box 52 Row E, in case you are wondering. I could hardly contain myself.

The greatest rivalry in all of sports, and I was right there, sitting just off the on-deck circle of the much-hated Yankees. It was a rainy day, and the four of us fans had come prepared with ponchos. Mark Teixeira was in his typical early-season slump, batting in the .190s, which brought me joy. There's nothing better than watching the overpaid mercenaries of the evil empire underperform their obnoxious salaries. The Sox were only playing .500 ball, but I didn't care. This was a dream come true for me. Unfortunately the dream didn't last long. The Yankees were doing their best to turn it into a nightmare, putting on a clinic between the raindrops. Tex hit three home runs that day enroute to a 14-3 crushing of the Sox. The more important part of the story, though, had nothing to do with the beatdown on the field.

During a rain delay, one security guard was posted just in front me. I'll never forget his name. Dan was about 6'5" and bald. I told him a quick version of my story about being a kid getting to be on the field, and what had happened to my prized baggy of dirt memorabilia. I asked, since we were in a rain delay, if he would allow me to go out on the field, just for a second, and scoop up some chalk and dirt. It was worth a shot, right? Predictably, he said he was sorry, but no fans were allowed on the field. I figured that was it, this had been my only chance and I simply couldn't make it happen. But then Dan looked over my shoulder and saw the plastic carrying bag from my rain-soaked poncho. He said, "I think we can do something. Why don't you hand me that poncho bag"? I handed it over immediately. This man who didn't know me and probably heard stories like this every game, walked over to the third base line, bent down, scooped up some dirt and chalk, and put it in the bag for me. I didn't even see him walk back over to me as my eyes were so filled up with tears, I couldn't contain myself. He handed me the bag and I hugged him out of instinct. I no longer cared about the game itself or the outcome.

Dan gave me back so much more than a bag of dirt that day. What he couldn't know was that my mom had passed away six years earlier, on October 16, 2004, at the age of 48 from Chronic myelomonocytic leukemia, a rare form of blood cancer. That same year, as we all know, was the year the Red Sox won it all for the first time in 86 years. To this day, I believe they won it because of her. I faithfully stayed up every night and watched every single game, every single pitch. From Dave Roberts stealing second, to the epic performance of my man David Ortiz, I was so thankful for every moment. It kept me from dwelling on the loss of Mom, helped me make it through one of the hardest times of my life.

Baseball, because it is always there in the background of our lives, has an amazing ability to freeze moments in time. It has the uncanny ability to be a calendar, photo album, or time capsule. The joy of being a little kid playing the game I loved with my friends, and the pride of winning the state championship, the awe of standing on hallowed ground at Fenway. The appreciation for a mother who loved me enough to clean my room and cried when she accidently tossed something out, because that was how much she cared.

A compassionate gesture from a kind man. A simple bag of dirt and chalk. Memories restored, full circle.

~DJ Hardaker, Graniteville, Vermont

I was almost 12 years old, living in Crawfordville, Georgia, a small town 80 miles from Atlanta and 50 miles from Augusta. It was April 8, 1974, and Hank Aaron came up to bat in the 4th inning against the Dodger's Al Downing. Of course, Hank was sitting on 714 career home runs, tied with Babe Ruth. I am sure the capacity crowd in Atlanta was as quiet as it was in my living room. People were divided regarding how they felt about the inevitable breaking of Ruth's record. There were baseball purists who thought that records are made to be broken, and there were those who didn't care to see records fall. Some simply couldn't abide a

Black man beating the Babe's record. In my town, in my house, there was no question about wanting this to happen.

Reception on our television was always spotty, depending on the weather and how you turned the antenna. It was a cloudy day, which thankfully made for good reception. I sat on my mom's easy chair in the living room, waiting for the pitch. When Hank hit that home run, I would like to say it was as noisy in my living room as it was in the stadium, but I was concentrating far more on circling the bases with him than listening. The couch was first base, the TV was second, another couch was third, and then I was at home plate, back in the easy chair. I will never forget that moment.

Many years later, in 1999, as director of the Negro Leagues Baseball Museum, I had the chance to meet my idol, Hank Aaron. It was the 25th anniversary of the day he broke that record. The Kansas City Royals brought him to the area for some functions, and I had the distinct honor of touring him through the museum. Preparing for this tour, I had been a wreck. I'd debated for an eternity what clothes I should wear to greet him.

At the museum, there was a huge media throng. As we toured, I showed Hank and his wife, Billie, a photo of when he was 17 years old, preparing to join the Indianapolis Clowns. It had been a long time since he'd seen that photo. He mentioned that before he had the nickname Hammerin' Hank, in the Negro Leagues he was called Pork Chops. I asked him about that, and he said it was probably the only thing he knew how to order off the menu! I remember so many things about that day, including his comment that the day had brought back some painful memories for him. He had been under constant threat of harm as he neared the record, and he had feared for his family.

After all the ceremonies, we went to the Gym Theater across the street from the museum. There was a public discussion hosted by sportswriters Jason Whitlock and Joe Poznanski. The place was filled. After the discussion, Hank, Billie, and I adjourned to an office room where we enjoyed a great meal of Gates BBQ ribs. I couldn't believe it. I was eating ribs with my all-time hero! To this day, on the occasions when I see Mr. Aaron, he always asks if I've brought ribs.

~Bob Kendrick, Kansas City, Missouri

On any September afternoon, the offer of free box seat tickets to a Cubs game at Wrigley Field would trump any other scheduled activity, especially school work. That was the case in 1975, a year after I had begun graduate school in Chicago. My classmate and friend, Don Musser, formerly a pastor in Pittsburgh, called the hotel where the visiting Pirates were staying and left a message for his former parishioner, Art Howe, a utility infielder for the Pirates. Within hours, Art offered Don two tickets for next day's game. Inviting me to join him, Don and I abandoned our studies for the afternoon, took the L to the Addison Street station, claimed our comp tickets, and sat in a sun-bleached box in the fourth or fifth row behind the first base dugout. The game proved to be historic. The Pirates won 22-0, the largest margin of victory for a shutout in major league history, and Rennie Stennett went 7 for 7, the only player since 1900 to collect seven hits in a nine-inning game.

The first inning set the tone for the game. Stennett led off with a double and scored pitches later on a single by Richie Hebner. Even John Candelaria, the Pirates' starting and winning pitcher who allowed only three singles, drove in two runs with a single of his own, knocking Cubs starter Rick Reuschel off the mound after retiring only one hitter among the first nine. Stennett, up again, lined a single to right. His day's hit barrage began to look like the Beatles' play list.

After Stennett singled for his sixth hit in the seventh, the umpire tossed the ball to the Pirates dugout. Most fans expected that his day was done. It wasn't. He scored the twenty-first run when Dave Parker, who'd earlier hit a monstrous home run that landed on the sidewalk across the street on Sheffield Avenue, singled him home. In his final at-bat the next inning, Stennett tripled to right. Perhaps tired from running the bases and scoring five runs, he was lifted for pinch-runner Willie Randolph, leaving the field to a standing ovation from the few faithful fans remaining from the official crowd of less than 5,000.

But Stennett's day was not quite done or was ours. Following the final out in the ninth, Art Howe, who regrettably didn't get into the game, signaled for Don and me to approach the dugout and presented Don with the ball from Stennett's sixth hit, which Stennett then signed to end his day's work.

What a game! In two and a half hours the Pirates tallied 22 runs, collecting 24 hits, 6 walks, and four additional base runners on three errors and a hit batter. It was an uncommon afternoon at Wrigley Field.

~Joseph L. Price, California, co-director of the Institute for Baseball Studies at Whittier College, author of *Rounding the Bases: Baseball and Religion in America*

First, full disclosure. My sister, Gail, went to high school with author Eric Gray, and I was a couple years ahead. We are Long Islanders! That means everything we do and think comes with an extra dollop of passion, angst, emotion. I am *not* surprised that Eric has turned his love for baseball into a book about the love of baseball, and that it is less about the triple play, more about the secular passion play. Which it certainly was for me.

Some of my earliest memories are the sounds of a televised game forming a lazy chord with buzzing insects and lawnmowers and screen doors slamming on summer days in our new suburban neighborhood filled with hope in the late '50s and early '60s. My dad would sit in his recliner with a beer and a bologna and mayonnaise sandwich, watching the TV in its place of honor in the living room. Years later, I'd realize he should have been out doing chores like the other dads, helping my mom around the house, but he was just a few years removed from hand to hand combat in Guadalcanal, where he'd landed after lying about his age at 16 and joining the Marines to get out of the orphanage. The game? That was his reward.

I was a little girl who did what was available to little girls in those days—I dreamed about boys. I applied all of what would later become producing and reporting skills in television and news reporting to cataloguing and curating those boys. And very early on? I decided Roger Maris and Mickey Mantle were worthy of my gaze. They were, of course, the two most charmed and star-dusted baseball players of their day, with Beach Boy looks and Babe Ruth stats. In 1961, they were chasing Ruth's home run record, completely unaware that 11-year-old me was chasing them, on the hunt and determined to bag a catch. Them.

I had a diary and autograph book, which I remember was pink and had a clasp. And no autographs.

Gail and I once met Harry Belafonte at the Forest Hills Stadium restaurant before his concert. That's my memory, anyway. Gail says it wasn't him. But who else could it have been in the largely segregated 1950s, who would charm two little girls and delight diners by paying us for each of the seven dwarfs we could name? Years later, I interviewed him for a show called Evening Magazine in Boston and reminded him of the encounter. But I didn't get his autograph. Or Louis Armstrong's. I have *no* idea how or why my dad and I were backstage at some club and I met the great man. I can picture him, so gentle, horn in his lap, looking down at me. I remember wearing my best church dress. Which was also what I wore when I met the Bronx Bombers.

We had to arrive at Yankee Stadium early to get to the railing. I wore my pink tulle confirmation dress for the occasion. Pictures would probably show unruly cowlicks and a wandering eye that two surgeries had not yet tamed, but in my mind's eye? I was a catch. Maris and Mantle came to the railing radiating sunshine and virility, like frisky racehorses. I remember feeling awe. I think they actually signed that pink autograph book, but I have no idea where it is.

In 1963, I went to another baseball cathedral, Shea Stadium, to see the Beatles. Dad drove Gail and me, then waited in the parking lot. I'd scored tickets as a very organized member of the Murray the K Fan Club. He was the New York DJ known as the 5th Beatle, and I approached getting those tickets the way young men of a certain stature approached getting in to Harvard. I didn't know about Harvard at the time. And of course I did not get the Beatles' autographs.

I wish I wish… I *wish* I'd talked to my dad about those times. He died way too young—refer back to the beers, bologna sandwiches, and hand to hand combat. But I realize now how often he was there in the background while I pushed my way to the railing.

Fast forward to 1975. I was a fledgling director for then-sports powerhouse TV 38 in Boston, which carried Bruins and Red Sox games. I got to second direct, which meant rolling slo-mo replays, cutting to commercials, and going to games. On April 22, I was at Fenway Park, home of the Red Sox, on Patriots Day, one of the most exciting days in Boston. In addition to re- enacting the start of the American Revolution in Lexington and Concord, the Sox home game always coincided with the Boston Marathon, the finish line a short distance from the park.

Pregame, I was down by the dugout when I heard on the radio that Bill Rogers, beloved Boston runner, was about to be the first from Massachusetts, the first hometown boy, to win the Marathon. I thought, with the same sudden force that had propelled me to the railing at Yankee Stadium over 10 years earlier, "This I gotta see." I started running through crowds of baseball and marathon fans, becoming aware of a sound accompanying me. A *click, click, click*. What was that? Over my shoulder, Bill Lee, famed Red Sox pitcher known as the Spaceman for reasons such as these. He was jogging right behind me, in full uniform, including cleats. With a mitt. With me running defense, we made our way to the old Eliot Lounge, where fabled bartender Tommy Leonard often served both Bills—Lee and Rogers. And we watched as Rogers turned the corner toward Boylston Street and a record-breaking victory.

I didn't have my autograph book, then, either. Within a year, these guys might be jokingly asking for *mine*, as I went on to host popular TV and radio shows, something that would have seemed impossible to me as a child. As was actually playing sports myself.

But what I learned through my love for baseball players has stayed with me for life, even as I got my opportunities, and it is this: Coming out to applaud, to cheer on, to catalogue and curate, to be in awe, is often just as satisfying as being the one crossing the finish line. And we all belong at the railing.

Little could Maris and Mantle have known how much they empowered that lazy-eyed little Long Island girl in her very best pink tulle skirt.
~Robin Young, Boston, Massachusetts, Host of NPR's Here and Now

Today, on Willie Mays' birthday, I am thinking back to 1962 when as an 11-year-old, I went to see the Giants play the Pirates at old Forbes Field. With me, I had a baseball given to me by my grandfather that I wanted Mr. Mays to sign. After the game, I went to the entrance of the dressing room and asked the attendant if he could ask Mr. Mays to sign my ball. When

Willie found out who the other two signatures on the ball were from, he actually came out of the dressing room to talk with me. I will never forget his act of kindness. Oh, and the other two signatures were Lou Gehrig and Honus Wagner.

~Vince Doran, McLean, VA

A simple, kind gesture

July 1997 was our first summer in Atlanta. I was seven months along with Connor, very pregnant. For whatever mind-boggling reason, we decided to go to our first Braves game on a hot, melt-the-make-up-off-your-face, muggy night. Our evening started out with us not knowing exactly where to park, and we wound up trekking a mile and a half. Did I mention I was pregnant? We sat down to watch the game, and my then-husband, Wayne, didn't seemed to notice how I was struggling, sweaty, and haggard.

Suddenly, a woman behind me tapped me on the shoulder and handed me the frozen ice cream cone she had just purchased. She said simply, "That's the first treat for your baby." I was so grateful for this little random act of kindness. It made me realize that we all have lovely people and moments in our lives, some expected, some complete surprises. We chatted a little during the game, and when it ended, we hugged, she wished me good luck, and I never saw her again.

I really don't remember anything about the game. I don't even know who the Braves were playing. But I will never go to a game without remembering this story and recalling that very kind woman's gift to my child that was so much more than ice cream.

~Peg Nicholls, Atlanta, GA

My dad, Ralph, passed away two years ago. He and I loved meeting players at spring training. Some players were easy to talk to, some were jerks. The guy who will forever be one of my favorite players of all time is

Eduardo Perez, not for anything he did on the diamond but for his one five-second gesture of kindness. We were on the east coast of Florida at a Cardinals practice. It had to be 95 degrees. Dad and I were trying to get the autograph of the supposed "next superstar of baseball," J.D. Drew. Drew wouldn't even acknowledge us, not a big surprise, but Dad wanted to continue to wait until he came off the field. We were standing by the fence sweating our butts off, and Eduardo came over to get a drink from the players' cooler. Without saying a word, he poured a drink into a cup and handed it to my dad. It sounds so minor, so simple, but as hot as it was, he was more worried about the senior citizen than himself. I later messaged him on Facebook and told him that story, and he was gracious enough to message me back. Dad talked about that day often in his final years, one of many, many great memories we shared.

-Joe Iorlano, Westerly, Rhode Island

In the summer of 2001, living and working as a contractor in Phoenix, Arizona, I scored four tickets to see the Diamondbacks play the Cubs at Bank One Ballpark, now called Chase Field. I took two clients to the game—Michael Del Castillo, a home builder, along with his future wife, and Jim McCullum, a road builder. We had pretty good seats a little north of first base, a couple of sections up. I am a die-hard Cubs fan, as was Michael's girlfriend. Michael and Jim are both big fans of the game, with Michael partial to the Angels and Jim a Dodgers fan.

The D-backs jumped on the Cubs, but the lead went back and forth. The crowd was pleasant, as is usual, but there was one kid that kept giving me a hard time because of my Cubs hat and shirt. I was good-natured about it and gave back when I could, but he really became obnoxious. He was 12 or 13, and his parents seemed embarrassed by his behavior, although they didn't do much to calm him down.

In the top of the 6th inning, Cubs Ron Coomer came up to bat. Michael had brought his glove and had it on. We all had beers to manage and were enjoying the game, talking back and forth, when Coomer fouled one off toward the first base side. Michael and I saw the ball come off the bat and, with amazing speed, slice toward the section below us. Incredibly, it skipped off three sets of hands, like a flat stone on calm water. Then the ball was right in front of us, and the next moment Michael was sitting there, stunned, the way a boxer looks when he gets knocked out, blinking and involuntarily nodding his head. The ball had hit him right in the forehead! You could see the imprint of the stitches within seconds. None of us spilled our beers, which were in-hand, but Michael never raised his glove. As he sat there dazed, the ball rolled and that annoying kid grabbed it. Medical staff was on Michael within minutes. It was impressive how quick, professional, and efficient they were. Michael checked out okay and soon was telling jokes and had the whole section laughing.

Now the kid was taunting us with the ball. Michael wanted it, but the kid was being a real prick about it. I thought his folks were going to take him home. In the middle of the 7th, I went to get some hot dogs. I noticed that the vendor at the top of the stairs had brand-new official league baseballs for sale, along with sharpies. I bought a ball and sharpie and, on a napkin, practiced signing Ron Coomer's name five or six times. I took the ball out of the box and signed it Ron Coomer, sticking the napkin and sharpie in my pocket. It didn't look half bad, although I had no idea what Ron's real signature looked like. At each section in the stands there is a volunteer who checks tickets and helps people get seated, usually retired folks who love to be at the ballpark. Ours was an older gentleman, and I said to him, "Could you please give this ball to the guy who got hit?" He figured out what I was up to and said he could. I asked him to say it was from Coomer, and not to let on who it was really from. He agreed, and from the top of the stairs I watched as he gave Michael the ball. He said, "I was asked to give you this."

A couple of minutes passed and I went back to our seats. Michael told me about the autographed ball he'd received and how great it was that they did that! I remarked about how classy it was of the opposing team, my beloved Cubbies. At this point, only the usher and I knew what was really going on.

In the bottom of the 8th, Michael and the kid were still jawing. Michael wanted the ball that actually hit him, willing to trade the autographed one for it. They debated back and forth and the kid finally agreed to the swap. They made the trade like a couple of kids, each hanging on until the other released grip of their respective balls. It was pretty funny. I was laughing so hard inside I thought I would give it away.

In the top of the 9th the kid became more obnoxious than ever, especially because Sosa had just struck out to end a threat. The D-backs won. We said our goodbyes and Michael and his gal turned one way to leave, and Jim and I went another way. The kid was still really giving it to me now, his parents looking apologetic and sheepish. With the parents looking on, and Jim and I going up the stairs with the exiting crowd, I said; "Hey kid, here's the pen I signed that ball with. I thought you might like to have it." I took the sharpie out and handed it to him. "Wattaya mean?" he asked. I repeated, "This is the pen I used to sign the ball that you traded for." He insisted Ron Coomer signed the ball. I said, "Nope, it was me." His folks were now intently watching, and I noticed them smiling a little. I said, "Yep, I signed that ball and had the usher give it to my friend." The kid basically called me a liar. I then reached into my pocket, pulled out the napkin, and said, "Here, you might as well have this, too. It's the napkin I practiced on. I think you'll find the signatures match perfectly." The parents were in full smile now as the kid stood there dumbfounded, looking at the signatures on the ball and napkin. A look came over his face, and he knew he'd been had. It was priceless. I smiled at him and said, "You just can't beat fun at the ole ballpark, can ya?" and departed. The parents shook my hand and said thanks.

This was on a Saturday. Michael didn't hear the story until Monday when we met on a project. He laughed so hard he could barely stand up. Jim was riding with me and we laughed the whole way back to Tucson.

It was a great day.

~Andy Rowe, Chino Valley, Arizona

I was a girl who loved baseball. Not softball mind you, hard ball. I usually played first base, sometimes third, but my passion was batting. I could hit the ball hard and far. I thrilled to the crack of the ball against the bat, the trademark up so as not to split it.

It was recess. I stood at the plate watching the pitcher wind up and release the ball. It headed into the strike zone. I shifted my weight to my right foot, gripped the handle of the bat and raised it ever so slightly over my shoulder into the air, tensed and ready to knock the ball far beyond the outfielder's reach. I swung full power, anticipating the sound of a home run. I was amazed when I heard, instead, a *smush*. It felt soft like hamburger, like modeling clay, like a wad of wet tissues. My head followed the arc of the bat to see what had gone wrong.

Jolene stood behind me, blood gushing from her face, her Orphan Annie eyes huge and vacant, fingers splayed in front of her face, afraid to touch what might be missing. For an endless moment the world stopped, a soundless tableau of school children at recess. Then in a collective breath, they swarmed toward the schoolhouse, the teacher and Jolene in the lead. I stood alone on home plate, stunned into silence, bat dangling limp at my side. I turned my back and walked slowly to my house a block from the schoolyard. No one was home. Dad was logging up in the Coast Range and only came home on weekends. Mom was seeing to Jolene. She was Jolene's teacher.

I sat on the edge of the front porch that fall afternoon, doubting my mom's love and Dad's judgement in insisting I be good at a boy's game. Most of all, I doubted me. How had I become capable of causing a sweet, harmless girl so much pain, maybe disfigurement? Maybe she would even die. All I had wanted, intended, was to show how good I was at baseball, as good as any boy. I'd felt strong and bold, confident of my batting skills. Now I felt betrayed, tricked by some unseen God that I now doubted, as well.

Jolene lived. Despite all the blood, she still had her head, her eyes, her brain, and her face, a bit worse for the blow, but fixable. A broken nose, a split lip, broken front teeth, and deep colorful bruising. For weeks I spent my allowance on presents for her. Coloring books and crayons, paper dolls, comic books, and candy you didn't have to chew. Jolene recovered and never allowed the cruelty of my act to alter her sweet disposition. She still thought I was cool. I could see it in her eyes and her now-crooked smile.

~Nancy Pyburn, Vancouver, Washington

MY PLAYER, MY TEAM, MY GAME: WHAT BASEBALL MEANS TO ME

This chapter, along with Family, means the most to me. The stories provide glimpses into what makes this game the National Pastime. Why, in my opinion, it is the game that folks feel most sentimental about, that invokes loving memories, that brings them, well…home. I knew how folks could remember endless stats, and going to games with their parents, but until I started collecting stories for this project, I just did not quite understand how important baseball was to so many. As it is for me.

Baseball was my first true love, from the time I was a kid imaging all my favorite players and imitating their at-bats. I even had a mean Julio Franco approach. The game changed for me over the years from Little League to playing in college, and then as a coach for over a decade. It has taught me more life lessons than anything else, especially on how to deal with failure. In how many other sports can you fail 70 percent of the time but still be considered a star? Baseball has taught me to never be fully satisfied with anything in life, especially oneself. There is always room for improvement.

I love arriving at a field before everyone else. I love the smell of the fresh-cut grass, the sounds of the sprinkler system spraying, the silence of the moment, but still feeling the energy that will arrive. I love seeing a player show up before everyone to take swings, and the sound of the crack of the bat in an empty stadium. I love the family aspect of the game, and the smile or joy you see on a child's face and notice it is the same smile you see on a senior citizen's face. I love going to games with my son but can't wait until the day I can do the same with my grandson. Looking into the stands, seeing a grandfather and grandson together watching and discussing the game has brought smiles, even tears, to my face. It is the one sport, and part of life, that while everything is evolving around us, remains the same. The game teaches us so much—character, competition, acceptance, humility, confidence, respect, loyalty, brotherhood, friendship, and kindness. It has brought people of different cultures, races, and religions together more than anything in this world.

I don't have a one-time baseball moment. Baseball has been both a reality and an escape from reality. Being at the ballfield is my refuge, home, enemy, and best friend. Sitting on a field before a game, taking in all the pregame smells of grass, sunflower seeds, and hotdogs, and imagining the echoes of what is about to take place is my serenity, my sanctuary, my peace. And peace is what we all are looking for.

-Joshua Adkins, Kingsport, Tennessee

Joshua, I, too, cannot wait to take my granddaughter to her first game.

I'm a die-hard Dodgers fan, and that means such incredible history—Jackie Robinson breaking the color barrier, Vin Scully the greatest announcer of all time, moving baseball westward, Kirk Gibson's home run. But because I grew up in the 1990s, there is one important thing to remember: *The Dodgers sucked for the entire decade.* This may be an overreaction, and Pirates fans may want to stone me, but the '90s saw the complete failure of an historic team, without yearly contenders or reassurance that the O'Malley family would guide us back. Fox stewarded the Dodgers like a drunken captain on the Titanic. But in 2004, the Dodgers finally won the National League West, featuring the incredible moment when Steve Finley hit a walk-off grand slam against the rival Giants. The Dodgers went on to lose to the Cardinals in the National League Division Series, but not before my favorite moment in sports. L.A. lost Games 1 and 2 in

St. Louis and were facing a sweep, but hell if I was going to miss a chance to see my Boys in Blue in the playoffs.

On the mound for the Dodgers in Game 3 was Jose Lima. At one point or another we've all been Jose Lima—undervalued, not quite skilled enough, doubted. He had been a steady presence all year in an effort to revive his career. He brought Lima Time to Dodger Stadium, pitching with the confidence of a Hall of Famer and bravado of Ali. He was fun and, in 2004, pretty good. The collective hearts of L.A. put their faith in Lima to save them from 16 straight years without a playoff victory. The Dodgers got a few runs on the board, and Lima was putting up zeroes. The 8th ended with L.A. up 4-0. Undoubtedly, Eric Gagne would come out of the left field bullpen. After all, Gagne ruled the world, and we didn't know then that he was juicing like a four-year-old on a sugar rush.

But that wasn't what happened. The bullpen gate didn't fly open. "Welcome to the Jungle" did not play. I vividly remember 56,000-plus fans looking to the bullpen, dumbfounded that the position players were running onto the field without Gagne. Then it happened. Lima emerged from the dugout, hand raised in the air, sprinting to the mound. All the emotion he had shown throughout the season in his struggle to save his career was somehow in beautiful unison with the decade-plus frustration of Dodgers fans. We were a family. We were in this together. The roar was electric, like a proud father at a Little League game who could not contain his screaming while watching his son win, multiplied by 56,000. Lima got the job done and the Dodgers finally had their playoff win. I broke a seat jumping up and down on it.

While all that was memorable, what came next, I will never forget.

Near the heart of Los Angeles, in that moment, there was a melting pot of true embrace and camaraderie. Blacks and Whites, Jews and Muslims, Catholics and Protestants, Mexicans and Asians. It just didn't matter. No one cared about the skin color or the beliefs of the person next to them. There were hugs, high-fives, and tears. We were all with Lima. He had brought the City of Angels together, if only for a brief, wonderful time.

~Lucas Mayer, Los Angeles, California

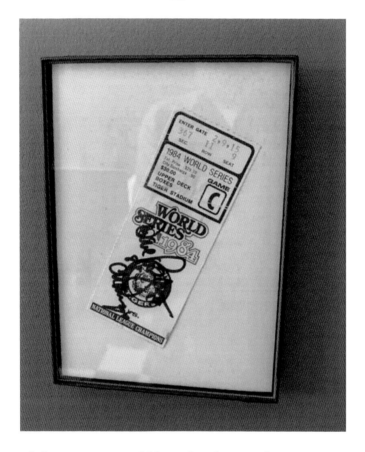

In 1984, I was 11 years old but already several years into my intense Tiger fandom. All signs said the Tigers would be a winner that year. From the get-go, I cut out the box score for each game and taped it to my wall.

The second half of the year would be tumultuous. My brother, Mike, and I made a very difficult decision to move from Mom's house to Dad's house in the fall. My parents had divorced in 1979 when I was six, and we had lived with Mom for the five years since.

Contrary to the memories you often hear about boys and their fathers, it was Mom who took us to Tiger Stadium every year to see at least one game, often more. We lived on the west side of the state (still do) and Mom hated long drives, so it became a tradition to stay at the Holiday Inn in Howell when we went to games. It broke up the drive and provided a fun sleepover for me and Mike. The hotel is still there; I think of those times every time I drive by. Some of my fondest childhood memories were from those games with Mike and Mom. When we made the decision to move in late summer of 1984, Mom took it very hard. There was a lot of tension between us and a lot of hurt.

Despite the feelings, when the Tigers won the playoff series, Mom submitted an application for World Series tickets. There was no Stubhub then, and the only resellers were standing outside the park as they still do today. There was no paying thousands for a $30 face-value ticket.

Mom's application was for tickets, all you could ask for, not for a specific game. Your name basically went into a hat and you hoped for the best. Mom got three tickets for Game 5, for less than $100 for all of them combined. They were in the upper deck, right field, foul territory. We had to actually root for the Padres to win one game so we could go. They did, and we went.

I remember the day like it was yesterday. Of course, we'd slept at the Holiday Inn the night before. "I'm So Excited" by the Pointer Sisters played on giant speakers all over downtown that afternoon. It felt like it was the only song being played that day. I still get goosebumps when I hear it.

After we'd announced we were moving, the times before that game were tense, and they remained so for a couple years after that game, for far too long. But on that day, we put it all aside. On that day it felt as though nothing had happened. We didn't talk about the move, didn't talk about the tension. We watched a team all three of us had grown up with win the World Championship. We saw Gibby hit two home runs, and Parrish—always my favorite—hit one. We smiled and laughed and high-fived until it hurt, with each other and with thousands we didn't know. Baseball has that power. It always has for me.

Since we sat in the upper deck, we couldn't rush the field when the game ended, but we yelled to someone to throw us some grass. Mom put it in a baggie and we brought it home and re-planted it. We could always spot it because it was darker than the other grass. Mike and I always showed it off to friends. Pitcher Dave Rozema later signed the ticket stub, saying it was one of the coolest things he'd ever signed.

The tension between us is now long gone. Bygones became bygones a few years later. The three of us are close again and talk baseball and the Tigers nonstop. We still talk about that day, that game, those memories. We never discuss the sad times, only the smiles, laughs, and high-fives. Only the greatest team we ever saw reside at The Corner win the greatest game we ever attended.

~Matthew Molter, Holland Michigan

My parents should have known better when I refused to play soccer as a young tyke. I was literally pulled through the passenger side window of our truck out onto the field. I remember a woman physically taking my leg and moving it so I would kick the soccer ball. I would coin my objection as a stoic protest, both in the mental and physical senses. My soccer career lasted one whole day, so it makes no sense to me why my parents, or even I, agreed to my participation in T-Ball.

I have few memories of the summer I played, but I do recall playing in the infield dirt. Rather than fielding ground balls or catching pop flies, I was more concerned about the shape of my star and perfecting my capital letter "A." Coaches tried to redirect my attention, which would work for a hot minute, but then I was back at my dirt calligraphy. Home videos also show my "enthusiasm" for the game. My dad decided to film one of our practices, but I have no idea why. The first few choppy minutes show me at first base, again playing in the dirt. Then the video cuts to me at bat. My batting stance needed serious work. I'm standing straight-legged, hands gripping the bat, elbows nearly touching the sides of my body. My coach tossed me an underhand pitch, and it went by me, followed by my swing about five seconds later. Hand-eye coordination problem? Probably. This was around the time we discovered I needed glasses. I had the mindset of

"Just bring out the Tee, please. I don't want to further embarrass myself as you try to get me to hit an underhand pitch. It's not happening, people."

Shockingly, my T-Ball career lasted a full season. Though I don't recall much about the game itself, I have fond memories surrounding it. I remember looking forward to the after-game treat, usually a melted Popsicle and a cool can of Shasta pop. After my games I would walk over to the other diamond to watch my older brother play Little League. I chased down foul balls with other kids and was rewarded with pieces of Super Bubble Gum from the concessions stand for bringing the balls back. It seemed like the whole town stopped what it was doing to head to the baseball diamonds to watch the summer baseball games. Mothers, fathers, grandparents, aunts, uncles, cousins, businessmen, and farmers. Everyone was there.

I am grateful for all my memories associated with baseball. Every time I catch a Royals game on T.V. or watch a local high school game, a comforting nostalgia settles over me. I believe most people enjoy baseball because of the fond memories the sport has given them. To me, it is almost like a feeling of peace, one that no other sport can offer. One day my husband and I will get to enjoy summers watching our children play this wonderful game. Of course, if I notice them playing in the dirt at second base, I'll kindly suggest a summer art class as well.

~Allison Clark, Tucson, Arizona

I am from France and moved with my wife and our two kids to Montreal in 2013. I had always been fascinated by North America and wanted to live there before it would be too hard to make my kids leave family and friends. My wife didn't speak any English, so Montreal was ideal for us. I started looking for activities for my children, especially a sport for my son to play. Hockey and football were too violent. Soccer, sure, but I wanted to find a sport native to North America. With baseball fields by our apartment, I signed my son up to play and volunteered to help coach. I started following baseball news and saw that a preseason game between the Blue Jays and Mets was scheduled at Olympic Stadium, home of the defunct Montreal Expos. I bought four tickets immediately, six months before game day.

On March 29, 2014, we were in the subway enroute to the big O. The closer we got, the more we saw fans with Expos gear. I didn't know what to expect. I had never seen the inside of the stadium and did not know how many fans would be there. What a crowd there was when we arrived, people chanting, "Let's go Expos," continuously. I still remember the sight of the stadium. It was huge. We were speechless, filled with a mixture of anxiety and excitement.

With players of both teams warming up on the field, the lights lowered and the announcer said, "Ladies and gentlemen, please welcome the best team in baseball in 1994" I wondered what was going on, as I didn't yet know the history of the Expos. People stood and started to applaud. Players of that 1994 team were introduced to a standing ovation, including Marquis Grissom, Moises Alou, Larry Walker, Darren Fletcher, Cliff Floyd, and of course manager Felipe Alou. A video of their exploits was broadcast on the scoreboard. It was really emotional, even if we didn't know much about that team.

The game itself was not spectacular, a victory 1-0 by the Blue Jays, but to see in person the speed the ball was pitched, to hear the sounds of the ball on the bat and in the gloves was amazing. After five innings, I moved around the stadium to take photos. The closer I got to the field the more impressed I was by the pitch speed. In the 7th inning everybody stood and started singing a short song I was hearing for the first time, something that seemed to be from the 1920s. Everyone applauded at the end. What was this? Did I miss something? Of course, as soon as I got back home, Google helped me to understand the 7th Inning Stretch, a contagious song for me ever since.

I didn't know what to expect that day, but what I saw changed me into a big fan of the game and its history. We were impressed by the crowd of 50,000 coming to watch a preseason game between two teams they didn't root for, chanting all game long, "Let's go Expos." It was such an unbelievably great atmosphere. We felt joy and happiness in every person's eyes, from very young kids to former fans. We could also feel the nostalgia and the desire to have a team back to Montreal, the desire becoming a will.

I have gotten involved in many fan groups both on the web and in Montreal, where people share our common passion, baseball and the return of a Major League Baseball team in the city that saw players like Jackie Robinson, Roberto Clemente, Gary Carter, Andre Dawson, Tim Raines, Pedro Martinez, and Dennis "El Presidente" Martinez' perfect game. Is Montreal only a hockey city? I can strongly affirm, *no*. Just go out in spring and summer and look at the kids playing baseball everywhere.

~Benoit Ripert, Provence, France

My love of baseball started when I was seven, having moved to Milwaukee. My soon-to-be best friend Sue's mom ran a Little League, and Sue asked if I played. Her big brother taught me all about Yount, Molitor, and Jim Ganter. I was hooked. After a move to Phoenix, I became a season ticket holder for the Giants Triple-A Firebirds. Since 2001, I have had total loyalty for the D'Backs.

Home games found me in the autograph line at The BOB—the Bank One Ballpark. Fans talked about who was pitching that night, what visiting superstar they hoped to see play, and who might come up from Triple-A. Baseball experts said the D'Backs had a good shot at the World Series. I thought it was crazy talk, but it intensified after the All-Star break. Could this inconsistent, never-dominant team actually get there and beat the big bats in the American League? Between the autograph search and hours waiting for bobbleheads, we were stand-in-line pros. It was like a neighborhood party with blankets, coolers full of water and snacks, and conversation. We made long-term friends standing in line that year. But there were dark times approaching as summer moved into fall. Sept 11th happened. Being so far away and not directly affected, I couldn't understand the magnitude of the event, nor comprehend why my game was not being played, nor truly fathom what my country was experiencing.

The D'Backs won the National League West, and I was back in line to get tickets for the National League Division Series against the Cardinals. But as Tony Womack hit that amazing single to left bringing home my old Firebird guy, Matt Williams, to win the game 2-1, where was I? On 4th Street standing in line for, you guessed it, more tickets. In order to get Series tickets for Games 6 and 7, we lined up at 5:30 a.m. the day before they went on sale. I dumped my 72-year-old mother at the curb, instructing her, "Get in line, I'm going to get some supplies for overnight and I'll be right back." I somehow convinced my sister, Mary, to spend the night with Mom and D'back Nation so I could function at work the next day. The next morning, as I dropped off coffee and donuts before going to work, I was told to never, *ever* ask this of them again. It had been impossible to sleep in the midst of a slumber party of thousands, especially when Jesse the trumpet player serenaded the crowd at 2:00 a.m.

I could talk all day about how the D'backs beat the Yankees, but you know, it is really about the journey, which included friends, a love of baseball, and a love of my D'backs.

~Maureen OBrien, Phoenix, Arizona

After over 50 years and attending hundreds of ball games, I had still never seen a no-hitter. I wasn't there on June 13, 2012, when Matt Cain stepped onto the AT&T mound, but I was watching on TV. My wife, Lynn, and I watched the whole thing, and our daughter, Rachel, was working at the park as usual for home games. As our collective favorite player, Matt Cain, was tossing more and more zeroes—0 hits, 0 runs, 0 errors, 0 walks—the tension and anxiety began to rise in our household. From 3000 miles away, four-way texts began with our son, David, who knew he should be going to sleep, but could not pass on the chance to watch history being made. Gregor Blanco's catch in the 7th was the first breathtaking moment. For the last play, a tough hop to Joaquin Arias, who had replaced Panda for defensive purposes, made him step backward, taking away any momentum toward first base. The play was made, Cain pumped his fist, and then came the phone call, a very brief one at 1:00 a.m. or so, from David. This was history, just the 22nd perfect game ever. It was our favorite player who had accomplished this feat and, it was obvious that once again, this magical game of baseball had connected the four of us, from our home in San Francisco to the press elevator in the park, to an apartment in D.C., to the pitcher's mound.

Five years later, Lynn and I got tickets for the last game of the 2017 season. Lynn likes to go to this game, Fan Appreciation Day, at which prizes are given away like water to racers in a marathon and players throw balls into the stands after the game. But we went that day because we knew this was the last game that Matt Cain would ever pitch. Several years of ineffectiveness, caused in part by the injuries that suddenly plagued the once-impervious Horse, had resulted in his decision at the relatively young age of 33 to hang 'em up rather than keep pushing to regain a past magic. We knew he would get the start one last time, after half a season of doing bullpen mop-up work. He did, and he was magnificent, reaching back and pitching like the Matt Cain of old. And, fittingly, befitting the term coined from his name, he got "Cained," receiving no run support. He pitched five innings, the last reputedly on fumes and adrenalin, and took the loss.

Still our guy, I thought, as today I watched the ceremonies inducting him onto the Giants Wall of Fame. And it still makes me a little teary when I read this story. He will be my last ever favorite player.

~Eric Gray, San Francisco, California

In 2012, I was working in a restaurant in Kenosha, Wisconsin, and for one night I was temporarily transferred to another location in Carol Stream, Illinois, a suburb of Chicago. The playoffs were underway, and I was listening to the Orioles vs. Rangers Wild Card game on the radio while closing out for the night. I finished my paperwork as the 9th inning began, and as I locked the door to go home, I heard a familiar voice. I looked over to the nearby convenience store and there was a guy in his car in the parking lot listening to the same game. I went over, said hi, and asked him if he had a dog in the race. I stood by his car, listening and talking about the happenings in Major League Baseball. After a couple at-bats, he offered his passenger seat so we could sit and listen together. It seemed like a long inning while we sat and talked baseball and Portillos—my favorite restaurant, where he happened to work. After the game ended, we sat and continued to talk baseball for another 20 minutes before I got going. Of all the people I had dealt with that day, it felt nice that the last one was a complete stranger to whom I gave 45 minutes of my life talking about and listening to baseball. I love how baseball can bring people together like that, complete strangers who can chat like old friends because of a game. It's one of my favorite memories.

~Shawn Cusack, Oak Creek, Wisconsin

Nothing illustrates the emotional rollercoaster of baseball better than two nights in 2012. After thirty-three years without baseball, Washington, D.C. finally had a major league team. For several mediocre seasons, the team played like an expansion franchise, but suddenly, with homegrown names like Harper, Strasburg, and Storen, who had come up through the system together, the Nationals were in the playoffs.

Having wrapped up its first division title, the Nationals were down two games to one to the Cardinals, heading into a potential elimination game at home. In a very controversial decision, the Nats had shut down Strasburg in his first year back from Tommy John surgery. The Game 4 starting assignment went to Ross Detweiler, a journeyman spot starter and long relief man this season. He pitched the game of his life. In the bottom of the 9th, after fouling off numerous pitchers, Nats' Jayson Werth lined the game-winning home run off of Lance Lynn. I have never seen, or been part of, a crowd so deliriously happy. Strangers were hugging, high-fiving, and spilling beer all over each other. What a great example of the speed and tension of playoff baseball. It was the single happiest moment I have had at a major league game.

Game 5 was played on a chilly night, Nationals Gio Gonzalez vs. Cardinals ace Adam Wainwright. After three innings, the Nationals led 6-0 and the park felt like the world's largest cocktail party. But the Cardinals chipped away at the lead. Going into the 9th, the score was 7-5. Out through the swinging bullpen door strode reliable closer Drew Storen. Half a dozen times he was one strike away from closing out the Series, but the Cardinals would not go down. The most memorable at-bat was the one ending in a walk to David Freese, followed by hits from Descalso and Kozma…and that was the game. For the fans in the stadium and all around the D.C. area, it was like the New Year's party that never came.

Since that day, I've had periodic dreams of sitting in section 205, where I sat that game, of Storen getting that last strike, and the park erupting in pandemonium. Too bad I wake up and nothing has changed.

These two back-to-back games represent, for me, the incredible speed and tension and rollercoaster of the emotions in playoff baseball. They illustrate the transition from delirious high to slow, torturous death. It is what I love about baseball, and for me, no sport captures these emotions in quite the same way.

~Len Foxwell, Easton, Maryland

My early childhood was spent in Brooklyn. That was a long time ago, yet the images remain very clear. My world revolved around the Dodgers. I would leave home, walk down Bedford Avenue to Ebbets Field, and hang out and watch the folks who could afford to attend games. It was similar to people on Waveland Avenue by Wrigley Field. There was no television then, and games were not even broadcast regularly on the radio. It is hard for young people today to imagine a time without instantaneous news, but that was my reality growing up.

The memory that stands out for me most involves my favorite uncle, Peter Kobak, who knew someone in the St. Louis Cardinals organization. On September 21, 1934, Uncle Peter managed to get me into the Cardinals clubhouse before a doubleheader against the Dodgers. What a thrill that was! Here I was, a 10-year-old kid, standing around talking with the Dean brothers, Leo "The Lip" Durocher, manager Frankie Frisch, Enos "Country" Slaughter, Joe "Ducky" Medwick, and Rip Collins. They were referred to as the "Gashouse Gang." Some of them asked if I was rooting for them. "*No*," I strongly replied. "I am a Dodgers fan!" They thought I was a cute kid, and they all signed a baseball for me anyway. Of course, as many folks can relate to, my mom threw that ball away when I was in the Navy during WW ll. As she put it, "It was an old baseball with some writing on it." I never left anything of value at home after that.

Anyway, back to that doubleheader. Jay Hanna "Dizzy" Dean tossed a three-hitter in the first game, shutting out my Dodgers. As if competing in a friendly rivalry with his brother, Paul "Daffy" Dean pitched a no-hitter in the second game of the twin bill. Dizzy was later heard saying to his brother in the clubhouse, "Gee, Paul, if I'da known you was goin' to throw a no-hitter, I'da thrown one too." The Dodgers were a wonderful group, but not the best team in the league. Shortstop Lonnie Frey committed six errors in a single game and was traded to the Reds, and pitcher Van Lingo Mungo lost 20 games. But on that day there were two amazing pitching performances, by brothers, on the same day. What a day of baseball.

The Dodgers' glory years with Jackie, Pee Wee, Duke, Camilli, Erskine, Dixie Walker, Campanella, Lavagetto, Newcomb, and Koufax, were still two decades and 3000 miles away. The games were called by the great Red Barber, Al Helfer, and of course, Vin Scully. Dazzy Vance ended his career with the Dodgers, and Babe Ruth served briefly as their batting coach. And then there was the great betrayal when the Dodgers moved to Los Angeles, but that story is for another time. I am grateful for Ebbets Field and the players who helped me to understand "You can't win them all." Long ago I moved to Chicago, and I can't wait for the Cubs to be in the World Series. But those Dodgers, and that one day at Ebbets Field, I will remember them always.

~Jerry Hausmann, Evanston, Illinois

As I play
I hear rumbling crowds
and I see bright lights
and smell the pure green grass

As I play
I am thinking
I am ready in attack position
the game I play begins

As I play
I dive for the catch
I reach for the ball
and I deliver a pitch across the plate

As I play
the game of baseball
my life is mine
and I'm in control
~Austin Karp, Tarpon Springs, Florida

Growing up in Oregon, I was not exposed to Major League Baseball. When my husband and I moved to the Bay Area, I found myself starting to follow the Oakland A's simply because I lived there. My interest became a passion when my son, Ethan, began playing at a serious level.

It is the vulnerability that draws me to baseball. Whether standing at the plate waiting for the pitch, keeping the runner on first as you prepare to pitch to the batter, or being in the field with the ball coming your way, all eyes are on you. This vulnerability leads to intensity for the observer as well as the player. I find myself feeling the players' pain or elation, depending on the outcome of their performance. I've become an active observer rather than a passive one, and I keep coming back for more.

~Karen Hopkins, Oakland, California

How does a love for baseball develop? You hear tales of Ebbets Field and cowbells, Comiskey Park and Nancy Faust's organ, eating your first Dodger Dog, or being a bum in the bleachers at Wrigley. Be it Koufax, Ted Williams, Reggie's three bombs in '77, or Junior's backwards cap, something, someone, turned all fans' eyes for that first time, and baseball became their love. Mine? It was a little-known outfielder from Puerto Rico, Pepe Mangual, who played from 1972 to 1977 with the Expos and Mets. My first live game started my love affair. A walk-off grand slam? Nah, he had no pop. Steal of home? He had speed, but nothing that dramatic. Game-saving catch? He was a decent center fielder, but, again, no.

On Friday September 5, 1975, a young, hopeful, but not terribly talented last place Expos team took on the first place Pirates in a twi-night doubleheader. It was my first time inside "Parc", Jarry Park, which until then had been nothing but a dream castle on the TV set to a nine-year-old boy who'd started loving baseball in 1974. In the opener, Bruce Kison was wild and didn't make it out of the first. Bob Moose, who would tragically die 13 months later, came in to toss 5 2/3 innings. The Expos led 2-0 lead going into the 8th, but a Richie Zisk two-run shot, my first live home run, and Willie Stargell's pinch single gave the Pirates a 3-2 lead. The Expos tied it, and into extra innings we went! Pittsburgh could not plate after rookie Art Howe hit into a double play.

My young blood was pumping, and Jarry Park was rocking to the house organ with 15,000-plus fans on their feet as the Expos came up. Young side-arming Kent Tekulve, a future Expos-killer, took the mound. Walks, wild pitches, and passed balls got Pete Mackanin to third, Jim Lyttle to second, and Jerry White to first, the bases loaded for center fielder, Pepe Mangual. Pepe entered the game as a pinch-hitter in the 7th inning hitting a nondescript .247, but what would a kid know other than it was the bottom of the 10th and the bases were loaded? Bruce Froemming was the umpire behind the plate. I cannot recall how many total pitches were thrown, but the count was 2-2 as Pepe fouled off pitch after pitch, every fan on their feet screaming, willing Pepe to not fail.

I was in awe and wanted, in that moment, more than anything ever, to win the game. It had been a horrific week in my life, filled with trauma. A young boy from small town Towanda, Pennsylvania, I went to visit my grandparents not knowing my parents were splitting up, and that I'd never return home. I was to stay in Montreal, a new kid in school, with French-speaking folks hating English-speaking people and vice versa, mere months before a hated Separatist Government would come to power, forever changing the Quebec landscape. It was a terrifying experience for this small-town kid.

None of that mattered right now. I just needed Pepe to win it for us! He worked the count full, then fouled off two more. I couldn't take it anymore. The next pitch was "ju-ussst" a little outside, as Bob Uecker might say. Froemming motioned ball four, and the Expos mobbed Pepe as he trotted to first and Mackanin walked home. A 4-3 Expo victory! For that small, scared, nine-year-old boy who would have to face his new life and surroundings once again on Monday morning, nothing else mattered. I found love in Montreal, the love of the Expos, the love of Pepe Mangual my new could-do-no-wrong-hero, and my greatest new love, one that would last a lifetime without fail, baseball.

-Patrick Guttin, Sandpoint, Idaho

I grew up with baseball in Cranston, Rhode Island. My father idolized Carl Yastrzemski and the Impossible Dream Boston Red Sox of 1967. He first learned true heartbreak, not from a girl, but from the Sox, who lost the World Series not only in '67 while he was a teenager, but again as a young man in 1975. In 1986, when the Sox were winning Game 6 against the Mets, he woke five-year-old me from a deep slumber to witness something with him that he'd never seen in his lifetime, or his father in his—the Red Sox winning the Series. Instead, he allowed me the opportunity to witness something all too common, the Sox blowing a lead and snatching defeat from the jaws of victory. I remember asking, "Why would you wake me up to see that? Why would you want me to get so happy and then make me cry?" He didn't have an answer.

Two years later, Dad took my younger brother and me to our first major league game after having been to only AAA games at McCoy Stadium in Pawtucket, Rhode Island. We were going to Fenway Park! Even at seven years old, I amazed family and parents' friends with my knowledge of baseball trivia. I loved reading about its history and the legends of the game. And I was about see a field that had been home to the Greatest Hitter Who Ever Lived, Ted Williams. Cy Young, Ty Cobb, Walter Johnson, Babe Ruth, Joe DiMaggio, Mickey Mantle, Stan Musial, and yes, my dad's favorite, Yaz, had all played on that field alongside stars who stood head and shoulders above all others.

It was June 26, 1988, and we were running late getting to the game. We walked up the concourse and Dad specifically took us on a route that would ensure the first thing we'd see was The Wall. The Green Monster, the 37-foot-high green wall in left field that was defended so elegantly by Dad's hero, Yaz. Just as we walked up the steps, the crowd stood and roared as future Hall of Famer Jim Rice, who took over for Yaz in left field, blasted a pitch high over the wall and into the net protecting the cars on the street. That was it. If I wasn't hooked on baseball before, that moment sealed the deal.

The greatest performance I ever witnessed also occurred at Fenway, when Pedro Martinez struck out 16 Atlanta Braves in a three-hit, complete game masterpiece against another Hall of Famer, Tom Glavine, blemished only by a Ryan Klesko home run that just barely curled around the Pesky Pole in right. The Dominican flag waved proudly in the stands as it did with every Pedro start. I experienced this once more in 2015 when I sat on the lawn in Cooperstown, New York, to see Pedro inducted into the Baseball Hall of Fame.

Baseball has always been a part of my life and it always will be. I continue to study and analyze its complexity daily, but also appreciate its simplicity. As major league hit king Pete Rose once said, "See the ball, hit the ball." It creates so many passionate debates among fans and elicits the greatest of stories. I make the trek every year to Induction Weekend in Cooperstown and enjoy chatting with other fans almost as much as seeing the legends themselves. I look forward to having a son one day, and to introduce him to the game I so deeply love. Hopefully, however, I won't wake him up from a deep sleep so he can watch his favorite team blow the World Series.

~Matthew Mendillo, New Egypt, New Jersey

My husband is an avid A's fan. I have always followed them, but never went all fan girl. I'm much too shy for that. We went to the final game of the 2012 season, and it was so exciting! The energy in the stadium was infectious. I can only believe that the players must have felt our support because they rallied to win that game in a huge way, snatching the division title from the Rangers. We stayed well after the final out was made, watching them celebrate in the locker room on Diamond vision, wanting to catch them one more time on this magical day. They delivered, and the fans who stayed saw them take final group photos in their champagne-soaked uniforms. It was amazing! I will never forget the way I felt that day. It was overwhelming, and still brings tears to my eyes to recall it. Absolutely awesome!

~Lourdes D., Portland, Oregon

My grandparents meant the world to me. I was too young to truly appreciate just how much of an impact they would have on me, and probably didn't show them as much gratitude as I should have. That's the thing about human beings, we don't know what we have till it's gone.

My paternal grandfather was named Noble Riddle. Never was a man more aptly named. A working man, he grew up and lived in the mountains in southeastern Kentucky, settled in small town McRoberts, and was married to my Granny Vina for over 50 years. Papaw never lost his temper, never raised his voice, a godly man but never judgmental, he owned his mistakes. Papaw was an intellectual, an introspective and well-read man, wise beyond my comprehension, and we hit it off like gangbusters. He wrote me letters while I was in boot camp, always addressed to "Master Clinton Riddle," in the old style of addressing young bachelors. I always got a kick out of that. And when we visited him, he always called me Doc. I idolized him.

As a kid, I constantly had my nose stuck in a book—novels, textbooks, encyclopedias, anything I could get. Never remotely caring about sports until I was 14, I didn't spend years playing Little League or Pop Warner football. Papaw had served as a radioman on a Coast Guard ship in the Pacific Theatre during World War II, and I wanted to be just like him, although I chose to go Navy. My dad had carried a field radio in Vietnam. Initially wanting to become a shipboard communications officer, I ended up taking a much different path, enlisting as a hospital corpsman. I've never regretted that.

Papaw was a baseball fan. He would turn on the Reds games and we'd watch together. I was interested in the game simply because he was. He told me stories of seeing barnstorming teams in Pacific ports, teams with all-time greats like Johnny Mize. He'd mentioned Mize, so I became interested in Mize. Papaw took the time to relay these experiences to me. His mention of Mize, DiMaggio, and Musial, and the 1970s Reds greats like Perez, Concepcion, Rose, and Bench sparked my interest in baseball. Papaw loved the game, which stoked my fascination.

Already a history buff, I decided to learn about it. I read everything I could find on the history of baseball, starting with almanacs and record books, reading about names I'd never heard of performing feats I couldn't imagine. Suddenly, I was back in the early 1900s, with the Giants, A's, and Dodgers, John McGraw, Rogers Hornsby, Ty Cobb, and Tris Speaker. Papaw's stories made that history come alive in the mind of a bookish child with a wild imagination. It was simple, if he talked about it, I wanted to learn about it. Through our common interests, we became closer and learned more about one another.

This was no gradual thing but a head-first dive. I sought out games on TV. The Reds, the Braves, the Cubs, any game I could find, as long as Papaw would watch with me. I entered fandom the long way around, learning its history before I had even picked a favorite team or player.

A lot of us have someone in our lives that fills that same role. In another life, Papaw could have been a leader of men, a captain of industry. Anything would have been within his reach, but he chose to simply be a dependable man who led his life with a heart of love for God and neighbor. He may as well have been Moses come down from the mountain to a 13-year-old kid with more knowledge than was remotely useful, but little true wisdom, and no idea what the real world was like. We could have had any mutual interest—farming, or woodworking (he did that, too), anything. It just happened to be baseball. I fell in love with the game because I loved my grandfather.

In October of 1993, about to enter Hospital Corps School, I was home on leave from boot camp in Great Lakes. Papaw was dying from a cancer that had metastasized to his brain and liver. My parents and I visited him in McRoberts, in the home he and Vina had shared for more than 50 years. Weak and lying in bed, he sat up a bit as we spoke for a little while. We looked at each other, this time man-to-man, and we both knew this would be our last time together. He asked how boot camp went, and I told him it was a breeze. I'd played three sports in high school, all because of a seed of interest he'd unknowingly planted, so I was in good enough shape to handle boot camp. When our short conversation was over, and I'll never forget this, he said "Goodbye." "See you later," I replied, and I truly believe that.

Five weeks into Corps School, the call came. Noble Riddle was gone. I took the call in the hallway of our barracks, with dozens of other Corps School students busily going about their lives. I handled it without tears. Papaw would have wanted that. The Red Cross representative offered to fly me back for the funeral. I declined. I wanted to remember him as I'd known him, not as he was now. I think he would have wanted that, too.

I wanted to model my life after him in so many ways, failing more times than I could count, but he was always my benchmark of success. Much of the way he lived his life was reflected in my father's life, as well. I only hoped I could be half the man he was.

Now a rabid baseball nut, a fan of both the game and its history, I had chosen favorite players from decades past, even though they'd died long before I was born, because I believed they were like my Papaw—Christy Mathewson and Lou Gehrig. All-time greats, to be sure, but more to the point, they reminded me of him. My interest in the game was now my own, aside from our shared experiences. Honestly, I don't think he necessarily intended or expected that I'd become a fan like him.

I regret that I didn't spend more time with him or know more about him than I did. We lived three hours away, and for a kid, that trip seemed like going to another world. Ultimately, it wasn't the game that was important, it was the man who loved it.

That was 28 years ago, and he's been in my heart and my mind, every day since. When I watch a game, or read about its history, it comes alive in a way that he made possible. He always showed me a great deal of respect, like we were contemporaries instead of grandfather and grandson. I've stayed in medicine now for 28 years, and I write about the game from time to time. I even kept the nickname Doc because that's what he called me. I sometimes wonder if I'll ever have the sort of influence on anyone as Papaw did for me or write anything to spark the interest in baseball that he created in me. Someday, I hope.

~Clinton Riddle, Lexington, Kentucky

Tales of Love About the Other Willie

Everyone should have a favorite baseball player, and I think that I have the best as my hero, Willie McCovey. My father told me about going to Game 7 of the 1962 World Series with my grandfather, but he wasn't very descriptive about the experience. I know of course how it ended, tying and winning runs on base for the Giants, McCovey lining out to Yankee second baseman, Bobby Richardson.

I became a fan in 1978. It was like all the planets aligned. The Giants had an exciting year with a combination of good pitching, solid defense, and timely hitting, a core of good young players and some veterans. Willie Mac had returned to the Giants in 1977, had a great year, and was named Comeback Player of the Year. Unfortunately, the team faded in September of '78 and Willie's performance declined. But he was the connection between the great Giants teams of the 1960s and the 1978 Giants, a team that inspired lots of kids to become Giants fans.

I discovered an accidental hobby one day hanging out with my friends, Jonathan and Lincoln Mitchell. Looking through the Sunday newspaper in December 1980, we saw that Willie would be signing autographs. The only thing I had for him to sign was a 1979 San Francisco Giants media guide. His became the first autograph in that guide. Thirty-five years later, in 2015, the project was completed with the autograph of the last player, Hector "Heity" Cruz. It had certainly been a fun quest.

In 1986, Dad asked what I wanted for my 21st birthday. I replied I wanted to see McCovey inducted into Cooperstown. Dad said he would fly me to New York, then I could stay with my sister and brother-in-law, Laura and Michael, at their apartment in Hoboken, New Jersey, and take the bus to Cooperstown for the ceremony. I was ecstatic. I got to see New York City and spend a weekend in Boston, too.

Michael and I went to a Mets game the night before Cooperstown. With rain delays, we didn't get home until 2:00 a.m. and had to wake up again at 4:00 a.m. to return to Manhattan to catch the bus. We slept most of the way, but I kept waking up to see where we were, avoid oversleeping, and wind up in Canada. When we arrived, we went straight to the Hall of Fame Museum. It was spectacular. That night, we camped out across the street from the Hall on the porch, under the eaves of the Cooperstown library. We rose the next morning to watch the induction ceremony. I was thrilled and proud to be there representing Giants fans, to see my hero, Willie McCovey, inducted into the Hall of Fame.

Some years later, working on a graduate school research paper and listening to the radio, I heard that McCovey would be guesting at the station's lunchtime oldies show. I called to ask if I could come get his autograph. They gave no guarantee but said to come by. I asked Willie if he could please sign my McCovey picture, and he did, writing, "To Charles, Best Wishes, Willie McCovey." I have that picture to this day. Riding the elevator with him, I said nothing, I was so in awe of him. He drove away in a red sports car, honking his horn and waving goodbye.

Over the years, I got autographs at card shows and went to the annual Willie Mac Award ceremony, honoring the team's most inspirational player as voted by the fans. One Christmas, I received a box from my then-wife and my family. It was the certification of a plaque in my name at McCovey Cove. Several years ago, Willie sat outside of the ballpark, waiting to go on a radio broadcast. I stood there talking to him, but he said very little. I told him how I had seen him play when I was a kid, and that I'd gone to his Hall of Fame induction ceremony. He didn't respond. I had a ball in my pocket and asked if he would sign it. The security guard sternly said, "No autographs." Willie spoke up, "No, I'll sign a ball for him," pointing to me, and "for no one else." I thanked him for his kindness.

One of my friends is a Giants executive, but I don't take advantage of our friendship. Several years ago, I dropped off a picture I'd taken of Willie at Giants Photo Day in 1978. I had forgotten about it since so much time had passed. Last August, it arrived back in my mailbox, signed by Willie. It was beautiful. I received a message from my friend telling me it was probably Willie's last autograph.

In October 2019, as I left the gym, my phone blew up with messages. My hero had died. I sat at the bus stop and started crying, unable to stop. He'd lived up to all my expectations of what a hero should be. He was kind, quiet, and a giant Giant. The next day, I went to his statue at McCovey Cove to leave flowers. A reporter asked what Willie meant to me and I again started to cry. I proudly went to his memorial service at AT&T Park. Willie will remain my hero for the rest of my days.

~Charles Fracchia, San Francisco, California

When the Giants came west, they established their top farm team in Phoenix, which joined the Sacramento Solons in the Pacific Coast League. One evening early in the 1959 season, my parents took me to see the Solons and the Giants play. Phoenix' big left-hander at first base was impressive just to look at. In his first at-bat, he hit one over the scoreboard in left-center, followed by another to right-center. When a Solon hit a smash to his right, he seemingly pulled the ball out of right field to make the out. I thought, "This guy won't be here long." He wasn't. The Giants soon called him up, even with another budding Hall of Famer, Cepeda, playing first. In his first game, the new guy went 4-4 against Phillies' All-Star Robin Roberts, including two triples. Already a Giants fan, I now had a favorite player: Willie McCovey.

The 1962 World Series, the Giants vs. the Yankees, was played in the daytime, making watching games problematic for a sophomore in school. I had P.E. as the famous Game 7 entered its final innings. The coaches, not wanting to miss it either, played the radio through the loudspeaker. My hero came to the plate. "It's a line drive..." Willie had tied, or maybe won, the game! "Richardson jumps and makes the catch." No! It can't be true! A few days later, Bay Area native Charles Schultze drew his daily Peanuts cartoon, where the first three frames had Charlie Brown looking forlorn. In the 4th frame, he lifts his head and shouts, "Why couldn't McCovey have hit the ball a foot higher?!" I knew exactly how Charlie Brown felt.

In 1977, McCovey returned to the Giants, where he belonged. I went to a night game at Candlestick, and risking frostbite, I stayed till the end. In a close game with the Giants trailing, McCovey came up. This time no one caught his line drive, a walk-off hit for the Giants. I was delirious! It was the last game I saw him play, a perfect climax.

~Doug Kempster, Sacramento, California

I was fortunate to have tickets for the 2017 American League Division Series Game 2, Indians vs. Yankees, arranged by my nephew for my brother and me. A lifelong Indians fan, this would be my first time at a Tribe playoff game. It turned out to be, literally, the most exciting major league game of my life.

The stadium was packed. The Indians were coming off a 102-win season—including 22 wins in a row—and the division title. Playing in Cleveland, they beat the Yankees in the first game. Ace Corey Kluber would face former Indian C.C. Sabathia in Game 2. Kluber was unexpectedly not sharp, and the Yankees chased him before he completed three innings. The Indians quickly fell behind 8-3, and a hush fell over the crowd.

The Indians slowly crept back, and in the 6th inning, Francisco Lindor hit a grand slam, the ball hitting the right field foul pole, bringing them to within one. The crowd went into a frenzy and remained so until the 8th inning when Jay Bruce hit an opposite field home run, tying the game. The fans erupted again. I texted my sons, Scott and Jeff, "Do you believe this?!" Scott answered, "Unreal. What's it like in the stadium?" I replied, "The place is going wild." Watching from his apartment in Maryland, Scott's heart was pounding in excitement. In fact, years later, he still gets chills watching replays of those two mammoth home runs.

The rest of the game settled into a relievers' pitching duel, eventually going into extra innings. Both teams threatened along the way, but some terrific defensive plays prevented either team from breaking the tie. At one point, Indians catcher Yan Gomes picked off a Yankee at second base with a rifle throw from a seated position.

Finally, in the 13th inning, Gomes singled in the winning run, and the Indians won 9-8. Fans rejoiced, and nobody wanted to leave the stadium. I wondered if this magical game might lead to a magical ending with the Indians claiming their first World Series title since 1948. Alas, that was not to be. The Yankees won the next three games, and the Series. However, I suspect this will remain the greatest game I'll ever witness.

~Bob Tiell, Louisville, Kentucky, with an assist from Scott, Rockville, Maryland

I was born in the early 1980s as a military brat and we moved to a new base every three years. That made it hard to feel as if I had a home team. But because my father was from Georgia and the Braves were always on TBS, they were our go-to ball club even though they lost almost every game I watched. We lived in Germany from 1986 to 1990 and did our best to pay attention to Major League Baseball, but I couldn't really relate. In 1991 my father was stationed back in Georgia, and we moved mid-summer to our new house and school system. I began my last years of elementary school with new friends...and no idea what it meant to be a Braves fan. I would soon be introduced into what might have been the craziest few weeks of baseball excitement ever seen in the South when the Braves pulled off the impossible, going from worst to first.

My first week of school, I was not fully aware of what this meant. August was declared Braves month, with students allowed to bring their foam Tomahawks to classes, which began with the singing of the classic War Cry prior to any actual classwork. The first time it happened, I didn't even know the right pitch for the tune. My P.E. class consisted of walking or running (our choice) around the track while the coach beat an "Indian" drum and students continued to sing...for an hour. It was insane. If you didn't wear a Braves jersey or T-shirt on a game day, you were considered a traitor, subjected to all of the evils that little kids do or say to let you know that you are wrong. I quickly got a shirt and found myself caught up in the hysteria. After we beat the Pirates in a nail-biting Game 7, the pastor at our church somehow managed to fit it into his sermon as a lesson on perseverance.

Never able to stay up late unless there was a game, the family watched and supported the Braves until the end. I don't think I've ever hated a team more than the Minnesota Twins. As far as I'm concerned, they can burn in hell...although I am not sure our pastor would agree to that! They beat us in seven, in what some say was the greatest World Series ever played. I know that's how I feel, being the first time I understood what it meant to have a team. They're still my team, and I love the Braves.

~Adam Rivette, Atlanta, Georgia

Of all the great roads in the United States, there is none more significant for me than U.S. 192 in Florida. At its northern end are the hotels, resorts, and theme parks of Orlando where thousands of vacationing Brits spend their time, but head away from there, through the outskirts of Kissimmee, and on the edge of town you will see the light towers of Osceola County Stadium, spring home of the Houston Astros. This is where, on a glorious March afternoon in 2001, I discovered baseball.

Already a huge sports fan, I couldn't resist taking in a game, thanks to a kindly gentleman from upstate New York who patiently explained the rules and jargon "two on, one out," "double play," and "sac fly." They meant nothing to me back then, but I saw enough to become hooked. Now I spend two weeks every summer making road trips to different parts of the country, visiting as many different ballparks as I can.

What's so great about the game? First, there is the history and the way the game of today is indelibly linked to the traditions and players of the past. There is a reverence to the game itself found every bit as much in the purity of a college wood bat in front of a few hundred spectators as it is in the glory days of the big leagues. Then there are the stadiums, cathedrals of sheer beauty—Comerica Park in Detroit, Michigan, Lindquist Field in Ogden, Utah, and my favorite, Cardines Field in Newport, Rhode Island.

At Osceola County Stadium on that day in 2001, it had been foggy but in the late afternoon the mist rolled away and the sun shone. I sat in the back row of the stands and looked out across the bright green grass where young men in white and grey were lined up ready to face the flag. The scene was timeless and perfect, and there was nowhere I would rather have been.

Now if someone could just explain ERA to me again, I would be much obliged…

~Jon Green, Norwich, England

I hope, Jon, that I adequately explained Earned Run Average to you.

To be a Pirates Fan

I have always been a Pittsburgh Pirates fan, but it's been a long, bumpy road. I am 32 and they have had far more years being the laughing stock of baseball then actually playing .500 ball, let alone making the playoffs. I wasn't alive for the 1979 "We are Family" World Series win. I never saw Roberto Clemente play in person. I have only seen Bill Mazeroski's Game 7 World Series-winning walk-off home run on YouTube. I was about to turn 10 when Sid Bream was called safe at home in Game 7 of the 1992 National League Championship Series. During 20 years of losing, I grew to accept that the Pirates were, well, losers. With no memories of the good old days, losing became a normal part of baseball life.

I have dreamed my whole life of the Pirates winning the World Series, a dream that seemed would never come true. Things started to change in 2012 when they had their best roster and record in years and remained competitive for a few years after that. On Oct 1, 2013, my almost-10-year-old son watched his first Pirates playoff game, the first one I remembered. They rattled Cueto and won the Wild Card game, only to lose to St. Louis in the Division Series. I am waiting for them to become the World Series champs while representing The City of Champions, the only city in which all three professional sports team wear the same colors, black and gold.

~Anne Benson, Ambridge, Pennsylvania

As much as I love the ballpark and the many wonderful times I've had there over the years, the greatest memory of a game happened at PNC Park on October 1, 2013, for the National League Wild Card game. The Pirates, after decades of losing, made the post season as a Wild Card team against the Reds. I have never before or since heard a sporting event atmosphere quite like it was at that game. Frustration over 20 years of losing was unleashed on an unsuspecting Reds team and their ace starter, Johnny Cueto. The once laughed-at fans of the lowly Pirates were in a frenzy well before the lineups were introduced, and that electricity didn't end until well after the final pitch. The noise was intense. This was the same ballpark so accustomed to being empty that one August weekday afternoon the umpires had to stop the game because they were able to hear Bob Walk's radio broadcast out on the concourse discussing pitch selection from the plate. Not on that day. Over 40,000 fans donned in all black were going nuts. All those years of losing finally ended that day. We were proud again.

~JoJo Vinay, Jefferson Hills, Pennsylvania

DICK ALLEN TO THE HEAVEN OF FAME

That badass ballplayer
Played the better game
Parked his rawhide
Outside their fence

His best D against
Their offensiveness
Writing his Truth
In their dirt.

Then there was
His great Offense
Of being too big
For their b'riches

for DA and Frog.
~Ronnie Norpel, New York, New York

I was wearing a Cincinnati Reds cap when I met Eric. My wife and I were celebrating our 30th anniversary in San Francisco and had gone to the Giants game the night before. I seldom wear a hat, but I was going to be outside all day. My Reds hat is my chosen pride and joy for such occasions. My son moved to Louisville and went to a Reds game, surprising me when he came home with a fitted hat from the Great American Ball Park. It was my first Reds hat in over 40 years of rooting for them.

I was born in 1962 in Wichita Falls, Texas. I started playing Little League baseball in 1969, a light-hitting, weak-armed, utility infielder. I loved the game, including the mental aspect. Infield suited me well, as I had to think quickly when the ball was put into play. In the early 1970s I started following Major League Baseball. The Rangers had just moved to Texas and were not winning. I found a winner in the Reds who competed every year for the pennant, and I adopted them as my team. I checked their box score every morning in the local paper and followed player stats and league standings. It was through baseball that I discovered I was a numbers person.

My favorite players were Pete Rose, Johnny Bench, Joe Morgan, Dave Concepcion, and Tony Perez. I rode my bike to the store to buy baseball cards, always hoping that one of my favorite Reds players would be inside the pack, but always feeling unlucky, collecting fewer Reds than I thought I should have for the number of packs I bought. I organized all the cards, but my Reds were put in a special category. My favorite was a 1972 Pete Rose. I spent hours studying the stats on the backs of the cards. Later, as a young married man under financial stress, I talked my brother David into selling my cards to a friend of his. I hated to part with them, but I needed the cash. Several years later, David surprised me by returning them. He explained that he decided to buy them himself and just keep them because he knew how much they meant to me. What an amazing brother!

The playoffs provided an opportunity to see the Reds on television, rare in those years. I rushed home from school in the afternoon to watch early games, and if there was a late game my parents allowed me to stay up past my normal bedtime. I celebrated the 1975-76 championships by myself, not knowing any other Reds fans. There have been many down years since then, but I've stuck with the team.

It has been a four-decade love of the game and the Reds. I have never been to a game in Cincinnati, but one of these summers I will make a trek to see my beloved Reds in person. Until then, you can catch me on hat-wearing days representing my loyalty in my Reds cap.

-Darryl Smith, Huntington, Texas

In all reality, my dad is the reason I enjoy America's pastime. He introduced me to baseball and made me a rabid, no-matter-what, Cubs fan! Hey, there's always next season, right? Grandpa Harry Kent, the biggest die-hard Cubs fan I knew, never missed a game. When he lived with us as he went through cancer treatment, I often found him in the truck listening to the game on the radio when I got off the school bus. To think he sat there for hours to listen to the game sounds ridiculous today, but he loved his Cubs.

I believe baseball is the most genuine sport known to man. There's no time limit, no clock to beat, just you, the players, and the game. What an easy way to get lost in the moment! It's everything American, from nachos to bonding with your dad as you sit next to him in the nosebleed section and he teaches you everything he knows about the game. How can a girl not like the sport? It's played on a diamond! Some of my favorite movies are baseball movies, such as *A League of Their Own* and *Major League*.

I've played slow-pitch softball for 29 years. Even at 35, I look forward to the season starting and getting dirty. I was lucky to have Dad coach me for the majority of those years, Mom right there along with him, teaching me everything he knew to make me better in more ways than one. I'm the player, and the person, I am today because of them. The game has that effect, the ability to teach life lessons you carry throughout your life. Things like traditions, working as a team, work ethic, coping with pressure, dealing with success and failure, patience, and restraint. Baseball builds the character and ethical values you will need in life to survive this crazy world.

As I start my journey as a parent alongside my husband, I look forward to passing America's favorite pastime and all of its glory down to my son, Kolton, and daughter, Payton. They do, however, have a tough choice to make. I'm still a Cubs fan, but their dad is a Cardinals fan. I can only dream that one day they do the same as my parents did for me, carry on the tradition of baseball and family.

~Shelby Hagan, Bondurant, Iowa

I found baseball in 1949. My parents and I moved from Apache to Lawton, Oklahoma, because Dad got a job selling Hudson cars. We moved to 614 McKinley on the south side of Lawton. Tommy and Johnny Bateman lived across the street and four houses over. You may have heard of John Bateman—he had a 10-year career in the majors. But he wasn't a major leaguer then. He was nine, and Tommy and I were seven. Next to their house was a vacant lot where we played baseball morning, noon, and into the night.

Boston is the only other person I remember from that time, playing ball on that lot. I thought he was very wise and mature back then. Looking back on it, he was probably only 11 or 12, but to a seven-year-old, 11 can appear wise and mature. While I can't remember his face, I do remember two things that happened on the lot that etched Boston into my memory.

The first occurred in the early stages of my baseball education. Boston told the players where to go on the field, and he directed me to play third base. I walked over and stood on the base, not knowing that's not where a third baseman stands when playing his position. Boston told me where I was supposed to be before he got into the batter's box, then told me to move closer to home plate because he was going to bunt the ball. I did, and he again told me, "Move in closer. I'm going to bunt." I probably didn't even know what bunt meant, but I knew what move in closer meant, so I did.

Let me begin the next part of this story by saying...boys will be boys. He did not bunt the ball. He hit a line drive right at me that my totally inexperienced baseball ability was unable to catch. The ball hit me in the upper part of my stomach knocking the wind out of me. I don't remember the pain, but I do remember lying on the ground on my back gasping for air, and not having any luck at all filling up my lungs. Finally, Johnny grabbed my belt and started raising my mid-section off the ground causing air to return to my lungs. Tommy told me many years later, "I thought he had killed you."

I consider Boston wise because of how he completely changed my relationship to baseball. I write and throw right-handed, so I was batting right-handed. Even though it was 65 years ago that Boston said this, I can still hear his words. "Gale, you can't bat right-handed. You need to bat left-handed." It was amazing he said that, because I believe I really was meant to bat from the left side. This seems over the top, but I like to think I owe Boston a lot for making me into a poor man's Ty Cobb, Joe Jackson, and, of course, Ted Williams.

Tommy died in 2013, but he and I got together in 2010 after not seeing each other for many years. Being old men, we did what old men do, we began to reminisce. He said, "Do you remember that lot on McKinley St. where we used to play ball? The one that was next door to our house?" I replied that I did. In fact, I had recently driven by it, for what I called romantic baseball reasons. He then said excitedly, "How did we ever play baseball there? It's so small!" I looked at him and smiled. "Tommy, we were small, too."

~Gale McCray, Ft. Worth, Texas

When the Marlins franchise began, Viera, Florida, became their spring training home. Viera was 30 minutes from my house. I was born in 1992 and have been a Marlins fan from the very beginning. My grandfather would take me down to the field to meet and get autographs from players such as Conine, Sheffield, Santiago, and Renteria. For my birthday, he bought me a 1997 World Series ball signed by the entire Marlins team after their first Series title. Even when they moved to Jupiter, we made it a priority to go to at least one game each spring when they visited the Expos or Nationals in Viera. When they won the World Series in 2003, my parents were out of town, so I was staying with my grandmother. I recall as an 11-year-old sitting cross-legged in front of the TV late at night as Beckett tagged out Posada. I went crazy. The Marlins had never won their division, and have only been to the postseason twice, as wild card teams. But when they won it all, an overwhelming feeling came over me, making me realize why it was so important to cheer for your team whether they're doing well or not. When I watch baseball, regardless of the team, the feeling of joy I get while watching a game that I love with people I love overcomes everything else. There's something about hearing the *crack* of a bat while eating a hot dog or having a beer that makes me happy to just enjoy three hours away from life.

~Austin Purden, Melbourne, Florida

I grew up in the Sunset District of San Francisco, in what seemed like the greatest neighborhood in the world. It was a family-oriented environment where neighborhood kids could run freely and safely, and parents never had to worry. The people on our street were very close-knit and looked out for one another. One such family was Joe and Evelyn Rydberg and their seven children. Perhaps the most important thing in the world to them, besides their six daughters and one son, was baseball. They hailed from Oakdale, California, in the heart of the Gold Country. After meeting and falling in love, they married and moved to San Francisco in the 1930s, where they would make their home for more than 50 years. They raised their kids to love baseball, and in 1958 when the New York Giants moved west, Joe, Evelyn, and their children became the greatest, most devoted fans.

Rarely missing a home game, they were well-known in the section where they held season tickets just beyond the first base line near the bullpen at now defunct Candlestick Park. They especially loved Sunday games. As Joe sipped from cans of Coors beer and Evelyn lit up her Kool cigarettes, they followed each game with laser-like focus, keeping score of every pitch, every hit, and every run.

Joe never had a favorite player, but Willie McCovey was Evelyn's sun, moon, stars, and everything in between. When Willie lived near our neighborhood, she spotted him in our local market and followed him throughout the store! She claimed he had the most infectious smile in the world. In anticipation of baseball season each year, Joe and Evelyn traveled to Scottsdale, Arizona, to catch spring training, a true testament to their love of baseball and the Giants.

In 1977, Evelyn was diagnosed with a rare blood disorder that eventually led to cancer, a devastating blow to her family and the many friends who loved her dearly. Within a year, Evelyn barely had the strength to attend Giants games, and eventually stopped going. Her absence left a huge void in the section where she and Joe had enjoyed watching games for so many years.

On April 12, 1981, a Sunday filled with glorious sunshine perfect for a doubleheader, Evelyn passed away peacefully, surrounded by her husband, children, and grandchildren. Above the bed was a Giants poster, signed by many of the players just months before. She had admired it each day that it hung on the wall. Several weeks later, family and friends gathered to celebrate her life. Many shared fond memories of her, almost all of which included touching and beautiful references to Evelyn's love for baseball. At the conclusion of the service, everyone stood up, including the priest, and sang, "Take Me out to the Ball Game." Like a torrential rain covering every blade of grass on a baseball diamond, there wasn't a dry eye in the house.

This is dedicated to Mary Evelyn Rydberg (1917-1981), maybe the world's greatest baseball fan.

~Kitty Martin, San Francisco, California

It was Saturday, October 28, and I had just turned thirteen. I was suddenly a star pitcher and home run leader for my Little League team, the Yarmouth Mariners. This was a big deal for me, since I was used to being one of the worst players on the team. My older brother was home from college at the time. He had been a left-handed, power-hitting, first baseman, but now baseball was just a game he'd once played. But for my parents and younger brother, this was a day of baseball—Game 6 of the 1995 World Series. My Atlanta Braves were one win away from the championship. Ever since I'd opened my first pack of baseball cards in 1991, David Justice being the first card, I had been a diehard Braves and Justice fan, amassing a huge collection of his cards that only museums could rival. That day, I was a hopeful kid who had watched his team lose the Series in 1991 and 1992 and was terrified it was happening again. There was a lot of anger in my family and growing up I didn't appreciate this day for what it would be—one of the few moments the whole family gathered around, united on a single cause, present and supportive.

Talk during the pregame show that night focused on how Justice had made (possibly mis-understood) negative comments about Braves fans. I silently watched and agreed with his comments in the interview. Braves fans needed to be more excited, this was the World Series! Sitting in my living room with my family all around me, I didn't need any more convincing.

The game was tight from start to finish. Future Hall of Famer Tom Glavine pitched eight one-hit innings and the dominant Cleveland Indians lineup with the likes of Albert Belle, Eddie Murray, and Jim Thome, looked downright pedestrian. Unfortunately, the Braves didn't threaten to score until the 6th inning. I remember every moment vividly—repeatedly watching old footage has it all ingrained into my psyche. Left-hander Jim Poole took the mound, and Justice stepped to the plate to the sound of cheers mixed with boos and sent the third pitch—a belt-high fastball— back into the right-field bleachers. Fulton County Stadium erupted. I was jumping, running, screaming at the TV, arms raised, and everyone in my house was shouting and giving high-fives. My favorite player had just hit the most important home run in the history of one of baseball's oldest franchises.

But the game wasn't over.

Cleveland's bullpen kept it close into the 9th, behind by only one run. The Braves gave the ball to closer Mark Wohlers, he of the mullet, the stare, and the 103mph fastball. It was a gutsy move considering Glavine had been so dominant, but this is why teams have closers. I cringed. Kenny Lofton popped one up in foul territory past third base, and out of nowhere came diminutive Dominican Rafael Belliard to make a phenomenal catch to retire the lead-off man. Pinch-hitter Paul Sorrento popped out to Marquis Grissom in center. All I heard was the crowd. Carlos Baerga drove the first pitch to Grissom and I immediately knew. I've seen enough games to know if a ball is going to land or be caught. I jumped up, waiting, waiting... The catch made, Marquis came running in, arms held high. Wohlers was on the mound as the players huddled him. I saw Chipper Jones dive into the scrum, camera cutting to Justice arriving at the celebration he helped create, throwing his glove into the air and wrapping his arms around a teammate.

Absolute joy reigned in both Atlanta and my living room. I was surrounded by a family who, it turned out, would never be united for a singular purpose again. My parents would separate and then divorce. I went on to play high school baseball, softball, and recreational slo-pitch, as well as coach at a local high school. I went off to university and permanently settled hours from my hometown. I followed the rest of David Justice's career, including the 1997 Comeback Player of the Year and 2000 American League Championship Series MVP, but nothing compared to October of 1995 and those impossibly great Atlanta Braves.

~Matt Clairmont, New Minas, Nova Scotia, Canada

MICKEY, WILLIE, AND THE STARS OF THE GOLDEN AGE OF BASEBALL

This chapter is dedicated to Mantle, Mays, Aaron, Koufax, Banks, and other stars of the '50s and '60s, known as the Golden Age of Baseball, the era that I grew up in. We tend to idealize our eras as the best, to the point that, despite evidence and statistics which may point to the contrary, we "know" these were the greatest of all time. Are Trout, Harper, Griffey, Pujols, and Kershaw better than these guys? Perhaps history will show that to be the case, but to my g-g-generation (The Who), this is the greatest collection of stars. They shone brightly in our baseball sky. I acknowledge it skews heavily to my hero, No. 7, but other superstars are well represented.

Somehow, someway, I managed to have a ticket to the Yankees game on June 8, 1969. This was no ordinary game. It was Mickey Mantle Day at Yankee Stadium. I was going to the game at which his iconic No. 7 would be retired.

I was 16 years old, and my first love had been the Yankees—with all due respect to Adele, my 6th grade girlfriend, who has a story in this book. By 1969, my baseball affections were split between the Yankees and the Amazin' Mets who captivated the nation by winning the 1969 World Series. But on this day, nothing mattered more than being there to honor my first hero, the only sports hero I've ever had. Sitting in the upper deck down the left field line, I, along with 300,000 fans—you know what they say, far more people witness every major baseball event than the stadiums could

301

hold—sat in anxious anticipation. What would the festivities entail? Which Yankee greats—all of them, as it turned out—would be there to participate?

My memories of this day are faint, although research has helped. I don't know who I was with, but it must have been my dad. I don't remember the Yankees' opponent, or who won, though the internet told me the Yankees swept the White Sox in a doubleheader. I remember a 13½ minute standing ovation, though accounts range from 6 to 20 minutes. I was even wrong about what I was certain I accurately remembered—Mantle's golf cart drive around the park to kick off the festivities. That ride apparently occurred *after* the ceremonies. Incidentally, he passed by my section about 1½ minutes into a 2½ minute ride. None of these details are important, really. All that is important is that *I was there*, and I know my eyes were quite moist.

Was this my favorite game of all time? I talk about several games in my stories in these books, and I guess I am not prepared to make that call. I do know that, along with the 61,000-plus fans who really were there that day, I think of that day often, and still with moist eyes.

~Eric Gray, San Francisco, California

I was a San Francisco Giants batboy working out of the visitor's clubhouse at The Stick. It was 1972, and I was 14 years old. The Giants had traded Willie Mays to the Mets early in the season, and the Mets were in town for a midweek series, the great Mays returning for the first time not in a Giants uniform. I was in the third base dugout by myself getting things ready, and Mays walked onto the field, all alone. He was always the showman. As he got to the dugout, adoring fans clapping, he said, "Hey kid, grab a glove." I looked around, but the only glove I could find was an old catcher's glove. Me and my idol, Willie Mays, were soon playing catch in front of thousands of fans. I told myself, "Whatever you do, don't drop the ball or make a bad throw!" I will tell this to my grandchildren someday. Me and Willie Mays.

~Carl Alioto, Walnut Creek, California

Forty years ago, on a drizzly Monday night in Atlanta, Georgia, Henry Aaron took an Al Downing pitch over the left-center field wall and became the true all-time home run leader. Like so many of us, I watched the game as an 18-year-old, mesmerized by the enormity of the feat. A humble, quiet Black man working in the somewhat intolerant Deep South had just unseated the Great Bambino, who'd been larger than life, boisterous and excessive, iconic in every way.

Ten years earlier, I'd seen the Milwaukee Braves at Shea Stadium with my dad, who was the ultimate Willie Mays fan. Aaron made several dazzling plays and throws from right field, and homered in both games, prompting me to ask Dad if Aaron was as good as Mays. Dad replied, "Not quite," but in my mind, Aaron became my baseball hero. He seemed so relaxed, deliberate, and confident at all times, without any antics or self-serving behavior.

In 1991, having just finished reading his autobiography, I was saddened, angered, distressed, and ashamed to be a White man. The death threats and hate mail that he and his family endured was beyond anything I could ever understand. The man chased the ghost of Babe Ruth with the fear that, at any moment, a sniper in the Deep Southern night could end his life for simply doing his job. I cried as I read some of the threats. Thankfully, civil liberties and social justice were and are paramount to me, and I was never taught to be a racist. Right then and there, I vowed to reach out in some way to Mr. Aaron and let him know that the majority of us had nothing but the utmost respect and admiration for him, something that went way beyond the back of a baseball card.

In 1998, I had a few years under my belt as a small-town radio host, with thousands of CDs, a home studio, and a desire to communicate with Henry. I learned of his great love of Delta Blues, Aretha, and Motown, so I recorded a homespun radio show and sent it to the Atlanta Braves where he held a senior position. The tape was not just music, but also my narrative on the great game of baseball, racism, social injustice, and education.

I introduced myself as a fan, inserted my comments, and before long I had a finished product. Debbie has asked me if I thought he'd respond. I didn't. But more important, it hardly mattered. What mattered was that he received a gift of appreciation for his commitment to dignity and grace under pressure. To my surprise, a week later the phone rang, and I found myself chatting with Hank. He asked me how I got this great music to blend so effortlessly, one into the next. I responded, "How did you excel in baseball for 23 years?" We both laughed, and agreed they were gifts bestowed upon us.

Over the next few years we stayed in touch, and many a mixed tape accompanied him on his drives home to Mobile or on weekend fishing excursions. When he learned of my car accident in 1999, he called and sent me a get-well present. Can you imagine? In the summer of 2000, business brought me to Atlanta, and I called his secretary, Susan, to see if we could finally meet in person. She said he'd be thrilled, and we met at his first of many BMW dealerships. When he learned that I'd cabbed over and spent 50 bucks, he was upset that I hadn't asked to be picked up!

So here we were in his office, me and Hank. He was impeccably dressed, my height, and had a twinkle in his eye. He toured the facility with me, asked about my life, and made me feel that I was a welcomed friend. Again, can you imagine? At one point I asked him about the smaller parks, the dearth of pitching, tightly spun balls, and steroids. I pointed out that many of his typical 600 at-bats during a season came while facing Hall of Fame talent such as Koufax, Drysdale, Seaver, Gibson, Perry, Jenkins, Marichal, Bunning, and Carlton, along with a plethora of amazing B-level hurlers like Maloney, Veale, Sutton, and Koosman. I asked him if he still played today what his numbers would be. He thoughtfully stroked his chin and said, "Oh, .275 20- 70," meaning batting average, home runs, and runs batted in. I was taken aback since a typical Aaron year had been .305 35-110, so I questioned him. "Scott! I am 64 years old," he responded with a chuckle. A great line, a greater man, and a nice story for me to tell you.

We lost touch over the years, but every April 8, I think back to that rainy night in Georgia where a Southern gentleman rewrote history with style, grace, and humility. Forty years later, the ugliness of racism, intolerance, violence, and social injustice continues to rear its ugly head. For all of our modern discoveries, technological advances and medical cures, we just can't seem to figure out this piece quite yet. Maybe the next 40 will prove to be different.

~Scott Goldman, Croton-on-Hudson, New York

In 1962, I took two girls—the one I was dating and my boss's daughter—from Chicago to Milwaukee by train to see the Cubs play the Braves. It was Ladies Day, so my companions received mugs and another gift.

It had been a tough day for the Cubs. Joe Adcock hit a solo home run for the Braves in the 2nd inning. We all thought it was a routine fly to left, but it kept accelerating until it cleared the fence. The Cubs loaded the bases in the 9th, but George Altman's high fly ball was caught by the Braves center fielder, his back pressed to the fence. You know about those windy days in Chicago! The game ended in a 1-0 Braves win.

After the game, with time to spare, we walked around County Stadium and found the Cubs bus, then watched as the team left the clubhouse to board the bus. Ernie Banks was the first one out. He tossed his bag to the bus driver, turned to a group of kids, and began signing autographs. Player after player came out, some signing an autograph or two, then boarded the bus for the ride back to the Windy City. But Ernie kept signing autographs, talking to the kids, smiling, encouraging, just being Ernie.

Then the bus began to move and someone called out, "Ernie come on, or we're gonna have to leave you." He was class personified. Years later, I saw him on the Jim Rome TV program saying how today's players are missing a blessing by not signing autographs. He told of meeting a man in downtown Los Angeles who stopped him, pulled out his wallet, and brought out a ragged, tattered little piece of paper with Ernie's autograph. He gave Ernie the date and place where he'd signed it, in the early 1960s. Ernie signed another piece of paper for him so he would have a better-looking copy.

My date's father had met Banks many times, and said he was the most gracious person one could ever hope to meet. I had that day of watching Ernie sign those autographs and agreed. I loved him although I never met him, and he influenced my life considerably, as he did many others. For so many reasons, Ernie was my idol.

~Mike Shea, Keokuk, Iowa

From the first time I saw Roberto Clemente play for the Pittsburgh Pirates, I became a fan of the team and, more important, the man. I have a few recollections of The Great One. I saw him end two consecutive innings firing strikes from right field to home to throw out Dodger runners. I saw him hit a line drive into runner Willie Stargell's rear end. Home runs, defensive plays, throws, the whole gamut.

Ironically, the game that I most particularly recall was in 1966 which I watched on TV. Cardinals journeyman pitcher Barry Latman was facing Roberto. On a swing and a miss, Clemente's bat slipped out of his hands, landing near the pitcher's mound. Latman refused to pick up the errant bat. Bob Prince, the legendary announcer for the Pirates, picked up on this, knowing something was about to happen. Indeed, it did. On the next pitch, Clemente *destroyed* that ball, and it landed a good 425 feet over the center field wall. The things athletes can do when they are motivated!

~Dan Mendlovitz, St. Petersburg, Florida

Toward the end of the great Mickey Mantle's career, as he was enduring another of his many injuries and recoveries, I was at Yankee Stadium in a lower box near the field. He didn't start the game, but he pinch-hit in the late innings. As his name was announced, the roar of the crowd was, of course, tremendous. He stepped into the box and swung at a pitch, missing it. It looked bad, very un-Mickey-like. The guy in front of me, who had been cheering moments earlier, started yelling at him, calling him a bum.

It was amazing to me that someone would ever think, much less make, such a disparaging comment about such a true hero.

On the next pitch, Mickey hit it out of the park. The crowd went crazy, as did the man in front of me. Again, I was amazed how someone could be so incredibly fickle, how this one pitch, with a different outcome, could so quickly reshape how he felt about our collective idol. It made me think a lot about human behavior and realize that, sadly, for so many people, it is all about what they do in this exact moment.

~Joe Rinaldi, San Francisco, California

I witnessed Sandy Koufax at his best and his worst, just one year apart. On June 9, 1963, I was at Wrigley Field for what was supposed to be a great pitcher's duel between Koufax and Cub Dick Ellsworth, who was having the only good season of his career. The wind was blowing out that day and Sandy was KO'd in the 5th after giving up six earned runs and three home runs. He got a no-decision because Ellsworth gave up a bit more and was the losing pitcher in a 11-8 Dodger win.

But just one year before, on April 24, 1962, on spring break from high school, I was in the left field bleachers at Wrigley, sparsely populated in those days. Sandy pitched a complete game victory (10-2) for the Dodgers with 18 Ks. I never saw so many swinging strikeouts, mostly on that devastating overhand curve ball that he had. Most people think of his blazing fastball, but the curve was his put-away pitch.

That's the way I, and most people, remember Koufax. Far more great games than bad ones.

~Rich Wambach, St. Charles, Illinois

Stan Musial.
Stan the Man is dead.
A childhood hero
A demi-god who hit the ball a mile
And never stuck out.
Except one time.
I heard it on the radio and cried.
Stan the Man is dead.
~Greg Luecke, Napa, California

On September 29, 1963, I went to a game at Sportsman's Field to see the St. Louis Cardinals play the Cincinnati Reds. I was barely six years old, and this was to be Stan Musial's last game. In my mind I have an image of him batting as we sat in the upper deck between home and first base. I don't remember much, but the internet tells me that Jim Maloney was pitching for the Reds and that before the game, Stan the Man rode around the stadium in a red convertible and gave a thank you and goodbye speech to the only hometown fans he'd ever played for.

What I do remember, though, is him coming to the plate in the 6th for what would be his last at-bat. My teenage cousin, Mick, kept telling me to "pay attention" because it would be "something I would want to remember." Sure enough, Musial hit a single that scored Curt Flood. It was his 1,815th home-field hit, the exact same number as he it on the road. A pinch-runner, Gary Kolb, was sent in for him. The place went nuts. My cousin kept yelling, "Remember this!" He hammered the memory into me. And I do remember. Many thanks, Mick.
~Kevin Doyle, Denver, Colorado

Most children look for someone to emulate. When I grew up in the 1950s the hero you sought out was most often a baseball player. In Cleveland, the player many of us gravitated to was Rocco Domenico Colavito, the Indians power-hitting outfielder. Rocky was unique in many ways. Boys loved his ability to hit the ball farther than anyone else, preceded by practice swings ending with pointing the bat at the pitcher, preceded by stretching exercises that involved locking his arms over a bat behind his back. Girls loved his chin-dimpled, chiseled face, dark complexion, and sparkling eyes. Rocky was *the* hero of Cleveland baseball fans in 1957, 1958, and 1959, at the same level as Mickey Mantle was in New York. Rocky was the most publicly admired Indian since Rosen, Feller, and Boudreau, but we kids truly loved him—and love is greater than admiration as a fan.

How much did we love Rocky? During the 1959 season, the Indians were chasing the Chicago White Sox for the American League pennant. Indians catcher Russ Nixon and his family moved into our neighborhood in Mayfield Heights, Ohio. One day a rumor was hatched that on the Indians next home off day, Rocky's family would be visiting the Nixons at their home on East Miner Rd. The next home off day was five or six days away, giving a group of a dozen or so Rocky fans time to have a meeting to develop a plan to say hi to Rocky when he showed up. We developed a spy system, recruiting a group of undercover spies to keep an eye on the traffic turning off Mayfield Road onto East Miner. We established a series of hand signals beginning with thumbs up and thumbs down for the spies to use for passing along information. We hid behind bushes and in trees that day, all of us with binoculars, waiting for Rocky. No one, of course, considered that the rumor might be just that—a rumor. Though Rocky didn't show up, it was a great day. Nixon somehow heard about our antics and came outside and talked baseball with us, promising to tell Rocky we loved him.

The Indians lost the pennant to the White Sox, but we had great hopes for 1960. Soon spring training would begin and end, with only Easter Sunday to wade through before Opening Day. I spent weeks working out my excuse to stay home from school that Tuesday, picturing myself lying in bed, my transistor radio propped up on the windowsill, Jimmy Dudley and Bob Neal telling me about the heroics of the Indians against the Detroit

Tigers. To this day, my plan for that day is what I think about whenever I hear or read the saying, "Man plans and G-d laughs."

Easter Sunday, 1960—a day that will live in infamy for all Cleveland Indian fans, even to this day. My grandparents picked me up and we headed downtown, grandpa in his tailored suit and grandma in her stylish dress and white gloves, to see David Niven and Doris Day in *Please Don't Eat the Daisies*. My interest, even at age 10, was in seeing Day, but my attention wasn't merely on her while I waited for the movie to end and the Chinese restaurant's food that I would soon be eating. I also had time to finalize my plans to play hooky for Opening Day…and the Chinese food provided the perfect alibi. It was always good for a two-day stomach ache.

But at the movie, something was going on near the front of the theater. People were talking louder and louder, the conversation moving to the middle rows and then farther back. Then I heard it. Rocky Colavito had been traded to the Detroit Tigers for Harvey Kuenn. I remember thinking, "Didn't we at least get Al Kaline for Rocky?" I recall getting dizzy. I recall crying. I recall my grandpa swearing in Yiddish. I don't remember the rest of the movie or the rest of the day. I remember waking up in the middle of the night sobbing. And I remember waking up again around 11:30 a.m. My parents knew they could not send me to school for a couple of days. On Tuesday, I listened to the game—but Rocky Colavito was now a Tiger. I had no idea how to react when the Tigers won. But I had a creepy feeling that Indians baseball would never be the same. Hence, The Curse of Rocky Colavito.

~Sheldon Green, Cleveland, Ohio

I don't think I ever saw a player play as hard as Minnie Minoso. Late in his career, on May 11, 1962, he was playing left field for the St. Louis Cardinals against the visiting Dodgers. My family and I were sitting in the grandstands well down the third base line, with a great view of the outfield in Sportsman's Park. It was particularly lovely because Cards owner August Busch refused to allow any advertising in the stadium except for a massive neon Anheuser-Busch eagle that flapped whenever a Cardinal hit a home run. Dodger Duke Snider came up to pinch-hit and lined a shot to the left field wall. Minnie never slowed, never took his eye off the ball. He crashed headfirst into the concrete wall at full speed. It was frightening. He slumped to the ground, completely out. We later learned that he'd fractured his skull and dislocated his arm. It was an enormous example, however, of the heart with which he played the game.

Minoso was at least 40 when this injury occurred and nearing the end of his career. He came back later that season and played the next year and a few games the following year before retiring. But he then returned to play a couple of games in 1976 and in 1980, therefore making him a five-decade player. He never received all the acclaim he deserved, but I sure admired him throughout his great career.

~Damon Kerby, San Anselmo, California

I was introduced to baseball by my father in 1958 as a six- or seven-year-old when we lived in Springfield, Massachusetts, where Dad was stationed at an air base from 1957 to 1965. I immediately loved baseball and played it through my freshman year of high school. My interest waned a bit when I became fascinated with the Beatles and all the music of the era, but baseball was always there. I was the oldest of four boys, with my brother, Jim, only 14 months younger than me. I don't remember why, but I became a Red Sox fan and Jim chose the Yankees. He, of course, had more luck following his team. We went to Fenway occasionally, but Yankee Stadium just once. This is what happened on that one visit.

The White Sox were playing the Yankees on Wednesday afternoon, August 24, 1960. I had been pleased the year before when the White Sox won the pennant instead of the Yankees—a rarity in that era. Tony Kubek homered, and it went over us into the second deck in right, and the Yankees won. That put the Yanks into the lead in the standings, and it stayed that way for the rest of the season. But the most memorable thing took place in the street afterward.

We were ensnarled in traffic on a street adjacent to the stadium, sitting in the family station wagon. My father and one of his B-52 crewmates were in front, and Jim, three days short of eight years old, was sitting to the right of me in the back, our windows open. Along with sounds of bustling activity, there was the sound for a few minutes, - maybe for quite a while, of a man heckling someone. Eventually we realized he was saying something along the lines of "You're a bum, Mantle. How about you are striking out—" and on and on. My father said he remembered Mantle striking out four times that day, although the box score says he was 1-3 with a walk and a strikeout.

A Cadillac tailfin was at a standstill next to Jim's window just a few feet away. The driver's door opened and out stepped Mantle, who was Jim's idol of course. Mickey marched toward this heckler guy who was wearing a suit, I think, and had been walking along behind Mantle's car badgering him as we inched along. Mantle picked the guy up by the lapels and shook him, his biceps bulging out of a short sleeve shirt about a foot from Jim's face, yelling threats at the heckler. Just then a woman's voice—I don't know if it came from inside his car or from an onlooker—said something like, "No, no, Mickey, you're a good ballplayer!"

Mickey eventually dropped the guy and marched back to his car. Traffic had opened up a bit and he dramatically sped off. The guy was shaken, literally and figuratively, and with Mantle gone he made a show of talking tough. "I'll call a cop!" An onlooker then muttered, "You call a cop and I'll kill you."

-Anthony Parber, Mill Valley, California

In 1971, my dad, Fred Sheldon, let me send in for lottery tickets to the All-Star Game to be played in Detroit. Lo and behold, we won two upper deck center field seats. Dad loved baseball, and I loved going to games with him. This was such a great game, the first time I ever saw any National Leaguers in person. The National League outfield was Mays, Clemente, and Aaron. Wow!

Five Tigers were on the roster. This would be the first and only time that our Mr. Tiger, Al Kaline, would play in front of the home crowd in a mid-season classic. Many recall that six home runs were hit that day, especially the awesome shot Reggie hit off the right-center light tower. The moment that stands out for me was when Kaline ran out to right field, receiving a standing ovation that lasted about 10 minutes. As he stood there looking down at the ground, you knew he was crying with joy as a dream came true for him to play in an All-Star Game in front of his hometown fans. This remains a special memory for both Al and me.

~Carol Sheldon, Royal Oaks, Michigan

Growing up in Whittier, California, it was all about the Dodgers. From the roof of my house, you could see the lights of Dodger Stadium in Chavez Ravine. My dad would take my brothers and me to games. I thought Vin Scully had the greatest voice and was the smartest man around. I wanted to be a pitcher like Don Drysdale or Sandy Koufax.

Late in the 1962 season, we headed to a game against Giants. I admired Mays and Marichal, even though they were our rivals. I was 11, and in the hustle to get into the park I got separated from Dad and my brothers. All I knew to do was go back to the car, where I sat on the bumper and waited. Dad eventually came back and found me, and we got to ride a private elevator up to our seats.

Maury Wills was setting stolen base records that season, eclipsing Ty Cobb, and we all chanted "Go Maury, go Maury!" You could probably have heard us all the way to the ocean. He stole his 102nd base that day and finished with 104, then a modern era stolen-base record. What a team! What a year! What a night!

~Stephen Busch, Clayton, California

I met my idol, Mickey Mantle, in the early 1990s at the Cow Palace in San Francisco. He was shilling for an RV company. I brought my most prized sports item, my 1967 Mickey Mantle scrapbook, with box scores, newspaper articles, and photos from every game. It included my personal notes on every at-bat, i.e. grounded to right, homered in 5th, etc.

As I rummaged through the pages with him, including looking at a great photo of his 500th homer, Mick said, "Richard, this gives me goose bumps." I told Mickey he had done that for me every time he stepped up to the plate, and I gave him the book to keep. He said, "Thanks, Richard, this is going into my keepsake closet with the other 18 scrapbooks I have."

Some friends mocked me for giving away such a prized possession, with front and back covers emblazoned with Mickey's baseball cards from different years. But to this day I have no regrets, and truly believe it's the best scrapbook his family has and will continue to enjoy for years to come.

~Rich Walcoff, Petaluma, California

In 1966, as a 12-year-old kid growing up in L.A., my family went to Angels spring training games in Palm Springs every year. Spring training was more laid back in those days. Fans could sit for free behind a hill and players were very accessible. The Angels and Giants played often because their respective camps were located near each other, while most teams trained in Florida. One day I caught a Willie Mays foul ball, and I also had brought a new ball for players to sign. Players went directly from the locker room to the team bus, passing through a line of fans wanting autographs. I concentrated on the Giants since I was a National League, albeit Dodgers, fan and watched many games on TV from wind-driven Candlestick Park. I was in heaven gathering autographs from players like Tom Haller, Jim Ray Hart, Ollie Brown, and Willie McCovey. I really wanted Mays to sign the ball I had caught. I waited for an hour, and when all the players had boarded the bus, my parents lost patience. They insisted I must have missed Mays since the bus had left. They went to the car out in the far corner of the parking lot, but I continued to wait.

Twenty minutes later, out came Willie, still in his dirty uniform from the game. I was the only one left and he asked me, "What are you doing out here alone, and where are your people?" I explained I had been waiting for him so he could sign his foul ball. I realized he had no ride to his hotel, and I asked, as only a kid would, what had taken him so long, mentioning that his bus had already left. He said he moved a bit slower than the rest of the guys. He had interviews, and he enjoyed taking his time and making his own way back to the motel. As we talked, he walked over to a U-Haul flatbed truck with an open back and a shell. He said, "This is my ride." The cab and the bed were separated by a window, and Willie told the driver to start 'er up, he was ready for a shower. He asked me again, "Where are your people?"

I explained my parents' frustration and that they'd gone to the car. He asked if I would like a ride to the car. With that, he pulled me into the back of the truck and away we went. The conversation was Willie asking all about me. I felt he needed to know I was a Dodger fan, and we discussed that a bit. He said I could not help where I lived, and maybe one day I could see the Giants in Candlestick Park. That is the day I became a baseball fan rather than just a Dodgers fan. As we got to the car, I saw my frustrated Dad looking for me. He didn't notice the oncoming U-Haul. We pulled up and Willie jumped out to help me down. I took my signed ball and looked at my parents with what must have been a huge grin. Dad looked more than a bit surprised. Willie got back into the truck and away he went with no word to my folks.

I saved both balls for a year or so, until one day we needed a ball for over the line, and we ultimately used them both, hoping, naïvely, they wouldn't get dirty. We played on grass, and they were practically ruined. I of course regret it to this day. But it has always been my feeling that Willie would understand that the love of playing the game outweighs memorabilia. From what I've learned about Willie, I think he would approve.

~Marc Hertz, Penn Valley, California

THAT SPECIAL, FAMOUS, EMOTIONAL, MOMENTOUS, GROUNDBREAKING GAME

Some games are famous, perhaps infamous. I don't mean just because it was, say, the last game of the World Series. No, they are famous because they are recognized as something special. Maybe it is just a certain play that occurred, rather than the whole game. Mazeroski's World Series-ending home run. Babe Ruth's home run point. Mantle's leg being ripped up in his first season. Robinson's steal of home. Schilling's bloody sock. There are so many games that baseball fans know about, even if they happened decades before they were born. These games are part of baseball lore. Here are the accounts of some of those special, memorable games.

I am a native of the Chicagoland area and was raised a Cubs fan. I recall my first game in 1972, in which my first baseball sports hero, Joe Pepitone, played first base and hit a home run. The years 2015 and 2016 were nothing short of thrilling for Cubs fans. The overwhelming favorites to win the 2016 World Series with the best record in baseball, 103 wins, they made it to the Series against the Cleveland Indians. I thought it would be a quick series, but others thought it would go seven games.

When the Cubs evened the Series at three games each, my wife insisted I go to Cleveland for Game 7. Who was I to say no? Progressive Field was very lively with energy from fans of both teams. I sat in the upper deck next to Cleveland fans. We were very polite to each other, and I even apologized when I went crazy with Dexter Fowler's lead-off home run, acknowledging that I knew they would do the same when the Indians scored. In the 7th inning, my new Cleveland friends Bob and Jim, who like me were from Chicago via California, and I made our way down to the field level seats. When the rain stopped the game after the 9th inning, we went further down to the 5th row and stood for the rest of the game. The Cubs took the lead by two runs in the top of the 10th as the fans held their collective breath. I don't remember the first two outs, or how the Cubs gave up a run, but I vividly recall Mike Montgomery, with no career saves, coming in to get Michael Martinez to hit a routine grounder to Kris Bryant at third base. Bryant made the play with a perfect toss to Anthony Rizzo, who strategically stuffed the ball into his pocket. Before my eyes, my beloved Chicago Cubs were officially World Series Champions! Finally! Months later, it still seems surreal to me. I was there to watch the celebration, yet still can't believe it. I've waited for 44 years for this win to happen, and many Cubs fans never had that chance. Did it really happen? It most certainly did, the first time since 1908. No more Billy Goat curses or black cats or Murphy's Law to get in the way of this team anymore.

~Robb Tavill, Elmhurst, Illinois

On June 2, 2010, I attended a game at Comerica Park, the Detroit Tigers vs. the Cleveland Indians. Armando Galarraga was pitching for the Tigers, and the game was like any normal game…that is, until it reached the 6th inning when you started hearing the buzz of "perfect game" in the crowd. In the 9th, with the Tigers leading 3-0, Austin Jackson made an unbelievable catch in deep center field to keep it alive. With two outs, Jason Donald hit a ground ball that was fielded and tossed to Galarraga at first for the third out. However, first base umpire Jim Joyce blew the call. They never put a replay on the scoreboard, but everybody started booing all at once. At 1 hour 50 minutes, it was one of the shortest games I've ever attended, and at the same time the most amazing and controversial one, as well.

~Mark Hughes, Eaton Rapids, Michigan

For those of you who don't know this story, Joyce, who in a players' poll had been voted the best umpire in the game by a wide margin, was emotional and incredibly remorseful at his blown call, nullifying the perfect game. Galarraga was incredibly gracious in understanding "nobody's perfect." The two met at home plate to exchange lineup cards the next day. This event took on a life of its own, but what distinguishes this game was the amazing way that they dealt with this incident, an example of the best in sports.

I lived in Baltimore in the mid-1990s, a city still mad at baseball for the 1994 strike. Like many others, I had lost a job—a good job—at Camden Yards, bartending in the corporate suites. Before I worked my first day there, I got caught in the crossfire between players and owners. Validity of the complaints aside, it was hard to be anything other than supremely ticked off. I knew many people who worked at the ballpark and in the little pubs, restaurants, and parking lots all around it, who made great money when the O's were winning, less when they were losing, but zero while the players and owners argued. Add to this the first grumbles about steroids, and people were angry. The topic of baseball was generally met with hostility in Baltimore when play resumed in the spring of 1995, heightened by the fact that at the time, the Orioles were pretty bad. The only topic you could bring up that wouldn't get you side-eyed was Cal Ripken. The Record. The Streak. His near-record of most consecutive games played at this point was well over 2000, and fast approaching Lou Gehrig of the New York Yankees record of 2,130.

His streak crept up without much fanfare. You didn't talk about it, didn't want to jinx it, the way you don't mention that a team has 0 hits in the 7th inning. But talk began at the start of the 1995 season. People liked Cal Ripken, a hometown guy, or close enough. He seemed uncomplicated, humble, and most important, likeable, the kind of guy you'd run into at your local and have a couple of beers with. He crept closer to making history every day, doing something we all identify with, just going to work. This isn't to downplay his talent. Most of us have never thrown a fastball or doubled to center. But we all know what it's like to go and do your job day in and day out. When Ripken was on TV or in the paper, it was like seeing your neighbor or cousin. You felt like you knew him and wanted him to succeed.

As the season rolled on, the fanfare cranked up. One camera crew outside the Eutaw Street gates became two, then four, then a whole section of a parking lot. Dates started to be counted. Instead of buying tickets to a game in April, you bought tickets to game 2,131. The sports segment on the local news had a countdown clock. Crowds were bigger, noisier, and happier, as was the whole town. Everyone wanted to see this Everyman show up at work for another day. Still bitter about the strike and lost jobs, people had choice words for Peter Angelos or Bud Selig. But when it came to Cal Jr., none of that mattered. We wanted him to have that record.

That's how I ended up on an early September evening in an orange ocean together with a president, a couple of Hall of Famers, and a whole lot of other famous people. But once you got inside Camden Yards, you just became part of The Crowd. I can't tell you if it was hot or cold that night. As long as it wasn't raining, the weather didn't matter. I imagine some special arrangements must have been made with the fire marshal that night. Camden was more packed than I've ever seen, with people standing on the picnic tables by the bullpen, the ramp to the upper levels, and all along the Warehouse. If there was a single person in there in an Angels jersey, I sure didn't see him. Poor Angels. I can't imagine how it must have felt to be such an afterthought that night.

The crowd was magnificent, so loud, orange, and excited! "It was alive" is a hackneyed phrased, but that night it was as if the crowd was a living, breathing thing all of its own, not a collection of 40-something-thousand cheering people. We all shouted "O!" during the Anthem, a ritual only Orioles and Braves fans truly understood. We jumped to our feet, cheering and stamping when they announced the starting lineup and the super-familiar No. 9. We were loud, very loud, and that day it felt like the whole East Coast was an Orioles fan. Maybe the whole country!

Then it was the 5th inning, a play that I don't really remember, but how fitting that Cal himself hit the ball that, once fielded for an out, sealed the game as Official! The crowd held its communal breath, a deafening silence after all those cheers. All eyes were on the Warehouse. The Warehouse banners that had marked the days all season flipped. Game 2130 became 2131, and we celebrated!

So many cameras flashing all at once like the brightest blink, and the voice of the crowd rising as one. Chanting, jumping, and cheering, alive and moving, I don't think to this day I've ever been anywhere else so completely excited and happy. Ripken, almost sheepish, almost reluctant, trotted around the park, shaking hands with fans lucky enough to be in the front row. The rest of us jumped and traded high-fives with strangers in the next row, cheering all the while. It was so loud, like what it must be like to stand next to a jet engine. Every person in that park was on their feet, so happy and proud! It was just a few minutes, but it felt like it lasted for days.

Someone reminded me that Cal also hit a home run that day, but I don't remember it, or Mike Mussina pitching, even though he was the O's ace and my favorite pitcher. I only recall the banners and crowd, the thousands of cameras all flashing at once, and how excited we all were! We knew we were seeing history. It couldn't have happened at a better time. And of course, I remember Cal Ripken, the Ironman, who just by going to work every day like you or me, made Baltimore fall back in love with baseball.

~Patti Rogers, Washington, District of Columbia

One Event, Two Perspectives

It was a nice day for a ball game, great weather, yet what was even greater was the atmosphere lurking in the air. It was Game 1 of the 1988 World Series, the Oakland A's vs. the L.A. Dodgers. I was there at my first World Series game thanks to my little sister, Yolie, who had asked me to join her as she had gotten four *free* tickets to attend this wonderful game. So, there I was, with my brother, Ben, Yolie, and nephew Mark, part of a packed house at the most beautiful ballpark in the nation, Dodger

Stadium. I grew up in L.A. and, with my dear old Dad and brother Bob, attended countless games at this historic stadium. But in all those years, I had never ever been to a World Series game at the Ravine.

I was finally at my first World Series game, with great loge seats right on the first base line. The excitement of Game 1 couldn't have been better, with the crowd anticipating a win. It was a close game throughout, both teams battling hard. In the 9th inning, the best reliever in all of baseball was on the mound for the A's, Dennis Eckersley, facing the very injured Kirk Gibson at the plate. Then the nearly impossible happened. On a full count, the pitch that Eckersley thought would end the game and put the Dodgers at one game down was hit by Gibson, and hit hard, into the right field bleachers! And she was "Gone!" as Vin Scully called it. Gibson was feeling no pain rounding the bases, fist pumping, with the crowd going completely insane at what had just happened, everyone on their feet, clapping, hugging, high-fiving, just going crazy! The roar of witnessing this famous win by an injured Gibson homer was unbelievable.

The crowd that day, for what was possibly the most famous home run in major league history, must have cheered for a solid 15 or 20 minutes. It was a roar heard, I'm sure, a very long way from Dodger Stadium.

I still attend games today with a mini season package with my wife, Denise, better known to me as Blue, a nickname I gave her over three decades ago. Why? Who knows, perhaps it was a good omen, as she is a diehard Dodger Blue fan today. We both love our Boys in Blue, and love attending games together at our well-seasoned age of 64 years young!

-Joseph Ramirez, Bellflower, California

In memory of Joseph. Thank you, Denise, for allowing me to share this story

It was October 15, 1988, Game 1 of the World Series, Dodgers vs. A's. If you are a baseball fan, you already know what this story is about. I was in the press box as a columnist for the Los Angeles Daily News. Early in the game, Jose Canseco hit a grand slam home run so hard it dented the center field camera. After 7 innings, the A's were leading 4-3. Writers were on a deadline, so I did what all the others were doing, I wrote about how poorly the Dodgers had played. The story was written and ready to go, except for the final score.

Dennis Eckersley, the A's all-star closer, came in to finish the game. He quickly retired the first two batters, and but then did something that it seemed like he hadn't done in two months: he walked a batter, his former teammate, the power-hitting Mike Davis, who hadn't had a hit in the game, on four straight pitches. Due up was the pitcher, so it was clear there would be a pinch-hitter. But we were all sure it wouldn't be Kirk Gibson. Gibson was injured, both legs were hurting, and there had been a press release earlier in the day saying he would not be available. Yet there he was hobbling to the plate, and looking terrible on his first few swings, unable to get around on the pitch. On the eighth pitch, he took that seemingly half one-armed swing, hitting a walk-off home run, a fabulous moment, regarded as one of the greatest in World Series history.

All of the writers now had to throw out our mostly written stories and start all over again. We felt the terror of a looming deadline and had no idea how to do what we absolutely needed to do—get to the locker room to interview Gibson. With most fans remaining in their seats, getting to the escalator was easier than we had anticipated, but we knew interviewing Gibson would be a harder task. He was a tough interview, sometimes engaging, sometimes, well, not so much. What would he be like tonight?

We got to a makeshift interview room, and there was Gibson, waiting and standing still. Then he began a monologue in which he told us all about the events of the day. He essentially wrote the story for us. No one had to ask a question. He described all the dramatic circumstances leading to his at-bat. In five minutes, he told us everything we wanted and needed. Of course, the concourse was now filled with people trying to leave the park. We had to fight our way back to the press box to start our pieces, but somehow we were all able to file on time and then take a deep breath.

I think Kirk Gibson performed two miracles that day. First, that totally unexpected and amazing home run, and second, the equally unexpected cooperation that enabled us to finish our day's work. Of course, this game, and this at-bat, grew into legend, the gift that keeps on giving.

-Ron Rapoport, Los Angeles, California

My beloved grandfather, Ully, took me to the 1954 All-Star Game in Cleveland. We were two of 69,000 fans and sat in the center field bleachers. The American League won, in no small measure due to the four home runs hit by home city heroes, two by Al Rosen, and one each by Larry Doby and Ray Boone. Ray had been a member of the 1948 Indians World Champs but was traded to Detroit in 1953. The National League hit two homers, by Ted Kluszewski and Gus Bell of the Cincinnati Reds. That year, the Indians went on to win the pennant, but lost to the Giants in the World Series that included the Willie Mays' famous over-the-head catch off Vic Wertz's drive.

What an amazing day it was at the All-Star Game, with at least 15 future Hall of Famers between the two squads. Almost every name on both rosters is remembered today by baseball fans. Whitey Ford and Robin Roberts were the starting pitchers. Team members included Mays and Mantle, Spahn and Lemon, Jackie, Yogi, Ted and Duke, Stan the Man and Minnie Minoso, Alvin Dark, Nellie Fox, and Red Schoendienst. It was a list of eternal stars in the baseball pantheon.

The American League scored three runs in the 8th to take a lead it did not relinquish, winning 11-9. All-Star Game records were set for most homers by one and both teams in a single game, and most hits and most runs in a game.

~Tom Tomsick, Cincinnati, OH, author of *Strike Three*

Tuesday August 7, 2007 was the day that Barry Bonds hit homer number 756 to break Hank Aaron's record for career home runs. Of course, it was a big day for Giants fans and Bonds fans, both of which I am. However, what made that day so memorable was the experience I had getting into the ballpark.

It was a weeknight evening game, and my son and I drove to AT&T Park in San Francisco from Lafayette in the East Bay. The commuter traffic is always unpredictable, and the game had already started when we got to the parking lot south of McCovey Cove. We decided we'd better run if we wanted to see Bonds' first at-bat. But we weren't the only latecomers with that idea. As we crossed the Lefty O'Doul Bridge and saw people coming from other directions, we were caught up in a strange spectacle of everyone still outside the park running for entrance gates.

We felt very lucky to be walking down the steps to our seats as Barry took his first at-bat. As it turned out, he hit #756 in the 5th inning of the Giants game against the Washington Nationals. Having witnessed nearly all of his milestone home runs, the details of the celebration aren't that distinct in my memory. But I'll never forget sprinting to the gates with the thousand or so others consumed with the fear that we might be missing out on the historic moment.

~Dave Rey, Lafayette, California

With Alex Rodriguez the most talked-about nonparticipant for four months of the 2013 baseball season, it was fun to look back upon a game when A-Rod became the center of controversy for an on-field gaffe. It was a scene where I was a little too close for comfort, game 6 of the 2004 American League Championship Series between the New York Yankees and the Boston Red Sox. Two nights earlier, the Bronx Bombers had been one inning away from a sweep, but the resilient Red Sox were in the process of launching a comeback for the ages and erasing the Curse of the Bambino.

I attended the game as a volunteer runner for the photo pool, part of a small group who took turns collecting the on-field photographers' discs at the end of each half-inning. As the Yankees batted in the bottom of the 8th, I crouched near the visitors' dugout on the third base side. Curt Schilling had held the Bombers in check for seven frames, and the score was 4-2 when a slumping A-Rod stepped to the plate against reliever Bronson Arroyo with one out and Derek Jeter on first.

Instead of the game-tying home run Yankees fans wished for, Rodriguez's mighty swing produced a slow roller toward first base. Arroyo pounced on the ball and attempted to tag A-Rod, who slapped the pitcher's arm, knocking the ball loose and reaching base safely to keep the rally alive. Instantly, Bosox manager Terry Francona bolted out of the dugout claiming interference, and the umpires huddled. The brief conference produced a reversal of the call, and A-Rod was out.

Yankees fans did not take the decision well. Suddenly, balls and other debris began to rain down from the upper deck. I was a sitting duck. No aspirant for martyrdom, I beat a hasty retreat to shelter. The photographers would have to wait. Francona pulled his players from the field to protect them. After a delay, order was restored when NYPD officers took to the field in riot gear, an unprecedented action.

Boston's 4-2 triumph tied the American League Championship Series at three games apiece. I could have returned the next night, but this life-long Yankees fan saw that old man mo'(mentum), not Mariano Rivera, was on the other side. Game 7 was a 10-3 laugher, and the Sox then swept the World Series, completing a stunning eight-game winning streak.

A-Rod, after going 6-for-14 in the three Yankees victories, went 2-for-17 in the four losses. As for me, I kept my head while others were losing theirs.

~David Lieberfarb, Edison, New Jersey

I was one of the 31,395 fans who attended the last Expos game. When it was announced that the move to Washington was official, many fans (whatever was left of them) were anxious, and of course upset. To add salt to the wound, their opponents were the Florida Marlins, owned by Jeffrey Loria and David Samson, former owners of the Expos and, to many, the ones responsible for the death of the franchise in Montreal. My brother and I felt obligated to go to their last game. Expos manager Frank Robinson decided to start the unpopular Sun-Woo Kim instead of ace Livan Hernandez. Not surprisingly, Kim got knocked around by the Marlins' bats. I recall Miguel Cabrera hitting a monster home run over the left field bleachers. Over the course of the game, some fans got unruly and threw golf balls onto the field. Flyers with Commissioner Bud Selig's portrait on them, looking like wanted posters from the old West, were thrown down from the upper deck. As the game ended, there wasn't a dry eye anywhere, including my brother and me. It was the end of an era. Players expressed their emotions on the field. Brad Wilkerson was openly bawling. Tony Batista pointed both index fingers to the sky. It was a tumultuous time for the players and the fans.

~Paul Rapagna, Lachine, Canada

In July 1963, when I was eight, my father took me to watch my favorite baseball team, the Giants, play the Milwaukee Braves in San Francisco. It was the single greatest experience of my childhood. I would not realize until years later, just how significant that game was. Seven future Hall of Famers played in the game—Mathews, Aaron, Cepeda, Mays, McCovey, Spahn, and Marichal, no first names necessary. It ended on a Mays homer in the bottom of the 16th—perfect since Mays was my favorite player. Spahn and Marichal both pitched all 16 innings of this marathon, and I even got autographs from both Mays and McCovey. I just don't think life gets any better than that for an eight-year-old!

~Larry Mires, Buckeye, Arizona

Many readers know Marichal, 25 at the time, was to be removed after the 14th inning, but said something to the effect of, "If that 42-year-old *&$# is still out there, no one is taking me out"

It was the first baseball game in New York since the Twin Towers fell on September 11, 2001, Mets playing against the Braves. I was 30 years old, and my friend Michael and I got tickets the minute it was announced when the next game at Shea would be played. I was at my parents' place for dinner when I told my folks that I was going. My mother said to my father, "Stuart, tell your son that he's not going to that game." His response, "El, I could tell him, but nothing's gonna stop him from going." She didn't understand. I *had* to go.

It was a packed house, New York defiantly uniting against the enemy by continuing to live our lives. There was a serious air walking into Shea. Security was tight for the first time in ages. A precedent had been set. The awareness that we were no longer untouchable by our enemies had set in. I bought the new Mets cap that was on sale for the first time, all black with the American flag on the side. Mayor Giuliani threw out the first pitch. It was the first time I can remember nobody booing the longtime Yankees fan. All Mets wore FDNY, NYPD, and NY Port Authority caps. The American Flag was clearly seen on the back collars of the jerseys. No one needed prompting to stand and remove their caps for the National Anthem. It was the loudest I've ever heard the fans sing it.

The Braves took the lead in the 4th, and the Mets tied it right back. The Braves regained the lead in the 8th, somewhat quieting the crowd. In the bottom of the inning, Piazza came up after Alfonzo reached and was replaced by a pinch-runner. Piazza had doubled twice already, so the law of averages was that would be it for him. It was a 2-1 fastball that produced a crack of lightning, and thunder immediately followed, long before we saw the ball sail over just left of the straightaway center field fence. That time the thunder would not quit. It is the only time I can recall that Shea actually shook. It was a release of the floodgates of emotion. Such exultation among the fans, it had the atmosphere, and then some, of a World Series game.

We love sports because there are times they truly transcend being just a game. That night is forever burned into my memory, as much as the lesson my father understood on his deathbed about me—when you get knocked down, get up.

~Adam Beerman, Woodstock, Georgia

On October 31, 2001, I attended Game 4 of the Yankees vs. Diamondbacks World Series. Right after 9/11, the city had an eerie feel to it...and so did my entry into the stadium. My friend and I got separated, and I entered a gate I should not have been allowed to come through, security ultimately taking me to my section. Once in my seat, I noticed police everywhere. There appeared to be snipers on the roof behind the façade, and security was intense. The atmosphere was electric. The Yankees bleacher crowd, not known for its civility, yelled at other fans to stop talking or to take off their hats during the National Anthem, which was followed by a chant of "USA!" which started in the bleachers and echoed throughout the stadium. It was as if the entire stadium was announcing New York City's resilience to the world. This same scene played out during the seventh inning stretch when "God Bless America" was sung.

When the Yankees took the field in the 1st, the crowd chanted each player's name, starting from the pitcher, working around the infield and then the outfield, until that player turned and waved or tipped his cap, after which the crowd erupted in a loud cheer. It was absurdly exciting to be in the midst of the frenzy.

The game is a matter of record. Tino Martinez hit a home run that landed two rows away from where we sat. The crowd went insane, and the stadium shook as people jumped up and down. It felt like an earthquake. In the bottom of the 10th, Derek Jeter hit a home run to win the game, the ball landing not far from where Tino's had landed. The crowd again erupted in a frenzy. The noise was twice as loud as it had been in the 9th. The stadium felt like it was physically bouncing. Everyone was screaming, and I could not hear the people next to me or even my own voice. It was by far the loudest, most electric event I have ever attended. After the game, nobody left. The crowd just screamed until the players went off the field. Given the close timing to a true national tragedy, the way the game ended, and the crowd that day, I will never forget that game, and I doubt I will ever experience anything close to it again. I do still have the ticket stub.

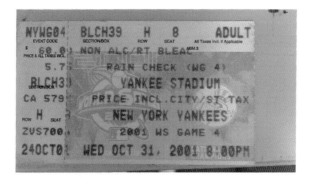

~Tim Smith, San Francisco, California

On September 28, 1960, my dad pulled me out of school and took me to Fenway Park for Ted Williams' last game there. It was a cold, raw, rainy day. The Sox were well out of the pennant race, but Ted homered in his last at-bat. He went out to left field in the top of the 9th, but was replaced by either Gene Stephens or Carroll Hardy, his designated caddies. He wouldn't, and didn't, tip his cap to the less than 10,000 fans still there.

What we didn't know was that he told broadcaster and fishing buddy, Curt Gowdy, in advance, and in confidence, that he wasn't going to New York for the final series of the season but finishing his career at home in Boston. In the excitement of the homer in the 8th inning, Gowdy spilled the beans in the play-by-play, saying Williams had "homered in his final at-bat in the major leagues."

That cold, rainy day stays with me, not just because of Ted's last game and at-bat, but more because of my bonding with my dad. It was a cherished moment, the best Red Sox game I ever saw, until 2004.

~Neal Milden, Raritan, New Jersey

329

On October 24, 2002, I was an 11-year-old on my way to school, as I did most mornings. But when the school bell rang, my dad picked me up to go to Game 5 of the 2002 World Series at AT&T Park, the Giants hosting the Angels. This was my first playoff game, and, of course, my first World Series game. We sat behind the third base dugout with a good view of home plate. The Giants were leading in the bottom of the 7th inning, and with JT Snow and David Bell on base, Kenny Lofton hit a shot off the wall. Everyone was standing, and what most of us saw, as much as Snow coming toward home and Bell not far behind, was Manager Dusty Baker's three-year-old son, Darren, the bat boy, running out to home plate to pick up Lofton's bat. He was right on course to get the bat just after Snow scored…and would surely be trampled by Bell. As JT crossed home plate, he scooped up Darren by his arm, getting him out of the way of a world of hurt. Watch the video on YouTube, it is amazing.

As you can imagine, there was as much chatter in the stands about Darren and JT's alertness and miracle as about what became irrelevant runs. The Giants went on to win the game 16-4 with Jeff Kent hitting two home runs, and now led the Series three games to two. Major League Baseball later changed the minimum age to be a bat boy. Dusty evidently was yelled at by *his* mom. Giants and Angels fans, and many others, remember what happened in Game 6, and I have no need to discuss it here. But I am pretty sure that everyone in the park that day for Game 5, and everyone watching it on TV, will never forget that play.

~Mike Massocca, San Francisco, California

JUST ANOTHER DAY
AT THE PARK

Announcers frequently say that every day, every game, you may see something that has never been seen before. That may be a bit of an exaggeration, but you never know. Maybe it's a stadium promotion, some incredibly bad base-running, or an astonishing catch. Maybe it's something that happened in the stands. Here is a collection of things that people have seen at games. Some took place around the bases, others in the bleachers. But all are different and unique.

My favorite baseball memory took place at a Mariners game against the visiting Yankees. My stepdad gets good tickets for advertising with the team, so we were sitting between home plate and first base, in maybe the 15th row. Prime real estate! Mom, my stepdad, a friend, and I were watching the game when someone hopped the fence between plays. I'd seen people on the field before, and it is always entertaining watching them zig-zag around trying to avoid the police. The cops finally caught this guy and hauled him off, and the game continued. Just 15 minutes later, another guy hopped the fence! Again, the police ran around chasing this guy who was whooping and hollering, making the most of his 15 seconds of fame. Now everyone in the crowd was attentive, wondering if it would happen again. Well, the flood gates had opened and a woman jumped onto the field. At this point, all of the ushers who stand at the top of the stairs to hold people back during plays moved down the aisles, watching like hawks for more potential runners. Much good they did, because lo and behold, half an hour later another person was on the field, this time a *streaker!* Buck naked, this guy was running around and the police were chasing him, but this time with a towel. It was like the most hilarious reverse of a bull and matador! The best part of the whole thing was that when the cops finally grabbed him and wrapped him in the towel, he waited until he was about halfway off the field to shake his hips and lose the towel one last time. I don't think I've ever seen a crowd more attentive than for the rest of that game. Speaking of the game, we were tied with the Yankees until that point, and the game then went into extra innings. It was so satisfying to see the Mariners crush them in the 13th inning with an epic home run. Definitely the best game of my life!

~Erika Duncan, Mountain View, California

Two New York guys of the same age don't know each other, but both brought something to this combo plate.

It was June 24, 1970. I was a teenager living in New York, and I went to a doubleheader at Yankee Stadium. The Yankees were terrible, as were the equally woeful visiting Cleveland Indians. This Wednesday afternoon saw a stadium less than half full, yet what a series of interesting events occurred!

The first game was rather mundane until the late innings. Tony Horton—not to be confused with Willie Horton of the Tigers—was a big, home run-hitting first baseman for Cleveland. The Yankees had a relief pitcher named Steve Hamilton, a skinny 6'7" lefty (he had played briefly in the NBA in the '50s) who, nearing the end of his career, had lost a lot of his stuff. Still effective against left-handed hitters, he was now very hittable against righties. In those days, clubs carried only 10 pitchers, so they usually faced multiple batters. To compensate, Hamilton had developed a pitch for righties that he called a "Folly Floater," a high, slow lob. He would start his wind-up, almost come to a stop, hold the ball up for the hitter to see, and then lob it in like a slow softball pitch. Horton, who had hit three homers against the Yankees during the prior month, apparently had been asked about the Folly Floater before the game and had stated that he would crawl back to the dugout if Hamilton got him out with it. The Yankees trailed, and Hamilton came in to pitch to Horton. He threw a floater that seemed to take five seconds to reach home plate—think softball pitch in a league that has no limit on arc, like 15 feet in the air. Horton fouled it back. Obviously ticked, Horton asked for another and Hamilton complied. Another floater, and Horton hit another pop foul, but catcher Thurman Munson made the catch. Horton threw down his bat and helmet in disgust and when he neared the dugout, true to his word, he got down on his hands and knees and crawled to the dugout with the crowd roaring.

But wait, there's more. Lots of crazy things this doubleheader.

Yankees center fielder Bobby Murcer homered in his last at-bat of the first game, and in the second game, he homered in his first at-bat, walked in his next, then hit another homer, for three consecutive home runs, since walks do not count as at-bats. I clearly recall his last at-bat. Everyone was buzzing with the realization that he had hit three consecutive home runs. Sure enough, Murcer launched a line drive to deep right into the bleachers. Definitely one for the record books! Of course, he also had to retrieve a ball hit by an Indians batter deep into center field beyond the monuments to Ruth, Gehrig, and Huggins which were on the field at that time.

But wait, you know there's more!

There was a huge brawl at home plate when Vada Pinson collided with Yankees pitcher Stan Bahnsen.

But the most bizarre event of the day occurred in the 5th inning of the second game. Ray Fosse, Indians catcher and rising star before his run-in with Pete Rose in the All-Star game, was crouching behind home plate, and some idiot in the upper deck threw a cherry bomb or a large fire cracker toward the field. It exploded under Fosse, who rolled in agony. The culprit was apprehended and taken away in handcuffs with the crowd cheering his arrest.

Altogether an amazing day!

The teams split that day if anyone cares.

~Alan Fram, Arlington, Virginia, then Bronx, New York

~Joel Goldman, Moraga, California then Hastings-on-Hudson, New York

My son, Adam, was maybe 10 years old, since it hadn't been too long that he'd been able to sit through an entire Giants game at Candlestick Park. I always brought my own peanuts to games, taken from a five-pound bag purchased at Safeway. But this time, a game against the Dodgers, I'd decided to bring in the whole bag. We ran into someone we knew who, to be nice, bought us a Bag o' Nuts. He tossed them to us, up two rows and four seats over. To be a gracious recipient, I kept the ones I'd brought in my backpack.

An obnoxious Dodgers fan sat four rows down, directly in front of us. When anything went the Dodgers' way, he would stand up and taunt the Giants fans. Sometimes he stood longer than necessary, blocking peoples' view of the game. Finally I'd had enough and nailed him in the back of his noggin with a peanut. He quickly turned around, but I played innocent so he had no clue who'd hit him. This went on a few more times, and then he whirled around in time to catch me in the act. He was ticked off and threw more than a handful of peanuts our way, hitting us and the people around us.

I reached into my pack, pulled out the unopened 5 lb. bag, put it in my right hand, stood up, cocked my arm, and started a throwing motion as if to propel the whole bag in his direction. I didn't see everyone's reaction, but my son, Adam, about had a heart attack. Obviously, I would never have let the projectile fly. The Dodgers fan laughed, and everything was fine after that.

Nowadays, I guess it would probably evolve into a fist fight and an eventual ejection from the premises.

~Steve G., San Francisco, California

One Fourth of July, I was at a minor league game of the Lancaster, California, Jethawks. For one of the later between-innings distractions, when the high desert evening air was considerably cooler, they pitted two slightly overweight fellows in their thirties against each other in a kind of contest you would only see at a minor league game. The rules of the contest were simple: race down the first base line, peel off your shirt, open the ice chest, pull out the folded, frozen-solid T-shirt, break up the ice in the T-shirt enough to put it on, and then do so.

In the estimation of the sellout crowd that night, the winner was probably the guy who finished second.

~Douglas B. Wilkins, San Francisco, California

Around 1965, I was a member of the School Patrol at my Atlantic Avenue Elementary School in Forest Hills near Pittsburgh, Pennsylvania. I was a sergeant and got to wear a white belt and a green badge. Every year the Pirates held a day when they invited School Patrol members from the area to attend a game. That year, we were way up in the center field stands. Someone hit a long fly ball which went foul into the upper deck along the first base side. There must have been a group from a Catholic school seated up there, because we saw many nuns in full black habits among them. Well, a couple of those sisters flew up out of their seats, habits flying, reaching for that ball, and one caught it! I am Jewish, but I lived in a neighborhood with a Catholic church and school, and believe me, I had never seen a nun move like that. They were awesome! I just wish I could have heard the reactions from their students.

~Lois, Forest Hills, Pennsylvania

My former high school, Golden West in Visalia, California, was a perennial varsity baseball powerhouse with many championships under their belt. I was lucky enough to be the stadium PA announcer for more than two decades, and I saw a lot of great baseball. Being paid to watch the game *and* talk over the loudspeakers with nobody telling me to shut-up was, well...heaven.

The teams were always well coached and successful, but the school district wouldn't buy a scoreboard worth spit. It was nothing more than a postage stamp with tiny light bulbs, which often either broke down or wouldn't light up the correct number of bulbs for the ball-strike count. Maybe the score was correct...and then maybe it wasn't. The stadium was located by the St. Johns River, the riverbanks heavily populated with ground squirrels which, we were told, had an affinity for electrical wire. They were twice blamed for eating the wiring to the AC chillers on campus, creating some rather hot classrooms and very unhappy teachers and students.

At one game, our scoreboard was in rare form. Balls were lit up as strikes, the score would jump two or three runs instead of one at a time, or it wouldn't work at all so nobody was able to tell how many outs there were. That day's umpire had deluded himself into thinking this high school ballpark was really Yankee Stadium and was becoming visibly upset...with me. He kept motioning to the scoreboard, then the press box, then back to the coaches in our dugout, and so on. Finally, at the second batter in the 3rd or 4th inning, this home plate ump walked toward the backstop fence below the press box, and believing I was purposely trying to show him up, gave me the heave-ho.

At first, I had no idea what he was doing. Throw out the stadium announcer...seriously? I stood up, extended my arms with palms up and asked, "What the heck?" He *really* didn't like that, pointed at me again and vigorously threw me out again. I was going to the showers until our coach, thankfully a good friend of mine, went to the ump, and after a rather heated discussion and much explaining how these evil squirrels had likely just decimated our postage stamp of a scoreboard, it was decided I could stay. They would keep score on the field instead. Gee. What a great idea. Now, why didn't I think of that?

Thus, certain tragedy was averted—the ejection of the stadium announcer—at least until the next game.

~Tim McGlasson, Visalia, California

On August 12, 2000, I was at the Mets vs. Giants game at Shea Stadium. With Jeff Kent and Ellis Burks on second and third, and one out for the Giants, a flyball was hit to left. Benny Agbayani made the catch and…handed the ball to a kid in the stands. The Giants runners were off like it was a track meet. Agbayani discovered a little late that there were only two outs. He ran back and grabbed the ball from the kid, but both runners scored on the play. This was in the 5th inning, and the rest of the evening the Mets players kept saying, "Hey, Benny! We're playing three outs this inning." Fortunately for the Mets, it didn't hurt them. They ended up winning anyway. And going to the World Series.

~Matt Purtill, Ankeny, Iowa

Sometimes it isn't a sporting event itself that generates a lasting moment. Occasionally, it is something around the event that does. Such was the case with my most vivid childhood baseball memory. My grandparents lived in a small village a few minutes away from Hornell in upstate New York. Hornell, a small, picturesque city with about 10,000 inhabitants was then a railroad town. My grandfather, his brothers, and seemingly every other man in the area worked for the Erie Railroad, in its repair shop or yards. In the summer, it also had the Hornell Dodgers, a class A Dodger affiliate, in what was then the Pony League. They played in a small, beautiful stadium. Some of the notables who passed through were Dodgers pitcher Karl Spooner and legendary Maury Wills.

We lived in Buffalo, about two hours away, and frequently visited my grandparents in the summer. My grandfather, father, and I would often take in a Dodgers baseball game. In 1954 when I was 10, appearing before the game was a baseball trick artist. I had never heard or seen anything like this, although I had seen newsreels of Eddie Feigner's "King and His Court." This performer was Jackie Price. He'd apparently had a brief major league career, but his calling was to do baseball tricks. He could hold three balls in one hand and accurately throw them to three different fielders and stand on his head and throw two balls simultaneously to two fielders. The way he caught baseballs was also unique. He unbuttoned his shirt and caught them in the shirt, or with his glove behind his back and through his legs. Then he hung upside down by his heels and belted line drives into center field. However, it was his finale that was the most unique and riveting. He'd have a bazooka on the ground by home plate and a Jeep idling alongside it. He would launch a baseball high into the evening sky over center field, climb into the Jeep, race into the outfield and catch the ball while driving. The crowd went wild.

It was the single most memorable thing involving baseball that I'd ever seen. Perhaps, subconsciously, I thought that if this man could do that, I could learn to catch any baseball or football thrown in my general direction. The ensuing game was pretty anticlimactic after that exhibition. The following summer we planned our trip to my grandparents to coincide with Price's return to Hornell. His finale was the same, just as successfully accomplished, and just as good to watch the second time.

~Jim Bennett, Mt. Pleasant, South Carolina

And speaking of Eddie Feigner...

Back in the early 1980's, I was still playing amateur baseball for a small college town, Whitewater, Wisconsin. It was a team I had started with the help of a few friends who hadn't seen baseball in their town for over 20 years. A few years later, we actually had a pretty good team. As the player-manager, I was once invited by the Parks and Rec director of the nearby town of Elkhorn to join in a game of fast-pitch softball, facing the famous team of "The King and His Court." Despite never having played a game of fast-pitch softball in my life, and knowing who this other team was, I still accepted the invitation.

When I showed up that night, I got my first practice swings against an underhand pitcher and figured I would just give my best, not exactly knowing what lay ahead. I was a newcomer, so not surprised to be on the bench to start the game, but I was assured that everyone would get to play about half.

We had a very good pitcher and a couple other guys who played fast-pitch on a regular basis, so by the middle of the game, we were still close in score. My turn came to bat, as I had subbed for the first baseman on defense the inning before. I'm a left-handed hitter and I prided myself on my ability to make contact against baseball pitchers, but as I mentioned, this would be a different kind of at-bat. Pitcher Eddie Feigner, the King, was over 60 years old at the time, and nearing the end of his shows. His team, or Court, consisted of only three other players, a catcher, first base-man, and shortstop, all part of his act. This was the usual setup.

The first pitch Eddie threw me was a riser. I had never in my life faced a pitch that went up, rather than dropping! Strike one. On the next pitch, the King went through his wind-up but didn't deliver the pitch as he nor-mally would, instead turning his body and flinging the pitch to me from behind his back! It came at me like a slow left-handed curve, dropping tremendously. There was no way I could have hit it, so I was glad that it dropped off the outside corner for ball one.

The next pitch was a riser that I fouled straight back to the screen, but now I had two strikes. I was not going to strike out! Another behind the back was ball two. Then another riser which I fouled off. Another behind the back was ball three, followed by a couple more fouled-off risers. Finally, a last riser which I popped up to shallow center field. With only four play-ers in the field, the shortstop raced toward center but couldn't quite get there in time, and it fell for an easy double. When I realized the King was still standing at the mound, I took off for third and was in easily with a triple! Eddie Feigner, wearing a microphone, made the most of it by an-nouncing to the crowd, "Hey, folks, look who just figured out that we don't have a third-baseman!"

So much for my becoming a great softball player. It was time to go back to hitting a smaller ball, one that didn't move around quite so much!

~Lynn Held, Stevens Point, Wisconsin

I fondly remember when my brother, "Tut," and I decided to see some games at Cooper Stadium in Columbus when Darryl Strawberry was doing a rehab stint in 1999 with the Clippers, a Yankees farm team. We were sitting way past first base, a good chunk down the line in right, and in the last row, but we didn't care. I think we went to every home game while Straw was there. Tut had been a big Mets fan growing up. One early evening, we realized that the sun was shining on us and that Tut was the only thing keeping it from blinding the opposing right-handed hitters' eyes. We knew this opportunity would not last long, so we waited until there were two strikes on the batter. Strike one. Ball one. Ball two. Strike two. Ball three. Right as the payoff pitch was being released, Tut moved aside. It was called strike three, and the hitter pointed his bat at us, visibly upset! It was the same with the next hitter. Both guys looked and pointed in our direction. We were definitely influencing the game. Ethical or not, it was the best I've ever felt at a baseball game. I can't even describe the emotion. Tut and I were never closer. We were trying to act cool, but the rest of the section had taken notice and was looking back at us and smirking. By that point, we were all smiles, too, and giving high-fives. The umpire even took off his mask, looked up at us and held up his arms to try to sway us. It was of no use. As the next batter walked to the plate, we thought, "Please be a righty." Yes! Foul ball. Strike two swinging. We knew what we had to do next.

~K. Kindberg, Burlingame, California

I grew up a fan of my hometown team, the Washington Senators, and was devastated when they moved to Texas. I transferred my allegiance to that team, but only as long as any Senators players who moved with the team still played for the Rangers. After that I became a fan of the other local team, the Baltimore Orioles.

I have so many memories from those years. I loved watching Eddie Murray. I went to the game when the great Red Sox outfielder, Carl Yastrzemski, made his last visit. A standing ovation was given to him by the appreciative and respectful Orioles fans at Memorial Stadium. I watched the Brewers and Don Sutton beat the O's and Jim Palmer to win the American League East in 1982. I got goose bumps and reveled along with so many others in 2005 when I saw the new Washington Nationals team wear caps with the Curly W during the team's first spring training game. Everyone at Nats games smiled because baseball was back in D.C..

One of my greatest memories had little to do with the game. In 2005, I took my wife, Linda, who is from Vietnam to her first game, Nationals vs. Mets. By 2010 she was a fan. That August, we went to "Pups in the Park" day and brought Cody, our 12-week-old pup. He wore a Nats jersey handed down from our previous dog, Phillip, with No. 00 on the back. We were asked if it would be okay if we were shown on the scoreboard between innings, as Linda was using a fan on the suffering little pup on a very hot D.C. day. That was Cody's, Linda's, and my 15 seconds of fame!

~Mark Hornbaker, Poolesville, Maryland

On July 11, 1990, I, my wife, Patti, and our kids were at the very first Turn Back the Clock day at Comiskey Park, a promotional game celebrating the final year of the park's existence. It was also a make-up game scheduled on the day after the All-Star Game. There were 40,666 people in attendance, pretty close to a full house.

The White Sox wore 1917-style uniforms to commemorate the year of their last World Series victory. Their opponents, the Milwaukee Brewers, wore regular road uniforms. To help foster an early-baseball atmosphere, ballpark ushers dressed in the styles of the day and some had megaphones to announce lineups. The scoreboard was mostly shut off, and there was minimal use of the loudspeaker system, so it really was a throwback game in many respects. Many fans even wore clothing of that year past, with a pregame parade of people in period costumes. Patti even recognized some of the costumes from a costume shop for which she had done some sewing.

General Admission ticket prices were $0.50 and all others were half price. The movie *Field of Dreams* had been out for about a year, so the whole style of the day was not as much of a novelty as it might have been otherwise. Some people had signs saying, "Easing the pain," a reference to Joe Jackson in the movie. There was a definite bygone era feeling in the park.

The combination of the first Turn Back the Clock day anywhere, and the last year of Comiskey, made this a unique and somewhat emotional day, probably in a different way for each person there. The contrast between the emotions for this game and crowd noise, along with the novelty of a game filled with no sounds out of the PA system, was very interesting and almost eerie. This was the park that the players portrayed in *Field of Dreams* actually played in, the home of the 1917 White Sox—who were nicknamed the Black Sox after the scandal—and this weighed heavily on me. Of course, the movie was all fiction, but I remember getting a real sense of the presence of the 1917 Sox, as if they really were there watching, enhanced by the fact that they had actually played there. Who knows, maybe they were. But that's me, and I'm an emotional sort. The signs people carried referring to the movie added to the emotions. Everything combined to provide a tingle of magic to the day.

As I write this, I can still hear James Earl Jones' line from the movie as he sat in the first base bleachers holding his Baseball Encyclopedia, "There is just something about this game." As far as *that* game, the Sox blew a big 7th inning lead and lost the game. Fortunately, we had to leave early, and I didn't see it.

~John Roeder, Oak Park, Illinois

During the early spring of 1962, I went to Cleveland to visit my cousin, Lenny. It was April and freezing, but we went to Cleveland Municipal, a cavernous old stadium, to see the Indians play the Kansas City Athletics.

The A's were owned by the legendary Charlie Finley, one of baseball's showman owners. The weird thing was that even though we were in Cleveland, it was KC Bat Day so they gave out green KC bats. The A's had a catcher named Doc Edwards, and before the game he came out of the bullpen riding on a donkey, trotting right up to home plate. Being eight years old, none of this seemed strange to me. As I got older, I realized what a strange event I had witnessed. We left in the 5th inning because by then it was about 30 degrees. I always tell my wife I have very few memories of my childhood, but I do remember that day. Maybe just because it was baseball.

~Joel Schechter, Buffalo, New York

On May 15, 1980, I was coaching a Little League team in Atlanta, Georgia. My team, the Athletics, was playing a regular season game against the Pirates. The crowd was small, only the parents of the players were there, so few people saw, and even fewer recognized, the amazing performance of 12-year-old Woody Vaughan, the Athletics' catcher.

The Pirates had a much worse record than ours, but that particular night they were better, winning 4-3. They were the home team and did not have to bat in the bottom of the 6th inning, so the Athletics recorded only 15 outs. Woody participated in 14 of them. Our pitchers struck out 10 Pirates, and under score-keeping protocol, the catcher is credited with a putout for each strikeout. Woody also had four assists in those five innings, which probably is not a record but compares well with the major league record set in 1883 of nine assists in a nine inning game. The amazing aspect is that Woody threw out a base runner at each base, including home plate! First, he cut down a base runner who attempted to steal second. Then he retrieved a wild pitch and threw to the pitcher covering home to retire a runner who'd tried to score from third. Next, he foiled a bunt attempt by throwing the batter out at first. Finally, he received a throw from the outfield too late to stop a run from scoring, but his relay to third nailed another runner trying to advance. That assist completed Woody's cycle.

In the major leagues, hitting for the cycle—a single, double, triple, and home run—in the same game is about as rare as a no-hit game. The feat is much rarer, if possible, in Little League, where games last only six innings. How likely is it that any other catcher ever threw for the cycle?

-Wynn Montgomery, Erie, Colorado

The Place: Chase Field in Phoenix, Arizona, home of the Arizona Diamondbacks

The Year: Around 2010

The Scene: The seventh inning stretch in a D'backs game against the San Diego Padres

The Rally Backs, D'back staff, were shooting T-shirts into the crowd with air guns. I had absolutely no interest in getting one. I calmly sat in my seat while two guys and their girlfriends in front of me were wildly jumping up and down hoping to get a prize. *Pow!* A shirt was launched right in my direction and hit me square in the left eye. *Ouch* big time. I have impact lenses after having had cataract surgery. I have noticed that in other ballparks ushers always check an area where a foul ball has reached to see if everything is okay. Not at Chase.

I checked with my eye surgeon when I returned home to the Los Angeles area and all was well. The T-shirt still hangs in a closet, never worn.

-Lee Watkins, Fullerton, California

On August 8, 2001, I went to my first Cubs game. I was 10 years old. The Cubs were playing the Rockies. Most of what I remember about that game are the usual first game experiences—the sights, the sounds, the nuances of watching a game in person. The organ was blaring, and the crowd was going wild. It wasn't a particularly great year for the Cubs, so maybe the crowd going mild would be a better way to put it. People were booing every Rockies pitchers' pickoff throw. It was all nothing special.

But then the game got interesting. Former Chicago Bear Steve McMichael led the crowd in the seventh inning stretch singing of "Take Me Out to the Ballgame," after which he proceeded, in what seemed to be a completely playful manner, to "threaten" the home plate umpire, Angel Hernandez, inciting the crowd. Hernandez ejected him, which of course further stirred the crowd. Had that ever happened before?

But wait, there's more.

The final play of the game was one of the most amazing plays of all time. With runners on first and second, Cubs batter Joe Girardi hit a single, and suddenly fielders and runners started slipping and falling, runners were in pickles between the bases, fielders not knowing where to throw the ball, just an unbelievable situation. The Cubs scored on that play. It is still one of my fondest memories, a very strange game. You can watch it here: https://www.youtube.com/watch?v=6htcE_vvZxg

~Jay Clancy, Round Lake Beach, Illinois

George Steinbrenner created a Yankees-brand credit card. There was a promotion to get the card in that after your first use, you got a cap and two free tickets to a game. I used mine once to buy gas and then threw it in a drawer. I was up $75 on George. It was a good day.

I used the tickets to take my son, Max, to a game against Toronto. Darryl Strawberry hit two home runs and the Yankees won. During the game, a group of seven guys behind us were playing "ball on the mound." They all ponied up $1 and gave it to the guy on the end. At the end of the inning, when the ball is typically tossed back toward the mound, if it rested anywhere on the mound, the guy with the money kept it. If the ball didn't rest on the mound, they would each pony up another dollar and the pot went to the next guy down the row. So, at the end of the inning when everyone else was starting to relax, these guys were going nuts. "Throw the freakin' ball, Girardi!" one of them yelled. Max asked if we could get in on it. I said, "It looks like fun but there's a good possibility of someone getting shot."

The game continued on. A foul ball landed about 10 rows in front of us. A little girl was about to pick it up when a big burly guy swept her aside and grabbed the ball. About 5,000 fans saw this happen and the chant started, "Give the kid the ball! Give the kid the ball!" The guy ignored the crowd. The chant changed, with fingers pointing. "Asshole! Asshole!" My son and I, arm in arm, joined the chant. The guys behind us had a pot of about $27, and they went down and offered it to the guy to give the girl the ball. He indignantly rejected the offer. That's when the hot dogs and beer cups started flying in his direction. And that's when I said, "Here comes security. Max, we gotta go!"

~Chris Barrett, West Palm Beach, Florida

It was early September in 1969, and I was 12 years old. The Mets, my Mets, were in a pennant race. The laughingstock of the baseball world for their entire seven-year history, they had pulled to within a game and a half of Chicago after trailing by as many as 10 games, just as the Cubs came into town.

My father, a butcher by trade, had scored four box seats in the mezzanine section at Shea one night, courtesy of his boss. I had been to a few games by this time, but that summer, baseball had taken over my life. The four seats meant we were all going, including my younger brother and my mother. After hurrying to finish dinner, I put on my yellow-trimmed Little League Pilots baseball uniform and my Mets hat. We had to wait in the car while Mom "got ready," as though she was going to a movie or a show. Back in the day, it took a long time to get that beehive hairdo to stand up like Marge Simpson's.

Our seats were just below the overhang of the upper deck. If you looked up, you could wave to the people above you. Mom had never been to a baseball game and barely understood what was going on. She certainly didn't comprehend the enormity of the game unfolding in front of her and was busy entertaining my brother while Dad and I were so engrossed in the game we barely knew they were with us.

Tom Seaver was pitching, and the Mets hit a few home runs, which caused Mom consternation because everyone was yelling and being raucous all around her. Near the end of the game, a black cat came out from under the stands and began walking near the Cubs dugout. As the crowd noticed what was going on and began reacting, the cat got scared and zigzagged across the Cubs players and Ron Santo in the on-deck circle, before disappearing back under the stands. Everyone was on their feet laughing and cheering! Years later, Mets icon Ed Kranepool would say that Shea Stadium had a lot of rats, so of course they had stray cats.

In the delirium following the appearance and disappearance of the cat, someone directly above us lost control of their beer cup and it slipped out of their hands. To this day, I don't know if Mom's hairdo had a bright red target on top, but that cup certainly locked onto its signal. Before landing, it flipped over completely, spilling the entire contents dead center on Mom's head! You know how there are times in your life when you are not supposed to think things are funny? Well, there was Mom, her hairdo turned from the beehive into the "wet dog," and we all had such a laugh, we were crying.

The Mets went on to win that game and would take over first place the next night, eventually winning their first World Series. To everyone else in the baseball world, this was the night of the famous Black Cat. To me, it will always be my mother's first—and last—baseball game!

~Paul DiSclafani, Massapequa, New York, author of *A View From the Bench*

WE HAVE OUR GOOD DAYS, WE HAVE OUR BAD DAYS

This is the chapter I intentionally did not use in my first book. I didn't want to go negative. When you are a kid, you assume your heroes are terrific people, but as we grow older, we sometimes see evidence to the contrary. In the course of hearing and reading so many stories about players, you learn that, with a few exceptions like Ernie Banks and Al Kaline, most ballplayers have their bad as well as their good moments. This chapter has become a combination of both positive and negative encounters from players and fans, from the bases to bleachers...and beyond.

On the last day of the season, I was there to see the Giants beat my team, the Dodgers, knocking them out of the playoffs. Fernando was pitching, and it started out rough with the Giants scoring early. That was common, but Valenzuela usually turned it around in later innings, as he did that day. Tommy Lasorda, whom I never viewed as a great manager, lifted Valenzuela with a batting average around .260 for pinch-hitter Jorge Orta, whose average was .133, despite Valenzuela mowing the Giants down. Orta struck out, and Lasorda put in Terry Forster who dished up an immediate home run to Joe Morgan. Season over.

In those days, visiting players walked to the locker room down the right field line. As an agitated Dodger fan, I walked with Tommy along that long walk to the exit, reminding him in a juvenile way of what he had done. I guess the fan in me, aka *fanatic*, came out in a negative way that day. I asked about the logic in his decision, among my other questions asked and opinions given. Lasorda, quiet and stoic, as is *not* his custom,

348

walked along the wall within 40 feet of me, not responding and not recognizing my presence. Until he reached the door. At that point I received what I had coming—the one-finger salute! He then disappeared, his message received and not one word spoken.

~Mark Hertz, Penn Valley, California

As a six-year-old kid living in San Diego, the Padres were an AAA team playing at nearby Westgate Park. I was a huge Giants fan. My grandfather would listen to Giants, Dodgers, Angels, and Padres games simultaneously on the radio. This drove me crazy. I couldn't process all the broadcasts at the same time, and I wondered who the heck cared about any game but the Giants anyway. My grandfather became frustrated with my frustration and asked me to put my money where my mouth was. I had accrued $7.15 in my allowance fund, and I bet it all on the Giants. The Giants won! This initiated a 17-year winning streak, at the end of which I had won $1,615. One of the last things my grandfather said to me before he passed was how much he enjoyed our wagering, and how the significance of each game had grown because of our wagers.

Years later, I moved my own family to Maine. We once drove to Beantown to watch the Red Sox play the White Sox. One of my high school mates, Rick Leach, was a reliever for the White Sox, so we met down the left field line during batting practice. My three-year-old son, Kyle, was munching Doritos while sitting on the wall, and up walked Bo Jackson. Bo picked up Kyle and the Doritos and walked out to the foot of the "Green Monster:, carrying on a baseball conversation the whole time. I took a picture, of course, which Kyle treasures to this day. Bo said he would "hit a home run for the kid," but unfortunately he took a golden sombrero instead.

~Gary Ray, Reno, Nevada

This baseball memory wasn't funny at the time, but years later, it seems quite amusing. It was 1958, probably early in the season because I remember it being a rather cool, though sunny, day. The Yankees had just lost a Sunday doubleheader to the Detroit Tigers, including one to Yankee-killer Frank Lary. I was walking around outside Yankee Stadium, hoping for some autographs, an activity I was never very successful at. This time proved to be no exception. Moose Skowron and Mickey Mantle were in Skowron's red convertible and, standing at the curb, I said, and this is an exact quote I remember almost 60 years later, "Oooh, Mr. Skowron, may I please have your autograph?" He replied, "Get the hell out of here, you little pisspot." Mantle thought this was hilarious. As a 12-year-old, I was left upset and speechless. Now, at least I can recall that I had a close encounter with these players!

~Steve Aaronson, Bethlehem, Pennsylvania

I know why the ground ball went through Bill Buckner's legs. In the summer of 1983, I was at an afternoon weekday game at Candlestick Park with a friend, the Cubs playing the Giants. The Giants were having an abysmal season and the stands were largely empty, so my friend and I moved from our cheap seats down to the railing just beyond the first base dugout. In the 3rd inning, a Giants batter hit a high, foul popup toward us. Buckner, the Cubs first baseman, raced over to catch it. I understood the rules, knowing that if he reached over the rail into the stands I could interfere. Still, I liked Buckner, and thought it was unfair that Steve Garvey got the accolades in hated L.A. even though Buckner had better stats. In the spirit of fairness, I yelled to my friend, "Let Buckner catch the ball!" He reached into the stands, but the ball was just beyond his glove. It hit the empty seat next to us and ricocheted back onto the field. I shouted, "Bill, we let you have a chance to catch it, let us have it!" Bill gave me a friendly smile, picked the ball up and took a step toward us. With a grateful grin, I stuck out my right hand. He extended his left hand, making a motion to give me the ball, but just as he was about to drop it in my hand, he pulled it back, turned, walked down the rail, and handed the ball to a man a few seats away from me. As he jogged back to his position he looked over his shoulder and flashed me a malicious grin. So, three years later, when the ball went through his legs in Game 6 of the World Series, I knew what had just happened. Karma had caught up with Bill Buckner. He really should have handed me that ball.

~Terry Gomes, San Francisco, California

Rickey Henderson had that famous way of swatting at fly balls when they came to him, called the "snatch catch." Instead of letting the ball just come into the glove, Henderson would stab at it and flick his glove as he caught it. Completely a showboat move. It drove me nuts. At one game, we were sitting right by the left field foul pole, and I was razzing him terribly. "Ricky be da greatest baseball playa eva," I yelled, and told him he was going to miss one. In the 4th inning, he swatted at one for a three-base error. I was just merciless.

After the game, I wanted to get Mark McGwire's autograph. My cousin had connections, so we were waiting by the locker room door when Rickey saw me and started swearing at me. I was actually afraid he might kick my ass, which I probably would have deserved.

Four years later, at a Cubs vs. Padres game on Father's Day, I sat in the bleachers, and Henderson was in left for the Padres. I immediately started in on him. Without turning around, he yelled, "Go the *&^% back to Minnesota!" My buddy and I were given free beer for that one by people in the bleachers.

That same day I saw Fernando, Sandberg, Gwynn, and Sosa. I sang with Harry Caray and watched Captain Kangaroo throw out the first pitch.

Five years ago, I was able to see past Henderson's attitude and just look at his talent and career. He is one of the five or six greatest players in the history of the game. I purchased his rookie card and his autographed A's and Yankees cards.

~Anonymous

I was a member of the Milwaukee Braves Knothole Club in 1964. Students, generally 10 to 13-year-old boys, took a school bus to the ballpark and got into games for $0.25. One game, the Philadelphia Phillies were visiting our hometown Braves. We sat in the bleachers, and former Braves outfielder Wes Covington was playing left field for the Phils. During a pitching change in the 7th or 8th, just as the relief pitcher—whom I somehow remember was Jack Baldshun—was coming in from the bullpen, some loudmouth above us yelled out to Covington, "You stunk with the Braves, and you guys are going to fold!" Wes turned around and extended his middle finger. Some of our younger members did not know what that was. I was not even sure what it meant. The guy who had provoked Covington's gesture told us, "That means he likes us!" Right. I know what it means now.

~Gerry Schuster, Milwaukee, Wisconsin

I am not sure if my experiences with meeting Pirates staff can be called a success. But I loved their announcer, Bob "Gunner" Prince, so one game, after sneaking in through the left field bleachers, I walked up the stairs where Gunner was announcing the game. As I got to the top, he came out and said, "Kid, what are you doing here?" I said, "Coming to see you." He replied "Well, you did. Now scram." I thought he was just the coolest with his wild sport coat.

As a 12-year-old, I met Pirates first baseman Dick Stuart. I went up to him and said, "You are one of my favorite players." He told me to *$#@ off. I told this to my friend, and from that day forward, he was aces in our book. We still laugh about it. Could you imagine that happening today? It would be all over CNN.

~Richard DeGrano, Jeannette, Pennsylvania

My baseball acquaintance began as a little girl in the Oakland Coliseum rooting for the Athletics during the Charlie Finley winning years. Rollie Fingers, Vida Blue, and Catfish Hunter were on the mound, and Reggie Jackson was there, too. A battle of facial hair raged, Reggie sporting a beard, and Rollie with his signature handlebar mustache. I went to the games with my older brother, my mother, and grandmother, all ardent fans with weekday day-game season tickets. Mom was very old-fashioned and didn't talk much with me about the facts of life. So, it was a precious moment when we sat together in the Wednesday noon sunshine, giggling while watching long-legged Dennis Eckersley, our closer with a totally unique wind-up, mutually admiring his fine physique.

Once in a while, something magical happens. Kansas City Royals right fielder Jeff Francoeur once had 20 personal pizzas delivered to the rowdy bleacher A's fans in section 149, and he got as many cheers as did the A's that day. Sleuthing online to understand this generosity of spirit, we discovered he had tossed a ball wrapped in a $100 bill to the fans the previous year, instructing them to buy bacon or beer. A good guy.

~Linda Hamilton, Oakland, California

It was 1957 and I was 12. Teams visiting the Phillies stayed at the Warwick Hotel on 15ᵗʰ and Locust in Philadelphia, the same hotel where the Dodgers tried to stay in 1949 but were refused entry. My friend, Ted, and I would take the trolley downtown to try to see ballplayers at the Warwick. One day when the Braves were in town we hit the jackpot. Red Schoendienst came in wearing an open-collared shirt and suit. When I said, "Hi Mr. Schoendienst!" he replied, "I'm not—" but I interrupted, "Sure you are. I'd recognize you anywhere." He still had red, though thinning, hair. He declined, but not impolitely, to give me his autograph. Big Warren Spahn approached, and I said, "Can I have your autograph, Mr.

Spahn, sir?" He gave a look that chilled me and said, "Don't sir me, kid!" With a lump in my throat, I apologized and asked again. His reply was, "No, you're a brat, kid." It was so odd. Billy Bruton came over, we talked for a second, and he asked me to buy him The Bulletin, giving me a quarter. The paper was $.15 and he gave me the change to keep. He was smiling and just a pleasure.

As they boarded the bus for the ride to the game, we stood nearby talking to players. I spoke through an open window with Braves shortstop, Johnny Logan, who was wearing a white and black tweed sport jacket. He asked me which team I was a fan of, and I admitted to being a Phillies fan. "That's good, kid, you should be loyal to your home team," he replied. Spahn sat down and told Logan to "Hit that kid for me." Logan looked at him like he was crazy, but Spahn kept going. Logan looked appalled and said, "Don't mind him," followed by, "Here, kid," taking out two tickets from his sport coat and handing them to me. He told me to come to that night's game and he would give me a ball.

Ted and I went to the game early and from the row by the field watched Logan and Andy Pafko playing pepper. I leaned over and called out, 'Hey, Johnny!" They walked over, Logan telling Pafko, "This is the kid I told you about." Pafko said, "Hi, kid," and Johnny told me to wait, returning only after he had a ball signed by almost the whole team.

Later in the hotel lobby, Joe Adcock, Eddie Matthews, and Fred Haney sat at a coffee table, some of them smoking cigars. We talked to them for several minutes. Adcock was a gentle giant, Haney was very nice, and Matthews was quiet but smiled. We went out to a little sandwich shop across the street and around the block, and watched them eat, with a few other players joining them. We followed Hank Aaron around the neighborhood, South Street, taking in the city as he walked. This was one of the best days of my life. I swear I never did or said anything disrespectful to Spahn. I was in awe of these guys, but Spahn was a pure SOB. I cried the day Logan died.

Two years later, when I moved in 1959 from Philly to New Jersey, unbeknownst to me, my mom, not wanting to pack everything, tossed a box of about 2000 baseball cards along with that 1957 World Champion Braves ball.

~Harold Kasselman, Vorhees, New Jersey, author of *A Pitch for Justice*

On June 6, 1994, I was at The Ballpark in Arlington, Texas, watching the Yankees smash the Rangers, a game which ended with the score 17-7. I was 10 years old and it was my first major league game. I grew up loving Nolan Ryan, for whom my son is named. After the game, I walked around the park with my family, taking in the sights. It was the stadium's opening season, and the ballpark was surrounded by only parking lots and unfinished buildings. We hung around until 11:00 p.m. and started to leave, heading for the ramp leading to the player's parking lot under the stadium. At the bottom was Jose Canseco standing behind his Camaro arguing with a woman I assumed was his girlfriend. I wondered if he had car trouble, and in my kid voice asked, "Mr. Canseco, do you need help, sir?" He started yelling at me and told me to "Get the &f$# out of here." To this day, my mother hates Jose Canseco. I don't remember being upset, just shocked. I still rooted for my Rangers. Canseco wasn't around too much longer.

~Nathan Crawford, Amarillo, Texas

It was preseason at the Polo Grounds when Cleveland usually played a few games with the Giants. The year was 1950, and I was 12. I had gathered with other kids, trying to get autographs from players before the Indians and the Giants went into the clubhouse to get ready for the game. I recognized Early Wynn and rushed toward him. He stopped me in mid-track, held up his arm, and in language extremely obscene and disgusting, told me to back off. It was so effusive and unnecessary that I rejoiced whenever he lost a game thereafter. A possible hero for me was crushed forever.

After that, I had no more interest in shagging for autographs, especially non-Giants!

~Norman Hall, Novato, California

A decade or so ago at a game at Safeco Stadium in Seattle, I was watching from center field behind the wall near the Mariner's bullpen. A member of our armed forces was also standing near the bullpen. David Aardsma, the Mariner's closer, grabbed a ball, passed it to the entire bullpen, everyone signing it, and handed it to the guy. It was an absolutely class move by Aardsma.

~Philip Leerar, Hudsonville, Michigan

My buddy, Christopher Hollis, and I were at an Astros game against the White Sox in Houston. We decided to go down to Lefty's pub, a field-level bar just on the other side of the fence from the players on the field. It was where you could smoke and get free peanuts…and heckle Albert Belle. Belle had recently been arrested for chasing trick-or-treaters in his Benz, so we decided to give him some. At the pub, we learned that his real name was Joey, and that he *detested* it. We quickly made 20-30 friends in the bar and spread the word. Imagine 30 drunk Astros fans hanging onto a chain link fence 10 feet from Belle, chanting, "Joey, Joey, Joey, trick-or-treat, Joey!" and the like. Well, Joey wasn't amused. He paced back and forth, glaring at us. During a pitching change we actually thought he was going to climb the fence and come after us! After the change, with the bases loaded, the next batter hit one through the gap to left. Belle was so discombobulated that the ball went under his glove, rolling all the way to fence, right in *front of my foot!* I pointed at the ball, shouting, "Get it Joey! Get it! It's right there, Joey!" Angrily, he picked it up and proceeded to throw it into the dugout. An inside-the-park home run! Dude, that was a great night at the park!

~Steve Benninga, Houston, Texas

I worked for the A's and Giants in the late 1970s and early '80s as a sound and cameraman, generally doing work for visiting teams for their feeds back home. This involved setting up cables and mics in the broadcast booths, arranging headsets and monitors, music cue-ins, and checking sound levels. This helped me take care of a personal interest of mine. My daughter was young, and she and my wife often came to the games. Long before the age of Skype, I'd ask the camera guys if, during cutaways between innings, they would get a shot of them so our family back in New York could see them live.

My hair was 1970s long, Geddy Lee of Rush long, and I was skinny. One day the Twins were visiting the A's, and their two broadcast color guys were Harmon Killebrew and Jimmy Piersall. Piersall apparently had had some mental health issues, and was known for antics on the field, such as running his 100th career home run backwards around the bases. As I set up, I suddenly felt a presence behind me. I turned around and saw Piersall looming. He began our dialogue with "Excuse me, sweetheart, I can't hear myself in this IFB (earpiece)." I replied that he could control that himself. He countered with, "Actually, I have a problem, and what's more, darlin', you need a Goddamn haircut." I responded with the first clever comment I could think of, "F$*# you."

At that point, Piersall got right in my face, demanding, "Who the f#&* do you think you are?" I told him I had seen *Fear Strikes Out*, the movie about him in which there was an allusion that he was gay, and said if he had a homosexual problem, he shouldn't take it out on me. Then he threw a punch at me, but before it connected, Killebrew, who had arms like tree trunks, picked up Piersall and told him, "Leave the kid alone." Thanks to The Killer, I managed to escape that potential disaster unscathed.

~Scott Ross, Santa Barbara, California

STORIES HANDED DOWN

One day, while emailing with my friend Roz, she casually mentioned that her father had been an usher at Yankee Stadium and had told her about being at the game when Lou Gehrig made his iconic farewell speech. My mouth flew open like I had just tasted pizza for the first time. That began an obsession to get stories of this type. Obviously, as time goes by, there will be fewer folks able to recount stories from the 1920s, '30s, and even the '40s, so this seemed like the best way to try to capture stories from this era. Unlike all the other chapters, those credited as the storytellers usually did not give them to me directly. A very favorite, and special, chapter.

Lou Gehrig was my favorite baseball player, pure and simple, a superstar before the word was invented, a tremendous player, a beloved teammate. You learned these things when you grew up a Yankees fan in New York in the 1920s and '30s. Even more, I respected him as a great man. The Iron Horse's career is well documented, as is his bout with amyotrophic lateral sclerosis, or ALS, now known as Lou Gehrig's disease, and how it forced him into early retirement and took his life far too soon. This was told in the movie *Pride of the Yankees* starring Gary Cooper.

I was at Lou Gehrig Appreciation Day on July 4, 1939. He had formally retired on June 21, and the Yankees wanted to honor him in a manner befitting a legend. The ceremony was held between games of a doubleheader against the Washington Senators. All the details, who attended, and Lou's speech, are all easy to find on the internet. Of course, his ultimate classic line, "Yet, today, I consider myself the luckiest man on the face of this earth," is now part of the American lexicon and the standard for all retirement speeches.

What you can't find on the internet is the emotions that people attending the game experienced. It is said that for every classic game, three times as many people claim to have attended as could fit in the stadium. But I really was at this game, and the depth of emotion in the crowd, the awe and honor and esteem which people had for Gehrig, all came tumbling forth in a torrent of respect and sadness. It was truly the greatest moment I ever had at a baseball game.

~Ben Fine, New York, New York, as told to his daughter, Roz Fine Itelson, San Francisco, California

When people asked me where I was from, my answer was always, "I was born in Yankee Stadium between the first and second games of a doubleheader!" My friends and I grew up in the Bronx, six blocks from the Stadium, during the Babe Ruth and Lou Gehrig era. We played sandlot ball in a park across the street from the players' entrance, hearing the roar of the crowd and wondering what happened. After the game, always late in the afternoon, we'd stop our own game when the Yankees walked by in their street clothes and run across the street to talk to them and try to get autographs. My favorite player was Gehrig, so I was especially excited at a Gehrig sighting, and did finally manage to obtain that cherished signature.

~Paul Hunter, New York, NY, as told to Bruce Hunter

I recall Dad frequently recounting the above early childhood memories and traditions when I began going to Yankee stadium with him and my grandfather during the Mickey Mantle and Roger Maris era. They were of course different names and different eras, but both were amazing duos wearing the same pinstripe uniforms.

~Bruce Hunter, Atlanta, Georgia

Bill Terry played his entire career with the New York Giants. Their first baseman from 1923-36, he was by any measure one of the best offensive players of his time, a three-time All-Star who consistently received consideration for the league's MVP Award. Most notably, Terry's league-leading .401 batting average in 1930 still marks the last time that a National League player batted over .400. He was elected to the National Baseball Hall of Fame in 1954, and his uniform number, No. 3, has been retired by the Giants.

Terry was an all-time great. He was also my father's favorite player. Although I undoubtedly heard numerous stories about Terry's skills, other than remembering the obvious, that he is the National League's last .400 hitter, no tales about Terry's outstanding play have stuck with me. Fortunately, however, my father left me with one indelible memory of Bill Terry, which had contributed to Terry being his favorite player.

As a boy who grew up in Brooklyn in the 1920s and 1930s, my father became a Giants fan, initially, I think, because the Giants were neither the Dodgers nor the Yankees. For whatever reason, he loved the Giants. Decades later, in the 1960s, he successfully indoctrinated me, even though we lived in central Pennsylvania during the later years of the Willie Mays era. The most memorable baseball stories from my childhood involved my father telling me about his riding the subway with his friends, Morty and Stumpy, armed with sardine sandwiches wrapped in waxed paper, to see the Giants play at the Polo Grounds. The best of the adventures ended with the three friends, along with numerous other 12 to 15-year-old boys, clamoring for the players' attention at the stairway leading to the Giants' clubhouse in center field.

Among the many times when Terry and other Giants obliged the young fans by engaging them in banter about the game, the story my father recounted most frequently was the one time when Terry did not. After a heartbreaking loss, when faced immediately afterward with the adoring and clamoring hoard, Terry responded abruptly and colorfully, "Ah shit, kids! Leave me alone." While such a salty response to young fans may result in a player being fined these days, this incident endeared Terry to my father. He loved that Terry revealed his real emotions and saw in that moment the intensity and the total disdain for losing that made Terry such a great player.

~Bill Blier, Washington, District of Columbia

My biggest radio blooper as a baseball announcer occurred when the Tigers were playing the Angels in Anaheim. It was late in the game, and I think it was Dave Collins who'd stolen home. I was describing the play and talked about how angry Tigers catcher Bill Freehan had been when they called the runner safe. I said, "Freehan is arguing with the umpire, and he is beating his meat." Oops. I, of course, meant to say beating his *mitt*. I was very concerned about losing my job or being reprimanded, but because it was a late game on the West Coast, thankfully I didn't catch much flack.

~Ernie Harwell, as told to Byron Hatch, Flint, Michigan

My father was born in Brooklyn and was a Dodgers fan by 1930. His friend, Bud, was a Giants fan. In May 1940, they went to see the Giants at the Polo Grounds. That day, Carl Hubbell pitched a one-hitter, but faced the minimum of 27 batters. This game shows up in "This day in baseball history" lists in newspapers.

The reason this was Dad and Bud's favorite game was that they had gone early to the stadium and Hubbell had ridden on their subway car to the game! He was standing, and his left arm hung crooked from his years of throwing screwballs.

~Steve Itelson, San Francisco, California

"I once saw Babe Ruth hit a home run in Sportsman's Park, probably in the 1926 World Series, that went completely out of the park. It hit the street on Grand Avenue, rolled up to the YMCA, and would have rolled right in the door if it'd had a quarter for the entrance fee."

~Damon Kerby, St. Louis Post-Dispatch baseball writer in the 1930's, as told to his son, Damon (on several occasions), San Anselmo, California

My favorite baseball story involves my dad, Jack, my grandfather, and Babe Ruth…although The Babe obviously had no idea of his involvement. And…the story may have been embellished a little over time. My grandfather, after whom I'm named, occasionally took my dad to Yankees games when he was young. It was during the Depression, and as they didn't have much money, all they could afford was bleacher seats. My grandfather, an immigrant from Russia, now Ukraine, came here not knowing about baseball, but had become hooked after moving to the Bronx. He never really grasped everything about the game but was a huge Yankees fan until the end of his life. Dad, accordingly, became a Yankees fan, and never figured out why I chose the Mets instead. All I can guess is that we lived in Brooklyn while the Dodgers still played there, and when the Mets came into the league, they brought in former Dodgers Gil Hodges and Duke Snider to play for them. Either that, or it was a mild bit of rebellion against parental authority. Or both.

At a game, likely in the early 1930s, Babe Ruth came up and drilled a shot toward where Dad and my grandfather were sitting. Dad, a three-sport varsity high school athlete, knew the ball was coming his way. He was determined to catch it, and jumped up, yelling, "I got it!" or something like that. My grandfather, either out of a sense of protection or pride, said *he* was going to catch it, and moved Dad out of the way. Dad's favorite Yankees were Joe DiMaggio and Willie Randolph, but Grandpa particularly loved Ruth. Unfortunately, he had never played the game, so the only thing that he was going to catch the ball with was the middle of his forehead. So he ducked, the ball bounced away, and someone else got their hands on it.

I'm convinced that Dad would have caught the ball. Since then, no matter how many games members of my family have attended, we've never come close to catching a ball, foul ball or home run. It's the second Curse of the Bambino.

~Jack Raskin, as told to Joe Raskin, New York, New York

Forty-five years have come and gone since the New York Mets and Houston Colt 45s played their inaugural seasons as expansion teams in the National League. As expected, both teams were bad. But the 1962 Mets weren't just bad, they were classically bad. Perhaps it was because the Mets' first home game was played on Friday the 13th... As if their 40-120 won-lost record wasn't bad enough, the team was a disaster in ways the league standings could never come close to expressing. For instance, as a reward for being the most valuable player of the '62 Mets season, Richie Ashburn was given a boat by the club. The first time he tested the craft's seaworthiness, it sank. Or how about when, in his last major league at-bat while playing for the '62 Mets, Joe Pignatano hit into a triple play.

While the Mets rightfully cornered the market on expansion-team ineptitude and humorous anecdotes, good Houston Colt 45s stories seem hard to come by. Compared to the Mets, the Colts seemed to be a colorless, characterless expansion team that overachieved a tiny bit, finishing eighth in the 10-team National League. At least that's the impression one gets... until you start talking to Bob Lillis, an infielder from California who found himself playing in Houston when the Colt 45s started. Lillis was the prototypical expansion-draft player—a 31-year-old utilityman who was never a regular during his four years with Los Angeles and St. Louis. He spent the final six years of his baseball career in Houston, eventually managing the Astros from 1982 to 1985. Lillis, in a manner of speaking, kept the flame of the Colt 45s lit. He was there at the beginning and played his part in an experience that often toed the line between major league and bush league.

One didn't have to wait until the game began to notice that the Colt 45s were cut from a different cloth than the rest of Major League Baseball.

All you needed to do was watch them come out from an airplane. Most teams have their players dress in suits and ties on the road to present a professional look. But the owner of the Colt 45s, Roy Hofheinz, would have none of that. Because his team was representing Houston, not New York, he believed they should dress like Houston businessmen...in blue cowboy suits. Lillis once told me, "The day we traveled, we had blue cowboy outfits with black 10-gallon hats, and boots with orange lettering and decorations. We had string ties and cowboy shirts. Hofheinz felt we needed some identity, and all the guys had to wear them on the day of travel."

Although Lillis and his teammates didn't object to the idea of a team identity, the Wild Bill Cody look didn't go over too well. Lillis continued, "(We) didn't like it. Some of (the players) especially didn't like the boots. But we got fined if we didn't wear any part of it. I'll you a little story about the hat. I was sitting on the back of the bus with an open window signing autographs, and some little kid reached up, grabbed my hat, and started running down the street with it. I think he broke the world record for the 100-yard dash. I yelled, "He got my hat!' When I said that, everybody on the bus said 'Here, take mine! Take mine!' Nobody wanted to wear them." Hofheinz listened to the complaints and eventually backed off, allowing Colts players to wear normal business attire like every other team. But Lillis never threw out the suit. "I still have the cowboy outfit— the boots, the belt, the tie, the western shirts. I have everything but the 10-gallon hat that the kid took from me."

Like most expansion teams, the Colt 45s of 1962 didn't have a ton of talent. And the original Colt Stadium was a roofless structure hastily thrown together as a temporary residence for the team until the new domed stadium was completed. But the team did enjoy a slight home-field advantage that might have won them a few games here and there...if you could call dark clouds of ravenous mosquitoes an advantage. Insect spray was an absolute must at games. If an unfortunate visiting player neglected to put on repellent, he would be likely be too busy swatting and scratching to keep his head in the game.

"Those hot, humid evenings out there, I can remember in practice that we had to fog the field before we even got on it," said Lillis. "It was just miserable. You had to almost take a bath in that repellent to even get by during the night." According to Lillis, it wasn't just a matter of isolated insects here and there, mosquitoes swarmed at every Colt 45s home game. "It looked just like a fog bank coming over us sometimes.... I'm sure that's an exaggeration, but you've seen a flock of birds when they fly, they all fly in unison and change directions. That's about what it was like. And they were big." Club management tried to get rid of the mosquitoes, but to no avail. Lillis remembered watching exterminators working for hours before the game trying to make the players and fans more comfortable. "Usually, they had a guy with a backpack and a fogger, and he'd spray underneath the stands and the outfield."

There was, of course, more. If the mosquitoes didn't get to the players, the oppressive heat and humidity probably would. "We played some day games and day doubleheaders," Lillis remembered, "and you know four o'clock is basically the hottest time during the day during the summer, and you are out there playing a doubleheader.... it took its toll." One Sunday doubleheader against the Dodgers was not memorable for its on-field action—Los Angeles swept the Colts—but rather for the more than 70 people in the stands who were treated for heatstroke.

Focusing on youth from the beginning, in their second season they became the only team in major league history to start a game with nine rookies. In 1965 Hofheinz renamed the club the Astros, not because of a negative association with guns, but for business reasons and because Houston was home to the space program and Astros was a shorter version of Astronauts. Topps baseball cards from 1965 to 1968 didn't even include the team's new name, which was the only time in the manufacturer's history that it did not identify a team name.

The National League had granted Houston a franchise partially based on Hofheinz's vision for the future. Not only would the team eventually play in a real, thoroughly planned ballpark, but that park would be domed and serve as part of a broader entertainment complex. When Harris County Domed Stadium—eventually renamed the Houston Astrodome—finally opened in 1965, it was billed as the Eighth Wonder of the World and featured the largest scoreboard in operation at the time, a roof, and sky-boxes, all baseball firsts.

During their inaugural 96- loss season, the Colts had a particularly hard time beating the Philadelphia Phillies, losing the first 17 games, dangerously close to becoming the first team ever to lose an entire season series. Front-office employee Bill Giles hatched a scheme to try to break this unfortunate streak, - a "Voodoo Night" promotion scheduled for September 4. Fans were asked to bring anything that might bring good luck to the Colts. As Lillis explained, "Bill Giles at the time hired an 'Evil-Eyed Knievel' … to come out and put the hex on the Phillies. It caused quite a stir around the club. I don't think it worked.

"([Knievel)] was a guy around town that who had a history... …his big thing was being able to put a hex on some of the sporting teams around town when they were having trouble.… Bill thought it was a good promotional event and took advantage of it." Lillis continued, "We didn't think too much of it. We were out trying to bust our tails and trying to win ballgames. We weren't very superstitious…you know, you have to do battle with the pitcher, and… nobody else can help you. I imagine some of [the players] thought it would work." "He made an appearance… it was quite hilarious when you think of it. He was going through his routine; he was, making …hex signs.… [The Phillies] were on the field and he was basically in the stands, and that was to stimulate the people more than anything else. I don't think the Phillies paid any attention to it. That was towards the end of the season,…. and we were just using that as a promotional event.,"

Whether it worked or not depends on whom you ask. The Colts did beat the Phillies that night, and Lillis knocked in the game's winning run with a two-run triple. But despite the promotional shenanigans of September 4, 1962, only 4,500 fans came to the stadium that night.

Lillis knew that the Colts, as an expansion team, would not only struggle to win games, but to win over fans, as well. "Since there have been expansion teams before, everybody pretty much knows what to expect the first few years. They don't except the club to come out winning, but they expect a good show and a good team trying to do the best they can." In other words, that first year, Houston fans should have been content with the fact that they had landed a Major League Baseball franchise, regardless of the team's initial performance on the field. But the Colts came out of the gate blazing. "When we started out that season, the first three games we played Chicago and we swept the series. We felt pretty good going into the start of the season. We did beat two teams that year [in the standings] and finished eighth. We managed to beat Chicago and the Mets. We felt good about our season even though we didn't win a lot of games."

The Mets, playing in the media capital of the world under charismatic manager Casey Stengel, quickly established a monopoly when it came to putrid play and silly stories. In a strange twist, the Colt 45s came to be somewhat obscured by their relative success. Unlike the Mets, the very name of the Houston expansion team has become a thing of the past, relegated to encyclopedias and throwback jerseys. Playing in a temporary stadium under a temporary name, and playing in the shadow of the legendarily hopeless Mets, the "other" expansion team of 1962 is easily overlooked. But in many ways, the '62 Colts were just as colorful as the '62 Mets. Especially when they wore blue cowboy suits.

~Evan Weiner, New York, New York

On July 17, 1941, I hopped a train outside of Pittsburgh, Pennsylvania, with my brother, Vince. Our destination was Cleveland, to see Joe DiMaggio continue his hitting streak, then currently at 56 games. There were over 67,000 people in the stadium that day to see the streak continue. In the 1st inning against pitcher Al Smith, DiMaggio hit a hard smash and third baseman Ken Keltner robbed him of a double. In the 4th, he drew a walk, and the crowd was not happy. In the 7th, he hit another blast down the third base line, and Keltner snagged it again, throwing him out by a step. I'd never seen a crowd so rowdy, nor a place so loud as at that moment. It seemed like all the Indians fans were pulling for DiMaggio, too, not against him. He hit into a double play in the 9th, thereby ending the greatest hitting streak in major league history.

~Domenic Finoli Greensburg, Pennsylvania as told to his son, David, Monroeville, Pennsylvania

My friend, Clarke, and I took his Uncle Neil to a Giants game, where Neil regaled us with stories of his childhood. Neil was the grandson of Hall of Famer Fred Clarke, and grew up on the family farm in Winfield, Kansas. Fred Clarke had played before and after the turn of the century with the Kentucky Colonels and Pittsburgh Pirates in a 21-year career in which he had a batting average of .312.

According to Neil, Fred's stories had often been self-effacing. One was about early in his managing career, in 1901 when he was a player-manager. He had a shortstop, Bones Ely, who drank a lot, often coming to the ballpark drunk. One day Fred said, "You come to the ballpark drunk one more time, and you are *done*." The next day Bones did, and Fred made good on his word. Bones was shipped out, and Honus Wagner was moved to shortstop. Fred said it was the smartest thing he ever did. But Fred admitted he wasn't always a good eye for talent. In 1905 or 1906, a raw-boned kid from Kansas came by and said he could pitch. Fred put a glove on and caught him for 20 or so pitches then sent him away, thinking he was way too raw. It was future Hall of Famer Walter "Big Train" Johnson.

The team had to barnstorm to make money. One day in a small town in Iowa, with a runner on second base, Fred was in left field and the hitter hit a ground ball through the hole. Fred wound up and heaved a flyer. He airmailed the catcher, the ball going over one fence and through a gate in a second fence. The following year, in the same exact same town, in the same exact situation, a ball was again hit to Fred. As he fielded the ball and came up throwing, he heard a loud call from the stands, *"Close the gate!"*

~Neil Sullivan, as told by his grandpa, Fred Clarke, then told to Neil's nephew, Clarke Funkhouer, and Clarke's friend, Ford Goodman, Hillsborough, CA, and Petaluma, CA

As everyone knows, Lou Gehrig retired early due to the onset of ALS symptoms. After playing in 2,130 consecutive major league games, Lou Gehrig was forced to hang up his cleats. His disease, ALS, later known as Lou Gehrig's Disease, was first diagnosed at the Mayo Clinic.

At the beginning of the 1939 season, major leaguers, including my dad, George Case, who played for the Washington Senators, had been puzzled by the rapid deterioration of Gehrig's baseball skills and power. On April 30, 1939, my father caught what turned out to be the last hit by Gehrig, a fly ball to center field in a game at Yankee Stadium. Days later, on May 2, before a Yankees game at Briggs Stadium in Detroit, Lou took himself out of the lineup.

That July, on Lou Gehrig Appreciation Day at Yankee Stadium, Gehrig gave his famous Luckiest Man speech. As a youngster, I recall my dad talking to me about Gehrig, his greatness as a player, and his subsequent devastating illness and early death. My dad was on the field that day. I remember him telling me that in the ceremony between games of a Washington Senators vs. Yankees doubleheader, all the players on both teams had tears in their eyes as The Iron Horse bid farewell to baseball. Less than two years later, Gehrig passed away. Dad was fortunate to have actually played against him and witnessed in person the amazing speech by an extraordinary man.

Ted Williams, the last major leaguer to hit over .400, and my dad played against one another beginning in Williams' rookie year. The "Splendid Splinter" is recognized as possibly Major League Baseball's all-time greatest hitter, but as great as he was, Williams was not really a complete ballplayer. He could often be seen in the outfield, working on his swing!

Dad was blessed with great natural speed. Ted once said to him, "Casey, if I had your foot, and you had my bat, they'd never get us out!" Dad said Williams had the best hand-eye coordination he ever saw, born with 20/10 vision whereas perfect vision is considered 20/20. This 20/10 vision enabled him to pick up the spin on a baseball 10 feet quicker than a batter with 20/20 vison, a huge advantage! That gift also provided Ted an advantage off the baseball field as a Marine Corps flight instructor during WWII, and a jet fighter pilot during the Korean conflict.

Williams had other interests outside of baseball. He was elected to the Fly-Fishing Hall of Fame and was a crack shot as a hunter. Dad loved to tell the following anecdote about Ted. One day, the Washington ball club arrived early at Fenway Park for batting practice. As the players entered the stadium, they heard gunshots. Ted was standing on the field in his uniform, holding a shotgun and shooting at the pigeons flying around Fenway!

I once ran into Ted Williams at a sporting goods show in Chicago when Ted was representing Sears and his own line of hunting and fishing equipment. When he walked past our athletic footwear booth, I stepped out into the aisle. "Excuse me, Ted, I'm George Case's son and I just wanted to say hello!" He stopped, looked at me with a big grin, and said, "Damn, I haven't seen you since you were a little kid. How's your old man?" After that, many of my business associates wanted to know how in the world I knew Ted Williams.

In 1936 at the Munich Olympics, Jesse Owens personally destroyed Adolph Hitler's myth of Aryan Supremacy by winning four gold medals. Owens was known as the "world's fastest human". Dad led the major leagues in stolen bases from 1939 to 1943. He had circled the bases in 13.5 seconds and had the reputation as the fastest man in baseball. In 1946, Dad was traded to the Cleveland Indians when Bill Veeck became the club's owner. Veeck, who would become widely known for his various and often zany promotions, decided that his first promotion in Cleveland would be to match the world's fastest human against Major League Baseball's fastest player. Jesse Owens against George Case! When he first told Dad his idea, Dad's first reaction was, "Bill, you have to be kidding!" Veeck replied, "No, George, I'm serious. I think you'll do well against him."

The race would be promoted by Cleveland newspapers and held at Cleveland Stadium between games of a St. Louis Browns vs Indians doubleheader on September 8, 1946. This brought out thousands of fans for otherwise rather meaningless games between the lowly Indians and Browns. The 100-yard race was to be run over the outfield grass with both Jesse and Dad in baseball uniforms and wearing baseball shoes. Jesse ran the 100 in 9.9 seconds, and my dad ran it in 10 seconds flat! It should be pointed out that Owens' world record set 10 years earlier at the Olympics was 9.4 seconds, and Dad was troubled by injuries that would force his retirement in 1947 at only 31 years old, so neither were in their prime. However, both were still *very fast*!

I had the good fortune to meet Jesse Owens in 1961 when I was a student at Rutgers University and Jesse was on a speaking tour of college campuses on behalf of the U.S. State Department. At the conclusion of his talk, I introduced myself. Jesse said he was delighted to meet me and wanted to share the following story. He said after the race, Dad challenged him to race around the bases. Jesse laughed and said, "No way, George, you're the best in the world at that, I only run in straight lines!"

~George Case, Yardley, Pennsylvania
George, thank you for sharing so many of your dad's stories.

My family has a long history with the love of baseball. My mom, Patricia, was and is a Tigers fan. She loved Mickey Lolich and skipped college classes to see him pitch in the 1968 World Series. Her professor caught her but let her go because he said he'd be doing the same thing! My dad, Joel "Bill" Greenbaum, had loved the New York Giants since 1952, with a later devotion to the Mets beginning in 1962. Coincidentally, as a vendor at Yankee Stadium years before he met Mom, Dad said that Lolich was the only pitcher in the bullpen to show courtesy to the vendors who had to cross the visitors bullpen, not making them rush to dodge warmup pitches.

Dad spoke about the first game he ever attended, which was on September 4, 1954, when the Giants with Ruben Gomez faced the Dodgers and Carl Erskine at the Polo Grounds. Erskine was shelled. This game featured names like Marv Grissom, Pete Wojey, and George "Shotgun" Shuba, who, several years earlier when playing for Dodgers minor league team, the Montreal Dodgers, offered perhaps the first congratulatory handshake to Jackie Robinson on Jackie's very first home run. Whitey Lockman had the first hit Dad saw his beloved Giants get in person.

But our family dedication to the nation's pastime goes several generations back.

As a kid, I was regaled with stories of old time major leaguers like Roger Bresnahan, Joe McGinnity, Buck Ewing, and most of all, John McGraw, names most people today don't know. My maternal grandfather, Jack Hart, was a semi-pro ballplayer in the late 1920s and early 1930s, and later a bird-dog scout for the Philadelphia A's and St. Louis Browns. My paternal great-grandfather, Joe, once told Dad about seeing Christy Mathewson pitch and John McGraw manage. But the best story of all came from my paternal grandfather, Jerome "Jerry" Greenbaum.

On May 8, 1929, Grandpa Jerry saw pitcher Carl Hubbell throw a no-hitter in his 18th start, an 11-0 win over the Pittsburgh Pirates. It was a cool day, about 8,000 people in attendance, and the game lasted one hour and 35 minutes. Mel Ott hit two home runs, to boost his league lead to six. Hubbell tamed Paul and Lloyd Waner, Pie Traynor and Travis Jackson. But what happened to grandpa was as unhappily memorable as this historic game. The state of park concessions in those days in terms of refrigeration and heating was not at the level it is today. Grandpa Jerry ate what turned out to be a rancid hot dog in the 1st inning. From that point on, he was hanging on as hard as Hubbell, who endured a number of his teammates' errors. Great-grandpa Joe, who was at the game with his son, was just as insistent as Jerry about staying to the end of the game, as neither had ever seen a no-hitter. They managed to last until the end, although Jerry's ride home was spent hanging out of the side of the trolley. Specific details are left to your imagination. Still, despite the unpleasant ending, the play even beat out Game 6 of the 1986 World Series, where both Bill and Patricia were spectators and Mets fans.

Of course, you may be wondering how such names as Buck Ewing and Roger Connor figure into this. They'd have been before even Great-Grandpa Joe's time. But Joe, too, had a father, my great-great-grandfather,

Nathan Greenbaum. Most of the details of his first game have been lost to the pages of time, but it is known that it occurred in 1889 with Tim Keefe starting for the New York Giants against the Chicago Colts, or as Nathan called them, "Cap Anson's Mighty Colts." Whether Keefe won or not has been forgotten, but that game was what got the Greenbaum side of the family into baseball, and what has kept the family as baseball fans for over 140 years. Hearing about a Buck Ewing home run down the infamously-short right field foul line sometime in the 1890s will do that, I think.

~Nathan Greenbaum, as told to and seen by Joe Greenbaum, as told to and seen by Jerome Greenbaum, as told to and seen by Joel "Bill" Greenbaum, Bloomington, Indiana

~Jack Hart as told to Patricia H. Greenbaum and Joel "Bill" Greenbaum, as told to and by John-William Greenbaum, Bloomington, Indiana

My mom was born in St. Louis in 1910, and she was my main baseball influence. She used to tell me stories of the Gas House Gang and taught me to love Stan Musial. When she was about 90 and I was in my 50s, she shared the story of how she met Babe Ruth and shook his hand. The Yanks were in St. Louis to play the Browns in a day game. She went to the movies that same night at the Fox Theater, and when the movie was over, she stood up and, upon discovering the Babe sitting right behind her, she thrust out her hand and introduced herself. She told me The Babe was "just the nicest man." What she remembered most was that Babe's hand was what she called soft and flabby. I asked her, "Mom, why did you wait so long to tell me you'd met Babe Ruth?!" She shrugged and said, "Well, it just never came up before." RIP, Mom.

~David Moriah Ithaca, New York, as told by Loretta Morrissey

As a kid during the mid-1970s, many of my paper route customers were senior citizens, and I enjoyed listening to their stories. One that always

stuck out was Mr. Chillson's tale of his journey from Hartford County, Connecticut, to Chicago for the first Major League Baseball All-Star Game in 1933. He and a college buddy decided on a whim to head out, driving on the patchwork of poorly maintained network of roads to the promised land, Comiskey Park. He told of adventures stopping in small towns along the way, the eye-opening socio-cultural differences between the places, and the fun and sense of adventure that permeated the whole trip.

Arriving in Chicago, they stayed with a relative for a night, and then it was off to the big game. Mr. Chillson recalled being awestruck by seeing all the mythic legends of the game on one field. In that era before television and regular use of color photography, they had only ever seen their heroes in grainy black and white newspaper photos, or scratchy, sped-up newsreel highlights. Now, here right before them in living color, were Babe and Gehrig, Jimmie Foxx and Lefty Grove, and so many more. After the game was over, they duly piled back in the car for the long, circuitous journey home.

He spoke glowingly of these things, the 19-year-old in him coming back to life in his twinkling eyes as he shared these precious memories with me. Now, 45 years later, I can still see his face lighting up, animatedly telling me the tale. I was lucky, indeed, and glad I always took the time to listen.

~Kevin Crane, Enfield, Connecticut

AFTERWORD AND ACKNOWLEDGEMENTS

Well, book two is, as they say, in the books. It has been a sheer delight to put it together. Once again, I received far more wonderful stories than I could fit in one volume, but I loaded the bases and squeezed home some insurance runs. The final score is 370 stories, coming from 45 states and the District of Columbia plus seven other countries.

It goes without saying, and I hope understood by all, that my appreciation for everyone who contributed a story is immense. When I brag about these books—and I do—it is never from the perspective of "Look how great I am," but rather, "Look at all the amazing stories people were generous enough to share and trust me with." Whether stories were used in either book or not, my appreciation for every single one of them, and for you, dear reader, is equal.

Perry, Rick, Marie, Sherri, Claudia, Cheryl, Jim, you were on the front line of all the people who constantly encouraged people to send me stories or buy the first book. Friends hosted Lynn and me on our book tours around different parts of the country. Dean and Debbie, Laurie, Jennifer, Leslie, Moira and Peter, thank you for making your homes available to us in Milwaukee and Los Angeles, Philadelphia and Long Island. And thanks to my brother, Kevin, and his wife, Dana, for hosting us closer to home, and to Linda for making three facilities available to us. And thanks, as well, to those of you who helped me find cafés, book stores, and coffee shops at which to read. Your kindness is well noted and much appreciated.

My thanks again to Jack Jacobs at Palmetto Publishing, who believed in my project and gave me the green light to swing away with a second book before the first was completed; to Nina Bruhns for her astonishingly great editing and, except for right here, my adherence to her suggestions about eliminating semicolons; and to Alexandra LaPoint for keeping me and the project on track, coordinating the whole thing, and always being responsive to my questions.

A big thank you to my family for helping nourish my love of the game with company I love to be with. Baseball continues to be a family center, as evidenced by our Cain story. Yes, we love our Giants, but there is more to it than that. We love going to games. It is said that baseball is losing its appeal to younger people, but I don't recognize that from my world. Lynn and I, Rachel, David, and Lisa love going to games, and experiencing 2017 spring training in Phoenix was wonderful. Thanks to Lisa for her great back cover photo. And now there is a member of the next generation to be indoctrinated, Juliet. I implore David to wait until I can accompany them to her first game, hopefully this year, so I can sit her on my lap for nine innings, or at least two, and tell her everything I know about baseball. Okay, for that, maybe two innings is better!

Lynn deserves more of a shout-out than I have space for. I always get credit for the books, but I do my best to make sure that people know just how much she contributed. She took on a whole new career with the first book, doing the accounting, tech support, shipping and supplies consultant, web design, advertising, producer, roadie, and— Oh, hell, she is office manager/CFO/CEO all in one. She did tasks I didn't even know *had* to be done, much less how to do them. She was once again my sounding board for this book on stories, chapters, and, you know, everything. It was as if, forgive the dumb baseball analogy, she played every position on the field. Never once has she complained. When I feel guilty watching her spend full days on the grunt work, neglecting her own genealogy interests, her comment is always, "You've got your job, and I have mine." And most important, she has been unwaveringly supportive, helping manage every reading and signing even when she's heard the stories over and over. Holy cow, Phil Rizzuto, how did I get so lucky to hit that home run? She never for a second feels bad that I get the attention. I mean, how lucky can one man be? Thanks Lynn, I love you and promise I will continue to fight off every librarian and groupie completely and successfully. I have been so very lucky to share this journey with you.

Please continue to send me your stories or tell me your thoughts about the ones in this book. What touched you? What memories did it evoke? What could I do better? I hope to do a third volume. Oh, and if you have a concert or other music-related memory, send it to me, too! That next book is waiting to take the stage!

~Eric

eric.baseballstories@gmail.com or eric.concertstories@gmail.com

INDEX

Y

Z